Library of
Davidson College

POVERTY, ECONOMICS AND SOCIETY

Edited by
Helen Ginsburg

UNIVERSITY
PRESS OF
AMERICA

LANHAM • NEW YORK • LONDON

305.56
G493p

Copyright © 1981 by Helen Ginsburg

Copyright © 1972 by Little, Brown and Company (Inc.)

University Press of America,™ Inc.

4720 Boston Way
Lanham, MD 20706

3 Henrietta Street
London WC2E 8LU England

All rights reserved

Printed in the United States of America

Library of Congress Cataloging in Publication Data

Ginsburg, Helen, comp.
  Poverty, economics, and society.

  Bibliography: p.
  Includes index.
  1. Poor—United States—Addresses, essays,
lectures. 2. Poverty—Addresses, essays, lectures.
3. United States—Social conditions—1960-
—Addresses, essays, lectures.   I. Title.
HC110.P6G48   1981   305.5'6   80-6115
ISBN 0-8191-1385-9
ISBN 0-8191-1386-7 (pbk.)

86-2513

*To my husband Nathan, my mother Anna Lachs,
and to the memory of my father William Lachs.*

Preface

The United States is the richest and most powerful country the world has known. Yet poverty and inequality remain overriding domestic problems. Violence, racial conflict, and decaying cities are commonplace, the haunting symptoms of the extensive and dehumanizing poverty that American society has failed to eradicate. College students are bewildered and worried by the conflicts that threaten to destroy American society. Anxious to understand these conflicts, they are eager to examine the realities and controversies of our time. But the traditional textbook approach somehow transforms seething controversy into lifeless consensus and dispels students' eagerness without providing them with genuine understanding. Poverty is indeed a controversial issue, and this book points out the controversies rather than masking or minimizing them.

My special interest in poverty began in the period before the War on Poverty. In 1962 and 1963, I was a research associate for one of the first comprehensive studies on poverty in the post-World War II era. Oscar Ornati directed that study, "Poverty Amid Affluence," which was supported by the Twentieth Century Fund and carried out at the New School for Social Research in New York. Events since then have forced me to reexamine many of my previous views about the causes of poverty and the means of ending it.

I am convinced that economic factors are pivotal in the perpetuation of poverty. But, although an economist, I must admit that economics alone does not have all the answers. As Gunnar Myrdal has said in *Objectivity in Social Research,* "in reality, there are not economic, sociological or psychological problems, but simply problems, and . . . as a rule they are complex." Myrdal's truth is particularly applicable to poverty. Poverty, economics, and society are so inextricably related that my approach in this text is interdisciplinary. The book will be useful for courses in economics, sociology, social welfare, history, political science, urban studies, black studies, and integrated social sciences. It will also prove useful to people who work in social service, education, guidance, and the health services and to other citizens who are disturbed and perplexed by the stubborn persistence of poverty amidst affluence.

The book is divided into two sections. Part One traces the development of the major viewpoints about poverty from the seventeenth century through the New Deal and shows the economic, social, and political conditions in which they were nurtured as well as the controversies they engendered. Part Two focuses on contemporary American poverty and deals with the extent and causes of poverty, the people in poverty, the institutions that reinforce poverty, and the relationship between conflicting philosophies of poverty and current policy issues. Introductions to Part One, Part Two, and to each of the sixty-one selections provide background material that interweaves theory, history, policy, and contemporary issues. In order to keep the book within manageable size, I have given no coverage to the urgent problem of contemporary world poverty. To enhance readability and because of the introductory nature of this text, most of the original footnotes have been omitted.

The emphasis in Part Two on the relatedness of the economic, social, and political factors that perpetuate poverty reflects my present belief that contemporary American poverty is embedded in the structure of American society. As the reader will discover, I support the poor in their struggles to attain their rightful share of America's abundance. Their continued inability to attain that share has led me to investigate many institutions that commonly are assumed to reduce poverty. My findings often suggest opposite conclusions. Many readings in Part Two illustrate how these institutions actually can perpetuate poverty.

Student interest was a paramount consideration in selecting and editing these readings. I have learned much from my colleagues and students at Long Island University and welcome comments and suggestions from other students and instructors about the book.

Acknowledgments

I am indebted to many people and organizations for suggestions, shared insights, criticisms, encouragement, and other help in preparing this book. I would like to thank Oscar Ornati of New York University, Judith Gordon of Columbia University, Louis Menasches of the Polytechnic Institute of Brooklyn, Lorraine Lachs of Queens College, Bernard Newton and Jack Richardson of Long Island University, Lynn Turgeon of Hofstra University, Jerome Joffee, formerly of the Mobilization for Youth, and William Shneyer. Basil Dandison and Elizabeth Bates, both at Little, Brown and Company, gave me invaluable encouragement and assistance. The manuscript was skillfully typed by Marsha Schafler. Charles Rizzuto, formerly my student assistant, aided with library work. The staff members of the Long Island University Library, the New York Public Library, and the New School for Social Research Library were extremely helpful. Jack Richardson suggested that the book contain pictures. Many people helped me locate photographs, especially Jean Powers of the National Council of Churches, Charlotte LaRue of the Museum of the City of New York, the staff of the Picture Collection of the New York Public Library, and Robert Lassen. I owe an intellectual debt to the late Karl Polanyi and to the late R. H. Tawney, whose books have profoundly influenced my ideas about poverty and the rise of the market society, as expressed in Part One. I also acknowledge the assistance of the Brooklyn Center of Long Island University in the form of a research grant and a reduced teaching load.

My greatest debt of appreciation goes to my husband, Nathan Ginsburg. His penetrating criticisms and suggestions at every stage have greatly improved this book, which could not have been completed without his continuous cooperation and encouragement.

Finally, much as I appreciate the help of others (many of whom hold points of view that differ greatly from my own), I alone bear full responsibility for the final contents of this book.

Contents

Part One
Poverty: Perspectives from the Past   1

Chapter One
    The Preindustrial Society

1. Bloody Legislation Against Paupers   10
   Karl Marx

2. Should the Unemployed Be Hanged?   12
   Sir William Petty

3. The Origin of the Poor Law
   and the Law of Settlement   15
   Adam Smith

Chapter Two
    The Onslaught of Industrialism:
    Classical Economics, Critics, Social Thinkers

4. The High Earnings of Labor
   Are an Advantage to Society   19
   Adam Smith

5. A Plan for Social Reform   24
   Thomas Paine

6. Poverty Is Nature's Punishment
   for Overpopulation   30
   Thomas Robert Malthus

7. An Answer to Malthus   34
   William Godwin

8. Wages Should Be Left to the Fair
   and Free Competition of the Market ... 38
   David Ricardo

9. Change the Environment and Change the Man ... 44
   Robert Owen

10. The Distribution of Wealth Depends on
    the Laws and Customs of Society ... 50
    John Stuart Mill

Chapter Three
The Challenge of Marxism

11. The Attitude of the Bourgeoisie
    Towards the Proletariat ... 58
    Friedrich Engels

12. Relative Surplus Population
    and Capital Accumulation ... 69
    Karl Marx

Chapter Four
Black Poverty: Slavery and the Post–Civil War South

13. Life in the Slave Quarters
    and Life in the Big House ... 76
    Frederick Douglass

14. The Condition of Black People
    in the South, 1890 ... 80
    W. E. Burghardt DuBois

Chapter Five
Late Nineteenth and Early Twentieth Century Views of Poverty

15. Progress and Poverty ... 85
    Henry George

16. The Poor Are the Unfit ... 89
    Herbert Spencer

Contents

17.	Rerum Novarum *Pope Leo XIII*	92
18.	The Innuit Indians and the London Poor *Jack London*	96
19.	The Working Girls of New York *Jacob Riis*	98
20.	The Continued Progress of the Working Classes Under Capitalism *Alfred Marshall*	102
21.	Transferring Income from the Rich to the Poor *A. C. Pigou*	108

Chapter Six
The Great Depression and Its Aftermath

22.	One-Third of a Nation *Franklin Delano Roosevelt*	112
23.	Security for a People *Social Security Board*	115
24.	The General Theory of Employment, Interest, and Money *John Maynard Keynes*	117
25.	Business Is the First to Seek Relief *Fiorello H. LaGuardia*	121

Part Two
Contemporary Poverty in the United States   127

Chapter Seven
The Rediscovery of Poverty in the Affluent Society

26.	What Is Poverty? *Oscar Ornati*	140

27.	The Meaning of Poverty *President's Commission on Income Maintenance Programs*	143
28.	Hunger and Malnutrition in the United States *Clark Subcommittee, U.S. Senate*	153
29.	The Other America Revisited *Michael Harrington*	159
30.	Capitalism and Persistent Poverty *Paul A. Baran and Paul M. Sweezy*	164
31.	A View of the Poverty Program *Tom Hayden*	167

Chapter Eight
On Being Poor

32.	Facts and Fictions About the Poor *Elizabeth Herzog*	173
33.	The Welfare System *President's Commission on Income Maintenance Programs*	181
34.	Nigger *Dick Gregory*	191
35.	Why the Poor Remain Poor *President's Commission on Income Maintenance Programs*	194
36.	Congress and the Rats *U.S. Civil Rights Commission and Congressional Record*	207

Chapter Nine
The Invisible Poor: Far away or Forgotten

37.	Red Man's Heritage: The Lagoon of Excrement *Robert G. Sherrill*	211

Contents

38. Mississippi 217
    Leon Howell

39. Appalachia: The Corporate Fiefdom 223
    Harry M. Caudill

40. The Economics of Aging 227
    Special Committee on Aging, U.S. Senate

Chapter Ten
A Harvest of Shame

41. The Condition of Farm Workers
    and Small Farmers 233
    National Sharecroppers Fund

42. Farm Labor 242
    G. C. Henry

43. Letter from Delano 245
    Cesar Chavez

Chapter Eleven
Racism, Black Poverty, and Ghettos

44. How the Federal Government Builds Ghettos 249
    National Committee Against Discrimination in Housing

45. The Impact of Housing Patterns
    on Job Opportunities 254
    National Committee Against Discrimination in Housing

46. Menial Jobs and Black Poverty 258
    National Advisory Commission on Civil Disorders

47. For Sam Smith, Hospital Orderly:
    A Battle Whose Time Has Come 261
    John M. McClintock

48. Blame the Negro Child 264
    Doxey A. Wilkerson

49. Comparing the Immigrant
and the Negro Experience ... 270
National Advisory Commission on Civil Disorders

Chapter Twelve
Poverty, Inequality, and Unemployment

50. Poverty, Income Inequality, and Privilege ... 275
Robert L. Heilbroner

The Relationship Between Liberty and Equality

51. Liberalism and Egalitarianism ... 282
Milton Friedman

52. Equality and Liberty ... 283
R. H. Tawney

The Trade-off Between Unemployment and Inflation

53. Analytical Aspects of Unemployment ... 284
Walter Galenson

54. The No-Job Corps ... 288
Art Buchwald

Chapter Thirteen
The Paths from Poverty

55. The Alleviation of Poverty ... 291
Milton Friedman

56. A "Freedom Budget" ... 295
A. Philip Randolph Institute

57. Recommendations for National Action ... 301
National Advisory Commission on Civil Disorders

58.	The Myth and Irrationality of Black Capitalism *James Boggs*	**308**

The Peace Dividend:
Swords into Plowshares?

59.	Reorder National Priorities *National Commission on the Causes and Prevention of Violence*	**315**
60.	There Will Be No Peace Dividend *Daniel Patrick Moynihan*	**317**
61.	Why We Need Socialism in America *Michael Harrington*	**319**

Epilogue	**327**
Appendix	**329**
Suggestions for Further Reading	**333**
Index of Authors and Titles	**337**

Introduction

John Maynard Keynes once observed that "the ideas of economists and political philosophers, both when they are right and when they are wrong, are more powerful than is commonly understood."

The appropriateness of this statement to ideas about poverty is unassailable. Economic, social, and political thoughts about poverty have always exerted a strong influence over the minds and actions of different groups in society. Moreover, in various ways the theories of David Ricardo, Herbert Spencer, Karl Marx, and Keynes himself, for example, continue to shape and reshape the contradictory views held about the age-old problem of poverty.

Theories, especially the diverse and often opposing ones about poverty, are not born in a vacuum. Nor has the effect of these theories been neutral. Hence the purposes of this book are many. On the one hand, the book will acquaint readers with the facts and controversies of contemporary American poverty. But it will also show how theories about poverty evolved from specific economic, social, and political environments; it will point out the different assumptions, values, and goals implied by various theories; it will illustrate how these theories have been used by different groups and classes to promote their own economic, social, and political interests; and it will show the influence of the past on contemporary theories and policies.

Gunnar Myrdal has asserted that the social sciences are not independent of valuations. "Every study of a social problem, however limited in scope, is and must be determined by valuations. A 'disinterested' social science has never existed and, for logical reasons, can never exist." Differences in valuations, and in assumptions and goals, are and have been at the core of many theoretical and policy controversies about poverty. Many of these divergent valuations, assumptions, and goals stem from different interpretations about the nature of man and society and about their relationship to each other. They reflect different answers — whether explicit or implicit — to basic questions: Is poverty inevitable? Is poverty desirable? What are the causes of poverty? What is the nature of man? Are the poor innately inferior or equal to the rich? What is man's relationship to man and to society? Should I be my brother's keeper? What is the relationship between the State and the poor? What is the present or potential capacity of the economy to provide for all? Can we end poverty? Can we end inequality of income? Can we end inequality of status? Should we? If change is called for, how should it be achieved? What will bring about change? And finally, what kind of social and economic system should prevail?

Many selections spotlight different valuations, assumptions, and goals. Not every reading contains answers to all these questions, but most selections imply or clearly state some answers. The readings cover a wide spectrum of views. Consider the question of what economic system should prevail. The possibilities offered range from unregulated capitalism to regulated capitalism (with numerous variants of the welfare state or reform capitalism) to socialism.

Most of these views necessarily come from the pens of the nonpoor, for the poor seldom have had their own thoughts about poverty recorded. But this book does include selections in which the poor or the formerly poor describe from firsthand experience how it feels to be poor.

American poverty is sharply distinguishable from European poverty by its racial overtones, which no study of poverty can ignore. For although most poor Americans are white, blacks disproportionately swell the armies of the poor. From the earliest days of slavery to the present, black people have suffered from special racist oppression. Today poverty and racism are tightly intertwined. Any solution to poverty will have to confront racism in all its manifestations; it will have to develop methods of compensating for centuries of unequal treatment of blacks. Hence, I have given considerable coverage to racism and black poverty, with readings by many blacks as well as by whites.

In the pages that follow one can find thoughts expounded by rich and poor, capitalist and worker, believer and atheist, black and white, thinker and doer, revolutionary and government official. That they should clash is not surprising. That they should stimulate inquiry into the means of ending poverty and inequality is the hope of the editor.

Poverty, Economics, and Society

The Mulberry Bend,
New York, c. 1888
(Photograph by
Jacob A. Riis,
Museum of
the City of New York)

Sweatshop in a Ludlow Street tenement, New York, c. 1889 .(Photograph by Jacob A. Riis, Museum of the City of New York)

Cotton hoers, Mississippi, 1937 (FSA, Lange)

Plantation overseer and field hands, Mississippi Delta, 1936 (FSA, Lange)

Migrating family, Oklahoma, 1938 (Dorothea Lange, The Oakland Museum collection)

Part One

Poverty:
Perspectives from the Past

For the poor shall never cease out of the land: therefore, I command thee, saying, thou shalt open thine hand wide unto thy brother, to thy poor, and to thy needy, in thy land.

Deut. 15:11.

Is poverty inevitable? For thousands of years men thought that it was and had little reason to challenge that belief. The idea that poverty is natural and inevitable seemed to conform to reality. It became deeply etched in men's minds.

The Old Testament saying, "The poor shall never cease out of the land," was not questioned by Christianity. In the Middle Ages the Church set the moral tone for treatment of the poor in the Christian world — Christian charity. Relief of the needy was considered a primary obligation of the rich. Giving alms saved the soul of the rich as well as the body of the poor. The medieval Church accepted the inevitability of poverty and the permanent division of society into different strata. Religion told the poor to accept their fate on earth but promised them rewards in Heaven. Poverty was natural. The poor were not expected to rise to higher stations in life.

But if they were not expected to rise from the bottom, neither were the poor blamed for being on the bottom. The idea that the poor are responsible for their own poverty was nurtured in the market society. The centuries-long decline of feudalism and rise of capitalism was accompanied by sharp economic and social disruptions that brought new attitudes and policies toward the poor.

The earliest and most drastic changes occurred in England. New markets for wool in Flanders made sheep-raising extremely profitable and led to the transformation of the English countryside. As feudal lords became profit-oriented agricultural capitalists, they evicted large numbers of peasants from their leaseholds and also "enclosed" pastures and woodlots in which these peasants had had common rights for centuries. So land was converted from tillage and commons to profitable enclosed sheep pasturage, and masses of peasants, no longer able to gain sustenance from the land or to find other employment, were converted into paupers, beggars, and vagabonds.

In England most of the enclosures took place from the fifteenth through the nineteenth centuries. The resultant poverty was already evident by the fifteenth century. In the premarket society a bad harvest had often meant mass starvation, and there had always been the old, the widows, the orphans, and the infirm who required charity. Yet the humblest and poorest peasants had been able to maintain life most of the time and they had a place in society, even if only a low one. Now all that was changed. Now there was created a large and permanent group of able-bodied men with no place at all in society. In order to live they were forced to roam, to beg, to steal.

Profound changes in prevalent beliefs sprang from the proliferation of this new poverty in the emerging market society. Previously, the poor — at least in religious rhetoric — had been looked upon as God's friends, destined to inherit the earth. Now they were regarded as dangerous nuisances, idle by nature, whose fate was to be whipped, branded, enslaved, imprisoned, and even executed. Poverty had become a crime and paupers were criminals. Victims of economic forces beyond their control, they were held responsible for their poverty and punished.

CHAPTER ONE:
THE PREINDUSTRIAL SOCIETY

Karl Marx (Reading 1), the nineteenth century socialist theorist, unearthed some grotesque and inhumane sixteenth century English statutes and claimed that these laws served as a disciplining device necessary for building early capitalism.

Sir William Petty (Reading 2), a seventeenth century mercantilist economist writing when the poor were subjected to the punishments Marx describes, understood that not all the poor were lazy and also that lack of employment was a major cause of poverty. Petty's advocacy of more humane treatment was based on economic logic; he understood the potential benefit to the national economy of government-sponsored public works projects.

Punitive laws were only part of the total public policy toward the poor during this period. There was relief as well as repression. The monasteries had always administered charity to the needy, but with the Reformation in

England came confiscation of monastery lands and destruction of their philanthropic function. The new religion, with a harsher doctrine of poverty, did not look kindly on the poor. The Protestant ethic, a philosophy well suited to the economic needs of aspiring businessmen, was an exaltation of supreme individualism that contained scarcely any sense of society or community as a whole. Each man was on his own. Industriousness was the greatest of virtues, idleness the greatest of evils. Prosperity was a sign of righteousness, poverty of unworthiness.

Public rather than religious responsibility for relief of the poor dates from this period. Granting relief was a partial admission that there was such a thing as society and that it had some responsibility for its members, and a partial admission that economic and social as well as personal factors cause poverty. But there were other reasons, too. Economic misery had created widespread turmoil. And, as Frances Fox Piven and Richard A. Cloward point out in *Regulating the Poor* (1971), granting relief was also motivated by fear. Then as now, relief arrangements nearly always expanded after outbreaks of disorder.

The Elizabethan Poor Law of 1601 (also called the 43d of Elizabeth) firmly established the principle that the State is responsible for relief of the poor. The law set many patterns for relief that were destined to endure for centuries in England and also in America, where it was brought by the colonists. Vestiges of the 43d of Elizabeth are still embedded in American public assistance policies.

The Elizabethan Poor Law called for local financing and administration of relief for those legally settled in the parish and placed responsibility on relatives. The old, the blind, and the infirm were to be given relief. Orphans were to be apprenticed. The able-bodied poor were to be put to work or, if refusing, were to be banished to a house of correction or whipped.

As in America today, poverty was a national problem with national causes. Relying on local taxes called poor rates for financing relief exacerbated hostility toward the poor who had entered the towns in search of work. Every parish wanted to keep out the poor to keep down its poor rates. Reflecting a hardening stance, the Act of Settlement and Removal of 1662 permitted removal of any propertyless person to the parish of original residence, thus binding the poor to their parishes.

In 1971, when Governor Nelson Rockefeller signed into New York state law a one-year residency requirement for relief recipients, he was acting in the spirit of that law. So were the authorities who subsequently shipped several welfare recipients from New York City back to California, their former state of residence.

Writing in 1776, when the Poor Law and the Law of Settlement were still in effect, Adam Smith (Reading 3), Scotch political economist, attacked the Law of Settlement strenuously, first on libertarian grounds for restricting the freedom of movement of the poor, and then on economic grounds. Smith was a leading advocate of laissez-faire (noninterference of government in the economy) and free markets. He felt that hindering mobility prevented the formation of a national labor market that would freely adjust to changes in labor supply and demand.

But the continued spread of poverty during the initial transition to industrial capitalism led to widespread acceptance of the view that the Poor Law itself caused poverty by encouraging dependency. Putting paupers to work was stressed more and more as a punitive rather than as an employment measure. Work was punishment. The many workhouses that were established throughout England served as punitive institutions to discourage the poor from relying on assistance.

On the other hand, the positive benefits of poverty to individual factory owners were increasingly evident. Laborers could be persuaded to accept the lowest of wages. Orphaned pauper children as young as five or even four could be obtained by the newly established and prisonlike textile factories. As historian Paul Mantoux describes it in *The Industrial Revolution in the Eighteenth Century* (1961 ed.):

> . . . [Children] were more easily reduced to a state of passive obedience than grown men. They were also very cheap . . . the parishes . . . were only too anxious to get rid of their paupers. Regular bargains, beneficial to both parties if not to the children, who were dealt with as mere merchandise, were entered into between the spinners on the one hand and the Poor Law authorities on the other. Lots of fifty, eighty or a hundred children were supplied and sent like cattle to the factory where they remained imprisoned for many years. . . . At the beginning these "parish apprentices" were the only children employed in the factories. The workmen, very justifiably, refused to send their own. But unfortunately this resistance did not last long, and they were driven by want to a step which at first had so much horrified them.

CHAPTER TWO:
THE ONSLAUGHT OF INDUSTRIALISM

Adam Smith's advocacy (1776) of free markets — letting supply and demand set prices — was tinged with unwarranted optimism. Smith (Reading 4) explained that all groups in society would benefit from such freely operating markets. Workers might even gain high wages, a condition he thought would be advantageous to all classes.

In reality, the free market was setting low wages and high prices. The growing capitalist system was challenging the old tradition that morality should play a role in setting prices, the notion of the "just" wage and the "just" price that would permit a worker and his family to live decently. But with wages so low and food prices so high the laborer's life itself was threatened, and he protested violently against the market price. Food riots, burning of mills, plundering of shops and warehouses, disruption of wheat transportation — all sorts of direct action had radiated through the countryside. Riots reached a climax in 1795, with soaring food prices. The lesson of the French Revolution did not go unheeded.

Against this background emerged the Speenhamland decision of 1795. The Speenhamland system became operative in many country areas in England and bore some resemblance to President Nixon's Family Assistance Plan to subsidize the income of the working poor. Wages were subsidized from poor rates in accordance with variations in the price of bread. In effect, the working poor were to be permitted to live even if the market value of their wages dropped below subsistence level.

Some historians feel the Speenhamland plan saved England from revolution. Paul Mantoux claims that "its immediate object was attained, for the alleviation of workers' distress removed all danger of serious disturbance."

Three years before the Speenhamland decision roving revolutionary Thomas Paine had advocated (Reading 5) a sweeping plan to guarantee a minimum income to each citizen. With humanitarian fervor Paine declared that this was *to be granted not as a charity, but as a right.* The right to live in economic dignity and security is one of "the rights of man," as basic as the right to liberty that he loudly proclaimed on two continents. That his plan remained a vision rather than a fact was inevitable. Society's productive capacity was still too low; even had it not been so, the lower classes lacked the power to effect such unheard-of schemes. In the ensuing period of accelerating industrialization and mass misery, even the Speenhamland system was threatened as the rising capitalist class sought to abolish all relief for the poor.

The classical political economists Thomas Robert Malthus (Reading 6) and David Ricardo (Reading 8) were extremely influential in providing the upper classes with a theoretical base for their attack on the poor. Malthus and Ricardo accepted Smith's laissez-faire philosophy. But Malthus added a new and gloomy twist, with which Ricardo concurred. Malthus claimed to have discovered a virtually immutable law to prove the inevitability of poverty: Population growth tends to outstrip the food supply. The theory seemed to imply that poverty was due to the meagerness of nature but in fact shifted the blame onto the poor — "they are themselves the cause of their own poverty." The poor were the culprits who were guilty of overbreeding. Relief or high wages would only cause them to have more children; they needed the whip of necessity to work.

Malthus and Ricardo represent the extreme ideology of the market. The market reigns supreme. There is no society, only individual atomistic men, each alone, with his fate tied to the ups and downs of the market. "No person," said Malthus, "has any claim of *right* on society for subsistence if his labor will not purchase it." Malthus's proposal to abolish all relief to the poor became a political battle. In Parliament David Ricardo used new economic theories in his debates against the old Poor Law. The new Poor Law Reform Act of 1834 was a weaker version of Malthus's proposal. The industrialists had risen to political as well as economic power; their ideology was incorporated into law. Relief, which had been given increasingly outside the workhouse as a wage subsidy, could now be given only in the poorhouse, an institution created to evoke enough shame and horror to deter the poor from seeking support.

These views did not go unchallenged. William Godwin (Reading 7) accused Malthus of immorality by denying poor men the right to live. Increasingly, too, the nature of man became an important part of the debate about poverty. To Godwin man was ultimately perfectible. To Malthus and Ricardo poor men were basically degenerate and not likely to change. If poor men could not rise out of their debased condition, poverty was bound to be inevitable.

Robert Owen (Reading 9) was single-mindedly resolved to prove otherwise. His plan to end the degradation of poor men was based on his strong belief that men are shaped by their surroundings. Owen also raised another issue that was soon to become paramount, the relationship between poverty and the socioeconomic system. The classical economists Smith, Malthus, and Ricardo assumed that man is competitive and that the economic system works best when each competitively seeks to maximize his private gain. Owen questioned that assumption and regarded a cooperative society as economically and morally superior.

Unlike his predecessors, John Stuart Mill (Reading 10), a later classical economist, was sympathetic to the poor and to the possibilities of reorganizing society. Although private property was sacred to the other classicists (Malthus found it "absolutely necessary in order to attain any considerable produce"), Mill, though not a socialist, concluded that the nature of man was not an obstacle to socialism.

CHAPTER THREE:
THE CHALLENGE OF MARXISM

With the advent of Friedrich Engels and Karl Marx (Readings 11 and 12) discussion about poverty was no longer confined to the drawing rooms and to the halls of Parliament. Revolution was in the air and in 1848 abortive revolutions occurred on the European continent.

Marx and Engels, who were active revolutionaries as well as scholars, shaped arguments about poverty and society into an ideology of revolutionary socialism. Both men knew at first hand the horrors of the English

Industrial Revolution. Looking beyond the misery, Marx tried to awaken poor workers to the good news of socialism. His message was optimistic, clear, and urgent: Poverty is not inevitable at this point in history. In prior eras, when tools were simple, man's ability to produce was sharply limited. Most men were destined to be poor. Now capitalism, through technology, has given men the ability to live in abundance. But as a socioeconomic system rooted in private property and privilege it cannot abolish poverty. The system must be overthrown and succeeded by socialism. In sum, Marx brought to the poor the message of the possible: You do not have to be poor. But don't expect the capitalists to end your poverty. *You* will have to do that yourself by ending capitalism. For Marx, socialism, not poverty, was inevitable.

CHAPTER FOUR:
BLACK POVERTY

Although their ideas had great influence on American economic and social thought, none of the writers so far discussed were American. In America poverty had a dimension largely ignored in early classical and Marxist theories. While the Poor Law was debated, Frederick Douglass (Reading 13) and millions of his brothers were still slaves, enriching their masters. On attaining legal freedom, the ex-slave was landless and moneyless. Soon after he was stripped of civil, political, social, and human rights. So in the decades after the Civil War, when the United States was emerging as an industrial nation, the black people of the South, as W. E. B. DuBois observed (Reading 14), were being pushed into semipeonage.

CHAPTER FIVE: LATE NINETEENTH
AND EARLY TWENTIETH CENTURY VIEWS OF POVERTY

Also, in the last part of the nineteenth century and the beginning of the twentieth century, change was evident in America and in Britain. In some quarters there was more concern for the poor, elsewhere less. The philosophy of rugged individualism flourished. But social workers and reformers had discovered the poor. Wealth was exalted, and the age of big business had arrived. Capital and labor were in conflict; some workers seemed to have heard Marx's message. Mass immigration continued into America. The lot of the masses was said to be improving, and certain economists even claimed that poverty was on the way out.

During this era Herbert Spencer (Reading 16) and the Social Darwinists popularized still another reason why the poor should be left to rot in their misery: they were unfit and their elimination would purify the human race. Adding to the catalog of theories of poverty, Henry George (Reading 15) placed the blame on the monopolization of land and gained millions of adherents to a movement designed to end poverty by abolishing all taxes except one, that on land. Neoclassical economist Alfred Marshall (Reading 20) was pleased to see that the worst phase of English industrialism had passed and hopefully outlined the way in which capitalism would *gradually* raise the working classes out of poverty.

If Marshall was content to wait for progress to evolve, others were not. Socialist Jack London (Reading 18), looking at the same city of London as Alfred Marshall, was morally indignant about a civilization in which the poor had to plead for bread. Muckraker Jacob Riis (Reading 19), investigating New York's immigrant-filled slums, exposed comfortable America to the truth about how the other half lives and called for immediate reform. Pope Leo XIII (Reading 17), moved by compassion for the poor and fear of the socialists, told capital and labor to recognize each other's rights and asked the state to intervene to protect the poor. And A. C. Pigou (Reading 21), the last great neoclassical economist, recommended that the government tax the rich to give to the poor.

CHAPTER SIX:
THE GREAT DEPRESSION AND ITS AFTERMATH

By the 1930's optimism had vanished. The Great Depression tested not just economic and social theory but capitalism itself. More than the stock market had crashed. The system was in ruin. Poverty, mass unemployment, conflict, and chaos were everywhere. Thirteen million were out of work; miners earned $1.75 a day; soup kitchens and bread lines dotted the landscape; Francis Townsend and his aged followers called for $200 a month for all old people; and labor was picketing, marching, demonstrating, and sitting-in. When Franklin Delano Roosevelt (Reading 22) spoke of poverty, the American people knew what he was talking about.

John Maynard Keynes (Reading 24) gave theoretical arguments for government intervention in the economy. But with or without theory, in the depression measures were taken. Without alleviation of conditions capitalism might crumble, hastened to the grave by laissez-faire.

Minimum wage-and-hour laws, child labor laws, the right to form unions, and social security pensions all came out of the New Deal. The Social Security Act (Reading 23) did provide for old age pensions, through meager and regressively financed from the start. Equally important, the Act contained a public assistance proviso. Before, relief had been entirely a local responsibility, as in Elizabethan England, but with the collapse of private and public relief systems the federal government permanently assumed part of the burden of welfare.

Intervention in the economy included work projects and attempts to stimulate private business to pick up employment, much as Keynes had suggested. Yet despite all efforts, more than 8½ million people remained without jobs only seven months before the United States entered World War II. After the war Congress passed the Employment Act of 1946, but it was weaker than the original Full Employment Act supported by Fiorello LaGuardia (Reading 25) and other liberals.

Still, government's role in the economy had permanently expanded. By the decade after the end of World War II some economists announced the death of poverty in America and heralded the arrival of the affluent society.

Chapter One

The Preindustrial Society

1. Bloody Legislation Against Paupers

Karl Marx

Karl Marx (1818–1883), whose theories are fully developed in Reading 12, is often called the father of modern socialism. Yet this nineteenth century socialist spent most of his time studying capitalism.

During the transition from the feudal system to capitalism, peasants in England were forced off the land, pauperized, and eventually transformed into the proletariat as wage workers under capitalism. In this passage from Capital *(1867), Marx documents the brutal laws against sixteenth century paupers.*

The proletariat created by the breaking up of the bands of feudal retainers and by the forcible expropriation of the people from the soil, this "free" proletariat could not possibly be absorbed by the nascent manufactures as fast as it was thrown upon the world. On the other hand, these men, suddenly dragged from their wonted mode of life, could not as suddenly adapt themselves to the discipline of their new condition. They were turned *en masse* into beggars, robbers, vagabonds, partly from inclination, in most cases from stress of circumstances. Hence at the end of the 15th and during the whole of the 16th century, throughout Western Europe a bloody legislation against vagabondage. The fathers of the present working-class were chastised for their enforced transformation into vagabonds and paupers. Legislation treated them as "voluntary" criminals, and assumed that it

From Karl Marx, *Capital*, Vol. 1 (1867). Reprinted from the Random House, Inc., edition.

depended on their own goodwill to go on working under the old conditions that no longer existed.

In England this legislation began under Henry VII.

Henry VIII. 1530: Beggars old and unable to work receive a beggar's licence. On the other hand, whipping and imprisonment for sturdy vagabonds. They are to be tied to the carttail and whipped until the blood streams from their bodies, then to swear an oath to go back to their birthplace or to where they have lived in the last three years and to "put themselves to labour." What grim irony! In 27 Henry VIII, the former statute is repeated, but strengthened with new clauses. For the second arrest for vagabondage the whipping is to be repeated and half the ear sliced off; but for the third relapse the offender is to be executed as a hardened criminal and enemy of the common weal.

Edward VI.: A statute of the first year of his reign, 1547, ordains that if anyone refuses to work, he shall be condemned as a slave to the person who has denounced him as an idler. The master shall feed his slave on bread and water, weak broth and such refuse meat as he thinks fit. He has the right to force him to do any work, no matter how disgusting, with whip and chains. If the slave is absent a fortnight, he is condemned to slavery for life and is to be branded on forehead or back with the letter S; if he runs away thrice, he is to be executed as a felon. The master can sell him, bequeath him, let him out on hire as a slave, just as any other personal chattel or cattle. If the slaves attempt anything against the masters, they are also to be executed. Justices of the peace, on information, are to hunt the rascals down. If it happens that a vagabond has been idling about for three days, he is to be taken to his birthplace, branded with a redhot iron with the letter V on the breast and be set to work, in chains, in the streets or at some other labour. If the vagabond gives a false birthplace, he is then to become the slave for life of this place, of its inhabitants, or its corporation, and to be branded with an S. All persons have the right to take away the children of the vagabonds and to keep them as apprentices, the young men until the 24th year, the girls until the 20th. If they run away, they are to become up to this age the slaves of their masters, who can put them in irons, whip them, &c., if they like. Every master may put an iron ring round the neck, arms or legs of his slave, by which to know him more easily and to be more certain of him. The last part of the statute provides, that certain poor people may be employed by a place or by persons, who are willing to give them food and drink and to find them work. This kind of parish-slaves was kept up in England until far into the 19th century under the name of "roundsmen."

Elizabeth, 1572: Unlicensed beggars above 14 years of age are to be severely flogged and branded on the left ear unless some one will take them into service for two years; in case of a repetition of the offence, if they are over 18, they are to be executed, unless some one will take them into service for two years; but for the third offence they are to be executed without mercy as felons. Similar statutes: 18 Elizabeth, c. 13, and another of 1597.

James I: Any one wandering about and begging is declared a rogue and a vagabond. Justices of the peace in petty sessions are authorised to have them publicly whipped and for the first offence to imprison them for 6 months, for the second for 2 years. Whilst in prison they are to be whipped as much and as often as the justices of the peace think fit . . . Incorrigible and dangerous rogues are to be branded with an R on the left shoulder and set to hard labour, and if they are caught begging again, to be executed without mercy. These statutes, legally binding until the beginning of the 18th century, were only repealed by 12 Ann, c. 23.

Similar laws in France, where by the middle of the 17th century a kingdom of vagabonds (truands) was established in Paris. Even at the beginning of Louis XVI.'s reign (Ordinance of July 13th, 1777) every man in good health from 16 to 60 years of age, if without means of subsistence and not practising a trade, is to be sent to the galleys. Of the same nature are the statute of Charles V. for the Netherlands (October, 1537), the first edict of the States and Towns of Holland (March 10, 1614), the "Plakaat" of the United Provinces (June 26, 1649), &c.

Thus were the agricultural people, first forcibly expropriated from the soil, driven from their homes, turned into vagabonds, and then whipped, branded, tortured by laws grotesquely terrible, into the discipline necessary for the wage system.

2. Should the Unemployed Be Hanged?

Sir William Petty

Should the unemployed be hanged? Not according to Sir William Petty (1623–1687). Compared to the practice of that time, Petty's admonition that superfluous workers should neither be "starved, nor hanged, nor given away," seems almost beneficent. The law in England then decreed that, for a third offense, unlicensed beggars more than fourteen years old were to be executed without mercy. But Petty was motivated by economic logic, not humanitarianism. Although he was also a physician, a surveyor, and an inventor, Petty is remembered as a pioneer statistician and mercantilist economist. Mercantilist economic doctrines, reflecting the rise of merchant capitalism and the nation state, supported business interests and strong central government reg-

ulation of economic activity and stressed the economic and political advantages of a large population.

As a mercantilist, Petty considered the able-bodied unemployed poor to be a source of unutilized labor that could enrich the nation. Better to have the government provide them with useful work than to have them beg or steal, for the real cost to society would be the same in both cases. Petty even favored useless work over idleness to instill obedience and discipline in the poor and hence ensure social stability — shades of modern proposals to "cool off the ghettos."

Though the causes of unemployment were very different in seventeenth century England, Petty's prescription to have the idle build roads, public works, or even pyramids reads like a harbinger of Keynes's twentieth century antidote.

We enumerated six Branches of the Publick Charge, and have slightly spoken how four of them might be lessened; we come next to the other two Branches, whereof we shall rather recommend the augmentation.

The first of these two Branches I call, generally speaking, Care of the Poor, consisting of Receptacles for the aged, blind, lame, &c. in health; Hospitals for noisome, chronical, curable and uncurable, inward and outward Diseases. With others for acute and contagious. Others for Orphans, found and exposed Children; of which latter sort none should be refused, let the number be never so great, provided their names, families, and relations were well concealed: The choice of which Children being made at their being about eight or ten years old, might afford the King the fittest Instruments for all kind of his Affairs, and be as firmly obliged to be his faithful servants as his own natural Children.

This is no new nor rare thing, onely the neglect of it in these Countreys, is rather to be esteemed a rare and new project: Nor is it unknown what excellent fruits there have been of this Institution, of which we shall say much more, upon another occasion hereafter.

When all helpless and impotent Persons were thus provided for, and the lazy and thievish restrained and punished by the Minister of Justice, it follows now, that we finde out certain constant Employments for all other indigent people, who labouring according to the Rules upon them, may require a sufficiency of food and raiment. Their Children also (if small and impotent) as aforesaid, being provided for elsewhere.

But what will these Employments be? I answer, such as were reckoned as the sixth Branch of the Publick Expence, *viz.* making all Highways so broad, firm, and even, as whereby the charge and tedium of Travelling and Carriages may be greatly lessened. The cutting and scowring of Rivers into

From Sir William Petty, *A Discourse of Taxes and Contributions* (London, 1667).

Navigable; the planting of useful Trees for timber, delight, and fruit in convenient places.
The making of Bridges and Cawseys.
The working in Mines, Quarries, and Colleries.
The Manufactures of Iron, &c.

I pitch upon all these particulars, first, as works wanting in this Nation; secondly, as works of much labour, and little Art; and thirdly, as introductive of new Trades into *England,* to supply that of Cloth, which we have almost totally lost.

In the next place it will be asked, who shall pay these men? I answer, every body; for if there be 1000. men in a Territory, and if 100. of these can raise necessary food and raiment for the whole 1000. If 200. more make as much commodities, as other Nations will give either their commodities or money for, and if 400. more be employed in the ornaments, pleasure, and magnificence of the whole; if there be 200. Governours, Divines, Lawyers, Physicians, Merchants, and Retailers, making in all 900. the question is, since there is food enough for this supernumerary 100. also, how they should come by it? whether by begging, or by stealing; or whether they shall suffer themselves to starve, finding no fruit of their begging, or being taken in their stealing be put to death another way? Or whether they shall be given away to another Nation that will take them? I think 'tis plain, they ought neither to be starved, nor hanged, nor given away; now if they beg, they may pine for hunger to day, and be gorged and glutted to morrow, which will occasion Diseases and evil habits, the same may be said of stealing; moreover, perhaps they may get either by begging or stealing more than will suffice them, which will for ever after indispose them to labour, even upon the greatest occasion which may suddenly and unexpectedly happen.

For all these Reasons, it will be certainly the safer way to afford them the superfluity which would otherwise be lost and wasted, or wantonly spent: Or in case there be no overplus, then 'tis fit to retrench a little from the delicacy of others feeding in quantity or quality; few men spending less than double of what might suffice them as to the bare necessities of nature.

Now as to the work of these supernumeraries, let it be without expence of Foreign Commodities, and then 'tis no matter if it be employed to build a useless Pyramid upon *Salisbury Plain,* bring the Stones at *Stonehenge* to *Tower Hill,* or the like; for at worst this would keep their minds to discipline and obedience, and their bodies to a patience of more profitable labours when need shall require it.

In the next place, as an instance of the usefulness of what hath been propounded, I ask what benefit will the mending of High-wayes, the building of Bridges and Cawseys, with making of Rivers navigable produce, besides the pleasure and beauty of them? To which I also answer, as an instance of the premises, that the same, together with the numerous missions of Cattle and Sheep out of *Ireland,* shall produce a vaste superfluity of English Horses, the which because they have the many excellent qualities of beauty, strength, courage, swiftness, and patience concentrated in them, beyond the Horses of other places, would be a very vendible Commodity all over *Europe;* and such as depending upon the intrinsick nature of the English Soyle could not be counterfeited, nor taken away by others. Moreover, an Horse is such a Commodity as will carry both himself and his Merchant to the Market, be the same never so distant.

3. The Origin of the Poor Law and the Law of Settlement

Adam Smith

Adam Smith (1723–1790), whose theories are more fully discussed in Reading 4, is usually considered the founder of the classical school of economics. Smith, an advocate of laissez-faire (noninterference by the government in the economy), firmly believed that unregulated markets would produce most efficient results.

When Smith wrote The Wealth of Nations *(1776), there were two major laws in England regulating poor relief: The Elizabethan Poor Law of 1601 and the Law of Settlement of 1662. Smith describes the laws in this passage and attacks, in particular, the Law of Settlement for interfering with the optimum operation of the labor market. The law restricted labor mobility because it tied poor people to their parish of settlement, which alone had to grant them relief. If they went elsewhere to search for work they could be removed back to their original parish. No town welcomed a poor stranger. As now, every town wanted to cut its relief rolls.*

Whatever obstructs the free circulation of labour from one employment to another, obstructs that of stock likewise; the quantity of stock which can be employed in any branch of business depending very much upon that of the labour which can be employed in it. Corporation laws, however, give less obstruction to the free circulation of stock from one place to another than to

From Adam Smith, *The Wealth of Nations* (1776). Reprinted from the Random House, Inc., edition.

that of labour. It is every-where much easier for a wealthy merchant to obtain the privilege of trading in a town corporate, than for a poor artificer to obtain that of working in it.

The obstruction which corporation laws give to the free circulation of labour is common, I believe, to every part of Europe. That which is given to it by the poor laws is, so far as I know, peculiar to England. It consists in the difficulty which a poor man finds in obtaining a settlement, or even in being allowed to exercise his industry in any parish but that to which he belongs. It is the labour of artificers and manufacturers only of which the free circulation is obstructed by corporation laws. The difficulty of obtaining settlements obstructs even that of common labour. It may be worth while to give some account of the rise, progress, and present state of this disorder, the greatest perhaps of any in the police of England.

When by the destruction of monasteries the poor had been deprived of the charity of those religious houses, after some other ineffectual attempts for their relief, it was enacted by the 43d of Elizabeth, c. 2. that every parish should be bound to provide for its own poor; and that overseers of the poor should be annually appointed, who, with the church-wardens, should raise, by a parish rate, competent sums for this purpose.

By this statute the necessity of providing for their own poor was indispensably imposed upon every parish. Who were to be considered as the poor of each parish, became, therefore, a question of some importance. This question, after some variation, was at last determined by the 13th and 14th of Charles II. when it was enacted, that forty days undisturbed residence should gain any person a settlement in any parish; but that within that time it should be lawful for two justices of the peace, upon complaint made by the churchwardens or overseers of the poor, to remove any new inhabitant to the parish where he was last legally settled; unless he either rented a tenement of ten pounds a year, or could give such security for the discharge of the parish where he was then living, as those justices should judge sufficient.

Some frauds, it is said, were committed in consequence of this statute; parish officers sometimes bribing their own poor to go clandestinely to another parish and by keeping themselves concealed for forty days to gain a settlement there, to the discharge of that to which they properly belonged. It was enacted, therefore, by the 1st of James II. that the forty days undisturbed residence of any person necessary to gain a settlement, should be accounted only from the time of his delivering notice in writing, of the place of his abode and the number of his family, to one of the churchwardens or overseers of the parish where he came to dwell.

But parish officers, it seems, were not always more honest with regard to their own, than they had been with regard to other parishes, and sometimes connived at such intrusions, receiving the notice, and taking no proper steps in consequence of it. As every person in a parish, therefore, was supposed to have an interest to prevent as much as possible their being burdened by such intruders, it was further enacted by the 3d of William III. that the forty days residence should be accounted only from the publication of such notice in writing on Sunday in the church, immediately after divine service.

"After all," says Doctor Burn, "this kind of settlement, by continuing forty days after publication of notice in writing, is very seldom obtained; and the design of the acts is not so much for gaining of settlements, as for the avoiding of them by persons coming into a parish clandestinely: for the giving of notice is only putting a force upon the parish to remove. But if a person's situation is such, that it is doubtful whether he is actually removeable or not, he shall by giving of notice compel the parish either to allow him a settlement uncontested, by suffering him to continue forty days; or, by removing him, to try the right."

This statute, therefore, rendered it almost impracticable for a poor man to gain a new settlement in the old way, by forty days inhabitancy. But that it might not appear to preclude altogether the common people of one parish from ever establishing themselves with security in another, it appointed four other ways by which a settlement might be gained without any notice delivered or published. The first was, by being taxed to parish rates and paying them; the second, by being elected into an annual parish office, and serving in it a year; the third, by serving an apprenticeship in the parish; the fourth, by being hired into service there for a year, and continuing in the same service during the whole of it.

Nobody can gain a settlement by either of the two first ways, but by the public deed of the whole parish, who are too well aware of the consequences to adopt any new-comer who has nothing but his labour to support him, either by taxing him to parish rates, or by electing him into a parish office.

No married man can well gain any settlement in either of the two last ways. An apprentice is scarce ever married; and it is expressly enacted, that no married servant shall gain any settlement by being hired for a year. . . .

In order to restore in some measure that free circulation of labour which those different statutes had almost entirely taken away, the invention of certificates was fallen upon. By the 8th and 9th of William III. it was enacted, that if any person should bring a certificate from the parish where he was last legally settled, subscribed by the churchwardens and overseers of the poor, and allowed by two justices of the peace, that every other parish should be obliged to receive him; that he should not be removeable merely upon account of his being likely to become chargeable, but only upon his becoming actually chargeable, and that then the parish which granted the certificate should be obliged to pay the expence both of his maintenance and of his removal. And in order to give the most perfect security to the parish where such certificated man should come to reside, it was further enacted by the same statute, that he should gain no settlement there by any means whatever, except either by renting a tenement of ten pounds a year, or by serving upon his own account in an annual parish office for one whole year; and consequently neither by notice, nor by service, nor by apprenticeship, nor by paying parish rates [local taxes]. By the 12th of Queen Anne too, stat. 1. c. 18. it was further enacted, that neither the servants nor apprentices of such certificated man should gain any settlement in the parish where he resided under such certificate. . . .

The very unequal price of labour which we frequently find in England in places at no great distance from one another, is probably owing to the obstruction which the law of settlements gives to a poor man who would carry his industry from one parish to another without a certificate. A single man, indeed, who is healthy and industrious, may sometimes reside by sufferance without one; but a man with a wife and family who should attempt to do so, would in most parishes be sure of being removed, and if the single man should afterwards marry, he would generally be removed likewise. The scarcity of hands in one parish, therefore, cannot always be relieved by their superabundance in another, as it is constantly in Scotland, and, I believe, in all other countries where there is no difficulty of settlement. In such countries, though wages may sometimes rise a little in the neighbourhood of a great town, or wherever else there is an extraordinary demand for labour, and sink gradually as the distance from such places increases, till they fall back to the common rate of the country; yet we never meet with those sudden and unaccountable differences in the wages of neighbouring places which we sometimes find in England, where it is often more difficult for a poor man to pass the artificial boundary of a parish, than an arm of the sea or a ridge of high mountains, natural boundaries which sometimes separate very distinctly different rates of wages in other countries.

To remove a man who has committed no misdemeanour from the parish where he chuses to reside, is an evident violation of natural liberty and justice. The common people of England, however, so jealous of their liberty, but like the common people of most other countries never rightly understanding wherein it consists, have now for more than a century together suffered themselves to be exposed to this oppression without a remedy. Though men of reflection too have sometimes complained of the law of settlements as a public grievance; yet it has never been the object of any general popular clamour, such as that against general warrants, an abusive practice undoubtedly, but such a one as was not likely to occasion any general oppression. There is scarce a poor man in England of forty years of age, I will venture to say, who has not in some part of his life felt himself most cruelly oppressed by this ill-contrived law of settlements.

Chapter Two

The Onslaught of Industrialism: Classical Economics, Critics, Social Thinkers

4. The High Earnings of Labor Are an Advantage to Society

Adam Smith

Despite his many predecessors, Adam Smith (1723–1790) is widely acknowledged as the father of modern economics. Born in Scotland, the founder of the classical school of economics was for many years a professor of moral philosophy at Glasgow College. Smith was an optimist, perhaps because he wrote just before *the worst of the Industrial Revolution and did not anticipate the misery that was soon to prevail in Britain. Another reason for optimism was his faith in natural law; that faith permeates his well-known magnum opus,* The Wealth of Nations, *published in 1776. Newly discovered physical laws inspired his belief that there were natural laws of economics, whose unimpeded operation would result in progress. Hence Smith's advocacy of laissez-faire, or nonintervention by the government in the economy. In his model the best of all possible economic worlds would result if each man was free to act in his own self-interest. Competition, not regulation, would limit the power of businessmen.* The Wealth of Nations *became the Bible of the nascent industrial capitalists, who eagerly grasped the doctrine of laissez-faire which so conveniently served their interests.*

Where did the poor fit into Smith's schema? He assumed that there was a harmony of interests among all economic classes under capitalism. As this selection from The Wealth of Nations *shows, he favorably regarded high wages to spur industriousness, population growth, saving, large markets, and the further division of labor, on which all economic progress was thought to depend. The specter of rising population and the denigrating view of the poor so overriding in Malthus and Ricardo are absent from* The Wealth of Nations. *In Smith's eyes differences between rich and poor arise primarily from nurture, not nature; his proposal of schooling for the children of common people was a radical idea in England in 1776.*

The happy vision of a society in which all economic classes ride on the same upward escalator was later to be demolished by Malthus and Ricardo and by the full eruption of the Industrial Revolution.

The real recompence of labour, the real quantity of the necessaries and conveniencies of life which it can procure to the labourer, has, during the course of the present century, increased perhaps in a still greater proportion than its money price. Not only grain has become somewhat cheaper, but many other things, from which the industrious poor derive an agreeable and wholesome variety of food, have become a great deal cheaper. . . . The great improvements in the coarser manufactures of both linen and woollen cloth furnish the labourers with cheaper and better cloathing; and those in the manufactures of the coarser metals, with cheaper and better instruments of trade, as well as with many agreeable and convenient pieces of household furniture. . . .

Is this improvement in the circumstances of the lower ranks of the people to be regarded as an advantage or as an inconveniency to the society? The answer seems at first sight abundantly plain. Servants, labourers and workmen of different kinds, make up the far greater part of every great political society. But what improves the circumstances of the greater part can never be regarded as an inconveniency to the whole. No society can surely be flourishing and happy, of which the far greater part of the members are poor and miserable. It is but equity, besides, that they who feed, cloath and lodge the whole body of the people, should have such a share of the produce of their own labour as to be themselves tolerably well fed, cloathed and lodged.

Poverty, though it no doubt discourages, does not always prevent marriage. It seems even to be favourable to generation. A half-starved Highland woman frequently bears more than twenty children, while a pampered fine lady is often incapable of bearing any, and is generally exhausted by two or three. Barrenness, so frequent among women of fashion, is very rare among those of inferior station. Luxury in the fair sex, while it inflames perhaps the passion for enjoyment, seems always to weaken, and frequently to destroy altogether, the powers of generation.

From Adam Smith, *The Wealth of Nations* (1776). Reprinted from the Random House, Inc., edition.

But poverty, though it does not prevent the generation, is extremely unfavourable to the rearing of children. The tender plant is produced, but in so cold a soil, and so severe a climate, soon withers and dies. It is not uncommon, I have been frequently told, in the Highlands of Scotland for a mother who has borne twenty children not to have two alive. Several officers of great experience have assured me, that so far from recruiting their regiment, they have never been able to supply it with drums and fifes from all the soldiers' children that were born in it. A greater number of fine children, however, is seldom seen any where than about a barrack of soldiers. Very few of them, it seems, arrive at the age of thirteen or fourteen. In some places one half the children born die before they are four years of age; in many places before they are seven; and in almost all places before they are nine or ten. This great mortality, however, will every where be found chiefly among the children of the common people, who cannot afford to tend them with the same care as those of better station. Though their marriages are generally more fruitful than those of people of fashion, a smaller proportion of their children arrive at maturity. In foundling hospitals, and among the children brought up by parish charities, the mortality is still greater than among those of the common people.

Every species of animals naturally multiplies in proportion to the means of their subsistence, and no species can ever multiply beyond it. But in civilized society it is only among the inferior ranks of people that the scantiness of subsistence can set limits to the further multiplication of the human species; and it can do so in no other way than by destroying a great part of the children which their fruitful marriages produce.

The liberal reward of labour, by enabling them to provide better for their children, and consequently to bring up a greater number, naturally tends to widen and extend those limits. It deserves to be remarked too, that it necessarily does this as nearly as possible in the proportion which the demand for labour requires. If this demand is continually increasing, the reward of labour must necessarily encourage in such a manner the marriage and multiplication of labourers, as may enable them to supply that continually increasing demand by a continually increasing population. If the reward should at any time be less than what was requisite for this purpose, the deficiency of hands would soon raise it; and if it should at any time be more, their excessive multiplication would soon lower it to this necessary rate. The market would be so much under-stocked with labour in the one case, and so much over-stocked in the other, as would soon force back its price to that proper rate which the circumstances of the society required. It is in this manner that the demand for men, like that for any other commodity, necessarily regulates the production of men; quickens it when it goes on too slowly, and stops it when it advances too fast. It is this demand which regulates and determines the state of propagation in all the different countries of the world, in North America, in Europe, and in

China; which renders it rapidly progressive in the first, slow and gradual in the second, and altogether stationary in the last. . . .

The liberal reward of labour, therefore, as it is the effect of increasing wealth, so it is the cause of increasing population. To complain of it, is to lament over the necessary effect and cause of the greatest public prosperity.

It deserves to be remarked, perhaps, that it is in the progressive state, while the society is advancing to the further acquisition, rather than when it has acquired its full complement of riches, that the condition of the labouring poor, of the great body of the people, seems to be the happiest and the most comfortable. It is hard in the stationary, and miserable in the declining state. The progressive state is in reality the cheerful and the hearty state of all the different orders of the society. The stationary is dull; the declining melancholy.

The liberal reward of labour, as it encourages the propagation, so it increases the industry of the common people. The wages of labour are the encouragement of industry, which, like every other human quality, improves in proportion to the encouragement it receives. A plentiful subsistence increases the bodily strength of the labourer, and the comfortable hope of bettering his condition, and of ending his days perhaps in ease and plenty, animates him to exert that strength to the utmost. Where wages are high, accordingly, we shall always find the workmen more active, diligent, and expeditious, than where they are low. . . .

The difference of natural talents in different men is, in reality, much less than we are aware of; and the very different genius which appears to distinguish men of different professions, when grown up to maturity, is not upon many occasions so much the cause, as the effect of the division of labour. The difference between the most dissimilar characters, between a philosopher and a common street porter, for example, seems to arise not so much from nature, as from habit, custom, and education. When they came into the world, and for the first six or eight years of their existence, they were, perhaps, very much alike, and neither their parents nor playfellows could perceive any remarkable difference. About that age, or soon after, they come to be employed in very different occupations. The difference of talents comes then to be taken notice of, and widens by degrees, till at last the vanity of the philosopher is willing to acknowledge scarce any resemblance. But without the disposition to truck, barter, and exchange, every man must have procured to himself every necessary and conveniency of life which he wanted. All must have had the same duties to perform, and the same work to do, and there could have been no such difference of employment as could alone give occasion to any great difference of talents. . . .

The education of the common people requires, perhaps, in a civilized and commercial society, the attention of the public more than that of people of some rank and fortune. People of some rank and fortune are generally eighteen or nineteen years of age before they enter upon that particular business, profession, or trade, by which they propose to distinguish themselves in the world. They have before that full time to acquire, or at least to fit themselves for afterwards acquiring, every accomplishment which can recommend them to the public esteem, or render them worthy of it. Their parents or guardians are generally sufficiently anxious that they should be so accomplished, and are, in most cases, willing enough to lay out the expence which is necessary for that purpose. If they are not always properly educated, it is seldom from the want of expence laid out upon their education; but from the improper application of that expence. It is seldom from the want of masters; but from the negligence and incapacity of the masters who are to be had, and from the difficulty, or rather from the impossibility which there is, in the present state of things, of finding any better. The employments too in which people of some rank or fortune spend the greater part of their lives, are not, like those of the common people, simple and uniform. They are almost all of them extremely complicated, and such as exercise the head more than the hands. The understandings of those who are engaged in such employments of people of some rank and fortune, besides, are seldom such as harass them from morning to night. They generally have a good deal of leisure, during which they may perfect themselves in every branch either of useful or ornamental knowledge of which they may have laid the foundation, or for which they may have acquired some taste in the earlier part of life.

It is otherwise with the common people. They have little time to spare for education. Their parents can scarce afford to maintain them even in infancy. As soon as they are able to work, they must apply to some trade by which they can earn their subsistence. That trade too is generally so simple and uniform as to give little exercise to the understanding; while, at the same time, their labour is both so constant and so severe, that it leaves them little leisure and less inclination to apply to, or even to think of any thing else.

But though the common people cannot, in any civilized society, be so well instructed as people of some rank and fortune, the most essential parts of education, however, to read, write, and account, can be acquired at so early a period of life, that the greater part even of those who are to be bred to the lowest occupations, have time to acquire them before they can be employed in those occupations. For a very small expence the public can facilitate, can encourage, and can even impose upon almost the whole body of the people, the necessity of acquiring those most essential parts of education.

The public can facilitate this acquisition by establishing in every parish or district a little school, where children may be taught for a reward so moderate, that even a common labourer may afford it; the master being partly, but not wholly paid by the public; because, if he was wholly, or even principally paid by it he would soon learn to neglect his business....

The public can encourage the acquisition of those most essential parts of education by giving small premiums, and little badges of distinction, to the children of the common people who excel in them.

5. A Plan for Social Reform

Thomas Paine

"Hunger is not among the postponable wants," said Thomas Paine (1737–1809) in the Rights of Man, *a tract that proclaimed the natural equality of men. One of the eighteenth century's most influential political works, it was written in Paine's native England after he returned from America, where his fiery political pamphlets had rallied much-needed support for the Revolution.*

The first part of the Rights of Man *appeared in 1791 as a defense of the French Revolution. The second part, published in 1792, went beyond political rights and called for economic justice as well. It was an immediate success; nearly 200,000 copies were sold within a year. But then the book was banned as seditious libel and an order was issued for Paine's arrest. He fled to France and eventually returned to the United States.*

The Rights of Man *was not readily forgotten. Some copies circulated illegally while others were destroyed. But its egalitarian message remained etched in men's minds, especially in England, where it became a foundation text of the British working class movement.*

This selection from the second part of the Rights of Man, *with its scathing attack on tax inequities and lavish government support of the aristocracy, contains a far-reaching and detailed proposal for social reform and the alleviation of poverty. The cradle-to-grave plan contains the seeds of the modern welfare state and, like Paine, was well in advance of its time.*

When, in countries that are called civilised, we see age going to the workhouse and youth to the gallows, something must be wrong in the system of government. It would seem, by the exterior appearance of such countries,

From Thomas Paine, "Rights of Man," Part 2, in Moncure Daniel Conway, ed., *The Writings of Thomas Paine*, Vol. 2 (New York: G. P. Putnam's Sons, 1894).

that all was happiness; but there lies hidden from the eye of common observation, a mass of wretchedness, that has scarcely any other chance, than to expire in poverty or infamy. Its entrance into life is marked with the presage of its fate; and until this is remedied, it is in vain to punish.

Civil government does not exist in executions; but in making such provision for the instruction of youth and the support of age, as to exclude, as much as possible, profligacy from the one and despair from the other. Instead of this, the resources of a country are lavished upon kings, upon courts, upon hirelings, impostors and prostitutes; and even the poor themselves, with all their wants upon them, are compelled to support the fraud that oppresses them.

Why is it that scarcely any are executed but the poor? The fact is a proof, among other things, of a wretchedness in their condition. Bred up without morals, and cast upon the world without a prospect, they are the exposed sacrifice of vice and legal barbarity. The millions that are superfluously wasted upon governments are more than sufficient to reform those evils, and to benefit the condition of every man in a nation, not included within the purlieus of a court. This I hope to make appear in the progress of this work.

It is the nature of compassion to associate with misfortune. In taking up this subject I seek no recompense—I fear no consequence. Fortified with that proud integrity, that disdains to triumph or to yield, I will advocate the Rights of Man. . . .

Before the coming of the Hanoverians, the taxes were divided in nearly equal proportions between the land and articles of consumption, the land bearing rather the largest share: but since that æra nearly thirteen millions annually of new taxes have been thrown upon consumption. The consequence of which has been a constant encrease in the number and wretchedness of the poor, and in the amount of the poor-rates [local taxes to finance poor relief]. Yet here again the burthen does not fall in equal proportions on the aristocracy with the rest of the community. Their residences, whether in town or country, are not mixed with the habitations of the poor. They live apart from distress, and the expence of relieving it. It is in manufacturing towns and labouring villages that those burthens press the heaviest; in many of which it is one class of poor supporting another.

Several of the most heavy and productive taxes are so contrived, as to give an exemption to this pillar, thus standing in its own defence. The tax upon beer brewed for sale does not affect the aristocracy, who brew their own beer free from this duty. It falls only on those who have not conveniency or ability to brew, and who must purchase it in small quantities. But what will mankind think of the justice of taxation, when they know, that this tax alone, from which the aristocracy are from circumstances exempt, is nearly equal to the whole of the land-tax, being in the year 1788, and it is not less now, £1,666,152, and with its proportion of the taxes on malt and hops, it exceeds it.—That a single article, thus partially consumed, and that chiefly by the working part, should be subject to a tax, equal to that on the whole rental of a nation, is, perhaps, a fact not to be paralleled in the histories of revenues. . . .

. . . Were an estimation to be made of the charge of aristocracy to a nation, it will be found nearly equal to that of supporting the poor. The Duke of Richmond alone (and there are cases similar to his) takes away as much for himself as would maintain two thousand poor and aged persons. Is it, then, any wonder, that under such a system of government, taxes and rates have multiplied to their present extent?

In stating these matters, I speak an open and disinterested language, dictated by no passion but that of humanity. To me, who have not only refused offers, because I thought them improper, but have declined rewards I might with reputation have accepted, it is no wonder that meanness and imposition appear disgustful. Independence is my happiness, and I view things as they are, without regard to place or person; my country is the world, and my religion is to do good. . . .

. . . At the time when the taxes were very low, the poor were able to maintain themselves; and there were no poor-rates. In the present state of things a laboring man, with a wife or two or three children, does not pay less than between seven and eight pounds a year in taxes. He is not sensible of this, because it is disguised to him in the articles which he buys, and he thinks only of their dearness; but as the taxes take from him, at least, a fourth part of his yearly earnings, he is consequently disabled from providing for a family, especially, if himself, or any of them, are afflicted with sickness.

The first step, therefore, of practical relief, would be to abolish the poor-rates entirely, and in lieu thereof, to make a remission of taxes to the poor of double the amount of the present poor-rates, viz., four millions annually out of the surplus taxes. By this measure, the poor would be benefited two millions, and the house-keepers two millions. This alone would be equal to a reduction of one hundred and twenty millions of the National Debt, and consequently equal to the whole expence of the American War.

It will then remain to be considered, which is the most effectual mode of distributing this remission of four millions.

It is easily seen, that the poor are generally composed of large families of children, and old people past their labour. If these two classes are provided for, the remedy will so far reach to the full extent of the case, that what remains will be incidental, and, in a great measure, fail within the compass of benefit clubs, which, though of humble invention, merit to be ranked among the best of modern institutions.

Admitting England to contain seven millions of souls; if one-fifth thereof are of that class of poor which need support, the number will be one million four hundred thousand. Of this number, one hundred and forty thousand will be aged poor, as will be hereafter shewn, and for which a distinct provision will be proposed.

There will then remain one million two hundred and sixty thousand which, at five souls to each family, amount to two hundred and fifty-two thousand families, rendered poor from the expence of children and the weight of taxes. . . .

It is certain, that if the children are provided for, the parents are relieved of consequence, because it is from the expence of bringing up children that their poverty arises. . . .

I proceed to the mode of relief or distribution, which is,

To pay as a remission of taxes to every poor family, out of the surplus taxes, and in room of poor-rates, four pounds a year for every child under fourteen years of age; enjoining the parents of such children to send them to school, to learn reading, writing, and common arithmetic; the ministers of every parish, of every denomination to certify jointly to an office, for that purpose, that this duty is performed. . . .

By adopting this method, not only the poverty of the parents will be relieved, but ignorance will be banished from the rising generation, and the number of poor will hereafter become less, because their abilities, by the aid of education, will be greater. Many a youth, with good natural genius, who is apprenticed to a mechanical trade, such as a carpenter, joiner, millwright, shipwright, blacksmith, etc., is prevented getting forward the whole of his life from the want of a little common education when a boy.

I now proceed to the case of the aged.

I divide age into two classes. First, the approach of age, beginning at fifty. Secondly, old age commencing at sixty.

At fifty, though the mental faculties of man are in full vigor, and his judgment better than at any preceding date, the bodily powers for laborious life are on the decline. He cannot bear the same quantity of fatigue as at an earlier period. He begins to earn less, and is less capable of enduring wind and weather; and in those more retired employments where much sight is required, he fails apace, and sees himself, like an old horse, beginning to be turned adrift.

At sixty his labour ought to be over, at least from direct necessity. It is painful to see old age working itself to death, in what are called civilised countries, for daily bread. . . .

To provide for . . . persons who, at one time or other of their lives, after fifty years of age, may feel it necessary or comfortable to be better supported, than they can support themselves, and that not as a matter of grace and favour, but of right . . . I proceed to the mode of rendering their condition comfortable, which is:

To pay to every such person of the age of fifty years, and until he shall arrive at the age of sixty, the sum of six pounds *per annum* out of the surplus taxes, and ten pounds *per annum* during life after the age of sixty. . . .

This support, as already remarked, is not of the nature of a charity but of a right. Every person in England, male and female, pays on an average in taxes two pounds eight shillings and six pence *per annum* from the day of his (or her) birth; and, if the expence of collection be added, he pays two pounds eleven shillings and sixpence; consequently, at the end of fifty years he has paid one hundred and twenty-eight pounds fifteen shillings; and at sixty one hundred and fifty-four pounds ten shillings. Converting, therefore, his (or her) individual tax in a tontine, the money he shall receive after fifty years is but little more than the legal interest of the nett money he has paid. . . .

After all the above cases are provided for there will still be a number of families who, though not properly of the class of poor, yet find it difficult to give education to their children; and such children, under such a case, would be in a worse condition than if their parents were actually poor. A nation under a well-regulated government should permit none to remain uninstructed. It is monarchical and aristocratical government only that requires ignorance for its support.

Suppose, then, four hundred thousand children to be in this condition, which is a greater number than ought to be supposed after the provisions already made, the method will be:

To allow for each of those children ten shillings a year for the expense of schooling for six years each, which will give them six months schooling each year, and half a crown a year for paper and spelling books. . . .

Notwithstanding the great modes of relief which the best instituted and best principled government may devise, there will be a number of smaller cases, which it is good policy as well as beneficence in a nation to consider.

Were twenty shillings to be given immediately on the birth of a child, to every woman who should make the demand, and none will make it whose circumstances do not require it, it might relieve a great deal of instant distress. . . .

And twenty shillings to every new-married couple who should claim in like manner. . . .

Also [money] to be appropriated to defray the funeral expences of persons, who, travelling for work, may die at a distance from their friends. By relieving parishes from this charge, the sick stranger will be better treated.

I shall finish this part of the subject with a plan adapted to the particular condition of a metropolis, such as London.

Cases are continually occurring in a metropolis, different from those which occur in the country, and for which a different, or rather an additional, mode of relief is necessary. In the country, even in large towns, people have a knowledge of each other, and distress never rises to that extreme height it sometimes does in a metropolis. There is no such thing in the country as persons, in the literal sense of the word, starved to death, or dying with cold from the want of a lodging. Yet such cases, and others equally as miserable, happen in London.

Many a youth comes up to London full of expectations, and with little or no money, and unless he get immediate employment he is already half undone; and boys bred up in London without any means of a livelihood, and as it often happens of dissolute parents, are in a still worse condition; and servants long out of place are not much better off. In short, a world of little cases is continually arising, which busy or affluent life knows not of, to open the first door to distress. Hunger is not among the postponable wants, and a day, even a few hours, in such a condition is often the crisis of a life of ruin.

These circumstances which are the general cause of the little thefts and pilferings that lead to greater, may be prevented. . . . The plan will then be:

First,—To erect two or more buildings, or take some already erected, capable of containing at least six thousand persons, and to have in each of these places as many kinds of employment as can be contrived, so that every person who shall come may find something which he or she can do.

Secondly,—To receive all who shall come, without enquiring who or what they are. The only condition to be, that for so much, or so many hours' work, each person shall receive so many meals of wholesome food, and a warm lodging, at least as good as a barrack. That a certain portion of what each person's work shall be worth shall be reserved, and given to him or her, on their going away; and that each person shall stay as long or as short a time, or come as often as he chuse, on these conditions. . . .

By the operation of this plan, the poor laws, those instruments of civil torture, will be superseded, and the wasteful expence of litigation prevented. The hearts of the humane will not be shocked by ragged and hungry children, and persons of seventy and eighty years of age, begging for bread. The dying poor will not be dragged from place to place to breathe their last, as a reprisal of parish upon parish. Widows will have a maintenance for their children, and not be carted away, on the death of their husbands, like culprits and criminals; and children will no longer be considered as encreasing the distresses of their parents. The haunts of the wretched will be known, because it will be to their advantage; and the number of petty crimes, the offspring of distress and poverty, will be lessened. The poor, as well as the rich, will then be interested in the support of government, and the cause and apprehension of riots and tumults will cease.—Ye who sit in ease, and solace yourselves in plenty, and such there are in Turkey and Russia, as well as in England, and who say to yourselves, "Are we not well off?" have ye thought of these things? When ye do, ye will cease to speak and feel for yourselves alone.

6. Poverty Is Nature's Punishment for Overpopulation

Thomas Robert Malthus

It is not surprising that economics was dubbed "the dismal science" after Thomas Robert Malthus (1766–1834) expounded his theory of population. Malthus was an ordained minister who became a professor of history and political economy, and in the latter capacity he became famous as a courier of bad tidings to the poor. Not only was poverty widespread, but from his law of population Malthus also concluded that it was inevitable.

Malthus's interest in population came just as the Industrial Revolution in England was gathering momentum, strewing in its wake poverty, unemployment, and disease. The interest was engendered by a disagreement with his scholarly father, who retained an optimistic belief in the perfectibility of man and society in the face of proliferating misery. The father had been influenced by two political philosophers of egalitarianism, the Frenchman Marquis de Condorcet and the Englishman William Godwin. But the son set out to destroy their ideas, fearing that the ideals of the French Revolution might inspire the British underclasses to revolt. The Essay on Population, *which first appeared in 1798, was the fruit of that effort.*

The law of population Malthus put forth is well known: population, if unchecked, tends to outstrip the food supply. If there is no "moral restraint" to curb population growth (a possibility for salvation added to later editions), then famine, misery, pestilence, or war will do the job.

And the poor? They have only themselves to blame for their misery. Poverty is a natural punishment for overbreeding by the lower classes. They should not be given relief, for that will only cause them to have more children. And if given high wages, they will do the same thing.

Poverty was not invented by Malthus, but under his aegis it attained the sanctity of a natural law that should not be tampered with. Furthermore, poverty was regarded as useful as well as inevitable; it would serve to discipline the poor, who were seen as inherently slothful and unwilling to work without the goad of starvation.

The fact that poverty might be caused by economic factors beyond the control of the individual was scarcely considered. Not surprisingly, the message Malthus bore found a ready audience among the propertied classes. Now with good conscience they could deny thousands of years of religious teaching about their responsibility toward the poor. Now there need be no moral qualms about subhuman factory conditions or poverty wages. The upper class movement to abolish relief (and to reduce taxes) gained strength from Malthus's argument and finally accomplished its goal. In 1834 a new Poor Law in England stipulated that relief should only be granted in workhouses, where married couples were to be separated and conditions were deliberately to be made more unpleasant than anything existing elsewhere.

It is often claimed that Malthus softened his views about poverty in the later editions of his essay. The following passages are from the fifth edition of An Essay on the Principle of Population, *published in 1817, almost two decades after the original edition. The reader can decide how "soft" Malthus became in his attitude toward the poor.*

The rapidity with which the poor's rates [local taxes to finance poor relief] have increased of late years presents us indeed with the prospect of such an extraordinary proportion of paupers in the society, as would seem to be incredible in a nation flourishing in arts, agriculture and commerce, and with a government which has generally been allowed to be the best that has hitherto stood the test of experience.

Greatly as we may be shocked at such a prospect, and ardently as we may wish to remove it, the evil is now so deeply seated, and the relief given by the poor-laws so widely extended, that no man of humanity could venture to propose their immediate abolition. . . .

I have reflected much on the subject of the poor-laws, and hope therefore that I shall be excused in venturing to suggest a mode of their gradual abolition, to which I confess that at present I can see no material objection. Of this indeed I feel nearly convinced, that, should we ever become so sufficiently sensible of the widespreading tyranny, dependence, indolence and unhappiness which they create, as seriously to make an effort to abolish them, we shall be compelled by a sense of justice to adopt the principle, if not the plan, which I shall mention. It seems impossible to get

From T. R. Malthus, *An Essay on the Principles of Population,* Vol. 3, 5th ed. (London, 1817).

rid of so extensive a system of support, consistently with humanity, without applying ourselves directly to its vital principle, and endeavouring to counteract that deeply-seated cause which occasions the rapid growth of all such establishments, and invariably renders them inadequate to their object. As a previous step even to any considerable alteration in the present system, which would contract or stop the increase of the relief to be given, it appears to me that we are bound in justice and honour formally to disclaim the *right* of the poor to support.

To this end, I should propose a regulation to be made, declaring, that no child born from any marriage, taking place after the expiration of a year from the date of the law, and no illegitimate child born two years from the same date, should ever be entitled to parish assistance. And to give a more general knowledge of this law, and to enforce it more strongly on the minds of the lower classes of people, the clergyman of each parish should, after the publication of banns, read a short address, stating that strong obligation on every man to support his own children; the impropriety, and even immorality, of marrying without a prospect of being able to do this; the evils which had resulted to the poor themselves from the attempt which had been made to assist by public institutions in a duty which ought to be exclusively appropriated to parents; and the absolute necessity which had at length appeared of abandoning all such institutions, on account of their producing effects totally opposite to those which were intended.

This would operate as a fair, distinct and precise notice, which no man could well mistake; and, without pressing hard on any particular individuals, would at once throw off the rising generation from that miserable and helpless dependence upon the government and the rich, the moral as well as physical consequences of which are almost incalculable.

After the public notice which I have proposed had been given, and the system of poor-laws had ceased with regard to the rising generation, if any man chose to marry, without a prospect of being able to support a family, he should have the most perfect liberty so to do. Though to marry, in his case, is, in my opinion, clearly an immoral act, yet it is not one which society can justly take upon itself to prevent or punish; because the punishment provided for it by the laws of nature falls directly and most severely upon the individual who commits the act, and through him, only more remotely and feebly, on the society. When Nature will govern and punish for us, it is a very miserable ambition to wish to snatch the rod from her hands, and draw upon ourselves the odium of executioner. To the punishment therefore of Nature he should be left, the punishment of want. He has erred in the face of a most clear and precise warning, and can have no just reason to complain of any person but himself when he feels the consequences of his error. All parish assistance should be denied him; and he should be left to the uncertain support of private charity. He should be taught to know, that the laws of Nature, which are the laws of God, had doomed him and his family to suffer for disobeying their repeated admonitions; that he had no claim of *right* on society for the smallest portion of food, beyond that which his labour would fairly purchase; and that if he and his family were saved from feeling the natural consequences of his imprudence, he would owe it to the pity of some kind benefactor, to whom, therefore, he ought to be bound by the strongest ties of gratitude.

If this system were pursued, we need be under no apprehensions that the number of persons in extreme want would be beyond the power and the will of the benevolent to supply. The sphere for the exercise of private charity would, probably not be greater than it is at present; and the principal difficulty would be, to restrain the hand of benevolence from assisting those in distress in so indiscriminate a manner as to encourage indolence and want of foresight in others.

With regard to illegitimate children, after the proper notice had been given, they should not be allowed to have any claim to parish assistance, but be left entirely to the support of private charity. If the parents desert their child, they ought to be made answerable for the crime. The infant is, comparatively speaking, of little value to the society, as others will immediately supply its place. Its principal value is on account of its being the object of one of the most delightful passions in human nature — parental affection. But if this value be disregarded by those who are alone in a capacity to feel it, the society cannot be called upon to put itself in their place; and has no further business in its protection than to punish the crime of desertion or intentional ill treatment in the persons whose duty it is to provide for it.

At present the child is taken under the protection of the parish, and generally dies, at least in London, within the first year. The loss to the society is the same; but the crime is diluted by the number of people concerned, and the death passes as a visitation of Providence, instead of being considered as the necessary consequence of the conduct of its parents, for which they ought to be held responsible to God and to society. . . .

The circulation of Paine's Rights of Man, it is supposed, has done great mischief among the lower and middling classes of people in this country. . . .

Nothing would so effectually counteract the mischiefs . . . as a general knowledge of the real rights of man. What these rights are it is not my business to explain; but there is one right which man has generally been thought to possess, which I am confident he neither does nor can possess — a right to subsistence when his labour will not fairly purchase it. Our laws indeed say that he has this right, and bind the society to furnish employment and food to those who cannot get them in the regular market; but in so doing they attempt to reverse the laws of nature; and it is in consequence to be expected, not only that they should fail in their object, but that the poor, who were intended to be benefited, should suffer most cruelly from the inhuman deceit thus practiced against them. . . .

If the great truths on these subjects were more generally circulated, and the lower classes of people could be convinced that by the laws of nature, independently of any particular institutions, except the great one of property, which is absolutely necessary in order to attain any considerable produce, no person has any claim of *right* on society for subsistence if his labour will not purchase it, the greatest part of the mischievous declamation on the unjust institutions of society would fall powerless to the ground.

7. An Answer to Malthus

William Godwin

Malthus wrote his Essay on Population *as a frontal attack on the ideas of William Godwin (1756–1836). This English political thinker, who had been a minister in his youth, was one of the first philosophical anarchists. After turning from religion, Godwin put his supreme faith in the rationality, equality, and perfectibility of man. According to Godwin, human beings are shaped by their experiences and a more perfect society will produce more perfect people. Godwin denied the possibility of overpopulation, since he did not think that rational beings would propagate irrationally.*

These passages from Of Population *were written by Godwin as an answer to Malthus. They point out the moral implications of the policies advocated by Malthus. In Godwin's eyes these policies represent the antithesis of the Christian tenet to love thy neighbor as thyself. Ironically, this lesson in Christianity was used by Godwin, an ex-minister turned atheist, to instruct Malthus, who remained an ordained clergyman all his life.*

There was an old maxim, the repetition of which has been attended with some compunction in the minds of the tender-hearted and humane.

"He that will not work, neither shall he eat."

From William Godwin, *Of Population: An Enquiry Concerning the Power of Increase in the Numbers of Mankind, Being an Answer to Mr. Malthus's Essay on That Subject* (London, 1820).

But Mr. Malthus's proscription is of a very different sort, and includes, 1. man in his infancy and childhood, whose little hands are yet incapable of the labour that should procure him the necessaries of life: 2. the aged, whom length of years, and the hardships they have endured, have finally rendered as feeble as helpless infancy: 3. the sick, the cripple, the maimed, and those who labour under one or other of those diseases, which make the most fearful part of the picture of human life: 4. those who, being both able and willing to work, are yet, by the ill constitution of the society of which they are members, or by some of those revolutions to which perhaps all societies are liable, unable to procure employment. These are the persons, whom "in justice and honour" we are bound to inform, that they have no claim of right to the assistance of their prosperous neighbours.

There is no need of informing them, that they have no right, founded in political law, to assistance, except in those countries, and to that extent, where and to which a provision is made for that purpose, as by the poor-laws of England.

But Mr. Malthus's appeal is to a very different jurisdiction. He denies that they have any right in morality to the assistance of their neighbours.

There are two heads and springs of moral duty, as far as this country of England is concerned; the first of which is to be found in the records of the Christian religion, and the other in the instructions we derive from the light of nature. I should not think myself justifiable on the present occasion in over-looking the first.

The lessons of Christianity on this subject are plain and incontrovertible. We are there taught to "love our neighbours as ourselves," and to "do unto others as we would they should do unto us." When an ingenuous young man came to Jesus Christ, desirous to be instructed in his duties, he was referred to the commandments; and, having answered, "All these have I kept from my youth up; what lack I yet?" Christ bade him, "Go, sell all that he had, and give to the poor:" upon which "the young man went away sorrowful; for he had great possessions."

There is a kind of Oriental boldness in this, at least considered as a general exposition of the moral law: for it would be reasonable to answer, If it is my duty to render the greatest benefit to my fellow-creatures, and if my mind is well prepared to discharge this duty, it will probably be better done, by my devoting my income to this purpose, than by at once divesting myself of the principal.

But nothing can be more clear than the general tenour of revelation in this question. By it we are instructed that we are stewards, not proprietors, of the good things of this life, we are forbidden to pamper our appetites or our vanity, we are commanded to be fellow-workers with and impartial ministers of the bountiful principle of nature, and we are told that, when we have done all, we have done nothing of which we have any right to

Such are the dictates of the Christian revelation in this particular: and in all this there is nothing new, nothing that the light of nature did not as clearly and imperiously prescribe, to every one who was willing conscientiously to enquire into the law of morality. . . .

To the rich also he [Malthus] has read an important lesson. A great portion of this class of society are sufficiently indisposed to acts of charity, and eminently prone to the indulgence of their appetites and their vanity. But hitherto they had secretly reproached themselves with this, as an offence against God and man. Mr. Malthus has been the first man to perform the grateful task of reconciling their conduct and their consciences, and to shew them that, when they thought they were allowing themselves in vice, they were in reality conferring a most eminent and praiseworthy benefit upon the community. . . .

His plan is that of a law, "declaring, that no child born from any marriage, taking place after the expiration of a year from the date of the law, and no illegitimate child born two years from the same date, shall ever be entitled to parish assistance." "This," he says, "would amount to a fair, distinct and precise notice, which no man could well mistake." "No individual would be either deceived or injured and consequently no person could have a just right to complain."

For my own part, I profess myself at a loss to conceive of what earth the man was made, by whom this sentence was penned.

In the question of a child to be born into the world, and of the fortune that shall attend it, there are two parties concerned, the child and its parents. I own I was ignorant enough to imagine that the child was the most deeply concerned of the two.

Tristram Shandy has trifled in a very whimsical way with the idea of a scheme for baptising children before they are born. Mr. Malthus is the first man that has proposed the proclaiming children, and putting them out of the protection of the law, before they are born, for the purpose of preventing them from complaining afterwards. What has his "fair, distinct and precise notice" to do with them? . . .

Here then is a child that perishes with want perhaps as soon as he is born. Or he may drag on the load of existence for a varied length of way, from one to fourscore years. However long he may exist, he shall bear about him for ever the miseries, which arise from his being half-famished in the first stage of existence. And Mr. Malthus comes and tells him he "has no right to complain," for a "fair, distinct and precise notice" was given two years before he was born.

If Mr. Malthus and his disciples were to tell him, that general considerations of human weal, and the "principle of population" required that he should be thus deserted, that would be somewhat different. But to say, that a "fair, distinct and precise notice" was given two years before he was born, and *"therefore* no person has a just right to complain," what a mockery is it! . . .

But let us follow a little more closely Mr. Malthus's scheme for the gradual abolition of the poor-laws.

"To give a more general knowledge of this law, and to inforce it more strongly on the minds of the lower classes of people, I should propose that the clergyman of each parish should, after the publication of the bans of marriage, read a short address, stating the strong obligation on every man to support his own children; the impropriety, and even immorality, of marrying without a prospect of being able to do this; the evils which had resulted to the poor themselves, from the attempt which had been made to assist by public institutions in a duty which ought to be exclusively appropriated to parents; and the absolute necessity which had at length appeared of abandoning all such institutions, on account of their producing effects totally opposite to those which had been intended.

"This would operate as a fair, distinct and precise notice, which no man could well mistake."

It must be admitted that this is a strong measure. It strips human life of all those pleasing hues, and all that fascinating appearance, which, if not genuine, has at least served to reconcile thousands to their fate. Marriage is the grand holiday of our human nature; and, if the rest of the path-way of life is too often involved in horrors or in shades, this is the white spot, the little gleam of pure sunshine, which compensates for a thousand other hardships and calamities. It is indeed a bitter homily to the poor man, that Mr. Malthus proposes. However fair may be his hopes, no one who lives by the sweat of his brow, can be sure that he shall always be able, without assistance, to support a family. . . .

Never certainly was there so comfortable a preacher as Mr. Malthus. No wonder that his book is always to be found in the country-seats of the court of aldermen, and in the palaces of the great. Very appropriately has a retreat been provided for him by the commercial sovereigns of the regions of the East. What a revolution does his theory produce in the interior sentiments of the human breast! There were vices on the earth before Malthus. Men abounding in the good things of this world, indulged themselves unsparingly in all those caprices, which they well knew the mass of their species condemned, and which they more than suspected were worthy of condemnation. But they had a monitor, not only on their shelves, but in their bosoms, which said: "Rejoice, O thou rich man, in thy wealth; and let thy heart cheer thee in the multitude of thy possessions; walk thou in the ways of thy heart, and in the sight of thy eyes: but know, that for all these things God will bring thee into judgment."

Mr. Malthus has reversed all this. He has undertaken to shew, that while they thought they were giving way to their vices, and were drawing down the "curses, not loud, but deep," of the bystanders, they were in reality public benefactors, and that the more they wasted, the more they saved. He has encouraged them to persist in their generous plan of conduct, undismayed by the lamentable misconstructions of their starving fellow-creatures. Nature (not Mr. Malthus's Nature) had planted within us a secret monitor, which, when we wandered from the path of decency and duty, admonished us with a soft and gentle, but articulate voice, and bade us recollect ourselves. But Mr. Malthus stimulates us to drive away this better genius. He reconciles us to the worst and most prodigal appetites of our sensual faculty, and bids us call them by the names of patriotism and philanthropy. It is sufficiently remarkable that, when he enumerates the eleven ways in which vice and misery act to keep down the excess of population, he does not betray his cause, or put the extravagance of the rich and great into his catalogue. It is true, for this it seems is not vice.

8. Wages Should Be Left to the Fair and Free Competition of the Market

David Ricardo

David Ricardo (1772–1823) was one of the most distinguished economists of all times. Ricardian economics dominated the classical school of economics for fifty years and Ricardo's abstract deductive method of theorizing left a permanent imprint on economics. Ironically, although he was a staunch supporter of capitalism, Ricardo by his economic reasoning exerted a strong influence on Karl Marx, who adapted many of Ricardo's ideas and incorporated them into a theory of the inevitable downfall of capitalism.

Ricardo came from a rich family. Nevertheless, his formal schooling ended at the age of fourteen when he entered the business world. As a successful stockbroker, Ricardo amassed a fortune, part of which he used to buy landed estates. His wealth also enabled him to purchase a seat in Parliament, which he occupied from 1818 to 1823, and to retire from business to pursue his scholarly interest in economics.

Ricardo's major concern in economics was to discover the laws that determine the distribution of income among economic classes: labor, capitalist, and landowner. He reasoned that rising population, a fixed supply of land, and eventually diminishing returns in agriculture would cause rents to rise continuously. The main winners, the landlords, would reap an ever-increasing proportion of the national in-

come. Neither laborers nor capitalists would come out well, since they could only share what was left after the landlords took their bounty. If one group received more the other would receive less. And the workers had the least cause for rejoicing. Wages would "naturally" oscillate around the minimum cost of subsistence. If they rose above that level, population would increase. If they fell below that level, population would decrease. In either case, wages would gravitate toward the subsistence level.

Was there a way out of the "iron law of wages?" Yes, there was a thin reed of hope, if workers would have fewer children. Or if they would acquire a greater taste for comforts. In the latter case the subsistence level, which Ricardo considered to be determined by psychological as well as physiological factors, could rise. But Ricardo had little faith in the poor, and so he continued to believe that the iron law of wages would, in fact, prevail. The poor were doomed by their own reprehensible behavior to remain poor. To compound the misery, nonbehavioral, hard economic facts would make poverty even more inescapable. For Ricardo became firmly convinced that machinery might cause technological unemployment and hence worsen the lot of workers, a possibility he had long denied.

Ricardo focused on the conflict of economic interests and shattered Smith's construct of a harmonious world. But agreeing with his friend Malthus, Ricardo opposed any interference with the operation of "natural laws" even if they resulted in eternal misery for the poor. He therefore opposed minimum wage laws and all poor relief.

"On Wages" and "On Machinery" are passages from On the Principles of Political Economy and Taxation (3d edition), 1821. The last selection is the official summary report of a speech against a poor-law bill made by Ricardo in the House of Commons in 1819. In Parliament, as in his economic writings, Ricardo consistently opposed aid to the poor.

ON WAGES

Labour, like all other things which are purchased and sold, and which may be increased or diminished in quantity, has its natural and its market price. The natural price of labour is that price which is necessary to enable the labourers, one with another, to subsist and to perpetuate their race, without either increase or diminution.

The power of the labourer to support himself, and the family which may be necessary to keep up the number of labourers, does not depend on the

From David Ricardo, *On the Principles of Political Economy and Taxation* (London, 1821).

quantity of money which he may receive for wages, but on the quantity of food, necessaries, and conveniences become essential to him from habit, which that money will purchase. The natural price of labour, therefore, depends on the price of the food necessaries, and conveniences required for the support of the labourer and his family. With a rise in the price of food and necessaries, the natural price of labour will rise; with the fall in their price, the natural price of labour will fall. . . .

The market price of labour is the price which is really paid for it, from the natural operation of the proportion of the supply to the demand; labour is dear when it is scarce, and cheap when it is plentiful. However much the market price of labour may deviate from its natural price, it has, like commodities, a tendency to conform to it.

It is when the market price of labour exceeds its natural price, that the condition of the labourer is flourishing and happy, that he has it in his power to command a greater proportion of the necessaries and enjoyments of life, and therefore to rear a healthy and numerous family. When, however, by the encouragement which high wages give to the increase of population, the number of labourers is increased, wages again fall to their natural price, and indeed from a re-action sometimes fall below it.

When the market price of labour is below its natural price, the condition of the labourers is most wretched: then poverty deprives them of those comforts which custom renders absolute necessaries. It is only after their privations have reduced their number, or the demand for labour has increased, that the market price of labour will rise to its natural price, and that the labourer will have the moderate comforts which the natural rate of wages will afford.

Notwithstanding the tendency of wages to conform to their natural rate, their market rate may, in an improving society, for an indefinite period, be constantly above it; for no sooner may the impulse, which an increased capital gives to a new demand for labour be obeyed, then another increase of capital may produce the same effect; and thus, if the increase of capital be gradual and constant, the demand for labour may give a continued stimulus to an increase of people. . . .

It is not to be understood that the natural price of labour, estimated even in food and necessaries, is absolutely fixed and constant. It varies at different times in the same country, and very materially differs in different countries. It essentially depends on the habits and customs of the people. An English labourer would consider his wages under their natural rate, and too scanty to support a family, if they enabled him to purchase no other food than potatoes, and to live in no better habitation than a mud cabin; yet these moderate demands of nature are often deemed sufficient in countries where "man's life is cheap," and his wants easily satisfied. Many of the conveniences now enjoyed in an English cottage, would have been thought luxuries at an earlier period of our history. . . .

The friends of humanity cannot but wish that in all countries the labouring classes should have a taste for comforts and enjoyments, and that they should be stimulated by all legal means in their exertions to procure them. There cannot be a better security against a superabundant population. In those countries, where the labouring classes have the fewest wants, and are contented with the cheapest food, the people are exposed to the greatest vicissitudes and miseries. They have no place of refuge from calamity; they cannot seek safety in a lower station; they are already so low, that they can fall no lower. On any deficiency of the chief article of their subsistence, there are few substitutes of which they can avail themselves, and dearth to them is attended with almost all the evils of famine. . . .

These then are the laws by which wages are regulated, and by which the happiness of far the greatest part of every community is governed. Like all other contracts, wages should be left to the fair and free competition of the market, and should never be controlled by the interference of the legislature.

The clear and direct tendency of the poor laws, is in direct opposition to these obvious principles: it is not, as the legislature benevolently intended, to amend the condition of the poor, but to deteriorate the condition of both poor and rich; instead of making the poor rich, they are calculated to make the rich poor; and whilst the present laws are in force, it is quite in the natural order of things that the fund for the maintenance of the poor should progressively increase, till it has absorbed all the net revenue of the country, or at least so much of it as the state shall leave to us, after satisfying its own never failing demands for the public expenditure.

This pernicious tendency of these laws is no longer a mystery, since it has been fully developed by the able hand of Mr. Malthus; and every friend to the poor must ardently wish for their abolition. Unfortunately, however, they have been so long established, and the habits of the poor have been so formed upon their operation, that to eradicate them with safety from our political system, requires the most cautious and skilful management. It is agreed by all who are most friendly to a repeal of these laws, that if it be desirable to prevent the most overwhelming distress to those for whose benefit they were erroneously enacted, their abolition should be effected by the most gradual steps.

It is a truth which admits not a doubt, that the comforts and well-being of the poor cannot be permanently secured without some regard on their part, or some effort on the part of the legislature, to regulate the increase of their numbers, and to render less frequent among them early and improvident marriages. The operation of the system of poor laws has been directly contrary to this. They have rendered restraint superfluous, and have invited imprudence, by offering it a portion of the wages of prudence and industry.

The nature of the evil points out the remedy. By gradually contracting the sphere of the poor laws; by impressing on the poor the value of independence, by teaching them that they must look not to systematic or casual charity, but to their own exertions for support, that prudence and forethought are neither unnecessary nor unprofitable virtues, we shall by degrees approach a sounder and more healthful state.

No scheme for the amendment of the poor laws merits the least attention, which has not their abolition for its ultimate object; and he is the best friend to the poor, and to the cause of humanity, who can point out how this end can be attained with the most security, and at the same time with the least violence.

ON MACHINERY

Ever since I first turned my attention to questions of political economy, I have been of opinion, that such an application of machinery to any branch of production, as should have the effect of saving labour, was a general good, accompanied only with that portion of inconvenience which in most cases attends the removal of capital and labour from one employment to another. It appeared to me, that provided the landlords had the same money rents, they would be benefited by the reduction in the prices of some of the commodities on which those rents were expended, and which reduction of price could not fail to be the consequence of the employment of machinery. The capitalist, I thought, was eventually benefited precisely in the same manner. He, indeed, who made the discovery of the machine, or who first usefully applied it, would enjoy an additional advantage, by making great profits for a time; but, in proportion as the machine came into general use, the price of the commodity produced, would, from the effects of competition, sink to its cost of production, when the capitalist would get the same money profits as before, and he would only participate in the general advantage, as a consumer, by being enabled, with the same money revenue, to command an additional quantity of comforts and enjoyments. The class of labourers also, I thought, was equally benefited by the use of machinery, as they would have the means of buying more commodities with the same money wages, and I thought that no reduction of wages would take place, because the capitalist would have the power of demanding and employing the same quantity of labour as before, although he might be under the necessity of employing it in the production of a new, or at any rate of a different commodity. If, by improved machinery, with the employment of the same quantity of labour, the quantity of stockings could be quadrupled, and the demand for stockings were only doubled, some labourers would necessarily be discharged from the stocking trade; but as the capital which employed them was still in being, and as it was the interest of those who had it to employ it productively, it appeared to me that it would be employed on the production of some other commodity, useful to the society, for which there could not fail to be a demand; for I was, and am, deeply impressed with the truth of the observation of Adam Smith, that "the desire for food is limited in every man, by the narrow capacity of the human stomach, but the desire of the conveniences, and ornaments of building, dress, equipage and household furniture, seems to have no limit or certain boundary." As, then, it appeared to me that there would be the same demand for labour as before, and that wages would be no lower, I thought that the labouring class would, equally with the other classes, participate in the advantage, from the general cheapness of commodities arising from the use of machinery.

These were my opinions, and they continue unaltered, as far as regards the landlord and the capitalist; but I am convinced, that the substitution of machinery for human labour, is often very injurious to the interests of the class of labourers. . . .

My mistake arose from the supposition, that whenever the net income of a society increased, its gross income would also increase; I now, however, see reason to be satisfied that one fund, from which landlords and capitalists derive their revenue, may increase, while the other, that upon which the labouring class mainly depend, may diminish, and therefore it follows, if I am right, that the same cause which may increase the net revenue of the country, may at the same time render the population redundant, and deteriorate the condition of the labourer. . . .

All I wish to prove, is, that the discovery and use of machinery may be attended with a diminution of gross produce; and whenever that is the case, it will be injurious to the labouring class, as some of their number will be thrown out of employment, and population will become redundant, compared with the funds which are to employ it.

REPORT OF RICARDO'S SPEECH ON A POOR LAW BILL*

Session 1819: House of Commons
Poor Rates Misapplication Bill, 25 March 1819

Mr. Sturges Bourne moved for leave to bring in a bill, which, he declared, was intended to prevent the payment of the wages of labour out of the poor rates; no relief should in future be given to able-bodied labourers in employment, but their children should be provided for and set to work.

Mr. Ricardo thought, that the two great evils for which it was desirable

---

* From Piero Sraffa, ed., and M. H. Dobb, collab., *The Works and Correspondence of David Ricardo: Speeches and Evidence,* Vol. 5 (Cambridge: Cambridge University Press for the Royal Economic Society, 1952). This is the official summary of Ricardo's speech, made at the time the speech was given in the House of Commons.

to provide a remedy, were, the tendency towards a redundant population, and the inadequacy of the wages to the support of the labouring classes; and he apprehended, that the measure now proposed would not afford any security against the continuance of these evils. On the contrary, he thought that, if a provision were made for all the children of the poor, it would only increase the evil; for if parents felt assured that an asylum would be provided for their children, in which they would be treated with humanity and tenderness, there would then be no check to that increase of population which was so apt to take place among the labouring classes. With regard to the other evil, the inadequacy of the wages, it ought to be remembered, that if this measure should have the effect of raising them, they would still be no more than the wages of a single man, and would never rise so high as to afford a provision for a man with a family.

9. Change the Environment and Change the Man

Robert Owen

All his life, Robert Owen (1771–1858) cherished the belief that men are shaped by their environment and that better conditions would create better men. Owen's career was diverse. But whether as factory owner, pioneer factory reformer, social experimenter, or utopian socialist,[1] he never lost that faith, not even in the darkest days of the Industrial Revolution when men like Malthus were blaming the poor for their poverty and degradation.

Ironically, Welsh-born Owen was a self-made man. At 9 he left school to work. By 29 he owned one of the largest spinning mills in Scotland, at New Lanark. But Owen was dissatisfied with mere money-making. He wanted to prove that the poor could be remade with education and a new environment, so he turned New Lanark

---

[1] Utopian socialism is a term used to denote the various plans of late eighteenth century and of early and mid-nineteenth century social reformers who felt that the ills of society could be eliminated through some form of voluntary association. Marx dubbed them "utopian" because they relied on convincing the upper classes of the superiority of socialism. Marx considered his own form of socialism "scientific" because he believed in the existence of scientific laws governing society. And he became convinced that he had discovered laws showing that contradictions within capitalism would inevitably cause the downfall of that system and the rise of socialism. Socialism was inevitable, according to Marx, and you did not have to win over the upper classes to the cause.

into an experimental model community. Instead of slums and ignorance there were decent homes for workers, the first preschool nursery in Britain, and free schools for all children from 5 to 10 years old. Owen's factory innovations were considered absurd. He paid higher wages, reduced the workday from 17 to 10 hours, and banned children under 10 (instead of 6 years) from work.

The experiment proved both successful and profitable and New Lanark became world-famous. Owen had hoped that other industrialists would adopt his paternalistic methods. But they did not. Nor did the British government, despite rising unemployment, establish the self-supporting "villages of cooperation" for the poor that Owen advocated to replace the degrading and dehumanizing dole. In this selection Owen describes the organization of a proposed village in which there is to be great emphasis on rational education for children. It is part of the plan that he presented to Parliament in 1817.

The plan was defeated but not Owen, who became even more convinced of the evil of the competitive social system and the need for the reorganization of society along cooperative lines. Owen tried to implement these ideas in America, where he organized a short-lived cooperative community in Indiana. After his return to England he became the leader of a large working-class movement. Some of his followers founded the consumers' cooperative movement in the never-realized hope that consumers' cooperatives would become forerunners of working-class "villages of cooperation."

My Lords and Gentlemen, having been requested by you to draw up a detailed Report of a Plan for the general Relief of the Manufacturing and Labouring Poor, I have the honour to submit the following.

In order to do justice to this interesting subject, it is necessary to trace the operation of those leading causes, to which the distress now existing to an unprecedented extent in this country, and in other countries in no very slight degree, is to be ascribed: the evil will be found to flow from a state of things to which the progress of society has given birth; — a development of this will therefore suggest the means of counteracting it.

The immediate cause of the present distress is the depreciation of human labour. This has been occasioned by the general introduction of mechanism into the manufactures of Europe and America; but principally into those of Britain, where the change was greatly accelerated by the inventions of Arkwright and Watt. . . .

From Robert Owen, *Report to the Committee of the Association for the Relief of the Manufacturing and Laboring Poor,* laid before the Committee of the House of Commons on the Poor Laws (London, 1817).

I proceed, therefore, with the subject, and shall endeavour to show in what manner advantageous employment can be found for all the poor and working classes, under an arrangement which will permit mechanical improvements to be carried to any extent.

Under the existing laws, the unemployed working classes are maintained by, and consume part of the property and produce of, the wealthy and industrious, while their powers of body and mind remain unproductive. They frequently acquire the bad habits which ignorance and idleness never fail to produce; they amalgamate with the regular poor, and become a nuisance to society. . . .

. . . Any plan for the amelioration of the poor should combine means to prevent their children from acquiring bad habits, and to give them good ones — to provide useful training and instruction for them — to provide proper labour for the adults — to direct their labour and expenditure, so as to produce the greatest benefit to themselves and to society; and to place them under such circumstances as shall remove them from unnecessary temptations, and closely unite their interest and duty.

These advantages cannot be given either to individuals, or families, separately, or to large congregated numbers.

They can be effectually introduced into practice only under arrangements that would unite in one establishment a population of from 500 to 1500 persons, averaging about 1000. . . .

It is evident, that while the poor are suffered to remain under the circumstances in which they have hitherto existed, they, and their children with very few exceptions, will continue unaltered to succeeding generations.

In order to effect any radically beneficial change in their character, they must be removed from the influence of such circumstances, and placed under those which, being congenial to the natural constitution of man, and the well-being of society, cannot fail to produce that amelioration in their condition, which all classes have so great an interest in promoting.

Such circumstances, after incessant application to the subject, I have endeavoured to combine in the arrangement of the establishment represented in the drawings, so far as the present state of society will permit. These I will now attempt to explain more particularly.

Each lodging-room is to accommodate a man, his wife, and two children under three years of age; and to be such as will permit them to have much more comfort than the dwellings of the poor usually afford. It is intended that the children above three years of age should attend the school, eat in the mess-room, and sleep in the dormitories, the parents being of course permitted to see and converse with them at meals, and all other proper times. That before they leave school they shall be well instructed in all necessary and useful knowledge; that every possible means should be adopted to prevent the acquirement of bad habits, from their parents or otherwise; that no pains should be spared to impress upon them such habits and dispositions as may be most conducive to their happiness through life, as well as render them useful and valuable members of the community to which they belong.

It is proposed that the women should be employed, in the first place, in the care of their infants, and in keeping their dwellings in the best order. 2dly, In cultivating the gardens to raise vegetables for the supply of the public kitchen. 3dly, In attending to such of the branches of the various manufactures as women can well undertake; but not to be employed more than four or five hours in the day. 4thly, In making up clothing for the inmates of the establishment. 5thly, In attending occasionally, and in rotation, in the public kitchen, mess-rooms, and dormitories; and when properly instructed, in superintending some parts of the education of the children in the schools.

It is proposed that the elder children should be trained to assist in gardening and manufacturing for a portion of the day, according to their strength; and that the men should be employed, all of them, in agriculture, and also in manufactures or some other occupation for the benefit of the establishment.

The ignorance of the poor, their ill training, and want of a rational education, make it necessary that those of the present generation should be actively and regularly occupied through the day in some essentially useful work; yet in such a manner as that their employment should be healthy and productive. The plan which has been described will most amply admit of this. . . .

It is impossible to find language sufficiently strong to express the inconsistency, as well as the injustice, of our present proceedings towards the poor and working classes. They are left in gross ignorance. They are permitted to be trained up in habits of vice, and in the commission of crimes; and, as if purposely to keep them in ignorance and vice, and goad them on to commit criminal acts, they are perpetually surrounded with temptations which cannot fail to produce all those effects.

The system, or rather want of system, which exists with regard to the management of the poor has been emphatically condemned by a long and painful experience.

The immense sums annually raised for their relief are lavished in utter disregard of every principle of public justice or œconomy. They offer greater reward for idleness and vice than for industry and virtue; and thus directly operate to increase the degradation and misery of the classes whom they are designed to serve. No sum, however enormous, administered after this manner, could be productive of any other result: rather will pauperism and wretchedness increase along with the increase of an expenditure thus applied.

The poor and unemployed working classes however cannot, must not, be abandoned to their fate, lest the consequences entail misfortune on us all. Instead of being left as they now are, to the dominion of ignorance, and to the influence of circumstances which are fatal to their industry and morals — a situation in which it is easy to perceive the inefficacy, or rather the injuriousness, of granting them a provision in a mere pecuniary shape — they should, on the contrary, be afforded the means of procuring a certain and comfortable subsistence by their labour, under a system which will not only direct that labour and its earnings to the best advantage, but, at the same time, place them under circumstances the most favourable to the growth of morals and of happiness. In short, instead of allowing their habits to proceed under the worst influence possible, or rather as it were to be left to chance, thus producing unintentionally crimes that render necessary the severities of our penal code, — let a system for the prevention of pauperism and of crimes be adopted, and the operation of our penal code will soon be restricted to very narrow limits.

The outlines of such a plan, it is presumed, have been, however imperfectly, suggested and sketched in this Report.

It may be hoped that the Government of this country is now sufficiently alive to the necessity of abandoning the principle on which all our legislative measures on this subject have hitherto proceeded; for no thing short of this can place the empire in permanent safety. Until the preventive principle shall become the basis of legislative proceedings, it will be rain to look for any measures beyond partial temporary expedients, which will leave society unimproved, or involve it in a much worse state. . . .

A summary of the advantages to be derived from the execution of such a plan may be presented under the following heads:

1. Expensive as such a system for the unemployed poor may appear to a superficial observer, it will be found on mature investigation by those who understand all the consequences of such a combination, to be by far the most œconomical that has yet been devised.

2. Many of the unemployed poor are now in a state of gross ignorance, and have been trained in bad habits, — evils which, under the present system, are likely to continue for endless generations. The arrangements proposed offer the most certain means, in a manner gratifying to all the parties interested, and to every liberal mind, of overcoming both their ignorance and their bad habits in one generation.

3. The greatest evils in society arise from mankind being trained in principles of disunion. The proposed measures offer to unite men in the

pursuit of common objects for their mutual benefit, by presenting an easy practicable plan for gradually withdrawing the causes of difference among individuals, and of making their interest and duty very generally the same.

4. This system will also afford the most simple and effectual means of giving the best habits and sentiments to all the children of the unemployed poor, accordingly as society shall be able to determine what habits and sentiments, or what character, ought to be given to them.

5. It will likewise offer the most powerful means of improving the habits and general conduct of the present unemployed adult poor, who have been grossly neglected by society from their infancy.

6. Owing to the peculiar arrangement of the plan, it will give to the poor, in return for their labour, more valuable, substantial, and permanent comfort than they have ever yet been able to obtain.

7. In one generation it will supersede the necessity for poor rates, or any pecuniary gifts of charity, by preventing any one from being poor, or subject to such unnecessary degradation.

8. It will offer the means of gradually increasing the population of such unpopulous districts of Europe and America as may be deemed necessary; — of enabling a much greater population to subsist in comfort on a given spot, if requisite, than existed before; — in short, of increasing the strength and political power of the country in which it shall be adopted, more than tenfold.

9. It is so easy, that it may be put into practice with less ability and exertion than are necessary to establish a new manufacture in a new situation. Many individuals of ordinary talents have formed establishments which possess combinations much more complex. In fact, there would not be any thing required which is not daily performed in common society, and which, under the proposed arrangement, might not be much more easily accomplished.

10. It will effectually relieve the manufacturing and labouring poor from their present deep distress, without violently or prematurely interfering with the existing institutions of society.

11. It will permit mechanical inventions and improvements to be carried to any extent; for by the proposed arrangement every improvement in mechanism would be rendered subservient to, and in aid of, human labour.

12. and lastly. Every part of society would be essentially benefited by this change in the condition of the poor. Some plan founded on such principles as have been developed herein, appears absolutely necessary to secure the well-being of society; as well as to prevent the afflicting spectacle of thousands pining in want, and amidst a superabundance of means to well-train, educate, employ, and support in comfort, a population of at least four times the present numbers.

10. The Distribution of Wealth Depends on the Laws and Customs of Society

John Stuart Mill

John Stuart Mill (1806–1873), the noted philosopher and political theorist, was also the leading mid-nineteenth century British economist. Mill was a classical economist. But when his humanitarian ideals conflicted with his dismal economic interpretations, as often happened, he tried to reconcile the apparent contradictions. In doing so, Mill seriously weakened some basic premises of classical economics.

How did this dichotomy in thought influence Mill's analysis of poverty? True to the classical tradition, he thought that population growth was the main cause of poverty. But unlike Ricardo and Malthus, Mill maintained that man does have considerable control over his destiny. Thus, he felt confident that workers would recognize the danger of overpopulation and produce fewer offspring. (With improved living conditions, birth rates did start to drop in most Western nations in the last part of the nineteenth century.)

Like other classical economists, Mill believed in the existence of natural laws of production. But he parted company with the classicists by denying that there were immutable laws of distribution. Instead, he felt that society was bound by laws of production but could distribute its wealth in any way it desired.

Having rejected fixed laws of distribution, Mill went on to consider alternatives to the market system. In contrast to other classical economists, he did not assume the permanency of capitalism and its institutions; whereas the others were completely hostile to communism, Mill examined that system (the Utopian, not the Marxian variety) seriously and sympathetically.

We can see from this reading that Mill acknowledged the feasibility of organizing society under communistic principles and recognized the sufferings caused by capitalism. But he felt that a humane form of capitalism had never really been tried, and he wanted to give the existing system another chance. So he became a reformer and as such wandered from the path of pure laissez-faire capitalism laid out by Malthus and Ricardo. Mill actively supported labor unions, despite lingering doubts about their ability to raise wages and eliminate poverty. He also favored other reforms such as inheritance taxes, women's rights, and government regulation of working hours and child labor.

OF PROPERTY

The principles which have been set forth in the first part of this Treatise, are, in certain respects, strongly distinguished from those, on the consideration of which we are now about to enter. The laws and conditions of the production of wealth, partake of the character of physical truths. There is nothing optional or arbitrary in them. Whatever mankind produce, must be produced in the modes, and under the conditions, imposed by the constitution of external things, and by the inherent properties of their own bodily and mental structure. Whether they like it or not, their productions will be limited by the amount of their previous accumulation, and, that being given, it will be proportional to their energy, their skill, the perfection of their machinery, and their judicious use of the advantages of combined labour. Whether they like it or not, a double quantity of labour will not raise, on the same land, a double quantity of food, unless some improvement takes place in the processes of cultivation. Whether they like it or not, the unproductive expenditure of individuals will *pro tanto* tend to impoverish the community, and only their productive expenditure will enrich it. The opinions, or the wishes, which may exist on these different matters, do not control the things themselves. We cannot, indeed, foresee to what extent the modes of production may be altered, or the productiveness of labour increased, by future extensions of our knowledge of the laws of nature suggesting new processes of industry of which we have at present no conception. But howsoever we may succeed in making for ourselves more space within the limits set by the constitution of things, we know that there must be limits. We cannot alter the ultimate properties either of matter or mind, but can only employ those properties more or less successfully, to bring about the events in which we are interested.

It is not so with the Distribution of Wealth. That is a matter of human institution solely. The things once there, mankind, individually or collectively, can do with them as they like. They can place them at the disposal of whomsoever they please, and on whatever terms. Further, in the social state, in every state except total solitude, any disposal whatever of them can only take place by the consent of society, or rather of those who dispose of its active force. Even when a person has produced by his individual toil, unaided by any one, he cannot keep, unless by the permission of society. Not only can society take it from him, but individuals could and would take it from him, if society only remained passive; if it did not either interfere *en masse,* or employ and pay people for the purpose of preventing him from being disturbed in the possession. The distribution of wealth, therefore, depends on the laws and customs of society. The rules by which it is determined, are what the opinions and feelings of the ruling portion of the community make them, and are very different in different ages and countries; and might be still more different, if mankind so chose.

OF COMMUNISM

Whatever may be the merits or defects of these various [socialist and communist] schemes, they cannot be truly said to be impracticable. No reasonable person can doubt that a village community, composed of a few thousand inhabitants cultivating in joint ownership the same extent of land which at present feeds the number of people, and producing by combined labour and the most improved processes the manufactured articles which they required, could raise an amount of productions sufficient to maintain them in comfort; and would find the means of obtaining, and if need be, exacting, the quantity of labour necessary for this purpose, from every member of the association who was capable of work.

The objection ordinarily made to a system of community of property and equal distribution of the produce, that each person would be incessantly occupied in evading his fair share of the work, points, undoubtedly, to a real difficulty. But those who urge this objection, forget to how great an extent the same difficulty exists under the system on which nine-tenths of the business of society is now conducted. The objection supposes, that honest and efficient labour is only to be had from those who are themselves individually to reap the benefit of their own exertions. But how small a part of all the labour performed in England, from the lowest paid to the highest, is done by persons working for their own benefit. From the Irish reaper or hodman to the chief justice or the minister of state, nearly all the work of society is remunerated by day wages or fixed salaries. A factory operative has less personal interest in his work than a member of a Communist association, since he is not, like him, working for a partnership of which he is himself a member. . . .

. . . Even the labourer who loses his employment by idleness or negligence, has nothing worse to suffer, in the most unfavourable case, than the discipline of a workhouse, and if the desire to avoid this be a sufficient motive in the one system, it would be sufficient in the other. I am not undervaluing the strength of the incitement given to labour when the whole or a large share of the benefit of extra exertion belongs to the labourer. But under the present system of industry this incitement, in the great majority of cases, does not exist. If Communistic labour might be less vigorous than that of a peasant proprietor, or a workman labouring on his own account, it would probably be more energetic than that of a labourer for hire, who has no personal interest in the matter at all. The neglect by the uneducated classes of labourers for hire, of the duties which they engage to perform, is in the present state of society most flagrant. Now it is an admitted condition of the Communist scheme that all shall be educated: and this being supposed, the duties of the members of the association would doubtless be as diligently performed as those of the generality of salaried officers in the middle or higher classes; who are not supposed to be necessarily unfaithful to their trust, because so long as they are not dismissed, their pay is the same in however lax a manner their duty is fulfilled. Undoubtedly, as a general rule, remuneration by fixed salaries does not in any class of functionaries produce the maximum of zeal: and this is as much as can be reasonably alleged against Communistic labour.

That even this inferiority would necessarily exist, is by no means so certain as is assumed by those who are little used to carry their minds beyond the state of things with which they are familiar. Mankind are capable of a far greater amount of public spirit than the present age is accustomed to suppose possible. History bears witness to the success with which large bodies of human beings may be trained to feel the public interest their own. And no soil could be more favourable to the growth of such a feeling, than a Communist association, since all the ambition, and the bodily and mental activity, which are now exerted in the pursuit of separate and self-regarding interests, would require another sphere of employment, and would naturally find it in the pursuit of the general benefit of the community. The same cause, so often assigned in explanation of the devotion of the Catholic priest or monk to the interest of his order — that he has no interest apart from it — would, under Communism, attach the citizen to the community. And independently of the public motive, every member of the association would be amenable to the most universal, and one of the strongest, of personal motives, that of public opinion. The force of this motive in deterring from any act or omission positively reproved by the community, no one is likely to deny; but the power also of emulation, in exciting to the most strenuous exertions for the sale of the approbation and admiration of others, is borne witness to by experience in every situation in which human beings publicly compete with one another, even if it be in things frivolous, or from which the public derive no benefit. A contest, who can do most for the common good, is not the kind of competition which Socialists repudiate. To what extent, therefore, the energy of labour would be diminished by Communism, or whether in the long run it would be diminished at all, must be considered for the present an undecided question.

Another of the objections to Communism is similar to that, so often urged against poor-laws: that if every member of the community were assured of subsistence for himself and any number of children, on the sole condition of willingness to work, prudential restraint on the multiplication of mankind would be at an end, and population would start forward at a rate which would reduce the community through successive stages of increasing discomfort to actual starvation. There would certainly be much ground for this apprehension if Communism provided no motives of restraint, equivalent to those which it would take away. But Communism is precisely the state of things in which opinion might be expected to declare itself with greatest intensity against this kind of selfish intemperance. An augmentation of numbers which diminished the comfort or increased the toil of the mass, would then cause (which now it does not) immediate and unmistakeable inconvenience to every individual in the association; inconvenience which could not then be imputed to the avarice of employers, or the unjust privileges of the rich. In such altered circumstances opinion could not fail to reprobate, and if reprobation did not suffice, to repress by penalties of some description, this or any other culpable self-indulgence at the expense of the community. The Communistic scheme, instead of being peculiarly open to the objection drawn from danger of over-population, has the recommendation of tending in an especial degree to the prevention of that evil.

A more real difficulty is that of fairly apportioning the labour of the community among its members. There are many kinds of work, and by what standard are they to be measured one against another? Who is to judge how much cotton spinning, or distributing goods from the stores, or bricklaying, or chimney sweeping, is equivalent to so much ploughing? The difficulty of making the adjustment between different qualities of labour is so strongly felt by Communist writers, that they have usually thought it necessary to provide that all should work by turns at every description of useful labour: an arrangement which by putting an end to the division of employments, would sacrifice so much of the advantage of co-operative production as greatly to diminish the productiveness of labour. Besides, even in the same kind of work, nominal equality of labour would be so great a real inequality, that the feeling of justice would revolt against its being enforced. All persons are not equally fit for all labour; and the same quantity of labour is an unequal burthen on the weak and the strong, the hardy and the delicate, the quick and the slow, the dull and the intelligent.

But these difficulties, though real, are not necessarily insuperable. The apportionment of work to the strength and capacities of individuals, the mitigation of a general rule to provide for cases in which it would operate harshly, are not problems to which human intelligence, guided by a sense of justice, would be inadequate. And the worst and most unjust arrangement which could be made of these points, under a system aiming at equality, would be so far short of the inequality and injustice with which labour (not to speak of remuneration) is now apportioned, as to be scarcely worth counting in the comparison. We must remember too that Communism, as a system of society, exists only in idea; that its difficulties, at present, are much better understood than its resources; and that the intellect of mankind is only beginning to contrive the means of organizing it in detail, so as to overcome the one and derive the greatest advantage from the other.

If, therefore, the choice were to be made between Communism with all its chances, and the present state of society with all its sufferings and injustices; if the institution of private property necessarily carried with it as a consequence, that the produce of labour should be apportioned as we now see it, almost in an inverse ratio to the labour — the largest portions to those who have never worked at all, the next largest to those whose work is almost nominal, and so in a descending scale, the remuneration dwindles as the work grows harder and more disagreeable, until the most fatiguing and exhausting bodily labour cannot count with certainty on being able to earn even the necessaries of life; if this, or Communism, were the alternative, all the difficulties, great or small, of Communism, would be but as dust in the balance. But to make the comparison applicable, we must compare Communism at its best, with the régime of individual property, not as it is, but as it might be made. The principle of private property has never yet had a fair trial in any country; and less so, perhaps, in this country than in some others. The social arrangements of modern Europe commenced from a distribution of property which was the result, not of just partition, or acquisition by industry, but of conquest and violence: and notwithstanding what industry has been doing for many centuries to modify the work of force, the system still retains many and large traces of its origin. The laws of property have never yet conformed to the principles on which the justification of private property rests. They have made property of things which never ought to be property, and absolute property where only a qualified property ought to exist. They have not held the balance fairly between human beings, but have heaped impediments upon some, to give advantage to others; they have purposely fostered inequalities, and prevented all from starting fair in the race. That all should indeed start on perfectly equal terms, is inconsistent with any law of private property: but if as much pains as has been taken to aggravate the inequality of chances arising from the natural working of the principle, had been taken to temper that inequality by every means not subversive to the principle itself; if the tendency of legislation had been to favour the diffusion, instead of the concentration of wealth — to encourage the subdivision of the large masses, instead of striving to keep them together; the principle of individual property would have been found to have no necessary connexion with the physical and social evils which almost all Socialist writers assume to be inseparable from it.

Private property, in every defence made of it, is supposed to mean, the guarantee to individuals of the fruits of their own labour and abstinence. The guarantee to them of the fruits of the labour and abstinence of others, transmitted to them without any merit or exertion of their own, is not of the essence of the institution, but a mere incidental consequence, which when it reaches a certain height, does not promote, but conflicts with the ends which render private property legitimate. To judge of the final destination of the institution of property, we must suppose everything rectified, which causes the institution to work in a manner opposed to that equitable principle, of proportion between remuneration and exertion, on which in every vindication of it that will bear the light, it is assumed to be grounded. We must also suppose two conditions realized, without which neither Communism nor any other laws or institutions could make the condition of the mass of mankind other than degraded and miserable. One of these conditions is, universal education; the other, a due limitation of the numbers of the community. With these, there could be no poverty even under the present social institutions: and these being supposed, the question of socialism is not, as generally stated by Socialists, a question of flying to the sole refuge against the evils which now bear down humanity; but a mere question of comparative advantages, which futurity must determine. We are too ignorant either of what individual agency in its best form, or Socialism in its best form, can accomplish, to be qualified to decide which of the two will be the ultimate form of human society.

If a conjecture may be hazarded, the decision will probably depend mainly on one consideration, viz. which of the two systems is consistent with the greatest amount of human liberty and spontaneity. After the means of subsistence are assured, the next in strength of the personal wants of human beings is liberty; and (unlike the physical wants, which as civilization advances become more moderate and more amenable to control) it increases instead of diminishing in intensity, as the intelligence and the moral faculties are more developed. The perfection both of social arrangements and of practical morality would be, to secure to all persons complete independence and freedom of action, subject to no restriction but that of not doing injury to others: and the education which taught or the social institutions which required them to exchange the control of their own actions for any amount of comfort or affluence, or to renounce liberty for the sake of equality, would deprive them of one of the most elevated characteristics of human nature. It remains to be discovered how far the preservation of this characteristic would be found compatible with the Communistic organization of society. No doubt, this, like all other objections to the Socialist schemes, is vastly exaggerated. The members of the association need not be required to live together more than they do now, nor need they be controlled in the disposal of their individual share of the produce, and of the probably large amount of leisure which, if they limited their production to things really worth producing, they would possess. Individuals need not be chained to an occupation, or to a particular locality. The restraints of Communism would be freedom in comparison with the present condition of the majority of the human race. The generality of labourers in this and most other countries, have as little choice of occupation or freedom of locomotion, are practically as dependent on fixed rules and on the will of others, as they could be on any system short of actual slavery; to say nothing of the entire domestic subjection of one half the species, to which it is the signal honour of Owenism and most other forms of Socialism that they assign equal rights, in all respects, with those of the hitherto dominant sex. But it is not by comparison with the present bad state of society that the claims of Communism can be estimated; nor is it sufficient that it should promise greater personal and mental freedom than is now enjoyed by those who have not enough of either to deserve the name. The question is, whether there would be any asylum left for individuality of character; whether public opinion would not be a tyrannical yoke; whether the absolute dependence of each on all, and surveillance of each by all, would not grind all down into a tame uniformity of thoughts, feelings, and actions. This is already one of the glaring evils of the existing state of society, notwithstanding a much greater diversity of education and pursuits, and a much less absolute dependence of the individual on the mass, than would exist in the Communistic régime. No society in which eccentricity is a matter of reproach, can be in a wholesome state. It is yet to be ascertained whether the Communistic scheme would be consistent with that multiform development of human nature, those manifold unlikenesses, that diversity of tastes and talents, and variety of intellectual points of view, which not only form a great part of the interest of human life, but by bringing intellects into stimulating collision, and by presenting to each innumerable notions that he would not have conceived of himself, are the mainspring of mental and moral progression.

Chapter Three

The Challenge of Marxism

11. The Attitude of the Bourgeoisie Towards the Proletariat

Friedrich Engels

Friedrich Engels (1820–1895), cofounder, with Karl Marx, of Marxian or "scientific" socialism, had an unlikely background for a career as a revolutionary socialist. German-born Engels was the son of a wealthy and conservative manufacturer. Like his fellow countryman, friend, and collaborator Karl Marx, Engels spent most of his adult life in England.

Both Engels and Marx were theoreticians for and active participants in the revolutionary socialist movements of their time. The relationship between them was personal and intellectual. Engels even subsidized Marx, who was often reduced to dire poverty, so that he might continue to write. Their friendship continued until Marx's death. Their intellectual collaboration continued even beyond the grave, for Engels edited many of Marx's best-known manuscripts after his death.

Engels first arrived in England in 1842, sent there to manage his family's factory in Manchester. England was then the world's foremost industrial power and Engels was impressed by her unparalleled industrial progress. But, with his observant eye, he missed little and was even more profoundly impressed by the suffering and exploitation of the working classes: Wretchedness. Starvation. Squalor. Overwork (fourteen, fifteen, even sixteen hours a day). Child labor (four- and five-year-olds in the mines and mills). Overcrowded hovels (seven, ten, twenty to a room). Filth. No sanitation. Epidemics. Cholera, the scourge of the slums. And a bourgeoisie intent upon making money regardless of social consequences.

As a response to his first encounter with English industrial capitalism, young Engels wrote The Condition of the Working Class in England in 1844 *(published in 1845). The book attracted wide attention and is a classic portrayal of the horrors of working-class life during the Industrial Revolution in England. More than that, it is a condemnation of capitalism, a system which brutally oppressed the workers whose labor it required. In Engels's view humanity inevitably perishes and brutality flourishes in a system based on maximizing private profit.*

Excerpts from two chapters of this classic are reproduced here. In the first short passage Engels describes child labor in the mines. The second selection, which furnished the title of this reading, is from the concluding chapter of the book and describes the callous attitude of the bourgeoisie toward the proletariat and the barbaric treatment of the poor in the workhouses of England. It ends with an apocalyptic warning of bitter class divisions: "It is too late for a peaceful solution" in the war of the poor against the rich. The passage contains the seeds of thought expressed in the world-famous The Communist Manifesto, *written by Marx and Engels in 1848 for the newly formed Communist League, in which they urged workers to unite, overthrow oppressive capitalism, and establish communism. That was their solution to the problem of poverty.*

THE MINING PROLETARIAT

In the North of England, on the borders of Northumberland and Durham, are the extensive lead mines of Alston Moor. The reports from this district agree almost wholly with those from Cornwall. Here, too, there are complaints of want of oxygen, excessive dust, powder smoke, carbonic acid gas and sulphur in the atmosphere of the workings. In consequence, the miners here, as in Cornwall, are small of stature, and nearly all suffer from the thirtieth year throughout life from chest affections, which end, especially when this work is persisted in, as is almost always the case, in consumption, so greatly shortening the average of life of these people. . . . In this district we find again the lodging houses and sleeping places with which we have already become acquainted in the towns, and in quite as filthy, disgusting and overcrowded a state as there. Commissioner

From Frederick Engels, *The Condition of the Working Class in England in 1844.* Translated by Florence Kelley Wishnewetzky (New York: John Lovell Company, 1887). Reprinted by permission of George, Allen and Unwin, London.

Mitchell visited one such sleeping barrack, 18 feet long, 13 feet wide, and arranged for the reception of 42 men and 14 boys, or 56 persons altogether, one-half of whom slept above the other in berths as on shipboard. There was no opening for the escape of the foul air; and, although no one had slept in this pen for three nights preceding the visit, the smell and the atmosphere were such that Commissioner Mitchell could not endure it a moment. What must it be through a hot summer night, with fifty-six occupants! And this is not the steerage of an American slave ship, it is the dwelling of free born Britons! . . .

In the coal and iron mines which are worked in pretty much the same way, children of four, five and seven years are employed. They are set to transporting the ore or coal loosened by the miner from its place to the horse path or the main shaft, and to opening and shutting the doors (which separate the divisions of the mine and regulate its ventilation) for the passage of workers and material. For watching the doors the smallest children are usually employed, who thus pass twelve hours daily, in the dark, alone, sitting usually in damp passages without even having work enough to save them from the stupefying, brutalizing tedium of doing nothing. The transport of coal and iron-stone, on the other hand, is very hard labor, the stuff being shoved in large tubs, without wheels, over the uneven floor of the mine; often over moist clay, or through water, and frequently up steep inclines and through paths so low roofed that the workers are forced to creep on hand and knees. For this more wearing labor, therefore, older children and half-grown girls are employed. One man or two boys per tub are employed, according to circumstances; and, if two boys, one pushes and the other pulls. The loosening of the ore or coal, which is done by men or strong youths of sixteen years or more, is also very weary work. The usual working day is eleven to twelve hours, often longer; in Scotland it reaches fourteen hours, and double time is frequent, when all the employees are at work below ground twenty-four, and even thirty-six hours at a stretch. Set times for meals are almost unknown, so that these people eat when hunger and time permit.

The standard of living of the miners is in general described as fairly good and their wages high in comparison with those of the agricultural laborers surrounding them (who, however, live at starvation rates), except in certain parts of Scotland and in the Irish mines where great misery prevails. . . .

THE ATTITUDE OF THE BOURGEOISIE TOWARDS THE PROLETARIAT

I have never seen a class so deeply demoralised, so incurably debased by selfishness, so corroded within, so incapable of progress, as the English bourgeoisie; and I mean by this, especially the bourgeoisie proper, particularly the Liberal, Corn Law repealing bourgeoisie. For it nothing exists in this world, except for the sake of money, itself not excluded. It knows no bliss save that of rapid gain, no pain save that of losing gold. In the presence of this avarice and lust of gain, it is not possible for a single human sentiment or opinion to remain untainted. True, these English bourgeois are good husbands and family men, and have all sorts of other private virtues, and appear, in ordinary intercourse, as decent and respectable as all other bourgeois; even in business they are better to deal with than the Germans; they do not higgle and haggle so much as our own pettifogging merchants; but how does this help matters? Ultimately it is self-interest, and especially money gain, which alone determines them. I once went into Manchester with such a bourgeois and spoke to him of the bad unwholesome method of building, the frightful condition of the working people's quarters, and asserted that I had never seen so ill-built a city. The man listened quietly to the end, and said at the corner where we parted: "And yet there is a great deal of money made here; good morning, sir." It is utterly indifferent to the English bourgeois whether his workingmen starve or not, if only he makes money. All the conditions of life are measured by money, and what brings no money is nonsense, unpractical, idealistic bosh. . . . He cannot comprehend that he holds any other relation to the operatives than that of purchase and sale; he sees in them, not human beings but hands, as he constantly calls them to their faces; he insists, as Carlyle says, the "Cash Payment" is the only nexus between man and man. Even the relation between himself and his wife is, in ninety-nine cases out of a hundred, mere "Cash Payment." Money determines the worth of the man; he is "worth ten thousand pounds." He who has money is of "the better sort of people," is "influential," and what *he* does counts for something in his social circle. The huckstering spirit penetrates the whole language, all relations are expressed in business terms, in economic categories. Supply and demand are the formulas according to which the logic of the English bourgeois judges all human life. Hence free competition in every respect, hence the regime of *laissez-faire, laissez-aller* in government, in medicine, in education, and soon to be in religion, too, as the State church collapses more and more. Free competition will suffer no limitation, no State supervision, the whole State is but a burden to it, it would reach its highest perfection in a wholly ungoverned anarchic society, where each might exploit the other to his heart's content. Since, however, the bourgeoisie cannot dispense with government, but must have it to hold the equally indispensable proletariat in check, it turns the power of government against the proletariat and keeps out of its way as far as possible.

Let no one believe, however, that the "cultivated" Englishman openly brags with his egotism. On the contrary, he conceals it under the vilest hypocrisy. What? The wealthy English fail to remember the poor? They who have founded philanthropic institutions, such as no other country can boast of! Philanthropic institutions forsooth! As though you rendered the proletarians a service in first sucking out their very life-blood and then practicing your self-complacent, pharisaic philanthropy upon them, placing yourselves before the world as mighty benefactors of humanity when you give back to the plundered victims the hundredth part of what belongs to them! Charity which degrades him who gives more than him who takes; charity which treads the downtrodden still deeper in the dust, which demands that the degraded, the Pariah cast out by society, shall first surrender the last that remains to him, his very claim to manhood, shall first beg for mercy before your mercy deigns to press, in the shape of an alms, the brand of degradation upon his brow. . . .

. . . Let us turn now to the manner in which the bourgeoisie as a party, as the power of the State, conducts itself towards the proletariat. Laws are necessary only because there are persons in existence who own nothing; and although this is directly expressed in but few laws, as for instance those against vagabonds, and tramps, in which the proletariat as such is outlawed, yet enmity to the proletariat is so emphatically the basis of the law that the judges, and especially the Justices of the Peace who are bourgeois themselves and with whom the proletariat comes most in contact, find this meaning in the laws without further consideration. If a rich man is brought up, or rather summoned to appear before the court, the judge regrets that he is obliged to impose so much trouble, treats the matter as favorably as possible and, if he is forced to condemn the accused, does so with extreme regret, etc., etc., and the end of it all is a miserable fine which the bourgeois throws upon the table with contempt and then departs. But if a poor devil gets into such a position as involves appearing before the Justice of the Peace, he has almost always spent the night in the station-house, with a crowd of his peers, is regarded from the beginning as guilty; his defense is set aside with a contemptuous "Oh! we know the excuses," and a fine imposed which he cannot pay and must work out with several months on the treadmill. And if nothing can be proved against him, he is sent to the treadmill, none the less, "as a rogue and a vagabond." The partisanship of the Justices of the Peace, especially in the country, surpasses all description, and it is so much the order of the day that all cases which are not too utterly flagrant are quietly reported by the newspapers, without comment. Nor is any thing else to be expected. For on the one hand, these Dogberries do merely construe the law according to the intent of the framers and, on the other, they are, themselves bourgeois who see the foundation of all true order in the interests of their class. And the conduct of the police corresponds to that of the Justices of the Peace. The bourgeois may do what he will and the policeman remains ever polite, adhering strictly to the law, but the proletarian is roughly, brutally treated; his poverty both casts the suspicion of every sort of crime upon him and cuts him off from legal redress against any caprice of the administrators of the law; for him, therefore, the protecting forms of the law do not exist, the police force their way into his house without further ceremony, arrest and abuse him; and only when a workingmen's association, such as the miners, engages a Roberts, does it become evident how little the protective side of the law exists for the workingmen, how frequently he has to bear all the burdens of the law without enjoying its benefits. . . .

The most open declaration of war of the bourgeoisie upon the proletariat is Malthus' Law of Population and the New Poor Law framed in accordance with it. We have already alluded several times to the theory of Malthus. We may sum up its final result in these few words that the earth is perennially overpopulated, whence poverty, misery, distress and immorality must prevail; that it is the lot, the eternal destiny of mankind, to exist in too great numbers and therefore in diverse classes, of which some are rich, educated and moral, and others more or less poor, distressed, ignorant and immoral. Hence it follows in practice, and Malthus himself drew this conclusion, that charities and poor rates are, properly speaking, nonsense, since they serve only to maintain and stimulate the increase of the surplus population whose competition crushes down wages for the employed; that the employment of the poor by the Poor Law Guardians is equally unreasonable since only a fixed quantity of the products of labor can be consumed, and for every unemployed laborer thus furnished employment another hitherto employed, must be driven into enforced idleness whence private undertakings suffer at cost of Poor Law industry; that, in other words, the whole problem is not how to support the surplus population, but how to restrain it as far as possible. Malthus declares in plain English that the right to live, a right previously asserted in favor of every man in the world, is nonsense. . . .

Since, however, the rich hold all the power, the proletarians must submit, if they will not good-temperedly perceive it for themselves, to have the law actually declare them superfluous. This has been done by the New Poor Law. The Old Poor Law which rested upon the Act of 1601, (the 43d of Elizabeth), naively started from the notion that it is the duty of the parish to provide for the maintenance of the poor. Whoever had no work received relief, and the poor man regarded the parish as pledged to protect him from starvation. He demanded his weekly relief as his right, not as a favor, and this became, at last, too much for the bourgeoisie. In 1833, when the bourgeoisie had just come into power through the Reform Bill, and pauperism in the country districts had just reached its full development, the bourgeoisie began the reform of the Poor Law according to its own point of view. A commission was appointed, which investigated the administration of the Poor Laws, and revealed a multitude of abuses. It was discovered that the whole working class in the country was pauperized and more or less dependent upon the rates from which they receive relief when wages were low; it was found that this system by which the unemployed were maintained, the ill-paid and the parents of large families relieved, fathers of illegitimate children required to pay alimony and poverty, in general, recognized as needing protection — it was found that this system was ruining the nation, was:

> A check upon industry, a reward for improvident marriage, a stimulus to increased population and a means of counterbalancing the effect of an increased population upon wages; a national provision for discouraging the honest and industrious, and protecting the lazy, vicious and improvident; calculated to destroy the bonds of family life, hinder systematically the accumulation of capital, scatter that which is already accumulated and ruin the taxpayers. Moreover, in the provision of aliment, it sets a premium upon illegitimate children.

(Words of the Report of the Poor Law Commissioner). This description of the action of the Old Poor Law is certainly correct; relief fosters laziness and increase of "surplus population." Under present social conditions it is perfectly clear that the poor man is compelled to be an egotist, and when he can choose, living equally well in either case, he prefers doing nothing to working. But what follows therefrom? That our present social conditions are good for nothing, and not as the Malthusian Commissioners conclude, that poverty is a crime and as such to be visited with heinous penalties which may serve as a warning to others.

But these wise Malthusians were so thoroughly convinced of the infallibility of their theory that they did not for one moment hesitate to cast the poor into the Procrustean bed of their economic notions and treat them with the most revolting cruelty. Convinced with Malthus and the rest of the adherents of free competition that it is best to let each one take care of himself, they would have preferred to abolish the Poor Laws altogether. Since, however, they had neither the courage nor the authority to do this, they proposed a Poor Law constructed as far as possible in harmony with the doctrine of Malthus, which is yet more barbarous than that of *laissez-faire,* because it interferes actively in cases in which the latter is passive. We have seen how Malthus characterizes poverty or rather the want of employment, as a crime under the title "superfluity," and recommends for it punishment by starvation. The commissioners were not quite so barbarous; death outright by starvation was something too terrible even for a Poor Law Commissioner. "Good," said they, "we grant you poor a right to exist, but only to exist; the right to multiply you have not, nor the right to exist as befits human beings. You are a pest, and if we cannot get rid of you as we do of other pests, you shall feel, at least, that you are a pest, and you shall at least be held in check, kept from bringing into the world other 'surplus' either directly or through inducing in others laziness and want of employment. Live you shall, but live as an awful warning to all those who might have inducements to become 'superfluous.' "

They accordingly brought in the New Poor Law, which was passed by Parliament in 1834, and continues in force down to the present day. All relief in money and provisions was abolished; the only relief allowed was admission to the workhouses immediately built. The regulations for these workhouses, or as the people call them, Poor Law Bastilles, is such as to frighten away every one who has the slightest prospect of life without this form of public charity. To make sure that relief be applied for only in the most extreme cases and after every other effort had failed, the workhouse has been made the most repulsive residence which the refined ingenuity of a Malthusian can invent. The food is worse than that of the most ill-paid workingman while employed, and the work harder, or they might prefer the workhouse to their wretched existence outside. Meat, especially fresh meat, is rarely furnished, chiefly potatoes, the worse possible bread and oat-meal porridge, little or no beer. The food of criminal prisoners is better, as a rule, so that the paupers frequently commit some offense for the purpose of getting into jail. For the workhouse is a jail, too; he who does not finish his task gets nothing to eat; he who wishes to go out must ask permission, which is granted or not, according to his behavior or the inspector's whim; tobacco is forbidden, also the receipt of gifts from relatives or friends outside the house; the paupers wear a workhouse uniform, and are handed over helpless and without redress, to the caprice of the inspectors. To prevent their labor from competing with that of outside concerns, they are set to rather useless tasks; the men break stones "as much as a strong man can accomplish with effort in a day"; the women, children and aged men pick oakum, for I know not what insignificant use. To prevent the "superfluous" from multiplying and "demoralized" parents from influencing their children, families are broken up; the husband is placed in one wing, the wife in another, the children in a third, and they are perimtted to see one another only at stated times after long intervals, and then only when they have, in the opinion of the officials, behaved well. And in order to shut off the external world from contamination by pauperism within these bastilles, the inmates are permitted to receive visits only with the consent of the officials, and in the reception rooms, to communicate in general with the world outside only by leave and under supervision.

. . . In practise, the spirit and not the letter of the law is followed in the treatment of the poor, as in the following few examples:

In the workhouse at Greenwich, in the summer of 1843, a boy five years old was punished by being shut into the dead-room, where he had to sleep upon the lids of the coffins. In the workhouse at Herne, the same punishment was inflicted upon a little girl for wetting the bed at night, and this method of punishment seems to be a favorite one. This workhouse, which stands in one of the most beautiful regions of Kent, is peculiar in so far as its windows open only upon the court, and but two, newly introduced, afford the inmates a glimpse of the outer world. The author who relates this in the *Illuminated Magazine,* closes his description with the words: "If God punished men for crimes as man punishes man for poverty, then woe to the sons of Adam!"

. . . In the St. Pancras workhouse in London (where the cheap shirts are made), an epileptic died of suffocation during an attack in bed, no one coming to his relief; in the same house four to six, sometimes eight children, slept in one bed. In Shoreditch workhouse, a man was placed together with a fever patient violently ill, in a bed teeming with vermin. In Bethnal Green workhouse, London, a woman in the sixth month of pregnancy was shut up in the reception-room with her two-year-old child, from February 28th to March 20th, without being admitted into the workhouse itself, and without a trace of a bed or the means of satisfying the most natural wants. Her husband, who was brought into the workhouse, begged to have his wife released from this imprisonment, whereupon he received twenty-four hours imprisonment with bread and water as the penalty of his insolence. . . . In Stockport, July 31st, 1844, a man seventy-two years old, was brought before the Justice of the Peace for refusing to break stones, and insisting that by reason of his age and a stiff knee, he was unfit for this work. In vain did he offer to undertake any work adapted to his physical strength; he was sentenced to two weeks upon the treadmill. In the workhouse at Basford, an inspecting official found that the sheets had not been changed in thirteen weeks, shirts in four weeks, stockings in two to ten months, so that of forty-five boys but three had stockings, and all their shirts were in tatters. The beds swarmed with vermin, and the tableware was washed in the slop-pails. In the West of London workhouse, a porter who had infected four girls with syphilis was not discharged, and another who had concealed a deaf and dumb girl four days and nights in his bed was also retained.

As in life, so in death. The poor are dumped into the earth like infected cattle. The pauper burial ground of St. Brides, London, is a bare morass in use as a cemetery since the time of Charles II., and filled with heaps of bones; every Wednesday the paupers are thrown into a ditch fourteen feet deep, a curate rattles through the Litany at the top of his speed; the ditch is loosely covered in, to be re-opened the next Wednesday, and filled with corpses as long as one more can be forced in. The putrefaction thus engendered contaminates the whole neighborhood. In Manchester, the pauper burial ground lies opposite to the Old Town, along the Irk; this, too, is a rough, desolate place. About two years ago, a railroad was carried through it. If it had been a respectable cemetery, how the bourgeoisie and the clergy would have shrieked over the desecration! But it was a pauper burial ground, the resting-place of the outcast and superfluous, so no one concerned himself about the matter. It was not even thought worth while to convey the partially decayed bodies to the other side of the cemetery; they were heaped up just as it happened, and piles were driven into newly-made graves, so that water oozed out of the swampy ground, pregnant with putrifying matter, and filled the neighborhood with the most revolting and injurious gases. The disgusting brutality which accompanied this work I cannot describe in further detail.

Can any one wonder that the poor decline to accept public relief under these conditions? That they starve rather than enter these bastilles? I have the reports of five cases in which persons actually starving, when the guardians refused them outdoor relief, went back to their miserable homes and died of starvation rather than enter these hells. Thus far have the Poor Law Commissioners attained their object. At the same time, however, the workhouses have intensified more than any other measure of the party in power the hatred of the working class against the property holders, who very generally admire the New Poor Law.

From Newcastle to Dover, there is but one voice among the workers, the voice of hatred against the new law. The bourgeoisie has formulated so clearly in this law, its conception of its duties towards the proletariat, that it has been appreciated even by the dullest. So frankly, so boldly had the conception never yet been formulated, that the non-possessing class exists solely for the purpose of being exploited and of starving when the property holders can no longer make use of it. Hence it is that this New Poor Law has contributed so greatly to accelerate the labor movement, and especially to spread Chartism; and, as it is carried out most extensively in the country, it facilitates the development of the proletarian movement which is arising in the agricultural districts. . . .

. . . Prophecy is nowhere so easy as in England, where all the component elements of society are clearly defined and sharply separated. The revolution must come; it is already too late to bring about a peaceful solution; but it can be made more gentle than that prophesied in the foregoing pages. This depends, however, more upon the development of the proletariat than upon that of the bourgeoisie. In proportion, as the proletariat absorbs socialistic and communistic elements, will the revolution diminish in bloodshed, revenge and savagery. Communism stands, in principle, above the breach between bourgeoisie and proletariat, recognizes only its historic significance for the present, but not its justification for the future; wishes, indeed, to bridge over this chasm, to do away with all class antagonisms. Hence it recognizes as justified so long as the struggle exists, the exasperation of the proletariat towards its oppressors as a necessity, as the most important lever for a labor movement just beginning; but it goes beyond this exasperation, because communism is a question of humanity and not of the workers alone. Besides, it does not occur to any communist to wish to revenge himself upon individuals, or to believe that, in general, the single bourgeois can act otherwise, under existing circumstances, than he does act. English Socialism, (*i.e.,* Communism), rests directly upon the irresponsibility of the individual. Thus the more the English workers absorb communistic ideas, the more superfluous becomes their present bitterness which, should it continue so violent as at present, could accomplish nothing; and the more their action against the bourgeoisie will lose its savage cruelty. If, indeed, it were possible to make the whole proletariat communistic before the war breaks out, the end would be very peaceful; but that is no longer possible, the time has gone by. Meanwhile, I think that before the outbreak of open, declared war of the poor against the rich, there will be enough intelligent comprehension of the social question among the proletariat, to enable the communistic party, with the help of events, to conquer the brutal element of the revolution and prevent a "Ninth Thermidor." In any case, the experience of the French will not have been undergone in vain, and most of the Chartist leaders are, moreover, already communists. And as Communism stands above the strife between bourgeoisie and proletariat, it will be easier for the better elements of the bourgeoisie (which are, however, deplorably few, and can look for recruits only among the rising generation), to unite with it than with purely proletarian Chartism.

If these conclusions have not been sufficiently established in the course of the present work, there may be other opportunities for demonstrating that they are necessary consequences of the historical development of England. But this I maintain, the war of the poor against the rich now carried on in detail and indirectly will become direct and universal. It is too late for a peaceful solution. The classes are divided more and more sharply, the spirit of resistance penetrates the workers, the bitterness intensifies, the guerilla skirmishes become concentrated in more important battles, and soon a slight impulse will suffice to set the avalanche in motion. Then, indeed, will the war cry resound through the land: "War to the palaces, peace to the cottages!" — but then it will be too late for the rich to beware.

12. Relative Surplus Population and Capital Accumulation

Karl Marx

Karl Marx (1818–1883) was an angry man and a brilliant man. Above all he was a man with a mission. The most influential modern socialist theorist was determined to prove that the death of inhumane capitalism and the birth of humane socialism were inevitable. Marx's penetrating analysis of capitalism remains the most formidable intellectual indictment yet developed against that system.

Marx, like his collaborator and friend Friedrich Engels, was born in Germany. He came from a comfortable, liberal, middle-class family and was well educated. But even with a Ph.D. in philosophy, he was barred from university teaching because of his radical views. So he became a journalist. His participation in revolutionary movements made him unwelcome in Germany and then in France and Belgium. In 1850 he settled permanently in England. Marx associated with revolutionary movements all his life. He coauthored The Communist Manifesto (1848) with Engels and helped found the First International in 1864. But Marx always remained an indefatigable scholar. Day after day, year after year, he meticulously studied historical, philosophical, political, and economic volumes in the British Museum in London. Then he wove seemingly disparate strands into a grandiose, unified theory of society and history.

According to Marx, during most of history human society has been divided into sharply opposing classes. The classes differ — slave owner and slave under slavery, lord and serf under feudalism, bourgeoisie and proletariat (capitalist and worker) under capitalism. But always there is an exploiting class and an exploited class, and always their interests conflict. In each epoch power is held by the class that owns the means of production. Under capitalism, workers, although in the majority, do not own the machines. Consequently they are exploited by a small minority, the capitalist owners, and the conflict of interest between these classes is irreconcilable.

The classical economists, whom Marx had studied, assumed that capitalism would last forever. But not Marx. Change was the rule of history and capitalism was no exception to the rule. It too would pass as had its predecessors, slavery and feudalism. Exploitation of workers would worsen. Capitalists, in their drive for profit, would pay subsistence wages. They would also introduce more and more cost-

cutting machinery, but workers would not benefit from improved technology. Instead, surplus labor would swell the ranks of the unemployed, forming an industrial reserve army. This would also hold down the wages of the employed. Demand would sag, causing ever-worsening crises. Finally, the sick system would collapse, destroyed mostly by its internal contradictions. But there would also be a revolution led by class-conscious workers. Socialism, then communism, would follow, with no private profits or private ownership of the means of production. Technology would bring abundance, not poverty.

In the following passage from Capital, the best-known of Marx's many works, he discusses the relation between the relative surplus population and capitalist accumulation. Malthus and Ricardo assumed that overpopulation caused poverty and resulted from the tendency of workers to have too many children. Marx claims that capitalism doesn't need workers to produce surplus population. Capitalism inevitably produces a surplus population that is doomed to the most wretched poverty.

For Marx both poverty and wealth were generated by the capitalist system. For poverty to end, capitalism must end. That was the message Marx gave to millions of people throughout the world.

The labouring population therefore produces, along with the accumulation of capital produced by it, the means by which itself is made relatively superfluous, is turned into a relative surplus population; and it does this to an always increasing extent. This is a law of population peculiar to the capitalist mode of production; and in fact every special historic mode of production has its own special laws of population, historically valid within its limits alone. An abstract law of population exists for plants and animals only, and only in so far as man has not interfered with them.

But if a surplus labouring population is a necessary product of accumulation or of the development of wealth on a capitalist basis, this surplus population becomes, conversely, the lever of capitalistic accumulation, nay, a condition of existence of the capitalist mode of production. It forms a disposable industrial reserve army, that belongs to capital quite as absolutely as if the latter had bred it at its own cost. Independently of the limits of the actual increase of population, it creates, for the changing needs of the self-expansion of capital, a mass of human material always ready for exploitation. With accumulation, and the development of the productiveness of labour that accompanies it, the power of sudden expansion of

From Karl Marx, *Capital*, Vol. 1 (1867). Reprinted from the Random House, Inc., edition.

capital grows also; it grows, not merely because the elasticity of the capital already functioning increases, not merely because the absolute wealth of society expands, of which capital only forms an elastic part, not merely because credit, under every special stimulus, at once places an unusual part of this wealth at the disposal of production in the form of additional capital; it grows, also, because the technical conditions of the process of production themselves — machinery, means of transport, &c. — now admit of the rapidest transformation of masses of surplus product into additional means of production. The mass of social wealth, overflowing with the advance of accumulation, and transformable into additional capital, thrusts itself frantically into old branches of production, whose market suddenly expands, or into newly formed branches, such as railways, &c., the need for which grows out of the development of the old ones. In all such cases, there must be the possibility of throwing great masses of men suddenly on the decisive points without injury to the scale of production in other spheres. Over-population supplies these masses. The course characteristic of modern industry, viz., a decennial cycle (interrupted by smaller oscillations), of periods of average activity, production at high pressure, crisis and stagnation, depends on the constant formation, the greater or less absorption, and the re-formation of the industrial reserve army of surplus population. In their turn, the varying phases of the industrial cycle recruit the surplus population, and become one of the most energetic agents of its reproduction. This peculiar course of modern industry, which occurs in no earlier period of human history, was also impossible in the childhood of capitalist production. The composition of capital changed but very slowly. With its accumulation, therefore, there kept pace, on the whole, a corresponding growth in the demand for labour. Slow as was the advance of accumulation compared with that of more modern times, it found a check in the natural limits of the exploitable labouring population, limits which could only be got rid of by forcible means to be mentioned later. The expansion by fits and starts of the scale of production is the preliminary to its equally sudden contraction; the latter again evokes the former, but the former is impossible without disposable human material, without an increase in the number of labourers independently of the absolute growth of the population. This increase is effected by the simple process that constantly "sets free" a part of the labourers; by methods which lessen the number of labourers employed in proportion to the increased production. The whole form of the movement of modern industry depends, therefore, upon the constant transformation of a part of the labouring population into unemployed or half-employed hands. . . .

The industrial reserve army, during the periods of stagnation and average prosperity, weighs down the active labour-army; during the periods of over-production and paroxysm, it holds its pretensions in check. Relative surplus-population is therefore the pivot upon which the law of demand and supply of labour works. It confines the field of action of this law within the limits absolutely convenient to the activity of exploitation and to the domination of capital. . . .

The relative surplus population exists in every possible form. Every labourer belongs to it during the time when he is only partially employed or wholly unemployed. Not taking into account the great periodically recurring forms that the changing phases of the industrial cycle impress on it, now an acute form during the crisis, then again a chronic form during dull times — it has always three forms, the floating, the latent, the stagnant.

In the centres of modern industry — factories, manufacturers, ironworks, mines, &c. — the labourers are sometimes repelled, sometimes attracted again in greater masses, the number of those employed increasing on the whole, although in a constantly decreasing proportion to the scale of production. Here the surplus population exists in the floating form.

In the automatic factories, as in all the great workshops, where machinery enters as a factor, or where only the modern divisions of labour is carried out, large numbers of boys are employed up to the age of maturity. When this term is once reached, only a very small number continue to find employment in the same branches of industry, whilst the majority are regularly discharged. This majority forms an element of the floating surplus-population, growing with the extension of those branches of industry. Part of them emigrates, following in fact capital that has emigrated. One consequence is that the female population grows more rapidly than the male, *teste* England. That the natural increase of the number of labourers does not satisfy the requirements of the accumulation of capital, and yet all the time is in excess of them, is a contradiction inherent to the movement of capital itself. It wants larger numbers of youthful labourers, a smaller number of adults. The contradiction is not more glaring than that other one that there is a complaint of the want of hands, while at the same time many thousands are out of work, because the division of labour chains them to a particular branch of industry.

The consumption of labour-power by capital is, besides, so rapid that the labourer, half-way through his life, has already more or less completely lived himself out. He falls into the ranks of the supernumeraries, or is thrust down from a higher to a lower step in the scale. It is precisely among the workpeople of modern industry that we meet with the shortest duration of life. Dr. Lee, Medical Officer of Health for Manchester, stated "that the average age at death of the Manchester . . . upper middle class was 38 years, while the average age at death of the labouring class was 17; while at Liverpool those figures were represented as 35 against 15. It thus appeared that the well-to-do classes had a lease of life which was more than double the value of that which fell to the lot of the less favoured citizens." In order to conform to these circumstances, the absolute increase of this section of the proletariat must take places under conditions that shall swell their numbers, although the individual elements are used up rapidly. Hence, rapid renewal of the generations of labourers (this law does not hold for the other classes of the population). This social need is met by early marriages, a necessary consequence of the conditions in which the labourers of modern industry live, and by the premium that the exploitation of children sets on their production.

As soon as capitalist production takes possession of agriculture, and in proportion to the extent to which it does so, the demand for an agricultural labouring population falls absolutely, while the accumulation of the capital employed in agriculture advances, without this repulsion being, as in non-agricultural industries, compensated by a greater attraction. Part of the agricultural population is therefore constantly on the point of passing over into an urban or manufacturing proletariat, and on the look-out for circumstances favourable to this transformation. (Manufacture is used here in the sense of all non-agricultural industries). This source of relative surplus-population is thus constantly flowing. But the constant flow towards the towns presupposes, in the country itself, a constant latent surplus-population, the extent of which becomes evident only when its channels of outlet open to exceptional width. The agricultural labourer is therefore reduced to the minimum of wages, and always stands with one foot already in the swamp of pauperism.

The third category of the relative surplus-population, the stagnant, forms a part of the active labour army, but with extremely irregular employment. Hence it furnishes to capital an inexhaustible reservoir of disposable labour-power. Its conditions of life sink below the average normal level of the working class; this makes it at once the broad basis of special branches of capitalist exploitation. It is characterized by maximum of working time, and minimum of wages. We have learnt to know its chief form under the rubric of "domestic industry." It recruits itself constantly from the supernumerary forces of modern industry and agriculture, and specially from those decaying branches of industry where handicraft is yielding to manufacture, manufacture to machinery. Its extent grows, as with the extent and energy of accumulation, the creation of a surplus population advances. But it forms at the same time a self-reproducing and self-perpetuating element of the working class, taking a proportionally greater part in the general increase of that class than the other elements. In fact, not only the number of births and deaths, but the absolute size of the families stand in inverse proportion to the height of wages, and therefore to the amount of means of subsistence of which the different categories of labourers dispose. This law of capitalistic society would sound absurd to savages, or even civilized colonists. It calls to mind the boundless reproduction of animals individually weak and constantly hunted down.

The lowest sediment of the relative surplus-population finally dwells in the sphere of pauperism. Exclusive of vagabonds, criminals, prostitutes, in a word, the "dangerous" classes, this layer of society consists of three categories. First, those able to work. One need only glance superficially at the statistics of English pauperism to find that the quantity of paupers increases with every crisis, and diminishes with every revival of trade. Second, orphans and pauper children. These are candidates for the industrial reserve-army, and are, in times of great prosperity, as 1860, *e.g.*, speedily and in large numbers enrolled in the active army of labourers. Third, the demoralized and ragged, and those unable to work, chiefly people who succumb to their incapacity for adaptation, due to the division of labour; people who have passed the normal age of the labourer; the victims of industry, whose number increases with the increase of dangerous machinery, of mines, chemical works, &c., the mutilated, the sickly, the widows, &c. Pauperism is the hospital of the active labour-army and the dead weight of the industrial reserve-army. Its production is included in that of the relative surplus-population, its necessity in theirs; along with the surplus-population, pauperism forms a condition of capitalist production, and of the capitalist development of wealth. It enters into the *faux frais* of capitalist production; but capital knows how to throw these, for the most part, from its own shoulders on to those of the working-class and the lower middle class.

The greater the social wealth, the functioning capital, the extent and energy of its growth, and, therefore, also the absolute mass of the proletariat and the productiveness of its labour, the greater is the industrial reserve-army. The same causes which develop the expansive power of capital, developes also the labour-power at its disposal. The relative mass of the industrial reserve-army increases therefore with the potential energy of wealth. But the greater this reserve-army in proportion to the active labour-army, the greater is the mass of a consolidated surplus-population, whose misery is in inverse ratio to its torment of labour. The more extensive, finally, the lazurus-layers of the working-class, and the industrial reserve-army, the greater is official pauperism. *This is the absolute general law of capitalist accumulation.* Like all other laws it is modified in its working by many circumstances, the analysis of which does not concern us here.

The folly is now patent of the economic wisdom that preaches to the labourers the accommodation of their number to the requirements of capital. The mechanism of capitalist production and accumulation constantly affects this adjustment. The first word of this adaptation is the creation of a relative surplus-population, or industrial reserve-army. Its last word is the misery of constantly extending strata of the active army of labour, and the dead weight of pauperism.

The law by which a constantly increasing quantity of means of production, thanks to the advance in the productiveness of social labour, may be set in movement by a progressively diminishing expenditure of human power, this law, in a capitalist society — where the labourer does not employ the means of production, but the means of production employ the labourer — undergoes a complete inversion and is expressed thus: the higher the productiveness of labour, the greater is the pressure of the labourers on the means of employment, the more precarious, therefore, becomes their condition of existence, viz., the sale of their own labour-power for the increasing of another's wealth, or for the self-expansion of capital. The fact that the means of production, and the productiveness of labour, increase more rapidly than the productive population, expresses itself, therefore, capitalistically in the inverse form that the labouring population always increases more rapidly than the conditions under which capital can employ this increase for its own self-expansion.

We saw [earlier], when analysing the production of relative surplus-value: within the capitalist system all methods for raising the social productiveness of labour are brought about at the cost of the individual labourer; all means for the development of production transform themselves into means of domination over, and exploitation of, the producers; they mutilate the labourer into a fragment of a man, degrade him to the level of an appendage of a machine, destroy every remnant of charm in his work and turn it into a hated toil; they estrange from him the intellectual potentialities of the labour-process in the same proportion as science is incorporated in it as an independent power; they distort the conditions under which he works, subject him during the labour-process to a despotism the more hateful for its meanness; they transform his life-time into working-time, and drag his wife and child beneath the wheels of the Juggernaut of capital. But all methods for the production of surplus value are at the same time methods of accumulation; and every extension of accumulation becomes again a means for the development of those methods. It follows therefore that in proportion as capital accumulates, the lot of the labourer, be his payment high or low, must grow worse. The law, finally, that always equilibrates the relative surplus-population, or industrial reserve army, to the extent and energy of accumulation, this law rivets the labourer to capital more firmly than the wedges of Vulcan did Prometheus to the rock. It establishes an accumulation of misery, corresponding with accumulation of capital. Accumulation of wealth at one pole is, therefore, at the same time accumulation of misery, agony of toil, slavery, ignorance, brutality, mental degradation, at the opposite pole, *i.e.,* on the side of the class that produces its own product in the form of capital.

Chapter Four

Black Poverty: Slavery and the Post–Civil War South

13. Life in the Slave Quarters and Life in the Big House

Frederick Douglass

What was it like to be poor and also a slave? In this passage from his autobiography, Frederick Douglass (c. 1817–1895) paints a bleak picture of physical deprivation in the slave quarters and then juxtaposes it against a description of the opulence in the big house.

Douglass wrote about slavery from firsthand experience. Born into bondage, he escaped to freedom as a young man. Though largely self-educated, he rose to prominence as orator, writer, adviser to Lincoln, and Consul General to Haiti. His devotion to human rights led him to fight for many causes, including the abolition of slavery, equality for blacks, free education, temperance, and women's rights.

It was the boast of slaveholders that their slaves enjoyed more of the physical comforts of life than the peasantry of any country in the world. My experience contradicts this. The men and the women slaves on Col. Lloyd's farm received, as their monthly allowance of food, eight pounds of pickled pork, or its equivalent in fish. The pork was often tainted, and the

---

From Frederick Douglass, *Life and Times of Frederick Douglass* (1892). Copyright © 1962 by the Crowell-Collier Publishing Company. Reprinted with permission of The Macmillan Company. Editor's title.

fish were of the poorest quality. With their pork or fish, they had given them one bushel of Indian meal, unbolted, of which quite fifteen per cent was more fit for pigs than for men. With this, one pint of salt was given, and this was the entire monthly allowance of a full-grown slave, working constantly in the open field from morning till night every day in the month except Sunday. There is no kind of work which really requires a better supply of food to prevent physical exhaustion than the field-work of a slave. The yearly allowance of clothing was not more ample than the supply of food. It consisted of two tow-linen shirts, one pair of trousers of the same coarse material, for summer, and a woolen pair of trousers and a woolen jacket for winter, with one pair of yarn stockings and a pair of shoes of the coarsest description. Children under ten years old had neither shoes, stockings, jackets, nor trousers. They had two coarse tow-linen shirts per year, and when these were worn out they went naked till the next allowance day — and this was the condition of the little girls as well as of the boys.

As to beds, they had none. One coarse blanket was given them, and this only to the men and women. The children stuck themselves in holes and corners about the quarters, often in the corners of huge chimneys, with their feet in the ashes to keep them warm. The want of beds, however, was not considered a great privation by the field hands. Time to sleep was of far greater importance. For when the day's work was done most of these had their washing, mending, and cooking to do, and having few or no facilities for doing such things, very many of their needed sleeping hours were consumed in necessary preparations for the labors of the coming day. The sleeping apartments, if they could have been properly called such, had little regard to comfort or decency. Old and young, male and female, married and single, dropped down upon the common clay floor, each covering up with his or her blanket, their only protection from cold or exposure. The night, however, was shortened at both ends. The slaves worked often as long as they could see, and were late in cooking and mending for the coming day, and at the first gray streak of the morning they were summoned to the field by the overseer's horn. They were whipped for oversleeping more than for any other fault. Neither age nor sex found any favor. The overseer stood at the quarter door, armed with stick and whip, ready to deal heavy blows upon any who might be a little behind time. When the horn was blown there was a rush for the door, for the hindermost one was sure to get a blow from the overseer. Young mothers who worked in the field were allowed an hour about ten o'clock in the morning to go home to nurse their children. This was when they were not required to take them to the field with them, and leave them upon "turning row," or in the corner of the fences.

As a general rule the slaves did not come to their quarters to take their meals, but took their ashcake (called thus because baked in the ashes) and piece of pork, or their salt herrings, where they were at work.

But let us now leave the rough usage of the field, where vulgar coarseness and brutal cruelty flourished as rank as weeds in the tropics and where a vile wretch, in the shape of a man, rides, walks, and struts about, with whip in hand, dealing heavy blows and leaving deep gashes on the flesh of men and women, and turn our attention to the less repulsive slave life as it existed in the home of my childhood. Some idea of the splendor of that place sixty years ago has already been given. The contrast between the condition of the slaves and that of their masters was marvelously sharp and striking. There were pride, pomp, and luxury on the one hand, servility, dejection, and misery on the other.

The close-fisted stinginess that fed the poor slave on coarse cornmeal and tainted meat, that clothed him in crashy tow-linen and hurried him on to toil through the field in all weathers, with wind and rain beating through his tattered garments, and that scarcely gave even the young slavemother time to nurse her infant in the fence-corner, wholly vanished on approaching the sacred precincts of the Great House itself. There the scriptural phrase descriptive of the wealthy found exact illustration. The highly-favored inmates of this mansion were literally arrayed in "purple and fine linen, and fared sumptuously every day." The table of this house groaned under the blood-bought luxuries gathered with painstaking care at home and abroad. Fields, forests, rivers, and seas, were made tributary. Immense wealth and its lavish expenditures filled the Great House with all that could please the eye or tempt the taste. Fish, flesh, and fowl, were here in profusion. Chickens of all breeds, ducks of all kinds, wild and tame, the common and the huge muscovite, guinea fowls, turkeys, geese, and peafowls — all were fat and fattening for the destined vortex. Here the graceful swan, the mongrel, the black-necked wild goose, partridges, quails, pheasants, pigeons, and choice waterfowl with all their strange varieties, were caught in this huge net. Beef, veal, mutton, and venison, of the most select kinds and quality, rolled in bounteous profusion to this grand consumer. The teeming riches of the Chesapeake Bay, its rock perch, drums, crocus, trout, oysters, crabs and terrapin, were drawn hither to adorn the glittering table. The dairy, too, the finest then on the Eastern Shore of Maryland, supplied by cattle of the best English stock, imported for the express purpose, poured its rich donations of fragrant cheese, golden butter, and delicious cream to heighten the attractions of the gorgeous, unending round of feasting. Nor were the fruits of the earth overlooked. The fertile garden, many acres in size, constituting a separate establishment distinct from the common farm, with its scientific gardener direct from Scotland, a Mr. McDermott, and four men under his direction, was not behind, either in the abundance or in the delicacy of its contributions. The tender asparagus, the crispy celery, and the delicate cauliflower, eggplants, beets, lettuce, parsnips, peas, and French beans, early and late; radishes, cantaloupes, melons of all kinds; and the fruits of all climes and of every description, from the hardy apples of the North to the lemon and orange of the South, culminated at this point. Here were gathered figs, raisins, almonds, and grapes from Spain, wines and brandies from France, teas of various flavor from China, and rich, aromatic coffee from Java, all conspiring to swell the tide of high life, where pride and indolence lounged in magnificence and satiety.

Behind the tall-backed and elaborately wrought chairs stood the servants, fifteen in number, carefully selected, not only with a view to their capacity and adeptness, but with especial regard to their personal appearance, their graceful agility, and pleasing address. Some of these servants, armed with fans, wafted reviving breezes to the overheated brows of the alabaster ladies, whilst others watched with eager eye and fawn-like step, anticipating and supplying wants before they were sufficiently formed to be announced by word or sign. . . .

In the stables and carriage-houses were to be found the same evidences of pride and luxurious extravagance. Here were three splendid coaches, soft within and lustrous without. Here, too, were gigs, phaetons, barouches, sulkies and sleighs. Here were saddles and harness, beautifully wrought and richly mounted. Not less than thirty-five horses of the best approved blood, both for speed and beauty, were kept only for pleasure. The care of these horses constituted the entire occupation of two men, one or the other of them being always in the stable to answer any call which might be made from the Great House. Over the way from the stable was a house built expressly for the hounds, a pack of twenty-five or thirty, the fare for which would have made glad the hearts of a dozen slaves. Horses and hounds, however, were not the only consumers of the slave's toil. The hospitality practiced at the Lloyd's would have astonished and charmed many a health-seeking divine or merchant from the North. Viewed from his table, and *not* from the field, Colonel Lloyd was, indeed, a model of generous hospitality. . . . Viewed from Col. Lloyd's table, who could have said that his slaves were not well clad and well cared for? Who would have said they did not glory in being the slaves of such a master? Who but a fanatic could have seen any cause for sympathy for either master or slave?

14. The Condition of Black People in the South, 1890

W. E. Burghardt DuBois

Emancipation spelled the end of legal bondage for the black people of America. But freedom without land was a cruel joke that doomed the ex-slave to unrelenting poverty. William Edward Burghardt DuBois (1868–1963) was a foremost scholar, a founder of the National Association for the Advancement of Colored People, and a monumental and often controversial leader of black thought for more than six decades. In this passage from The Souls of Black Folk, *DuBois gives us a glimpse of life among the debt-ridden blacks of the Deep South at the turn of the century. Later many of the people described by DuBois joined the great trek north in search of a better life.*

Throughout his life DuBois was involved in both the intellectual and political struggles of blacks. His writings span many fields, especially sociology, history, economics, philosophy, and psychology. DuBois, who held a Ph.D. from Harvard University, was an early advocate of academic education for blacks and rejected Booker T. Washington's view that the black should concentrate on vocational education. In education, as in economics and politics, DuBois demanded no less than full equality for his people.

We seldom study the condition of the Negro to-day honestly and carefully. It is so much easier to assume that we know it all. Or perhaps, having already reached conclusions in our own minds, we are loth to have them disturbed by facts. And yet how little we really know of these millions, — of their daily lives and longings, of their homely joys and sorrows, of their real shortcomings and the meaning of their crimes! All this we can only learn by intimate contact with the masses, and not by wholesale arguments covering millions separate in time and space, and differing widely in training and culture. To-day, then, my reader, let us turn our faces to the Black Belt of Georgia and seek simply to know the condition of the black farm-laborers of one county there.

Here in 1890 lived ten thousand Negroes and two thousand whites. The

---

From W. E. Burghardt DuBois, *The Souls of Black Folk* (New York: Fawcett Publications, 1961), pp. 105–113. Reprinted by permission of Shirley Graham DuBois; further use without her permission is unauthorized. Editor's title, by permission.

country is rich, yet the people are poor. The keynote of the Black Belt is debt; not commercial credit, but debt in the sense of continued inability on the part of the mass of the population to make income cover expense. This is the direct heritage of the South from the wasteful economies of the slave *régime;* but it was emphasized and brought to a crisis by the Emancipation of the slaves. In 1860, Dougherty County had six thousand slaves, worth at least two and a half millions of dollars; its farms were estimated at three millions — making five and a half millions of property, the value of which depended largely on the slave system, and on the speculative demand for land once marvellously rich but already partially devitalized by careless and exhaustive culture. The war then meant a financial crash; in place of the five and a half millions of 1860, there remained in 1870 only farms valued at less than two millions. With this came increased competition in cotton culture from the rich lands of Texas; a steady fall in the normal price of cotton followed, from about fourteen cents a pound in 1860 until it reached four cents in 1898. Such a financial revolution was it that involved the owners of the cotton-belt in debt. And if things went ill with the master, how fared it with the man?

The plantations of Dougherty County in slavery days were not as imposing and aristocratic as those of Virginia. The Big House was smaller and usually one-storied, and sat very near the slave cabins. Sometimes these cabins stretched off on either side like wings; sometimes only on one side, forming a double row, or edging the road that turned into the plantation from the main thoroughfare. The form and disposition of the laborers' cabins throughout the Black Belt is to-day the same as in slavery days. Some live in the self-same cabins, others in cabins rebuilt on the sites of the old. All are sprinkled in little groups over the face of the land, centering about some dilapidated Big House where the head-tenant or agent lives. The general character and arrangement of these dwellings remains on the whole unaltered. There were in the county, outside the corporate town of Albany, about fifteen hundred Negro families in 1898. Out of all these, only a single family occupied a house with seven rooms; only fourteen have five rooms or more. The mass live in one- and two-room homes. . . .

All over the face of the land is the one-room cabin, — now standing in the shadow of the Big House, now staring at the dusty road, now rising dark and sombre amid the green of the cotton-fields.

Among this people there is no leisure class. We often forget that in the United States over half the youth and adults are not in the world earning incomes, but are making homes, learning of the world, or resting after the heat of the strife. But here ninety-six per cent are toiling; no one with leisure to turn the bare and cheerless cabin into a home, no old folks to sit beside the fire and hand down traditions of the past; little of careless happy childhood and dreaming youth. The dull monotony of daily toil is broken only by the gayety of the thoughtless and the Saturday trip to town. The toil, like all farm toil, is monotonous, and here there are little machinery and few tools to relieve its burdensome drudgery. But with all this, it is work in the pure open air, and this is something in a day when fresh air is scarce.

The land on the whole is still fertile, despite long abuse. For nine or ten months in succession the crops will come if asked: garden vegetables in April, grain in May, melons in June and July, hay in August, sweet potatoes in September, and cotton from then to Christmas. And yet on two-thirds of the land there is but one crop, and that leaves the toilers in debt. Why is this?

Away down the Baysan road, where the broad flat fields are flanked by great oak forests, is a plantation; many thousands of acres it used to run, here and there, and beyond the great wood. Thirteen hundred human beings here obeyed the call of one, — were his in body, and largely in soul. One of them lives there yet, — a short, stocky man, his dull-brown face seamed and drawn, and his tightly curled hair gray-white. The crops? Just tolerable, he said; just tolerable. Getting on? No — he wasn't getting on at all. Smith of Albany "furnishes" him, and his rent is eight hundred pounds of cotton. Can't make anything at that. Why didn't he buy land! Humph! Takes money to buy land. And he turns away. Free! The most piteous thing amid all the black ruin of war-time, amid the broken fortunes of the masters, the blighted hopes of mothers and maidens, and the fall of an empire, — the most piteous thing amid all this was the black freedman who threw down his hoe because the world called him free. What did such a mockery of freedom mean? Not a cent of money, not an inch of land, not a mouthful of victuals, — not even ownership of the rags on his back. Free! On Saturday, once or twice a month, the old master, before the war, used to dole out bacon and meal to his Negroes. And after the first flush of freedom wore off, and his true helplessness dawned on the freedman, he came back and picked up his hoe, and old master still doled out his bacon and meal. The legal form of service was theoretically far different; in practice, task-work or "cropping" was substituted for daily toil in gangs; and the slave gradually became a metayer, or tenant on shares, in name, but a laborer with indeterminate wages in fact.

Still the price of cotton fell, and gradually the landlords deserted their plantations, and the reign of the merchant began. The merchant of the Black Belt is a contractor, and part despot. His store, which used most frequently to stand at the cross-roads and become the centre of a weekly village, has now moved to town; and thither the Negro tenant follows him. The merchant keeps everything, — clothes and shoes, coffee and sugar, pork and meal, canned and dried goods, wagons and ploughs, seed and fertilizer, — and what he has not in stock he can give you an order for at the store across the way. Here, then, comes the tenant, Sam Scott, after he has contracted with some absent landlord's agent for hiring forty acres of land; he fingers his hat nervously until the merchant finishes his morning chat with Colonel Saunders, and calls out, "Well, Sam, what do you want?" Sam wants him to "furnish" him, — *i.e.*, to advance him food and clothing for the year, and perhaps seed and tools, until his crop is raised and sold. If Sam seems a favorable subject, he and the merchant go to a lawyer, and Sam executes a chattel mortgage on his mule and wagon in return for seed and a week's rations. As soon as the green cotton-leaves appear above the ground, another mortgage is given on the "crop." Every Saturday, or at longer intervals, Sam calls upon the merchant for his "rations"; a family of five usually gets about thirty pounds of fat side-pork and a couple of bushels of cornmeal a month. Besides this, clothing and shoes must be furnished; if Sam or his family is sick, there are orders on the druggist and doctor; if the mule wants shoeing, an order on the blacksmith, etc. If Sam is a hard worker and crops promise well, he is often encouraged to buy more, — sugar, extra clothes, perhaps a buggy. But he is seldom encouraged to save. When cotton rose to ten cents last fall, the shrewd merchants of Dougherty County sold a thousand buggies in one season, mostly to black men.

The security offered for such transactions — a crop and chattel mortgage — may at first seem slight. And, indeed, the merchants tell many a true tale of shiftlessness and cheating; of cotton picked at night, mules disappearing, and tenants absconding. But on the whole the merchant of the Black Belt is the most prosperous man in the section. So skilfully and so closely has he drawn the bonds of the law about the tenant, that the black man has often simply to choose between pauperism and crime; he "waives" all homestead exemptions in his contract; he cannot touch his own mortgaged crop, which the laws put almost in the full control of the land-owner and of the merchant. When the crop is growing the merchant watches it like a hawk; as soon as it is ready for market he takes possession of it, sells it, pays the land-owner his rent, subtracts his bill for supplies, and if, as sometimes happens, there is anything left, he hands it over to the black serf for his Christmas celebration.

The direct result of this system is an all-cotton scheme of agriculture and the continued bankruptcy of the tenant. The currency of the Black Belt is cotton. It is a crop always salable for ready money, not usually subject to great yearly fluctuations in price, and one which the Negroes know how to raise. The landlord therefore demands his rent in cotton, and the merchant will accept mortgages on no other crop. There is no use asking the black tenant, then, to diversify his crops, — he cannot under this system. Moreover, the system is bound to bankrupt the tenant. . . .

. . . The Negro farmer started behind, — started in debt. This was not his choosing, but the crime of this happy-go-lucky nation which goes blundering along with its Reconstruction tragedies, its Spanish war interludes and Philippine matinees, just as though God really were dead. Once in debt, it is no easy matter for a whole race to emerge.

Chapter Five

Late Nineteenth and Early Twentieth Century Views of Poverty

15. Progress and Poverty

Henry George

Henry George (1839–1897) never forgot his own years of grinding poverty in California. A gold prospector, sailor, printer, journalist, and self-taught economist, George was indignant that debasing want flourished amid bountiful wealth, and he vowed never to rest until he discovered the cause and remedies for such inequalities.

Progress and Poverty *was the result of that relentless quest. In his analysis George was deeply influenced by Ricardo's law of rent (that rising population with fixed amount of land means rising rents). But his suggested cure was unlike anything Ricardo ever advocated. According to George, poverty stems from the private ownership and monopolization of land. As a nation grows, large unearned incomes from rising land values accrue to unproductive landowners, whose prosperity is paid for by the capitalists and workers. But labor's degrading poverty can easily be eliminated. George's solution? A single tax on unearned rent. No other taxes are needed and free competition should be restored.*

Progress and Poverty *was an immediate hit. Millions of copies were sold and the movement for a single tax on land spread rapidly. George lectured widely in the United States and abroad. And as Labor Party candidate for mayor of New York, he received more votes as runner-up than did the Republican Theodore Roosevelt.*

George's panacea for poverty obscured many significant issues, especially the growing power of the capitalists and their large profits from manufacturing, trade, finance, and transportation. There are few advocates of the single tax today. But in our increasingly urbanized and slum-ridden nation the unresolved problem of escalating land values again commands attention and gives many of George's insights a contemporary relevance.

This association of poverty with progress is the great enigma of our times. It is the central fact from which spring industrial, social, and political difficulties that perplex the world, and with which statesmanship and philanthropy and education grapple in vain. From it come the clouds that overhang the future of the most progressive and self-reliant nations. It is the riddle which the Sphinx of Fate puts to our civilization, and which not to answer is to be destroyed. So long as all the increased wealth which modern progress brings goes but to build up great fortunes, to increase luxury and make sharper the contrast between the House of Have and the House of Want, progress is not real and cannot be permanent. The reaction must come. The tower leans from its foundations, and every new story but hastens the final catastrophe. To educate men who must be condemned to poverty, is but to make them restive; to base on a state of most glaring social inequality political institutions under which men are theoretically equal, is to stand a pyramid on its apex. . . .

I propose in the following pages to attempt to solve by the methods of political economy the great problem I have outlined. I propose to seek the law which associates poverty with progress, and increases want with advancing wealth; and I believe that in the explanation of this paradox we shall find the explanation of those recurring seasons of industrial and commercial paralysis which, viewed independently of their relations to more general phenomena, seem so inexplicable. . . .

Look over the world to-day. In countries the most widely differing — under conditions the most diverse as to government, as to industries, as to tariffs, as to currency — you will find distress among the working classes; but everywhere that you thus find distress and destitution in the midst of wealth you will find that the land is monopolized; that instead of being treated as the common property of the whole people, it is treated as the private property of individuals; that, for its use by labor, large revenues are extorted from the earnings of labor. Look over the world to-day, compar-

From Henry George, *Progress and Poverty* (1880). Reprinted from the Random House, Inc., edition.

ing different countries with each other, and you will see that it is not the abundance of capital or the productiveness of labor that makes wages high or low; but the extent to which the monopolizers of land can, in rent, levy tribute upon the earnings of labor. Is it not a notorious fact, known to the most ignorant, that new countries, where the aggregate wealth is small, but where land is cheap, are always better countries for the laboring classes than the rich countries, where land is dear? Wherever you find land relatively low, will you not find wages relatively high? And wherever land is high, will you not find wages low? As land increases in value, poverty deepens and pauperism appears. In the new settlements, where land is cheap, you will find no beggars, and the inequalities in condition are very slight. In the great cities, where land is so valuable that it is measured by the foot, you will find the extremes of poverty and of luxury. And this disparity in condition between the two extremes of the social scale may always be measured by the price of land. Land in New York is more valuable than in San Francisco; and in New York, the San Franciscan may see squalor and misery that will make him stand aghast. Land is more valuable in London than in New York; and in London, there is squalor and destitution worse than that of New York. . . .

We have traced the unequal distribution of wealth which is the curse and menace of modern civilization to the institution of private property in land. We have seen that so long as this institution exists no increase in productive power can permanently benefit the masses; but, on the contrary, must tend still further to depress their condition. We have examined all the remedies, short of the abolition of private property in land, which are currently relied on or proposed for the relief of poverty and the better distribution of wealth, and have found them all inefficacious or impracticable.

There is but one way to remove an evil — and that is, to remove its cause. Poverty deepens as wealth increases, and wages are forced down while productive power grows, because land, which is the source of all wealth and the field of all labor, is monopolized. To extirpate poverty, to make wages what justice commands they should be, the full earnings of the laborer, we must therefore substitute for the individual ownership of land a common ownership. Nothing else will go to the cause of the evil — in nothing else is there the slightest hope.

This, then, is the remedy for the unjust and unequal distribution of wealth apparent in modern civilization, and for all the evils which flow from it: *we must make land common property.*

. . . I do not propose either to purchase or to confiscate private property in land. The first would be unjust; the second, needless. Let the individuals who now hold it still retain, if they want to, possession of what they are pleased to call *their* land. Let them continue to call it *their* land. Let them buy and sell, and bequeath and devise it. We may safely leave them the shell, if we take the kernel. *It is not necessary to confiscate land; it is only necessary to confiscate rent.*

Nor to take rent for public uses is it necessary that the State should bother with the letting of lands, and assume the chances of the favoritism, collusion, and corruption this might involve. It is not necessary that any new machinery should be created. The machinery already exists. Instead of extending it, all we have to do is to simplify and reduce it. By leaving to land owners a percentage of rent which would probably be much less than the cost and loss involved in attempting to rent lands through State agency, and by making use of this existing machinery, we may, without jar or shock, assert the common right to land by taking rent for public uses.

We already take some rent in taxation. We have only to make some changes in our modes of taxation to take it all.

What I, therefore, propose, as the simple yet sovereign remedy, which will raise wages, increase the earnings of capital, extirpate pauperism, abolish poverty, give remunerative employment to whoever wishes it, afford free scope to human powers, lessen crime, elevate morals, and taste, and intelligence, purify government and carry civilization to yet nobler heights, is — *to appropriate rent by taxation.*

In this way the State may become the universal landlord without calling herself so, and without assuming a single new function. In form, the ownership of land would remain just as now. No owner of land need be dispossessed, and no restriction need be placed upon the amount of land any one could hold. For, rent being taken by the State in taxes, land, no matter in whose name it stood, or in what parcels it was held, would be really common property, and every member of the community would participate in the advantages of its ownership.

Now, insomuch as the taxation of rent, or land values, must necessarily be increased just as we abolish other taxes, we may put the proposition into practical form by proposing — *to abolish all taxation save that upon land values.*

As we have seen, the value of land is at the beginning of society nothing, but as society develops by the increase of population and the advance of the arts, it becomes greater and greater. In every civilized country, even the newest, the value of the land taken as a whole is sufficient to bear the entire expenses of government. In the better developed countries it is much more than sufficient. Hence it will not be enough merely to place all taxes upon the value of land. It will be necessary, where rent exceeds the present governmental revenues, commensurately to increase the amount demanded in taxation, and to continue this increase as society progresses and rent advances. But this is so natural and easy a matter, that it may be considered as involved, or at least understood, in the proposition to put all taxes on the value of land. That is the first step, upon which the practical struggle must be made. When the hare is once caught and killed, cooking him will follow as a matter of course. When the common right to land is so far appreciated that all taxes are abolished save those which fall upon rent, there is no danger of much more than is necessary to induce them to collect the public revenues being left to individual land holders.

Experience has taught me (for I have been for some years endeavoring to popularize this proposition) that wherever the idea of concentrating all taxation upon land values finds lodgment sufficient to induce consideration, it invariably makes way, but there are few of the classes most to be benefited by it, who at first, or even for a long time afterwards, see its full significance and power. It is difficult for workingmen to get over the idea that there is a real antagonism between capital and labor. It is difficult for small farmers and homestead owners to get over the idea that to put all taxes on the value of land would be unduly to tax them. It is difficult for both classes to get over the idea that to exempt capital from taxation would be to make the rich richer and the poor poorer. These ideas spring from confused thought. But behind ignorance and prejudice there is a powerful interest, which has hitherto dominated literature, education, and opinion. A great wrong always dies hard, and the great wrong which in every civilized country condemns the masses of men to poverty and want, will not die without a bitter struggle.

16. The Poor Are the Unfit

Herbert Spencer

Contempt for the poor is at the heart of the ideology of Social Darwinism, the misapplication of evolutionary concepts to human society. The phrase "survival of the fittest," which epitomizes Social Darwinist thinking, originated with Herbert Spencer (1820–1903), the prominent British philosopher and sociologist. Charles Darwin's findings were used by Spencer and his disciples to fortify their views, but it was Malthus rather than Darwin whose ideas originally inspired him. Spencer began writing about social selection in 1850, almost ten years before the publication of Darwin's Origin of Species *in 1859.*

Spencer argued that the weak and the inferior are weeded out in the evolutionary process. Nature's rule is the survival of the fittest. The poor are unfit, so mankind benefits when they are eliminated. A philosophical anarchist, Spencer believed that government was, at best, a necessary evil. Thus, he pushed the case for complete laissez-faire even further than Malthus and Ricardo. Now evolutionary progress was at stake. There must be no government programs that might help the poor. No public relief. No public education. No public sanitation. No social legislation. These would only interfere with the process of natural selection and perpetuate the weak. In Spencer's view, private philanthropy was permissible, though ill advised. Why? Because the government must never hinder the rich from spending their money freely. Furthermore, privately operated charities could exclude the "unworthy" poor from aid.

Social Darwinism found its most fertile soil in America, the land of rugged individualism. Influential intellectuals such as sociologist William Graham Sumner embraced this ideology, along with business tycoons and many middle-class Americans. From the mid-nineteenth century until the New Deal, "survival of the fittest" was a powerful battle cry in the war against the poor. It was used to oppose social legislation and to justify indifference to the sordid living conditions of the masses. Remnants of the Social Darwinist philosophy linger on in many current attitudes toward the poor but seldom are expressed with as much candor as in the past.

And here we are brought face to face with the greatest of the difficulties attendant on all methods of mitigating distress. May we not by frequent aid to the worthy render them unworthy; and are we not almost certain by helping those who are already unworthy to make them more unworthy still? How shall we so regulate our pecuniary beneficence as to avoid assisting the incapables and the degraded to multiply?

I have in so many places commented on the impolicy, and indeed the cruelty, of bequeathing to posterity an increasing population of criminals and incapables, that I need not here insist that true beneficence will be so restrained as to avoid fostering the inferior at the expense of the superior — or, at any rate, so restrained as to minimize the mischief which fostering the inferior entails.

Under present circumstances the difficulty seems almost insurmountable. By the law-established and privately established agencies, coercive and

From Herbert Spencer, *The Principles of Ethics*, Vol. 1 (New York: D. Appleton and Company, 1904).

voluntary, which save the bad from the extreme results of their badness, there have been produced unmanageable multitudes of them, and to prevent further multiplication appears next to impossible. The yearly accumulating appliances for keeping alive those who will not do enough work to keep themselves alive, continually increase the evil. Each new effort to mitigate the penalties on improvidence, has the inevitable effect of adding to the number of the improvident. Whether assistance is given through State-machinery, or by Charitable societies, or privately, it is difficult to see how it can be restricted in such manner as to prevent the inferior from begetting more of the inferior.

If left to operate in all its sternness, the principle of the survival of the fittest, which, as ethically considered, we have seen to imply that each individual shall be left to experience the effects of his own nature and consequent conduct, would quickly clear away the degraded. But it is impracticable with our present sentiments to let it operate in all its sternness. No serious evil would result from relaxing its operation, if the degraded were to leave no progeny. A short-sighted beneficence might be allowed to save them from suffering, were a long-sighted beneficence assured that there would be born no more such. But how can it be thus assured? If, either by public action or by private action, aid were given to the feeble, the unhealthy, the deformed, the stupid, on condition that they did not marry, the result would manifestly be a great increase of illegitimacy; which, implying a still more unfavourable nurture of children, would result in still worse men and women. If instead of a "submerged tenth" there existed only a submerged fiftieth, it might be possible to deal with it effectually by private industrial institutions, or some kindred appliances. But the mass of effete humanity to be dealt with is so large as to make one despair: the problem seems insoluble.

Certainly, if solvable, it is to be solved only through suffering. Having, by unwise institutions, brought into existence large numbers who are unadapted to the requirements of social life, and are consequently sources of misery to themselves and others, we cannot repress and gradually diminish this body of relatively worthless people without inflicting much pain. Evil has been done and the penalty must be paid. Cure can come only through affliction. The artificial assuaging of distress by State-appliances, is a kind of social opium-eating, yielding temporary mitigation at the eventual cost of intenser misery. Increase of the anodyne dose inevitably leads by and by to increase of the evil; and the only rational course is that of bearing the misery which must be entailed for a time by desistance. The transition from State-beneficence to a healthy condition of self-help and private beneficence, must be like the transition from an opium-eating life to a normal life — painful but remedial.

17. Rerum Novarum

Pope Leo XIII

By the late nineteenth century, much of the impetus to end mass poverty in Europe took the form of the intensification of the struggle between capital and labor and the growth of the socialist movement. Most established religions had supported the upper classes and were indifferent to the plight of the masses. And now they faced the prospect of losing their lower class adherents to the socialists. The Roman Catholic Church met the challenge through the person of Pope Leo XIII (1810–1903), who was convinced of the dire need for social reform. The Pope's solution to the problem of mass poverty was social justice. In Rerum Novarum, *a landmark encyclical of the Catholic Church, he offered a compromise that rejected both socialism and laissez-faire capitalism. The encyclical upheld the right of private property but strongly condemned placing market values above human values. The encyclical justified state intervention in the economy on behalf of the poor and legitimized labor unions, both advanced positions at the time for a traditionally conservative institution.*

Rerum Novarum, *which is also known as* The Condition of Labor, *directly stimulated the development of the Catholic trade union movement in Europe. In America the labor movement benefited as Catholic workers became free to join unions without their previous fear of Church censure. Pope Leo's reaffirmation of the Church's opposition to socialism hindered that movement's growth and paved the way toward acceptance of the welfare state as a substitute.*

TO OUR VENERABLE BRETHREN, ALL PATRIARCHS,
PRIMATES, ARCHBISHOPS, AND BISHOPS
OF THE CATHOLIC WORLD, IN GRACE AND
COMMUNION WITH THE APOSTOLIC SEE

*Venerable Brethren, Health
and Apostolic Benediction:*

It is not surprising that the spirit of revolutionary change, which has so long been predominant in the nations of the world, should have passed beyond politics and made its influence felt in the cognate field of practical

From Pope Leo XIII, *Rerum Novarum (The Condition of Labor),* encyclical letter of 1891. Official translation.

economy. The elements of a conflict are unmistakable: the growth of industry, and the surprising discoveries of science; the changed relations of masters and workmen; the enormous fortunes of individuals, and the poverty of the masses; the increased self-reliance and the closer mutual combination of the working population; and, finally, a general moral deterioration. The momentous seriousness of the present state of things just now fills every mind with painful apprehension; wise men discuss it; practical men propose schemes; popular meetings, legislatures and sovereign princes all are occupied with it — and there is nothing which has a deeper hold on public attention.

Therefore, venerable brethren as on former occasions, when it seemed opportune to refute false teaching, we have addressed you in the interests of the Church and of the common weal, and have issued letter on "Political Power," on "Human Liberty," on the "Christian Constitution of the State," and on similar subjects, so now we have thought it useful to speak on *the "Condition of Labor."*

. . . All agree, and there can be no question whatever, that some remedy must be found, and quickly found, for the misery and wretchedness which press so heavily at this moment on the large majority of the very poor. The ancient workmen's guilds were destroyed in the last century, and no other organization took their place. Public institutions and the laws have repudiated the ancient religion. Hence by degrees it has come to pass that workingmen have been given over, isolated and defenceless, to the callousness of employers and the greed of unrestrained competition. The evil has been increased by rapacious usury, which, although more than once condemned by the Church, is nevertheless, under a different form but with the same guilt, still practised by avaricious and grasping men. And to this must be added the custom of working by contract, and the concentration of so many branches of trade in the hands of a few individuals, so that a small number of very rich men have been able to lay upon the masses of the poor a yoke little better than slavery itself.

To remedy these evils the *Socialists,* working on the poor man's envy of the rich, endeavor to destroy private property, and maintain that individual possessions should become the common property of all, to be administered by the State or by municipal bodies. They hold that, by thus transferring property from private persons to the community, the present evil state of things will be set to rights, because each citizen will then have his equal share of whatever there is to enjoy. But their proposals are so clearly futile for all practical purposes that if they were carried out the workingman himself would be among the first to suffer. Moreover they are emphatically unjust, because they would rob the lawful possessor, bring the State into a sphere that is not its own, and cause complete confusion in the community. . . .

Thus it is clear that the main tenet of *Socialism,* the community of goods, must be utterly rejected; for it would injure those whom it is intended to benefit, it would be contrary to the natural rights of mankind, and it would introduce confusion and disorder into the commonwealth. Our first and most fundamental principle, therefore, when we undertake to alleviate the condition of the masses, must be the inviolability of private property. . . .

. . . The great mistake that is made in the matter now under consideration, is to possess one-self of the idea that class is naturally hostile to class: that rich and poor are intended by nature to live at war with one another. So irrational and so false is this view, that the exact contrary is the truth. Just as the symmetry of the human body is the result of the disposition of the members of the body, so in a State it is ordained by nature that these two classes should exist in harmony and agreement, and should, as it were, fit into one another, so as to maintain the equilibrium of the body politic. Each requires the other; capital cannot do without labor, nor labor without capital. Mutual agreement results in pleasantness and good order: perpetual conflict necessarily produces confusion and outrage. . . .

. . . Religion teaches the rich man and the employer that their workpeople are not their slaves; that they must respect in every man his dignity as a man and as a Christian; that labor is nothing to be ashamed of, if we listen to right reason and to Christian philosophy, but is an honorable employment, enabling a man to sustain his life in an upright and creditable way; and that it is shameful and inhuman to treat men like chattels to make money by, or to look upon them merely as so much muscle or physical power. . . .

. . . We have insisted that, since it is the end of society to make men better, the chief good that society can be possessed of is virtue. Nevertheless, in all well-constituted States it is a by no means unimportant matter to provide those bodily and external commodities, *the use of which is necessary to virtuous action.* And in the provision of material well being, the labor of the poor — the exercise of their skill and the employment of their strength in the culture of the land and the workshops of trade — is most efficacious and altogether indispensable. Indeed, their coöperation in this respect is so important that it may be truly said that it is only by the labor of the workingman that States grow rich. Justice, therefore, demands that the interests of the poorer population be carefully watched over by the administration, so that they who contribute so largely to the advantage of the community may themselves share in the benefits they create — that being housed, clothed, and enabled to support life, they may find their existence less hard and more endurable. It follows that whatever shall appear to be conducive to the well being of those who work should receive favorable consideration. Let it not be feared that solicitude of this kind will injure any interest; on the contrary, it will be to the advantage of all; for it cannot but be good for the commonwealth to secure from misery those on whom it so largely depends.

Rights must be religiously respected wherever they are found; and it is the duty of the public authority to prevent and punish injury, and to protect each one in the possession of his own. Still, when there is question of protecting the rights of individuals, the poor and helpless have a claim to special consideration. The richer population have many ways of protecting themselves, and stand less in need of help from the State; those who are badly off have no resources of their own to fall back upon, and must chiefly rely upon the assistance of the State. And it is for this reason that wage earners, who are undoubtedly among the weak and necessitous, should be specially cared for and protected by the commonwealth. . . .

. . . *When work people have recourse to a strike,* it is frequently because the hours of labor are too long, or the work too hard, or because they consider their wages insufficient. The grave inconvenience of this not uncommon occurrence should be obviated by public remedial measure; for such paralysis of labor not only affects the masters and their work people, but is extremely injurious to trade, and to the general interests of the public; moreover, on such occasions violence and disorder are generally not far off, and thus it frequently happens that the public peace is threatened. The laws should be beforehand, and prevent these troubles from arising; they should lend their influence and authority to the removal in good time of the causes which lead to conflicts between masters and those whom they employ. . . .

If we turn now to things exterior and corporeal, the first concern of all is to *save the poor workers* from the cruelty of grasping speculators, who use human beings as mere instruments for making money. It is neither justice nor humanity so to grind men down with excessive labor as to stupefy their minds and wear out their bodies. Man's powers, like his general nature, are limited, and beyond these limits he cannot go. His strength is developed and increased by use and exercise, but only on condition of due intermission and proper rest. Daily labor, therefore, must be so regulated that it may not be protracted during longer hours than strength admits. . . .

Let it be granted, then, that as a rule workman and employer should make free agreements, and in particular should freely agree as to wages. Nevertheless, there is a dictate of nature more imperious and more ancient than any bargain between man and man, that the remuneration must be enough to support the wage earner in reasonable and frugal comfort. If through necessity or fear of a worse evil the workman accepts harder conditions because an employer or a contractor will give him no better, he is the victim of force and injustice. In these and similar questions, however, such as, for example, the hours of labor in different trades, the sanitary precautions to be observed in factories and workshops, etc. — in order to supersede undue interference on the part of the State, especially as circumstances, times, and localities differ so widely, it is advisable that recourse be had to societies or Boards such as we shall mention presently, or to some other method of safe guarding the interests of wage earners, the State to be asked for approval and protection. . . .

. . . Employers and workmen may themselves effect much in the matter of which we treat, by means of those *institutions and organizations* which afford opportune assistance to those in need, and which draw the two orders more closely together. Among these may be enumerated: Societies for mutual help: various foundations established by private persons for providing for the workman, and for his widow or his orphans, in sudden calamity, in sickness, and in the event of death; and what are called "patronages" or institutions for the care of boys and girls, for young people, and also for those of more mature age.

The most important of all are workmen's associations, for these virtually include all the rest. History attests what excellent results were effected by the artificers' guilds of a former day. They were the means not only of many advantages to the workmen, but in no small degree of the advancement of art, as numerous monuments remain to prove. Such associations should be adapted to the requirements of the age in which we live — an age of greater instruction, of different customs, and of more numerous requirements in daily life. It is gratifying to know that there are actually in existence not a few societies of this nature, consisting either of workmen alone or of workmen and employers together; but it were greatly to be desired that they should multiply and become more effective.

18. The Innuit Indians and the London Poor

Jack London

Jack London (1876–1916) was one of America's most popular novelists. Even today, his adventure stories such as The Call of the Wild *remain favorites with the young, few of whom are aware of the writer's more serious works.*

In the summer of 1902 the author impersonated a poor man and embarked on a social exploration of the poverty-stricken East End in London. There, in so-called "good times," he was appalled by the unending degradation and misery: old people searching garbage for food, the unemployed crying for bread, deformed children, shelters unfit for habitation.

The People of the Abyss, which London ranked among his most important works, records that experience. In the following passage from that book London contrasts life among the poor in a "civilized" nation with life among the primitive Innuit people he had known in Alaska and draws some unflattering conclusions about "civilization."

. . . It were well to look at the Social Abyss in its widest aspect, and to put certain questions to Civilization, by the answers to which Civilization must stand or fall. For instance, has Civilization bettered the lot of man? "Man" I use in its democratic sense, meaning the average man. So the question reshapes itself: *Has Civilization bettered the lot of the average man?*

Let us see. In Alaska, along the banks of the Yukon River, near its mouth, live the Innuit folk. They are a very primitive people, manifesting but mere glimmering adumbrations of that tremendous artifice, Civilization. Their capital amounts possibly to $10 per head. They hunt and fish for their food with bone-headed spears and arrows. They never suffer from lack of shelter. Their clothes, largely made from the skins of animals, are warm. They always have fuel for their fires, likewise timber for their houses, which they build partly underground, and in which they lie snugly during the periods of intense cold. In the summer they live in tents, open to every breeze and cool. They are healthy, and strong, and happy. Their one problem is food. They have their times of plenty and times of famine. In good times they feast; in bad times they die of starvation. But starvation, as a chronic condition, present with a large number of them all the time, is a thing unknown. Further, they have no debts.

In the United Kingdom, on the rim of the Western Ocean, live the English folk. They are a consummately civilized people. Their capital amounts to at least $1500 per head. They gain their food, not by hunting and fishing, but by toil at colossal artifices. For the most part, they suffer from lack of shelter. The greater number of them are vilely housed, do not have enough fuel to keep them warm, and are insufficiently clothed. A constant number never have any houses at all, and sleep shelterless under the stars. Many are to be found, winter and summer, shivering on the streets in their rags. They have good times and bad. In good times most of them manage to get enough to eat, in bad times they die of starvation. They are dying now, they were dying yesterday and last year, they will die tomorrow and next year, of starvation; for they, unlike the Innuit, suffer from a chronic condition of starvation. There are 40,000,000 of the English folk, and 939 out of every 1000 of them die in poverty, while a

From Jack London, *The People of the Abyss* (1903).

constant army of 8,000,000 struggles on the ragged edge of starvation. Further, each babe that is born, is born in debt to the sum of $110. This is because of an artifice called the National Debt.

In a fair comparison of the average Innuit and the average Englishman, it will be seen that life is less rigorous for the Innuit; that while the Innuit suffers only during bad times from starvation, the Englishman suffers during good times as well; that no Innuit lacks fuel, clothing, or housing, while the Englishman is in perpetual lack of these three essentials. In this connection it is well to instance the judgment of a man such as Huxley. From the knowledge gained as a medical officer in the East End of London, and as a scientist pursuing investigations among the most elemental savages, he concludes, "Were the alternative presented to me I would deliberately prefer the life of the savage to that of those people of Christian London.". . .

There can be no mistake. Civilization has increased man's producing power an hundred fold, and through mismanagement the men of Civilization live worse than the beasts, and have less to eat and wear and protect them from the elements than the savage Innuit in a frigid climate who lives today as he lived in the stone age ten thousand years ago.

19. The Working Girls of New York

Jacob Riis

Danish-born Jacob Riis (1849–1914) wrote the muckraking era's most popular exposés of poverty. Riis spent decades as a police reporter on New York's East Side, an experience that flavored his books about slums with a realism that shocked middle-class readers. His pioneering photographs of slum life added an additional sense of horror to his books. But Riis was no revolutionary. He was a reformer who called upon the comfortable classes to improve the living conditions of the masses because "slums are the hot beds of the epidemics that carry death to rich and poor alike."

Riis was a foremost proponent of the melting pot and felt strongly that immigrants should "Americanize" as he himself had done. Hence, he often exhibited a sense of superiority toward the foreign-born poor, who seemed to cling tenaciously to European languages and customs.

The following piece is from his most famous book, How the Other Half Lives. *Riis's most sympathetic portrayals are of women and children mired down in poverty. Even advocates of women's libera-*

> tion may find this description of working girls overly sentimental, but the extreme exploitation of women workers in 1890 is an undeniable fact.
>
> In addition to writing about slums and their inhabitants, Riis was the leading figure in the movement for tenement reform and for more parks and playgrounds.

. . . Six months have not passed since at a great public meeting in this city, the Working Women's Society reported: "It is a known fact that men's wages cannot fall below a limit upon which they can exist, but woman's wages have no limit, since the paths of shame are always open to her. It is simply impossible for any woman to live without assistance on the low salary a saleswoman earns, without depriving herself of real necessities . . . It is inevitable that they must in many instances resort to evil." It was only a few brief weeks before that verdict was uttered that the community was shocked by the story of a gentle and refined woman who, left in direst poverty to earn her own living alone among strangers, threw herself from her attic window, preferring death to dishonor. "I would have done any honest work, even to scrubbing," she wrote, drenched and starving, after a vain search for work in a driving storm. She had tramped the streets for weeks on her weary errand, and the only living wages that were offered her were the wages of sin. . . .

It is estimated that at least one hundred and fifty thousand women and girls earn their own living in New York; but there is reason to believe that this estimate falls far short of the truth when sufficient account is taken of the large number who are not wholly dependent upon their own labor, while contributing by it to the family's earnings. These alone constitute a large class of the women wage-earners, and it is characteristic of the situation that the very fact that some need not starve on their wages condemns the rest to that fate. The pay they are willing to accept all have to take. What the "everlasting law of supply and demand," that serves as such a convenient gag for public indignation, has to do with it, one learns from observation all along the road of inquiry into these real woman's wrongs. To take the case of the saleswomen for illustration: The investigation of the Working Women's Society disclosed the fact that wages averaging from $2 to $4.50 a week were reduced by excessive fines, the employers placing a value upon time lost that is not given to services rendered. A little girl, who received two dollars a week, made cash-sales amounting to $167 in a single day, while the receipts of a fifteen-dollar male clerk in the same

From *How the Other Half Lives* by Jacob Riis (1890). Copyright © 1957 by Hill and Wang, Inc. Reprinted by permission of Hill and Wang, Inc.

department footed up only $125; yet for some trivial mistake the girl was fined sixty cents out of her two dollars. The practice prevailed in some stores of dividing the fines between the superintendent and the time-keeper at the end of the year. In one instance they amounted to $3,000, and "the superintendent was heard to charge the time-keeper with not being strict enough in his duties." One of the causes for fine in a certain large store was sitting down. The law requiring seats for saleswomen, generally ignored, was obeyed faithfully in this establishment. The seats were there, but the girls were fined when found using them.

Cash-girls receiving $1.75 a week for work that at certain seasons lengthened their day to sixteen hours were sometimes required to pay for their aprons. A common cause for discharge from stores in which, on account of the oppressive heat and lack of ventilation, "girls fainted day after day and came out looking like corpses," was too long service. No other fault was found with the discharged saleswomen than that they had been long enough in the employ of the firm to justly expect an increase of salary. The reason was even given with brutal frankness, in some instances.

These facts give a slight idea of the hardships and the poor pay of a business that notoriously absorbs child-labor. The girls are sent to the store before they have fairly entered their teens, because the money they can earn there is needed for the support of the family. If the boys will not work, if the street tempts them from home, among the girls at least there must be no drones. To keep their places they are told to lie about their age and to say that they are over fourteen. The precaution is usually superfluous. The Women's Investigating Committee found the majority of the children employed in the stores to be under age, but heard only in a single instance of the truant officers calling. In that case they came once a year and sent the youngest children home; but in a month's time they were all back in their places, and were not again disturbed. When it comes to the factories, where hard bodily labor is added to long hours, stifling rooms, and starvation wages, matters are even worse. The Legislature has passed laws to prevent the employment of children, as it has forbidden saloon-keepers to sell them beer, and it has provided means of enforcing its mandate, so efficient, that the very number of factories in New York is *guessed* at as in the neighborhood of twelve thousand. Up till this summer, a single inspector was charged with the duty of keeping the run of them all, and of seeing to it that the law was respected by the owners.

Sixty cents is put as the average day's earnings of the 150,000, but into this computation enters the stylish "cashier's" two dollars a day, as well as the thirty cents of the poor little girl who pulls threads in an East Side factory, and, if anything, the average is probably too high. Such as it is, however, it represents board, rent, clothing, and "pleasure" to this army of workers. Here is the case of a woman employed in the manufacturing department of a Broadway house. It stands for a hundred like her own. She averages three dollars a week. Pays $1.50 for her room; for breakfast she has a cup of coffee; lunch she cannot afford. One meal a day is her allowance. This woman is young, she is pretty. She has "the world before her." Is it anything less than a miracle if she is guilty of nothing worse than the "early and improvident marriage," against which moralists exclaim as one of the prolific causes of the distress of the poor? . . .

The tenement and the competition of public institutions and farmers' wives and daughters, have done the tyrant shirt to death, but they have not bettered the lot of the needle-women. The sweater of the East Side has appropriated the flannel shirt. He turns them out to-day at forty-five cents a dozen, paying his Jewish workers from twenty to thirty-five cents. One of these testified before the State Board of Arbitration, during the shirtmakers' strike, that she worked eleven hours in the shop and four at home, and had never in the best of times made over six dollars a week. Another stated that she worked from 4 o'clock in the morning to 11 at night. These girls had to find their own thread and pay for their own machines out of their wages. The white shirt has gone to the public and private institutions that shelter large numbers of young girls, and to the country. There are not half as many shirtmakers in New York to-day as only a few years ago, and some of the largest firms have closed their city shops. The same is true of the manufacturers of underwear. One large Broadway firm has nearly all its work done by farmers' girls in Maine, who think themselves well off if they can earn two or three dollars a week to pay for a Sunday silk, or the wedding outfit, little dreaming of the part they are playing in starving their city sisters. Literally, they sew "with double thread, a shroud as well as a shirt." Their pin-money sets the rate of wages for thousands of poor sewing-girls in New York. The average earnings of the worker on underwear to-day do not exceed the three dollars which her competitor among the Eastern hills is willing to accept as the price of her play. The shirtmaker's pay is better only because the very finest custom work is all there is left for her to do. . . .

I have aimed to set down a few dry facts merely. They carry their own comment. Back of the shop with its weary, grinding toil — the home in the tenement, of which it was said in a report to the State Labor Bureau: "Decency and womanly reserve cannot be maintained there — what wonder so many fall away from virtue?" Of the outlook, what? Last Christmas Eve my business took me to an obscure street among the West Side tenements. An old woman had just fallen on the doorstep, stricken with paralysis. The doctor said she would never again move her right hand or foot. The whole side was dead. By her bedside, in their cheerless room, sat the patient's aged sister, a hopeless cripple, in dumb despair. Forty years ago the sisters had come, five in number then, with their mother, from the North of Ireland to make their home and earn a living among strangers. They were lace embroiderers and found work easily at good wages. All the rest had died as the years went by. The two remained and, firmly resolved to lead an honest life, worked on though wages fell and fell as age and toil stiffened their once nimble fingers and dimmed their sight. Then one of them dropped out, her hands palsied and her courage gone. Still the other toiled on, resting neither by night nor by day, that the sister might not want. Now that she too had been stricken, as she was going to the store for the work that was to keep them through the holidays, the battle was over at last. There was before them starvation, or the poorhouse. And the proud spirits of the sisters, helpless now, quailed at the outlook.

These were old, with life behind them. For them nothing was left but to sit in the shadow and wait. But of the thousands, who are travelling the road they trod to the end, with the hot blood of youth in their veins, with the love of life and of the beautiful world to which not even sixty cents a day can shut their eyes — who is to blame if their feet find the paths of shame that are "always open to them?" The very paths that have effaced the saving "limit," and to which it is declared to be "inevitable that they must in many instances resort." Let the moralist answer. Let the wise economist apply his rule of supply and demand, and let the answer be heard in this city of a thousand charities where justice goes begging.

20. The Continued Progress of the Working Classes Under Capitalism

Alfred Marshall

Alfred Marshall (1842–1924), the leading neoclassical economist, was drawn into economics from mathematics by a deep concern about poverty in England. Marshall taught at Cambridge for many years and is well remembered for his work in economic concepts such as equilibrium, supply and demand, elasticity, short-run and long-run. He stressed the self-adjusting nature of the free market system, particularly over long periods of time.

Living standards in England had risen during the last part of the nineteenth century. Hence, in sharp contrast to the pessimism of the earlier classical economists such as Malthus and Ricardo, optimism pervaded Marshall's outlook. According to Marshall, poverty was not a natural condition of the masses. It would gradually decline under capitalism, thus confounding the socialists, whose alternative he firmly rejected.

Exactly how would poverty recede under capitalism? Marshall recognized two types of poverty and foresaw two kinds of solutions. Ordinary poverty would be reduced by shifts in the supply and demand for labor caused by mechanization and widespread education. Mechanization would raise society's productivity and increase the demand for skilled labor. Education would end poverty because it would enable the children of unskilled workers to become more highly paid skilled workers. Also, since fewer unskilled workers would remain, their wages would rise.

What about the rest of the poor? Marshall tagged them the "Residuum" — shades of today's term "hard core." He attributed their poverty to personal characteristics rather than to society's shortcomings and felt they were "physically, mentally, or morally incapable of doing a good day's work" for "a good day's wage." Even so, Marshall felt that salvation was within their reach. Marshall pinned his main hope for all lower-class people on education and other forms of investment in human beings. But he thought that the Residuum would also need special treatment not required by the ordinary poor. Society might have to enforce certain child-rearing norms to prevent the transmission of undesirable traits from one generation to another. But, given these measures, the children of the Residuum were not doomed to eternal poverty. They could rise out of their class.

Marshall's solution, like many a current policy, focuses on adapting the poor to better jobs and middle-class life styles; it minimizes the role of income redistribution and leaves existing property relations undisturbed.

The main drift of this study of Distribution then suggests that the social and economic forces already at work are changing the distribution of wealth for the better: that they are persistent and increasing in strength; and that their influence is for the greater part cumulative; that the socioeconomic organism is more delicate and complex than at first sight appears; and that large ill-considered changes might result in grave disaster. In particular it suggests that the assumption and ownership by

Reprinted with permission of The Macmillan Company, New York, and Macmillan and Company, London, from *Principles of Economics*, 8th ed. by Alfred Marshall. Copyright 1948 by The Macmillan Company. Editor's title, by permission.

Government of all the means of production, even if brought about gradually and slowly, as the more responsible "Collectivists" propose, might cut deeper into the roots of social prosperity than appears at first sight.

Starting from the fact that the growth of the national dividend depends on the continued progress of invention and the accumulation of expensive appliances for production; we are bound to reflect that up to the present time nearly all of the innumerable inventions that have given us our command over nature have been made by independent workers; and that the contributions from Government officials all the world over have been relatively small. Further, nearly all the costly appliances for production which are now in collective ownership by national or local Governments, have been bought with resources borrowed mainly from the savings of business men and other private individuals. Oligarchic Governments have sometimes made great efforts to accumulate collective wealth; and it may be hoped that in the coming time, foresight and patience will become the common property of the main body of the working classes. But, as things are, too great a risk would be involved by entrusting to a pure democracy the accumulation of the resources needed for acquiring yet further command over nature.

There is therefore strong *primâ facie* cause for fearing that the collective ownership of the means of production would deaden the energies of mankind, and arrest economic progress; unless before its introduction the whole people had acquired a power of unselfish devotion to the public good which is now relatively rare. And, though this matter cannot be entered upon here, it might probably destroy much that is most beautiful and joyful in the private and domestic relations of life. These are the main reasons which cause patient students of economics generally to anticipate little good and much evil from schemes for sudden and violent reorganization of the economic, social and political conditions of life.

Further, we are bound to reflect that the distribution of the national dividend, though bad, is not nearly as bad as is commonly supposed. In fact there are many artisan households in England, and even more in the United States in spite of the colossal fortunes that are found there, which would lose by an equal distribution of the national income. Therefore the fortunes of the masses of the people, though they would of course be greatly improved *for the time* by the removal of all inequalities, would not be raised even temporarily at all near to the level which is assigned to them in socialistic anticipations of a Golden Age.

But this cautious attitude does not imply acquiescence in the present inequalities of wealth. The drift of economic science during many generations has been with increasing force towards the belief that there is no real necessity, and therefore no moral justification for extreme poverty side by side with great wealth. The inequalities of wealth though less than they are often represented to be, are a serious flaw in our economic organization. Any diminution of them which can be attained by means that would not sap the springs of free initiative and strength of character, and would not therefore materially check the growth of the national dividend, would seem to be a clear social gain. Though arithmetic warns us that it is impossible to raise all earnings beyond the level already reached by specially well-to-do artisan families, it is certainly desirable that those who are below that level should be raised, even at the expense of lowering in some degree those who are above it.

Prompt action is needed in regard to the large, though it may be hoped, now steadily diminishing, "Residuum" of persons who are physically, mentally, or morally incapable of doing a good day's work with which to earn a good day's wage. This class perhaps includes some others besides those who are absolutely "unemployable." But it is a class that needs exceptional treatment. The system of economic freedom is probably the best from both a moral and material point of view for those who are in fairly good health of mind and body. But the Residuum cannot turn it to good account: and if they are allowed to bring up children in their own pattern, then Anglo-Saxon freedom must work badly through them on the coming generation. It would be better for them and much better for the nation that they should come under a paternal discipline something like that which prevails in Germany.

The evil to be dealt with is so urgent that strong measures against it are eagerly to be desired. And the proposal that a minimum wage should be fixed by authority of Government below which no man may work, and another below which no woman may work, has claimed the attention of students for a long while. If it could be made effective, its benefits would be so great that it might be gladly accepted, in spite of the fear that it would lead to malingering and some other abuses; and that it would be used as a leverage for pressing for a rigid artificial standard of wages, in cases in which there was no exceptional justification for it. But, though great improvements in the details of the scheme have been made recently, and especially in the last two or three years, its central difficulties do not appear to have been fairly faced. There is scarcely any experience to guide us except that of Australasia. . . . A scheme, that has any claim to be ready for practical adoption, must be based on statistical estimates of the numbers of those who under it would be forced to seek the aid of the State, because their work was not worth the minimum wage; with special reference to the question how many of these might have supported life fairly well if it had been possible to work with nature, and to adjust in many cases the minimum wage to the family, instead of to the individual.

Turning then to those workers who have fairly good moral and physical stamina, it may be estimated roughly that those who are capable only of rather unskilled work constitute about a fourth of the population. And those who, though fit for the lower kinds of skilled work are neither fit for highly skilled work, nor able to act wisely and promptly in responsible positions, constitute about another fourth. If similar estimates had been made in England a century ago, the proportions would have been very different: more than a half would have been found unfit for any skilled labour at all, beyond the ordinary routine of agriculture; and perhaps less than a sixth part would have been fit for highly skilled or responsible work: for the education of the people was not then recognized as a national duty and a national economy. If this had been the only change the urgent demand for unskilled labour would have compelled employers to pay for it nearly the same wage as for skilled: the wages for skilled labour would have fallen a little and those for unskilled would have risen, until the two had nearly met.

Even as it is, something like this has happened: the wages of unskilled labour have risen faster than those of any other class, faster even than those of skilled labour. And this movement towards the equalization of earnings would have gone much faster, had not the work of purely unskilled labour been meanwhile annexed by automatic and other machinery faster even than that of skilled labour; so that there is less wholly unskilled work to be done now than formerly. . . .

Thus mechanical progress is a chief cause of the great differences that still exist between the earnings of different kinds of labour; and this may seem at first sight a severe indictment: but it is not. If mechanical progress had been much slower the real wages of unskilled labour would have been lower than they are now, not higher: for the growth of the national dividend would have been so much checked that even the skilled workers would generally have had to content themselves with less real purchasing power for an hour's work than the 6d. of the London bricklayer's labourer: and the unskilled labourers' wages would of course have been lower still. . . .

We have then to strive to keep mechanical progress in full swing: and to diminish the supply of labour, incapable of any but unskilled work; in order that the average income of the country may rise faster even than in the past, and the share of it got by each unskilled labourer may rise faster still. To that end we need to move in the same direction as in recent years, but more strenuously. Education must be made more thorough. The schoolmaster must learn that his main duty is not to impart knowledge, for a few shillings will buy more printed knowledge than a man's brain can hold. It is to educate character, faculties and activities; so that the children even of those parents who are not thoughtful themselves, may have a better chance of being trained up to become thoughtful parents of the next generation. To this end public money must flow freely. And it must flow freely to provide fresh air and space for wholesome play for the children in all working class quarters.

Thus the State seems to be required to contribute generously and even lavishly to that side of the wellbeing of the poorer working class which they cannot easily provide for themselves: and at the same time to insist that the inside of the houses be kept clean, and fit for those who will be needed in after years to act as strong and responsible citizens. The compulsory standard of cubic feet of air per head needs to be raised steadily though not violently: and this combined with a regulation that no row of high buildings be erected without adequate free space in front and behind, will hasten the movement, already in progress, of the working classes from the central districts of large towns, to places in which freer playroom is possible. Meanwhile public aid and control in medical and sanitary matters will work in another direction to lessen the weight that has hitherto pressed on the children of the poorer classes.

The children of unskilled workers need to be made capable of earning the wages of skilled work: and the children of skilled workers need by similar means to be made capable of doing still more responsible work. They will not gain much, they are indeed more likely to lose, by pushing themselves into the ranks of the lower middle class: for, as has already been observed, the mere power of writing and keeping accounts belongs really to a lower grade than skilled manual work; and has ranked above it in past times, merely because popular education has been neglected. There is often a social loss as well as a social gain when the children of any grade press into the grade above them. But the existence of our present lowest class is an almost unmixed evil: nothing should be done to promote the increase of its numbers, and children once born into it should be helped to rise out of it.

There is plenty of room in the upper ranks of the artisans; and there is abundant room for new comers in the upper ranks of the middle class. It is to the activity and resource of the leading minds in this class that most of those inventions and improvements are due, which enable the working man of to-day to have comforts and luxuries that were rare or unknown among the richest of a few generations ago: and without which indeed England could not supply her present population with a sufficiency even of common food. And it is a vast and wholly unmixed gain when the children of any class press within the relatively small charmed circle of those who create new ideas, and who embody those new ideas in solid constructions. Their profits are sometimes large: but taking one with another they have probably earned for the world a hundred times or more as much as they have earned for themselves.

It is true that many of the largest fortunes are made by speculation rather than by truly constructive work: and much of this speculation is associated with anti-social strategy, and even with evil manipulation of the sources from which ordinary investors derive their guidance. A remedy is not easy, and may never be perfect. Hasty attempts to control speculation by simple enactments have invariably proved either futile or mischievous: but this is one of those matters in which the rapidly increasing force of economic studies may be expected to render great service to the world in the course of this century.

In many other ways evil may be lessened by a wider understanding of the social possibilities of economic chivalry. A devotion to public wellbeing on the part of the rich may do much, as enlightenment spreads, to help the tax-gatherer in turning the resources of the rich to high account in the service of the poor, and may remove the worst evils of poverty from the land.

21. Transferring Income from the Rich to the Poor

A. C. Pigou

Arthur Cecil Pigou (1877–1959) succeeded Alfred Marshall at Cambridge and eventually became the chief exponent of neoclassical economics. Pigou pioneered in "welfare economics," a field whose central concern is how to maximize society's total well-being. He differed from Marshall in his approach to the alleviation of poverty, for Pigou advocated the redistribution of income and a guaranteed minimum income. Yet Pigou based his more radical proposal for income redistribution on the neoclassical idea of diminishing marginal utility. Each additional dollar of income adds relatively less to the recipient's total satisfaction. Hence, claims Pigou in this passage, the same dollar gives more satisfaction to a poor man than to a rich man, and transferring income from the rich to the poor would raise society's total satisfaction. (Pigou's reasoning is a theoretical justification for the progressive income tax.)

Most of Pigou's modern critics accept the law of diminishing marginal utility as valid but they claim that it is "unscientific" to compare satisfactions between different individuals. Those contemporary economists who claim that economics is and should be a value-free

A. C. Pigou

science think that Pigouvian welfare economics, which has influenced the philosophy of the welfare state, has strong ethical overtones. If he could reply, Pigou would probably concur.

If income is transferred from rich persons to poor persons the proportion in which different sorts of goods and services are provided will be changed. Expensive luxuries will give place to more necessary articles, rare wines to meat and bread, new machines and factories to clothes and improved small dwellings; and there will be other changes of a like sort. . . .

. . . It is evident that any transference of income from a relatively rich man to a relatively poor man of similar temperament, since it enables more intense wants to be satisfied at the expense of less intense wants, must increase the aggregate sum of satisfaction. The old "law of diminishing utility" thus leads securely to the proposition: Any cause which increases the absolute share of real income in the hands of the poor, provided that it does not lead to a contraction in the size of the national dividend from any point of view, will, in general, increase economic welfare. . . .

It must be conceded, of course, that, if the rich and the poor were two races with different mental constitutions, such that the rich were inherently capable of securing a greater amount of economic satisfaction from any given income than the poor, the possibility of increasing welfare by this type of change would be seriously doubtful. Furthermore, even without any assumption about inherent racial difference, it may be maintained that a rich man, from the nature of his upbringing and training, is capable of obtaining considerably more satisfaction from a given income — say a thousand pounds — than a poor man would be. For, if anybody accustomed to a given standard of living suddenly finds his income enlarged, he is apt to dissipate the extra income in forms of exciting pleasure, which, when their indirect, as well as their direct, effects are taken into account, may even lead to a positive loss of satisfaction. To this argument, however, there is a sufficient answer. It is true that at any given moment the tastes and temperament of persons who have long been poor are more or less adjusted to their environment, and that a sudden and sharp rise of income is likely to be followed by a good deal of foolish expenditure which involves little or no addition to economic welfare. If, however, the higher income is maintained for any length of time, this phase will pass. . . . In any case, to contend that the folly of poor persons is so great that a rise of income among them will not promote economic welfare in any degree is to press paradox beyond the point up to which discussion can reasonably be

From A. C. Pigou, *The Economics of Welfare,* 4th ed. (New York: St. Martin's Press, 1932). Reprinted by permission of St. Martin's Press and Macmillan and Company, London. Editor's title, by permission.

called upon to follow. . . . If the time is long enough to allow a new generation to grow up — the possession of such an income will make possible the development in them, through education and otherwise, of capacities and faculties adapted for the enjoyment of the enlarged income. Thus in the long run differences of temperament and taste between rich and poor are overcome by the very fact of a shifting of income between them. Plainly, therefore, they cannot be used as an argument to disprove the benefits of a tranference. . . .

There is general agreement among practical philanthropists that *some* minimum standard of conditions ought to be set up at a level high enough to make impossible the occurrence to anybody of extreme want; and that whatever transference of resources from relatively rich to relatively poor persons is necessary to secure this must be made, without reference to possible injurious consequences upon the magnitude of the dividend. This policy of practical philanthropists is justified by analysis, in the sense that it can be shown to be conducive to economic welfare on the whole, if we believe the misery that results to individuals from extreme want to be indefinitely large; for, then, the good of abolishing extreme want is not commensurable with any evils that may follow should a diminution of the dividend take place. Up to this point, therefore, there is no difficulty. But our discussion cannot stop at this point. It is necessary to ask, not merely whether economic welfare will be promoted by the establishment of *any* minimum standard, but also by *what* minimum standard it will be promoted most effectively. Now, above the level of extreme want, it is generally admitted that increments of income involve finite increments of satisfaction. Hence the direct good of transference and the indirect evil resulting from a diminished dividend are both finite quantities; and the correct formal answer to our question is that economic welfare is best promoted by a minimum standard raised to such a level that the direct good resulting from the transference of the marginal pound transferred to the poor just balances the indirect evil brought about by the consequent reduction of the dividend.

To derive from this formal answer a quantitative estimate of what the minimum standard of real income established in any particular country at any particular time ought to be, it would be necessary to obtain and to analyse a mass of detailed information, much of which is not, in present circumstances, accessible to students. One practical conclusion can, however, be safely drawn. This is that, other things being equal, the minimum can be advantageously set higher, the larger is the real income per head of the community. The reason, of course, is that every increase in average income implies a diminution in the number of people unable by their own efforts to attain to any given minimum standard; and, therefore, a diminution, both absolute and proportionate, in the damage to the dividend which an external guarantee of that standard threatens to bring about. It follows that, when we have to do with a group of pioneer workers in rough and adverse natural circumstances, the minimum standard may rightly be set at a low level. But, as inventions and discoveries progress, as capital is accumulated and Nature subdued, it should be correspondingly raised. Thus it is reasonable that, while a relatively poor country makes only a low provision for its "destitute" citizens, a relatively rich country should make a somewhat better provision for all who are "necessitous."

Chapter Six

The Great Depression and Its Aftermath

22. One-Third of a Nation

Franklin Delano Roosevelt

When Franklin Delano Roosevelt (1882–1945) entered the White House in 1933, the American economy lay prostrate. Banking and agriculture had collapsed. Mass unemployment afflicted one-fourth of the work force. The New Deal, which greatly expanded the role of the federal government in the economy and laid the foundation for our present social welfare system, was Roosevelt's response to the crisis of the Great Depression. He was elected for a second term (and afterward for a third and fourth term) and was given an overwhelming mandate to continue the New Deal.

In this passage from his famous Second Inaugural Address, delivered in January 1937, Roosevelt describes the mass poverty then afflicting one-third of the nation.

How far have we come since the 1930's? Not far enough if we use Roosevelt's own yardstick for progress: "[It] is not whether we add more to the abundance of those who have made much, it is whether we provide enough for those who have too little."

My fellow-countrymen:

When four years ago we met to inaugurate a President, the Republic, single-minded in anxiety, stood in spirit here. We dedicated ourselves to the fulfillment of a vision — to speed the time when there would be for all the

From Franklin D. Roosevelt, *Second Inaugural Address* (January 20, 1937).

people that security and peace essential to the pursuit of happiness. We of the Republic pledged ourselves to drive from the temple of our ancient faith those who had profaned it; to end by action, tireless and unafraid, the stagnation and despair of that day.

We did those first things first.

Our covenant with ourselves did not stop there. Instinctively we recognized a deeper need — the need to find through government the instrument of our united purpose to solve for the individual the ever-rising problems of a complex civilization.

Repeated attempts at their solution without the aid of government had left us baffled and bewildered. For, without that aid, we had been unable to create those moral controls over the services of science which are necessary to make science a useful servant instead of a ruthless master of mankind. To do this we knew that we must find practical controls over blind economic forces and blindly selfish men.

We of the Republic sensed the truth that democratic government has innate capacity to protect its people against disasters once considered inevitable — to solve problems once considered unsolvable. We would not admit that we could not find a way to master economic epidemics just as, after centuries of fatalistic suffering, we had found a way to master epidemics of disease. We refused to leave the problems of our common welfare to be solved by the winds of chance and the hurricanes of disaster. . . .

Our progress out of the depression is obvious.

But that is not all that you and I mean by the new order of things. Our pledge was not merely to do a patchwork job with second-hand materials. By using the new materials of social justice we have undertaken to erect on the old foundations a more enduring structure for the better use of future generations.

In that purpose we have been helped by achievements of mind and spirit. Old truths have been relearned, untruths have been unlearned. We have always known that heedless self-interest was bad morals; we know now that it is bad economics. Out of the collapse of a prosperity whose builders boasted their practicality has come the conviction that in the long run economic morality pays.

We are beginning to wipe out the line that divides the practical from the ideal, and in so doing we are fashioning an instrument of unimagined power for the establishment of a morally better world.

This new understanding undermines the old admiration of worldly success as such. We are beginning to abandon our tolerance of the abuse of power by those who betray for profit the elementary decencies of life.

In this process evil things formerly accepted will not be so easily condoned. Hard-headedness will not so easily excuse hard-heartedness. We are moving toward an era of good feeling. But we realize that there can be no era of good feeling save among men of good-will.

For these reasons I am justified in believing that the greatest change we have witnessed has been the change in the moral climate of America.

Among men of good-will, science and democracy together offer an ever-richer life and ever-larger satisfaction to the individual. With this change in our moral climate and our rediscovered ability to improve our economic order, we have set our feet upon the road of enduring progress.

Shall we pause now and turn our back upon the road that lies ahead? Shall we call this the promised land? Or shall we continue on our way? For "each age is a dream that is dying, or one that is coming to birth." . . .

Let us ask again: Have we reached the goal of our vision of that fourth day of March 1933? Have we found our happy valley?

I see a great nation, upon a great continent, blessed with a great wealth of natural resources. Its hundred and thirty million people are at peace among themselves; they are making their country a good neighbor among the nations. I see a United States which can demonstrate that, under democratic methods of government, national wealth can be translated into a spreading volume of human comforts hitherto unknown — and the lowest standard of living can be raised far above the level of mere subsistence.

But here is the challenge to our democracy: In this nation I see tens of millions of its citizens — a substantial part of its whole population — who at this very moment are denied the greater part of what the very lowest standards of today call the necessities of life.

I see millions of families trying to live on incomes so meager that the pall of family disaster hangs over them day by day.

I see millions whose daily lives in city and on farm continue under conditions labeled indecent by a so-called polite society half a century ago.

I see millions denied education, recreation and the opportunity to better their lot and the lot of their children.

I see millions lacking the means to buy the products of farm and factory and by their poverty denying work and productiveness to many other millions.

I see one-third of a nation ill-housed, ill-clad, ill-nourished.

It is not in despair that I paint you that picture. I paint it for you in hope, because the nation, seeing and understanding the injustice in it, proposes to paint it out. We are determined to make every American citizen the subject of his country's interest and concern, and we will never regard any faithful law-abiding group within our borders as superfluous. The test of our progress is not whether we add more to the abundance of those who have much, it is whether we provide enough for those who have too little.

23. Security for a People

Social Security Board

The Great Depression brutally exposed the economic insecurity that beset the average worker in our private enterprise society.

The Social Security Act of 1935, reformist in approach, belatedly acknowledged the need for the government to cushion some of life's economic hazards within the context of the private enterprise system.

The philosophy of the Act, which laid the groundwork for our current Social Security, welfare, and unemployment insurance systems, is given in this passage from the First Annual Report of the Social Security Board. *Unfortunately, after three and one-half decades, the promise of basic economic security remains unfulfilled for many Americans, and low-income wage earners pay an especially steep tax to help finance Social Security pensions.*

An attempt to find security for a people is among the oldest of political obligations and the greatest of the tasks of a state. The Declaration of Independence sets down as self-evident the right of a people "to provide new guards for a future security." The avowed object of the Constitution of the United States is "to secure the blessings of liberty to ourselves and our posterity."

But what is security? It is no blessing to be had for the asking. It is no gift of the government through a single legislative act. It is no abstraction too nebulous for definition. Security begins with bread and butter. But a mere subsistence is no security for the American citizen. The Nation is rich in natural resources; it possesses a developing technology; it has a varied abundance of human capacities to turn to account. Security is more than a condition of material well-being. An opportunity to earn a living, to be a member of the community, to have a part in the government is basic. In positive terms, the security of a people is the sum of the arrangements set up by business, by the government, and by society through which the things we cherish are safeguarded against the hazards we, as individuals, cannot control.

Above all, security is not static. The march of the decades brings changed conditions. Old problems have to be freshly stated, established safeguards to be supplanted by new. But there is still the necessity of

From *First Annual Report of the Social Security Board, Fiscal Year Ended June 30, 1936* (Washington, D.C.: U.S. Government Printing Office, 1937).

serving a people in their lives and properties, their liberties and opportunities. As we have met the exigencies which changing times have brought, the domain of security has been enriched and enlarged. As the way opens ahead, we must secure its wider opportunities.

The quest of security is a task for the whole of the people. It must be worked out within a system which is distinctly American. That system does not offer the individual a life of security. It grants him an opportunity and imposes upon him the obligation to find security for himself. There can be no obligation without opportunity. And for opportunity the individual must look to private enterprise. Upon it he is dependent for a job, an income, a chance to get ahead, a place to put his savings. If agriculture, industry, and business are articulated into an orderly and smoothly running system, the more fundamental part of the problem is solved. To the extent to which they are not so articulated, an obligation rests upon the government. Agriculture and industry must be aided to provide the opportunities out of which the security of the people is to be created. Thus, the security of a people is a great cooperative enterprise. The citizens, the economic system, and the government are partners in this national provision.

In this endeavor the government has its distinctive part. Its task is to quicken opportunity, to set up barriers against industrial shock, to care for the needy for whom private enterprise cannot provide. Its policies must be directed to all groups in society. The nation is an intricate organization of activities. Interests, occupations, and sections have different tasks to perform in a national economy. The security of each must be promoted within the circumstances peculiar to it.

The Social Security Act was passed as a single measure to promote the realization of this broad aim. Its meaning and significance are to be discovered in its relationship to the society it serves. It does not usurp the role of private enterprise. It recognizes work and a wage as the best security which the worker can find for himself. The act provides not a complete security in itself but a necessary complement to the security afforded by private enterprise and a complement to other measures of government directed to the same end. The plan would make a sorry go of it if the whole burden of keeping a people from destitution fell upon its provisions. In fact, it is the reasonable certainty of what industry can provide that makes it possible for government to undertake its task. It carries no threat to the way of individual thrift. On the contrary, it enlarges the opportunities and lessens the hazards of personal provision.

Here is the key to the Social Security Act. It hedges the major hazards of life about with safeguards which neither the individual alone nor industry unaided can provide. The life of the worker is continuous. The income from his job obeys the tides of the market; his expenses click on endlessly with the clock. This is the case for unemployment compensation. The worker's living comes from his job; yet his life is likely to outlast the skills which he can market. Neither wages nor savings can be depended upon to protect him against want in old age. The way of individual provision is beset with too many perils for safety. This is the case for old-age benefits. A number of hazards which no one can control lie in the path of every man and every woman — a dependent childhood, blindness, disability, the need for maternity care, an indigent old age. This is the case for public assistance and special services for health and welfare.

We cannot achieve security for a nation without promoting the security of the groups which make it up. But interests are interlocked. The well-being of industry reaches the farmer in a more plentiful supply of cheaper goods, just as an increase in the stream of farm income sets wheels turning and wage earners to work. As in war, so in public policy, forces must be massed at certain points of stress to protect the safety of all.

It is within this broad conception of the security of a people that the Board has endeavored to carry out the responsibilities allocated to it in the Social Security Act.

24. The General Theory of Employment, Interest, and Money

John Maynard Keynes

John Maynard Keynes (1883–1946), often called the father of the New Economics, is widely regarded as the most influential economist of the twentieth century. The theoretical tools and concepts he developed permeate the thinking of most contemporary nonsocialist economists, despite vast differences among Keynesians.

The General Theory of Employment, Interest and Money (1936), Keynes's most significant work, is a landmark in economics. The book was a response to the inability of neoclassical theory to explain the Great Depression. The neoclassical economists had assumed that a capitalist economy has a natural tendency to reach equilibrium at full employment. But Keynes, an Englishman trained in the neoclassical tradition at Cambridge, looked at the devastating unemployment then spreading throughout the capitalist world and found neoclassical economics completely inadequate for dealing with the problems of the times.

Keynes asked probing questions. What causes a capitalist economy to grind to a halt, leaving millions without work? Why do factories close for lack of sales, while the unemployed clamor for jobs and the income with which to buy the wares of these same factories? Nearly a century before, Karl Marx had asked similar questions. Marx, a foe of capitalism, had concluded that worsening depressions were inevitable under capitalism and would eventually hasten the collapse of the system. Needless to say, Marx was deliberately ignored by mainstream economists. But Keynes, a defender of capitalism, sought the means to prop up the ailing economic system. He was not ignored.

The neoclassical economists believed in laissez-faire. The government should not interfere in the economy. Hands off. The economy will find its own way back to full employment.

So Keynes had to forge his own theories and remedies. According to his analysis, an advanced capitalist economy has a tendency to reach equilibrium with high unemployment. And there is no built-in mechanism to bring about full employment. Hence, argued Keynes, laissez-faire must end. Government expenditures must compensate for inadequate private demand. With enough government spending, full employment can be attained.

Keynes reasoned that any government expenditures, if sufficient, would stimulate employment. Money could be spent on housing, pyramid-building, or war. The employment impact of beneficial, wasteful, or harmful expenditures would be similar. Only the social consequences would vary.

Such were Keynes's views about unemployment, which he regarded as the overriding issue of the day. But what about poverty? Ironically, our century's most distinguished economist had little to say about poverty per se as distinct from unemployment. Keynes did, however, discuss the question of the unequal distribution of wealth and income.

In the following passages from The General Theory of Employment, Interest and Money *Keynes expounds some of his ideas about government expenditures and income inequality. He acknowledges that his economic analysis has weakened any theoretical justification for large concentrations of income. The classicists and neoclassicists had assumed that saving was a virtue and defended large inequalities of income on the grounds that the rich save more than the poor. But Keynes points out that too much saving and too little spending cause advanced capitalism to falter. Hence, he claims, saving is no longer a virtue, and income inequality cannot be defended on the basis of economic theory.*

Ironically — perhaps because he was upper class — Keynes does not call for complete income equality. Rather, he justifies income inequality (though not to the extent then existing in England) on the basis of social and psychological factors.

Today, Keynesian tools — the use of government expenditures and taxation to control the level of employment and unemployment — are powerful and firmly embedded in the economies of the United States and most capitalist countries. But, like Keynes himself, many capitalist governments consider the questions of inequality of income to be subsidiary. More important to them is the goal of stabilizing the economic system at politically acceptable levels of unemployment. And in the United States in the post–World War II era the military establishment has received the lion's share of federal expenditures.

. . . For a man who has been long unemployed some measure of labour, instead of involving disutility, may have a positive utility. If this is accepted, the above reasoning shows how "wasteful" loan expenditure may nevertheless enrich the community on balance. Pyramid-building, earthquakes, even wars may serve to increase wealth, if the education of our statesmen on the principles of the classical economics stands in the way of anything better. . . .

If the Treasury were to fill old bottles with banknotes, bury them at suitable depths in disused coalmines which are then filled up to the surface with town rubbish, and leave it to private enterprise on well-tried principles of laissez-faire to dig the notes up again (the right to do so being obtained, of course, by tendering for leases of the note-bearing territory), there need be no more unemployment and, with the help of the repercussions, the real income of the community, and its capital wealth also, would probably become a good deal greater than it actually is. It would, indeed, be more sensible to build houses and the like; but if there are political and practical difficulties in the way of this, the above would be better than nothing.

The outstanding faults of the economic society in which we live are its failure to provide for full employment and its arbitrary and inequitable distribution of wealth and incomes. The bearing of the foregoing theory on the first of these is obvious. But there are also two important respects in which it is relevant to the second.

Since the end of the nineteenth century significant progress towards the removal of very great disparities of wealth and income has been achieved through the instrument of direct taxation — income tax and surtax and death duties — especially in Great Britain. Many people would wish to see this process carried much further, but they are deterred by two considerations; partly by the fear of making skilful evasions too much worth while

From *The General Theory of Employment, Interest and Money* by John Maynard Keynes. Reprinted by permission of Harcourt Brace Jovanovich, Inc., and the Keynes trustees.

and also of diminishing unduly the motive towards risk-taking, but mainly, I think, by the belief that the growth of capital depends upon the strength of the motive towards individual saving and that for a large proportion of this growth we are dependent on the savings of the rich out of their superfluity. Our argument does not affect the first of these considerations. But it may considerably modify our attitude towards the second. For we have seen that, up to the point where full employment prevails, the growth of capital depends not at all on a low propensity to consume but is, on the contrary, held back by it; and only in conditions of full employment is a low propensity to consume conducive to the growth of capital. Moreover, experience suggests that in existing conditions saving by institutions and through sinking funds is more than adequate, and that measures for the redistribution of incomes in a way likely to raise the propensity to consume may prove positively favourable to the growth of capital. . . .

. . . Our argument leads towards the conclusion that in contemporary conditions the growth of wealth, so far from being dependent on the abstinence of the rich, as is commonly supposed, is more likely to be impeded by it. One of the chief social justifications of great inequality of wealth is, therefore, removed. I am not saying that there are no other reasons, unaffected by our theory, capable of justifying some measure of inequality in some circumstances. But it does dispose of the most important of the reasons why hitherto we have thought it prudent to move carefully. This particularly affects our attitude towards death duties; for there are certain justifications for inequality of incomes which do not apply equally to inequality of inheritances.

For my own part, I believe that there is social and psychological justification for significant inequalities of incomes and wealth, but not for such large disparities as exist to-day. There are valuable human activities which require the motive of money-making and the environment of private wealth-ownership for their full fruition. Moreover, dangerous human proclivities can be canalised into comparatively harmless channels by the existence of opportunities for money-making and private wealth, which, if they cannot be satisfied in this way, may find their outlet in cruelty, the reckless pursuit of personal power and authority, and other forms of self-aggrandisement. It is better that a man should tyrannise over his bank balance than over his fellow-citizens; and whilst the former is sometimes denounced as being but a means to the latter, sometimes at least it is an alternative. But it is not necessary for the stimulation of these activities and the satisfaction of these proclivities that the game should be played for such high stakes as at present. Much lower stakes will serve the purpose equally well, as soon as the players are accustomed to them. The task of transmuting human nature must not be confused with the task of managing it. Though in the ideal commonwealth men may have been taught or inspired or bred to take no interest in the stakes, it may still be wise and prudent statesmanship to allow the game to be played, subject to rules and limitations, so long as the average man, or even a significant section of the community, is in fact strongly addicted to the money-making passion.

25. Business Is the First to Seek Relief

Fiorello H. LaGuardia

World War II brought the full employment that the New Deal, for all its efforts, had failed to achieve. But the specter of postwar unemployment remained even as the unemployment rate plummeted from ten percent in 1941 to a low of about 1 percent in 1944.

In Congress those committed to permanently ending unemployment sponsored the Full Employment Bill of 1945, which called for federally guaranteed "useful, remunerative, regular, and full-time employment" for all Americans who were willing and able to work. The National Association of Manufacturers and other conservative businessmen and congressmen opposed and helped defeat the bill. An important but much weaker substitute was eventually passed. The Employment Act of 1946 commits the United States government to ensuring "maximum employment." In the 1960's maximum employment was interpreted by President Kennedy's Council of Economic Advisors to mean 4 percent unemployment. That is a far cry from the original 1945 proposal to have the government guarantee remunerative jobs to all. Such a guarantee, which does not and has never existed in the United States, would be a powerful weapon against poverty.

In this selection from the testimony of the colorful former mayor of New York, Fiorello H. LaGuardia (1882–1947), in support of the original bill, LaGuardia recalls how different it was during the depression, when he was a congressman. Then business was the first to seek relief — for itself.

Mayor LaGuardia: On behalf of the United States Conference of Mayors I endorse Senate 380 and ask for a favorable report to the Senate. . . .

Gentlemen, if there is any public official who understands what unemployment means, it is a mayor of a city. It comes right to his desk, it comes right to his office, it comes right to his home. I have been through this period of unemployment, first as a Member of the House, when a few of us

From *Hearings Before a Subcommittee of the Committee on Banking and Currency,* U.S. Senate, 79th Congress, 1st Session, on S. 380 (August 1945).

on bended knees begged for assistance because we saw what was coming and were told that it was not a Federal function.

The United States Conference of Mayors was born in adversity and poverty. It was created because of the critical situation of the unemployed in the cities of the United States, and the group met in Detroit called by the then mayor, Frank Murphy, who now graces the United States Supreme Court bench. They came to Washington, went to the President, came to Congress, and all that they got out of it was a bill permitting a municipality to go into bankruptcy. Those were terrible days. You were in the Senate at the time, Mr. Chairman, and I was in the House. Unemployment was increasing every day in every city in every part of the country. Banks were closing. When we adjourned in 1932 we didn't know what was going to happen — in 1933 — it was the old session that ended in March when the new President came in. Members of Congress went home with their last pay in cash. The banks were closed on March 4.

People forget that. Some of the very gentlemen who represent the same organization that came to President Roosevelt with hat in hand and tears in their eyes, pleading for protection, are now coming before you saying the same thing that they were saying prior to the crash of 1929. . . .

Gentlemen, I was a mayor when we had to provide for a million people, 350,000 families destitute. Oh, that was a terrible period, and it lasted a long time. The country would have gone to ruin if it had not been for the help we got from the Federal Government. The City of New York of its own funds spent from 60 to 70 millions dollars a year on relief, yes, of our own funds, in addition to WPA, which was the salvation of the country.

Some of the gentlemen will remember the ridicule and the sneers and the jeers and the abuse we got when we came to Washington and asked for help. All during that unemployment period the figures of the United States Conference of Mayors were accurate. We predicted each fiscal year exactly what we needed, and when the appropriations were less, we then informed the committees they would have to appropriate extra funds in deficiency bills. One year when the funds were running out — the story can be told now — the executive committee of the conference met in Washington and had to plead with the Navy Department to get a message to the President who was on a cruiser to tell him the story. He wired right back and asked for the additional appropriations. He knew the situation.

Now, I know the mind of the opposition, and I say that employment is the function of government. Call me anything you like, I stand by that. I will be perfectly frank about it.

Senator Murray: Mr. Mayor, during that period of unemployment you are referring to, did the leaders of finance and industry come forward with any program by which the American system was going to take care of that situation?

New York City (Steve Salmieri)

Fiorello H. LaGuardia

Mayor LaGuardia: Oh, yes. They had their program. "Just leave us alone. Don't interfere with business. The Government doesn't know."

Well, they were left alone. They were left alone more than at any time in the history of the country, and when they were left alone they crashed, and the whole thing came down.

Senator Murray: They came here then and asked for relief themselves, didn't they?

Mayor LaGuardia: They were the first to get the relief. I remember in the closing days of the Congress of 1932–33 when the first very crude, primitive, and limited RFC bill came through. The argument was then, "Oh, yes; you must give assistance from the top. It will trickle down. It will create employment." I said at the time it would not. I think I was one of the very few that opposed it on the floor of the House because it was not sufficiently broad and all-embracing. But, Senator, this is the interesting thing: These very same people who through that period — you know, that stop-pick-up prosperity period — said "everything is going fine."

Gentlemen, the American people have learned that you cannot feed surveys to children, and that ticker tape ain't spaghetti. Senator, in the early part of 1933 and 1934, when the Government was shoveling money into support banks, after the bank holidays, this is the funniest thing, the funniest thing that I have ever witnessed in all of my experience — I was over in Washington one day at the Mayflower. Two or three of my fellow townsmen, whose names every one of you would recognize, big bankers, big financiers. I met them in the lobby, and they said, "Mr. Mayor, this man Roosevelt is great. Why, he is sound." That was the time we were shoveling out money, you know, to hold the banks. In a couple of years, after they had gotten the wrinkles out of their bellies, he was a radical, he was interfering with Government. I have lived through that. They cannot kid me anymore. I am too old.

Now, I say that it is less costly and more constructive to deal with the problem as intended in S. 380, because you are going to deal with the problem in any case. The Congress will either do it now, intelligently, constructively, and economically, or you are going to do it in 6 months, in a year, or in 18 months, and it will be much more costly.

Why do I say that employment is the function of the Government? Because the function of Government is to protect and preserve life. If we have unemployment and do nothing about it and people become impoverished and hungry, become diseased, the Government has to step in and take care of them, or you have an epidemic of disease. If an unemployed man is hungry and nothing is done for him and he breaks into a store and steals food, the Government has to take care of him. The Government provides board and lodging in the penitentiary. The Government will have to take care of him.

Migrant camp, Long Island (Magnum Photos, Inc.)

Indian reservation, southwest (National Council of Churches)

West side of Chicago (Wide World Photos)

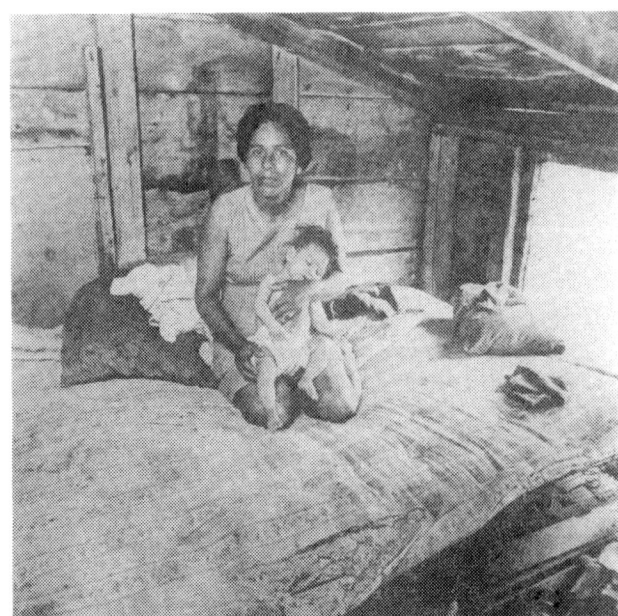

Migrant farmworker and child, Ohio (Larry O. Nighswander)

Part Two

Contemporary Poverty in the United States

Will the tired old, stale old excuses and evasions forever keep us paralyzed? Or will the might and wealth of this country once and for all be summoned to the side of the people we see in this book, so they can at last eat decently and work honorably — and so the rest of us in the cities can have at least one less important reason not to lie nervously, fearfully awake?

Robert Coles, Still Hungry in America

Why is there poverty in the midst of riches? That question — asked in the past by Karl Marx, by Henry George, by Pope Leo XIII, by Jacob Riis, and by many others — must be asked again. What accounts for poverty in the richest country in the world, a country whose Gross National Product exceeds $1 trillion? Surely not a lack of productive power. Hunger and malnutrition exist, but not because the nation lacks food. Millions are condemned to rural shacks and urban slums, but not because the nation cannot build houses. We cannot blame the meagerness of nature, nor can we blame a low level of technology. Such old justifications for poverty have no validity in the United States today. So we must identify and examine those social, economic, and political forces which prevent tens of millions of poor people from sharing in our society's abundance. This is the aim of this section on present-day poverty in the United States. And we shall begin by tracing the resurgence of interest in poverty in the 1960's.

THE REDISCOVERY OF POVERTY IN AMERICA

Strange as it now seems, post–World War II American society did not readily acknowledge the existence of domestic poverty. Not until the

1960's were middle-class Americans forced to recognize it. Then demonstrations, marches, riots, books, articles, and reports about poverty and hunger made all but the most recalcitrant admit that these evils had not disappeared from the United States. Middle-class reactions toward America's newly discovered poor were varied: Sympathy. Guilt. Self-righteousness. Apathy. Arrogance. Hostility. Hatred. But the popular myth that poverty had about disappeared from America received a near-mortal wound.

Characteristics of the Post–World War II Era

The myth made its debut in the years following World War II, when conditions were ripe for such a belief to take root. Little by little, concern about poverty faded. As an issue, it lost the political potency it had had in the New Deal days. The reasons for this are many and complex. The massive unemployment of the Great Depression had disappeared during World War II. But despite widespread predictions that peace would mean another depression, the much-feared collapse of the American economy never materialized. So fears about the economy melted away. Of course, the Cold War period (with its hot war in Korea) had started almost before the guns of World War II ceased. And the endless Cold War eventually led to large and growing military expenditures, which during this period became an established and accepted part of the peacetime economy. But employment remained high. And prosperity was in the air — so much so, that in 1958 the noted Harvard economist John Kenneth Galbraith proclaimed America "the affluent society."

Affluence seemed to be everywhere. Between 1950 and 1960, the median real income of American families[1] rose by 40 percent, and the number of autos soared from 36 to 57 million. Life styles changed drastically, as millions of white middle-class families — abetted by Federal highway and home mortgage programs — fled the cities for the suburbs. Outdoor barbecues. Patios. Two cars. Four-bedroom homes. Two bathrooms. Washing machines. Drying machines. Freezers. Air conditioners. Boats. Vacation homes. And even swimming pools. Not every suburban family had everything. But most had something and aspired to more. Pursuing the good life, who would think or care that millions still lived in rat-infested slums?

The political repressiveness at that time also contributed to the disappearance of poverty as a public issue. For in the heyday of McCarthyism and the witch-hunt, conformity was the watchword. Working to correct

---

[1] The median is the midpoint in a series — half the entries in the series are above and half below it. Thus, 50 percent of families receive more and 50 percent receive less than the median income. "Real" income means that changes in income have been adjusted for price changes.

flaws in American society — or even calling attention to them — was dangerous. Critics were labeled communist and subversive and threatened by the blacklist and jail. Clearly, the atmosphere was not conducive to an emphasis on poverty.

But poverty itself stubbornly refused to go away. Even Galbraith had recognized that. In *The Affluent Society* (1958) he discussed the persistence of poverty. But Galbraith underestimated its magnitude. Others underscored the severity of the problem, including, among others, economist Robert Lampman and author Michael Harrington. Lampman, in a 1959 study for the Joint Economic Committee of Congress, counted 32 million poor Americans while Harrington, in the influential *The Other America* (1962), estimated 40 to 50 million poor. It was Harrington who astutely observed that despite their large numbers, the poor were invisible to the more financially comfortable majority. For the middle classes had become more isolated from squalor and slums than ever before:

> The ordinary tourist . . . rides interstate turnpikes. He does not go into the valleys of Pennsylvania where the towns look like movie sets of Wales in the thirties. He does not see the company houses in rows, the rutted roads. . . . Then, too, beauty and myths are perennial masks of poverty. The traveler comes to the Appalachians in the lovely season. He sees the hills, the streams, the foliage — but not the poor. . . . Middle class women coming in from Suburbia on a rare trip may catch the merest glimpse of the Other America on the way to an evening at the theatre, but their children are segregated in suburban schools. The business or professional man may drive along the fringes of slums in a car or bus, but it is not an important experience for him.

Harrington was right. But not for long. Before the end of the 1960's the poor had become increasingly visible — in poor people's marches, in welfare rights organizations, in unionization campaigns, and in flames of protest in more than 150 ghettos.

It was logical that the civil rights movement, born of the most oppressed group in America, should become the vehicle for protest by the poor. But at the time, many liberals and intellectuals mistakenly assumed that organized labor would play the vanguard role it had played in the 1930's. Then, when millions of exploited industrial workers were battling for their rights, labor was the major catalyst for social ferment among the underdogs of America. But the 1950's were not the 1930's. Numerous factors made unions either unwilling or unable to organize the poorest and still unorganized workers. The antilabor Taft-Hartley Act of 1947, internal dissension over the issue of communism, racism, the desire for respectability, the very success of the new unions, the lack of an ideological commitment to the poor — each played a role in directing trade union energies inward toward extension of new benefits to already unionized workers rather than outward toward organizing the poorest. So, by labor's default and because of its own dynamism, the youthful civil rights movement became the torchbearer of social change that made the poor increasingly visible for all to see.

The Civil Rights Movement

The movement started in Montgomery, Alabama, a year and a half after the landmark Supreme Court decision on school desegregation. There, in December, 1955, Mrs. Rosa Parks, a black seamstress, refused a bus driver's order to give up her seat to a white man. The incident sparked a 361-day bus boycott by 17,000 blacks of Montgomery that catapulted Martin Luther King, Jr., leader of the boycott, into worldwide fame. The civil rights movement spread throughout the South, with school desegregation drives, boycotts, lunch-counter sit-ins, voter registration drives, and Freedom Rides. Black men, women, and children faced police brutality, dynamiting of their homes and churches, and even murder. When they were successful, the victory often had little meaning, for the typical southern black could neither afford a meal at a desegregated restaurant nor a night's lodging at an integrated hotel.

As the black revolution reached the northern ghettos, economic issues were no less important. Almost always, nationalist leaders such as Malcolm X found their greatest support among urban slum dwellers who were trapped by menial jobs, low wages, and chronic unemployment.

Since true political and social equality was not attainable without economic equality, the civil rights movement moved into the economic sphere. By August 1963 the new direction was official, with "Freedom and Jobs" the slogan of the historic March on Washington, in which more than 200,000 black (and some white) demonstrators participated.

The War Against Poverty

John F. Kennedy's short occupancy of the White House coincided with the build-up of these and other pressures. Kennedy's public interest in poverty started during his 1960 campaign. After touring destitute West Virginia, he won a crucial primary election in which the issue of depressed areas was important. Once in office, Kennedy voiced concern over depressed areas, poverty, and rising unemployment, which had escalated to nearly 7 percent by 1961, and considerably more in many industrial cities. Unemployment climbed to 9 percent in Buffalo, 10 percent in Youngstown, and 11 percent in Detroit and Pittsburgh, as the combined impact of automation and a sluggish economy threatened to strip industrial workers of their recent gains and push them into permanent unemployment and poverty.

Kennedy managed to secure passage of certain ameliorative legislation: a tax cut to stimulate the economy, federal assistance for depressed areas, and the Manpower Development and Training Act to provide the unemployed with retraining. But within the administration the impetus for an all-out attack on poverty came not from Kennedy but from economists Robert Lampman and Walter Heller, Chairman of the President's Council of Economic Advisers. However, since poverty was still not politically popular, Kennedy wavered on the issue until nearly the very end. As Sar A. Levitan, dean of the antipoverty program chroniclers, relates in *The Great Society's Poor Law* (1969):

> In the early fall of 1963 the notion of launching an antipoverty program received a temporary setback with widespread talk about "white backlash" as a reaction to the civil rights movement. Apparently some outside advisors had reached President Kennedy and urged him to inaugurate a program focusing on problems of suburbia as a central campaign theme for 1964. For a while Kennedy seemed to question the political wisdom of making an antipoverty program the theme of his reelection. . . . Kennedy refrained from committing himself to such a program until his last meeting with Heller, on November 19, 1963.

Three days later, a bullet in Dallas shattered Kennedy's plan to present a comprehensive antipoverty program to Congress.

The new President followed the path laid down belatedly by Kennedy. Lyndon B. Johnson signed "The Economic Opportunity Act of 1964" and officially launched the "War Against Poverty" one year after the August, 1963, March on Washington, during a summer of foreboding racial outbreaks.

If poverty was previously forgotten, soon the opposite seemed true. Economists, sociologists, community leaders, trade unionists, politicians, and others flocked to Washington to act as consultants or to man the battle stations of the newly created Office of Economic Opportunity (OEO).

The War Against Poverty was widely billed as a new approach to an old problem. New strategies were aimed to break the cycle of poverty and to make the poor more independent by upgrading their skills and earning power and by involving them in the fight against poverty. Consequently, the traditional income maintenance or direct cash approach was snubbed as an ineffectual means of ending poverty. But many of the poor — especially the aged, the ill or disabled, and fatherless families with dependent children — desperately needed more current income and the new programs could not give them that. The lack of a new and more adequate income maintenance program made the War Against Poverty considerably cheaper than it would otherwise have been, doubtless an important consideration for the Johnson administration. For it soon became apparent that the most costly war, an all-out war, was going to be waged against the Vietnamese, not against poverty. Only six months after declaring "War on Poverty,"

Johnson commenced the bombing of North Vietnam and eventually Vietnam war expenditures escalated to about $30 billion annually.

Funds did flow into the War Against Poverty, but a little was made to go a long way. In the first years of operation, from November, 1964, to June, 1968, the OEO allocated a total of about $5 billion to various highly publicized programs. The most controversial, the Community Action Program (CAP), financed local antipoverty boards in poor neighborhoods on which the poor themselves were to be mobilized in the fight against poverty. The popular Head Start program provided nursery schools to help poor children avoid later educational difficulties. The Job Corps and Neighborhood Youth Corps gave youths training or jobs. Volunteers in Service to America (VISTA), a domestic peace corps, sent young people to help the poor in Appalachia, in migrant workers' camps, in urban slums, and on Indian reservations. (Some non-OEO programs also were often considered to be part of the War Against Poverty — for example, those under the Area Redevelopment Act of 1961, the Manpower Redevelopment and Training Act of 1962, and the Appalachian Regional Development Act of 1965.)

The OEO did not lack opponents. Conservatives attacked the programs as a federal give-away that was putting money and power into the hands of the poor, the blacks, and the militants. And in fact many of the most talented and dynamic persons in poor communities were drawn into leadership positions in OEO-sponsored activities. But radical critics felt that drawing them into these activities may actually have neutralized the rising tide of militancy, at least in the short run. As black writer Joanne Grant relates in *Black Protest* (1968):

> Most of the militants in the Negro protest movement took the view that the extensive bureaucracy known as the Office of Economic Opportunity, with its hundreds of subsidiary local organizations through which federal funds were channeled, was in reality an elaborate system for co-opting movement activists. Movement community organizers saw the effort as an attempt to neutralize militancy by giving high-paying jobs to the most qualified of local leaders, in effect buying them off. Many Negro leaders saw the government's approach . . . as an attempt to deflect attention from the root causes of the Negro's condition to the effects. The reaction to the anti-poverty program was two-pronged. Many sought to continue their work independently; others sought to control it.

From its inception, opposition came from numerous mayors and local politicians who feared loss of their own political power if local antipoverty boards received funds directly from Washington. Any program that bypassed City Hall represented a threat to them. Opposition also came from some white workers who were not yet part of the affluent society. They felt that the government was ignoring their problems but taxing their hard-earned wages to subsidize undeserving blacks. These workers especially feared that blacks rising out of poverty would compete for their jobs.

The War Against Poverty was seriously devitalized during the Nixon administration. The Office of Economic Opportunity was retained, but most of the surviving programs were transferred to other government departments.

What did the War Against Poverty actually accomplish? Certainly, many individuals did benefit from specific programs. But for most of the poor nothing really basic changed. Today, ghettos are still ghettos. Appalachia is still Appalachia. And most of the poor are still poor, since OEO programs were primarily designed to change the poor — to make them fit better into the existing system — rather than to change the system. But one could not have realistically expected otherwise from a government-sponsored and financed program.

The War Against Poverty skirted the issue of the concentration of wealth and income in the nation. Power goes with wealth, and the rich were not about to hand their corporations and other property over to the poor. The poor lacked the political strength to bring about basic tax reform or adequate income maintenance legislation that might have had a significant impact on income distribution. Sending a VISTA worker to a slum, to an Indian Reservation, or to Appalachia could not accomplish that.

But the War Against Poverty can claim one major accomplishment. It helped to raise the expectations of the poor. Because many of these expectations were never fulfilled, it is still too soon to discern the ultimate impact of the War Against Poverty.

CHAPTER SEVEN: THE REDISCOVERY OF POVERTY IN THE AFFLUENT SOCIETY

The rediscovery of poverty reopened the question of the extent of poverty in the United States. Official government figures show that between 1959 and 1970 the number of people living in poverty dropped from 39.5 million to 25.5 million. But what do the figures mean? The size of any estimate of poverty depends on how you define poverty.

The government measurement of the extent of poverty is based on a Social Security Administration index with a range of income cut-offs or poverty lines that are adjusted for factors such as family size and place of residence. In 1970, when the poverty line for a family of four was set at $3,968, the U.S. Bureau of Labor Statistics estimated that an urban family of four required an income of about $6,960 to maintain a low living standard and approximately $10,666 to maintain a modest but adequate living standard. Obviously, if the government adopted the cost of either the low or the modest but adequate living standard as the poverty line, it would be acknowledging much more poverty than is officially recognized.

The official poverty threshold for a nonfarm family of four was set at $2,973 in 1959 and at $3,968 in 1970. So an urban family of four with $4,000 income in 1970 was not counted as poor. If you think that urban families with $4,000 or $5,000 or $6,000 or even more are still poor, your estimate of poverty in America would greatly exceed official government estimates. And you would probably be nearer to the truth. But why have you chosen one figure rather than another?

The implications of various approaches to the definition of poverty are discussed by economist Oscar Ornati (Reading 26). In "The Meaning of Poverty" (Reading 27) the President's Commission on Income Maintenance Programs shows precisely how the government arrives at its poverty figures and what it's like to live on a poverty income. Regardless of definition, poverty is so intense for millions of Americans that they suffer from hunger, malnutrition, and even starvation, as the hearings of the Clark Subcommittee of the U.S. Senate (Reading 28) disclosed. With intense poverty still rampant, Michael Harrington (Reading 29), whose book *The Other America* helped influence the War Against Poverty, wonders about that program. Harrington asks whether we may have "raised up hopes of the most abused only in order to knock them down again."

Finally, there are two views from the left. A penetrating critique of American capitalism is offered by Marxian economists Paul Baran and Paul Sweezy (Reading 30), who ask why poverty was forgotten in the 1950's. And Tom Hayden (Reading 31), writing in 1966, states why he thinks the War Against Poverty is doomed to failure.

CHAPTER EIGHT: ON BEING POOR

The literature about poverty abounds with distortions and half-truths about the poor. Elizabeth Herzog (Reading 32) of the U.S. Children's Bureau examines some of them, particularly those involving school achievement, family norms, and other aspects of the so-called culture of poverty. In "Why the Poor Remain Poor" (Reading 35), the President's Commission on Income Maintenance Programs observes that our economic and social structure virtually guarantee poverty for millions of Americans, so the Commission demolishes the Horatio Alger myth that the poor can raise themselves out of poverty by their own bootstraps.

Of all the stereotypes about the poor, those about welfare and its recipients are the cruelest. The usual image of the lazy welfare mother bears no resemblance to the portrait Dick Gregory (Reading 34) paints of his mother and the problems she faced when the Gregory family was forced to accept welfare. Indeed, despite all the controversy about welfare, few are aware of how the system actually operates. That is the subject of "The Welfare System" (Reading 33), also by the President's Commission on Income Maintenance Programs. And the strangest myth is that everyone is against poverty and slums. Would anyone oppose a program to rid the slums of rats? "Congress and the Rats" (Reading 36) offers some interesting insights into that myth about poverty.

CHAPTER NINE: THE INVISIBLE POOR

Not everyone is against poverty and slums, but who actually gains from poverty? Unfortunately the list is long: the white man who gained when he stole the red man's land; the southern planter enriched for hundreds of years by his exploitation of the black man; the corporations that have plundered Appalachia for their own profit; taxpayers who have refused to cut into their own affluence to finance adequate pensions for the aged. These are but a few of the beneficiaries. And the victims? Some are part of the army of the invisible poor that, even today, the affluent rarely see or think about. Some live in remote areas — the Indian reservations[2] visited by Robert Sherrill (Reading 37), the Delta country of Mississippi described by Leon Howell (Reading 38), or Appalachia, as reported by Harry M. Caudill (Reading 39). Others, like the aged poor, whose problems are analyzed by the U.S. Senate Special Committee on Aging (Reading 40), are hidden from view in every town and city.

CHAPTER TEN: A HARVEST OF SHAME

Agriculture is a stronghold of poverty. Average annual earnings of workers are only $1,500 (1970). Low-wage employers are the primary beneficiaries of the misery of the agricultural poor, but consumers also benefit, since food may cost less when it comes to the table from a harvest of shame.

Among the recent significant developments in agriculture recorded by James Pierce (Reading 41) of the National Sharecroppers' Fund is the attempt to unionize exploited farm laborers. Cesar Chavez (Reading 43), leader of migrants in California, has helped to bring visibility to poor farm workers. Chavez defends these workers' steadfast determination to organize for improved wages and working conditions, while G. C. Henry (Reading 42) of the agribusiness management understandably opposes unions, minimum wages, and similar protection for farm workers.

---

[2] Michael Harrington, who first used the term "invisible poor," did not include the plight of the Indian in his original edition of *The Other America* (1962). They were invisible even to him!

CHAPTER ELEVEN: RACISM, BLACK POVERTY, AND GHETTOS

Blacks are the largest of the poverty-stricken minority groups. Black poverty is the result of more than three centuries of injustices and exploitation — brutal slavery and semislavery and the denial of economic, social, and political equality. It arose from past injustice, but its perpetuation is guaranteed by present and continuing inequalities and injustices.

Whatever gains black people may have made during the 1960's, the attainment of economic equality with whites has not been among them. In 1970 median income of black families was only 61 percent that of white families. (See Appendix, Table 1.) Blacks in 1966 had a rate of poverty 3½ times higher than whites. (However the majority of the poor are white, because less than 12 percent of the nation's population is black.) But the white poor, who do not face the extra problem of racial discrimination, made greater gains during the 1960's. The Census Bureau noted in *The Extent of Poverty in the United States, 1959 to 1966* (May 1968) that:

> The poverty rate has also declined for both whites and nonwhites, but the gap between the two racial groups remained exceedingly wide. In 1966, after six consecutive years of economic expansion, 41 per cent of the nonwhite population was poor as compared with 12 per cent of the white. In 1959, the chances that a person would be living in poverty had been three times as great if he were nonwhite than if he were white, whereas in 1966 the chances were 3½ times as great.

Unfortunately, racism makes a substantial segment of the white population feel threatened by any black "advances," even illusory or token ones, and leads them to oppose government programs that might permit America's blacks to make real progress. This thinking is also found in the highest circles of government. For example, in March 1970 Daniel Moynihan, then counselor to President Nixon, claimed that "the American Negro is making extraordinary progress," and suggested that the "issue of race could benefit from a period of 'benign neglect.'" That policy has been consistently, though not benignly, pursued by the Nixon administration.

Without eradicating racism in the nation, blacks cannot achieve economic equality with whites. And until that happens there is no possibility of ending poverty in America. But so far most whites have been unwilling to relinquish their privileged position, so their racism contributes to the perpetuation of poverty.

Increasingly, black poverty means urban poverty. For over the past three decades changes in agriculture have pushed millions of southern blacks off the land and into cities. By the 1970 census, blacks made up more than 40 percent of the population of eleven of the nation's largest cities, including Washington, Gary, Atlanta, Detroit, and St. Louis. So if the ghetto poor are still invisible in the 1970's, it can only be because white America does not wish to see them.

A complete analysis of the economics of ghettos is beyond the scope of this book. But some significant aspects of ghetto economics are presented in this chapter.

The National Committee Against Discrimination in Housing (NCADH) shows "How the Federal Government Builds Ghettos" (Reading 44). And in "The Impact of Housing Patterns on Job Opportunities" (Reading 45) the NCADH explains how the increasing ghettoization of our metropolitan areas exacerbates the already grim employment situation of black workers. The staggering extent to which black workers are impoverished by low-wage jobs is documented by the National Advisory Commission on Civil Disorders (Reading 46). Recently some poor black workers instituted their own antipoverty program, a unionization campaign. A first-hand account of one such organizational struggle, that of black hospital workers in Baltimore, is given by John M. McClintock (Reading 47). Racial discrimination slashes employment opportunities and income even for well-educated blacks. But many blacks are also victims of insufficient schooling, so education is often advocated as a means of ending black poverty. But ghettos mean segregated schools and, as black educator Doxey A. Wilkerson explains in "Blame the Negro Child" (Reading 48), the educational system has worked against rather than for black children. Finally, a common but false analogy is dissected in "Comparing the Immigrant and the Negro Experience" (Reading 49). The piece shows how urban blacks are hindered by untold obstacles that the foreign-born did not encounter.

CHAPTER TWELVE:
POVERTY, INEQUALITY, AND UNEMPLOYMENT

Has the "affluence" of the postwar era or the War on Poverty altered the gross inequality of income that exists in our nation? Contrary to a common belief, the answer is no. As Table 1 indicates, the distribution of income has scarcely changed since 1947. The poorest twenty percent of American families received 5.0 percent of total income in 1947 and 5.4 percent in 1967. The richest 20 percent received 43.0 percent of total income in 1947 and 41.2 percent in 1967. Economic growth provided a larger pie, so the slices were bigger and living standards rose. But each group received about the same share in both years.

What causes income inequality? Actually, income inequality is a reflection of our society's unequal distribution of education, opportunity, jobs, and wealth. For example, under capitalism wealth is passed down from

Table 1. Percentage of Aggregate Income Received by Each Fifth and Top 5 Percent of Families in the United States, 1947–1967

Income of Families	1947	1950	1960	1967
Lowest (poorest) fifth	5.0%	4.5%	4.9%	5.4%
Second fifth	11.8	12.0	12.0	12.2
Middle fifth	17.0	17.4	17.6	17.5
Fourth fifth	23.1	23.5	23.6	23.7
Highest (richest) fifth	43.0	42.6	42.0	41.2
Total	100.0%	100.0%	100.0%	100.0%
Top 5 percent	17.2%	17.0%	16.8%	15.3%

Source: U.S. Bureau of the Census, *Statistical Abstract of the United States, 1969.*
Note: Because of rounding, figures may not total exactly 100 percent.

generation to generation and is even more unequally distributed than income. Wealth also begets wealth and generates income that is unequally distributed.

As New School economist Robert Heilbroner (Reading 50) points out, the top 2 percent of American families own between two-thirds and three-fourths of all corporate stock. So a fundamental question is whether poverty, inequality, and privilege are integral parts of American capitalism. Heilbroner believes that while massive poverty *may* be eliminated within three or four decades, the enormous concentration of wealth and privilege will not decrease within the structure of American capitalism. Of course, some people, like Milton Friedman (Reading 51), oppose measures that would lead to greater equality. Friedman feels that equality and liberty are conflicting goals. But R. H. Tawney (Reading 52) takes the opposite viewpoint.

All talk about eliminating poverty becomes meaningless when there are not enough jobs for everyone. However, when unemployment falls, prices tend to rise. This trade-off between unemployment and inflation is analyzed by Cornell economist Walter Galenson (Reading 53), who wonders why American society tolerates such high rates of unemployment: it is personalized in Art Buchwald's vignette of a worker (Reading 54) who wonders why *he* has become unemployed.

CHAPTER THIRTEEN:
THE PATHS FROM POVERTY

How can we end poverty in America? Many paths have been suggested but each one takes us to a different destination. For, in the final analysis, any proposed solution reflects some image of a preferred society.

Conservative Milton Friedman's (Reading 55) ideal is unregulated capitalism. Friedman's goals do not include the elimination of either poverty or economic inequalities, but he does want to alleviate poverty. So he advocates abolishing existing social welfare programs and replacing them with a negative income tax that would provide for a guaranteed minimum income — but at a figure so low that the poor would still be impoverished.

Suggestions for broad and comprehensive reforms within the context of capitalism are advocated by an establishment group, the National Advisory Commission on Civil Disorders (Reading 57) and by the liberal A. Philip Randolph Institute (Reading 56). These reforms could greatly improve the living standards of the poor, while still retaining class inequalities. But implementation would require massive government intervention on behalf of the poor which seems unlikely in the foreseeable future. Then, too, there is often little left in the public coffer for financing the many reforms that would be needed to improve conditions. With huge military budgets eating up so much of the nation's resources, the National Commission on the Causes and Prevention of Violence (Reading 59) advocates a reordering of national priorities. The Commission wants funds that now finance the war in Vietnam to be used for sorely needed domestic purposes. But Daniel Moynihan (Reading 60) does not think these funds will be available for such uses.

Black capitalism has often been advocated as a means of overcoming black poverty. Taking a negative view of that road, James Boggs (Reading 58) tells why he thinks the black community should adopt the socialist approach.

In 1962 Michael Harrington was instrumental in calling attention to the existence of domestic poverty. Now we see his provocative thoughts (Reading 61) on how to end poverty. Harrington's solution is socialism. Not that he opposes welfare-state reforms advocated by liberals, but his examination of how reforms operate in a class society convinces him that they cannot do the job. And, Harrington states, if we are to transcend the capitalist limits of today's welfare state, an attack on the systematic concentration of economic power is required.

Chapter Seven

The Rediscovery of Poverty in the Affluent Society

26. What Is Poverty?

Oscar Ornati

What is poverty? The answer is neither simple nor unambiguous. In the early 1960's economist Oscar Ornati, now professor at New York University, directed a major Twentieth Century Fund research project at the New School for Social Research. In this passage from the report on that research project, Ornati ponders on various ways of defining poverty. "Subjective," "objective," and "relative" poverty have distinct meanings. And poverty due to "insufficiency" is not the same as that involving "inequality." But the differences are more than academic, for, as Ornati wisely notes, how poverty is defined can reveal as much about a person's or a society's ideals as it does about the poor.

Poverty is variously defined as being "subjective," "objective," or "relative." It is viewed as involving "insufficiency" or "inequality" or both.

Subjective poverty refers to the individual's "feeling" rich or poor, according to the range of currently available goods and services he might reasonably expect to enjoy. Nobody, for instance, felt poor a hundred years ago who did not have electric light. Today it is taken for granted that even poor people in the United States should have electric light. It is an accepted

From Oscar Ornati, *Poverty amid Affluence: A Report of a Research Project Carried Out at the New School for Social Research* (New York: Twentieth Century Fund, 1966), pp. 1–3, 7, 16, 120–1. Editor's title, by permission.

part of the U.S. style of life at even the lowest level. Although electric light is not absolutely necessary to life, we feel deprived without it. Subjective poverty is also determined by a myriad of other psychological and sociological forces which have been analyzed in writings on social stratification and social status, and on status-seeking and life in the suburbs. . . .

Poverty is often treated as a matter of inequality. From this viewpoint, one can say that the poor are always with us. If the poor are defined as making up some part of the bottom of the income distribution, some kind of lower fifth, eighth, tenth, or whatever fraction might be chosen, their eternal permanence is guaranteed. This approach creates poverty by definition. . . .

In terms of insufficiency, poverty has traditionally been considered to be the condition of persons whose resources have been insufficient to satisfy minimum needs. The resources with which we have concerned ourselves have been the individuals' incomes — savings have been found to be almost insignificant for this group. In the determination of minimum needs, he who is "poor" is found traditionally to be the individual living below "minimum subsistence," the individual whose essential needs are not being "adequately" met, who lives in "deprivation." Having agreed that nobody should live below "subsistence" or be "deprived," we seem, as a nation, unable to agree as to exactly what we mean. Even the physical sciences are of small help in determining "minimum needs." One component of need, "adequate nutrition," for instance, is not scientifically definable. Among nutrition experts, estimated protein requirements are little more than intelligent guesswork; there is doubt about desirable intakes of calcium, iron, and vitamins. As one student of the subject has noted, "the problem is rather like that of trying to define 'adequate' individual height."

People differ with respect to their ideas of what constitutes need, their feeling of justice, their values. Their estimates of need will differ according to whether they are themselves poor or not poor, thrifty or lax, interested in things or ideas, conversant with or ignorant of the lives of the poor. Their explicit and implicit notions about the workings of the economy and the society become crucially important. They will view levels of poverty as unacceptable depending on whether they are by training economists, sociologists, or engineers; possibly on whether they were trained at Harvard or Chicago; whether or not "survival of the fittest" sums up their social outlook. . . .

Objectively, poverty can be measured in terms of the proportion of currently agreed-upon basic "necessities" that income can buy. Most necessary to human health and well-being, everybody will agree, are basic food, shelter, and clothing. Those who measure poverty quantitatively will concentrate their attention on these necessities. Those concerned with more than bare subsistence will ask another question — are all Americans sharing reasonably well in the current U.S. affluence? Such critics will be interested in income inequality as well as in insufficiency. In addition to lacking the barest necessities of life, being "poor" in the United States in the 1960's may also mean that one belongs to the bottom 20 per cent of the population that receives less than 5 per cent of total family personal income. One can be poor, then, from an insufficiency of food, clothing, and housing. Or one can be poor from having a much less than proportionate share in available goods and services. . . .

If poverty is defined in static terms, as in the President's annual economic report, an increasing rate of economic growth will obviously reduce poverty — eventually. With poverty defined in contemporary terms, as in this study, the matter is more complex. We have noted at each period the existence of circularity between accustomed styles of life and budget criteria. What does this mean to us today, as we talk about eliminating poverty? As living standards in general rise, including standards at the lowest end of the poverty band — for recipients of relief — we might ask: Are we not making the eradication of "poverty" impossible by continually jacking up the standards?

The answer to this question is clearly no. It is no for the reason that the definition of poverty in each generation represents not only the contemporary life style of the low income classes; it also represents a life style below which society agrees — in terms of dollars — that its citizens should not be allowed to fall. Definitions of poverty therefore reflect not only habitual expenditure at the poverty band level; they reflect current social ideals. If people are complacent about the living conditions of those within the poverty band, standards will not change much. If public opinion discerns great inequities in life styles on the poverty level, standards may improve. The test is whether people are willing to pay what it costs. Relief budgets and the other budgets of the poverty band — "minimum adequacy" and "minimum comfort" budgets — tell a great deal about U.S. ideals as well as the realities of life at low income levels.

Considering poverty for a moment in terms of inequality rather than insufficiency, anyone willing to look at the *Statistical Abstract of the United States* can readily see that the lowest 20 per cent of the population gets only about 5 per cent of the national income — and that their share has fallen slightly in recent years. Some such inequity will always exist — whether the lowest 20 per cent gets 5 per cent or 4 per cent or 6 per cent or whatever. In this sense, poverty is indeed eternal, just as physical and mental qualities are unequal, and hereditary advantages are usually unequal. If total national income rises, the proportion received by the bottom 20 per cent might very well remain at 5 per cent; but in terms of this study, poverty could conceivably be eliminated *if the increase sufficed to bring every family and every individual in the bottom 20 per cent up to what society currently accepts as minimal standards.*

There is another inequity: certain groups have become disproportionately and increasingly the primary victims of poverty. The statistical odds are clearly against them — non-whites, the young, the old, single people, female heads of families, rural farm families, southern families, residents of depressed areas. To the extent that current social ideals accept the notion that a little poverty is all right, so long as it happens to members — or even to most members — of certain groups, it reflects indifference. It may even reflect hypocrisy in people who with the next breath insist that America is a land of equal opportunity, that any man of ability can rise on his own. . . .

Whether those at the bottom of the income distribution are or are not poor depends on whether their income level is or is not, by objective standards, sufficient to cover their needs. This is so even though the standards of sufficiency themselves in turn depend both on the amount of income available to society and on society's income distribution. Precisely because of the interdependence of objective conditions and the determination of standards of sufficiency, it is essential to separate, as far as possible, the problem of income distribution from that of poverty and to note in detail changes in income distribution as well as changes in standards. Of course one can deal only with objective changes in income standards; the subjective impact of changes in income structure is beyond this study. All we can say is that while one man says, "My neighbor has more and I am thereby richer," another man says, "My neighbor has more and I am thereby poorer." That an individual's sense of happiness is dependent not only on his own level of consumption but also on what his neighbor consumes has long been known; but besides suggesting a certain "rationality" of "dog in the manger" type actions, this knowledge does not help us much.

27. The Meaning of Poverty

*President's Commission
on Income Maintenance Programs*

Can a family of four manage on less than $3,500 a year? Yes; but, as this excerpt from the Report of the President's Commission on Income Maintenance Programs shows, it's not much fun. In 1968, 25 million persons lived in households with incomes less than the official and unrealistically low poverty line, set that year at $3,553 for a non-

farm family of four. This passage shows how the government arrives at its estimate of poverty. (Defining poverty differently — setting a higher poverty line — would, of course, yield a much higher and more realistic estimate of the number of poor people in the United States.)

For these millions of poor Americans who live in decaying slums and rural shacks, life is a daily struggle for survival. A unique feature of the report is inclusion of the testimony of poor people at the Commission's public hearings. They give first-hand accounts of the panorama of human misery caused by the lack of money for basic food, clothing, shelter, and medical care.

THE POOR

The postwar period has witnessed a remarkable improvement in the material welfare of most Americans. Even with the effect of inflation taken into account, median family income grew by 76 percent between 1947 and 1967. The proportion of families enjoying a total income of $10,000 or more increased from 22 to 34 percent during the same period. And, in recent years, we have taken justifiable satisfaction in the reduction of poverty from 22 percent of the population in 1959 to 13 percent in 1968. But the fact remains that 25 million persons are still poor.

Thousands of pages of statistics about the poor have been tabulated and published. The poor have been measured, surveyed, and sorted into numerous categories, some of which are summarized in Table 1 for 1966. But in the end, the diversity of the poor overwhelms any simple attempt to describe them with statistics. What may be said simply is that millions of our fellow citizens are living in severe poverty, with few prospects for a better life, and often with little hope for the future.

To the poor, poverty is no statistical or sociological matter. Their condition exists as a daily fight for survival. This Commission has found their deprivation to be real, not a trick of rhetoric or statistics. And for many of the poor, their poverty is not a temporary situation, but an enduring fact of life.

THE POVERTY LIVING STANDARD

Any discussion of the poor must begin by defining those who are poor and those who are not. But it is obvious that any single standard or definition of poverty is arbitrary, and clearly subject to disagreement. The standard which this Commission has employed is the widely used poverty index,

From *Poverty amid Plenty: The American Paradox. The Report of the President's Commission on Income Maintenance Programs* (Washington, D.C.: U.S. Government Printing Office, November 1969).

Table 1. Selected Characteristics of the Poor and the Nonpoor, 1966

Characteristic	Number (millions)		Percent distribution	
	Poor	Nonpoor	Poor	Nonpoor
Age				
Total	30.0	163.9	100.0	100.0
Under 18 years	13.0	57.4	43.5	35.0
18–21	1.6	10.4	5.3	6.4
22–54	7.4	68.7	24.7	41.9
55–64	2.5	14.7	8.5	9.0
65 and over	5.4	12.6	18.0	7.7
Race				
Total	30.0	163.9	100.0	100.0
White	20.4	150.2	68.3	91.6
Nonwhite	9.5	13.7	31.7	8.4
Family status				
Total	30.0	163.9	100.0	100.0
Unrelated individuals	5.1	7.6	17.1	4.6
Family members	24.9	156.3	82.9	95.4
Head	6.1	42.8	20.3	26.1
Spouse	4.1	38.5	13.5	23.5
Other adult	2.1	17.7	7.2	10.8
Child under 18	12.6	57.3	42.0	35.0
Type of residence				
Total	30.0	163.9	100.0	100.0
Farm	2.5	8.5	8.2	5.2
Nonfarm	27.5	155.4	91.8	94.8
Rural	11.2	46.7	37.3	28.5
Urban	18.8	117.2	62.7	71.5

Source: Office of Economic Opportunity, unpublished tabulations from the Current Population Survey and draft report, "Dimensions of Poverty, 1964–1966."

developed by the Social Security Administration. This index is based on the Department of Agriculture's measure of the cost of a temporary low-budget, nutritious diet for households of various sizes. The poverty index is simply this food budget multiplied by three to reflect the fact that food typically represents one-third of the expenses of a low-income family. The resulting figure is the minimum income needed to buy a subsistence level of goods and services; the 25 million people whose incomes fall below the index are poor, while those above it are, officially at least, nonpoor. According to this poverty index, in 1968 a nonfarm family of four required a minimum income of $3,553 per year, or $2.43 per person per day to meet its basic expenses. Table 2 shows the poverty index for families of various sizes in 1968.

. . . In 1967 the poverty budget [for a nonfarm family of four] was $3,410. A moderate family budget developed by the Bureau of Labor Statistics required an income of $7,836 per year, or $1,300 less than the

Table 2. 1968 Poverty Thresholds

Family size	Poverty index Nonfarm	Farm
1	$1,748	$1,487
2	2,262	1,904
3	2,774	2,352
4	3,553	3,034
5	4,188	3,577
6	4,706	4,021
7 or more	5,789	4,916

median family income of $9,120 for nonfarm families of four. Neither budget makes allowance for any costs of employment or taxes paid. [The *total* cost of the Bureau of Labor Statistics moderate budget for four person families in 1967, *including* Social Security and Disability payments and personal taxes, was $9,076 in the urban United States.]

Clearly, the poor family must do without many of the things that families with an average income consider to be "necessities" — a car, an occasional dessert after meals, rugs, a bed for each family member, school supplies, or an occasional movie. Nothing can be budgeted for medical care or insurance.

This food budget requires more than a third of the poor family's income, but still allows only $1.00 a day for food per person. . . .

The poor family's budget provides only $91 a month for all housing costs — including rent, utilities, and household operation — for four persons. No allowance is included for the poor family to purchase household furnishings. In Head Start programs, for example, teachers found that many children never had eaten at a table. Thirty percent of families on welfare live in homes where each family member does not have a bed. . . .

Clothing school children is a major problem in poor families. Many poor children wear hand-me-down clothes which they receive from relatives, neighbors, and even teachers. Some clothing may be purchased at second-hand stores. But many poor children have to go to school on rainy days with no boots or raincoats — or stay home.

The poor family has $108 annually — about $9 a month — to spend on "luxuries": reading matter, recreation, education, gifts and contributions, tobacco, alcohol. But it is likely that this money will be spent on necessities, supplementing the meager food, clothing, and housing allowances. There is no room in the budget for luxuries — or emergencies.

Technically, an income at the poverty level should enable families to purchase the bare necessities of life. Yet an itemized budget drawn at that level clearly falls short of adequacy. There are many items for which no money is budgeted, although those items may be needed. Funds for them can only come out of sums already allotted to the basic necessities of life. As one witness told the Commission, "I either eat good and smell bad, or smell good and don't eat."[1] When another witness was asked how he made ends meet, he simply replied, "They don't meet."[2]

HOW THE POOR SURVIVE

Although the official poverty index level of income is inadequate, it has gained wide currency as a benchmark denoting the subsistence level of income. Yet many poor households have incomes well below that level. More than 70 percent of the poor families have incomes at least $500 under the poverty level and nearly half are more than $1,000 below the poverty line. The total amount by which the income of the poor fell below the poverty standard was $10.6 billion in 1966. This is 40 percent of the $26.5 billion in total income the poor would have had if all of them were living at the poverty line. . . .

Food

Many poor families are not fed adequately. To keep families from going hungry, poor women often use great ingenuity to reduce their food costs. They may buy at markets where day-old bread and damaged canned foods are sold at discounts. Many use cheaper dried milk despite their preference for liquid milk. They buy large amounts of inexpensive foods, like spaghetti and dried beans, that do not spoil and are nutritious. They use surplus commodities distributed by the Government when these goods are available to them, and Food Stamps when they can afford them. They may share transportation costs for shopping trips away from small neighborhood stores.

In spite of these efforts, the Department of Agriculture's 1965 Food Consumption Survey showed that 63 percent of households with incomes under $3,000 had inadequate diets. The Commission heard first-hand evidence to this effect throughout the country:

> I have to cut corners and now I am cutting down the middle. I don't have any corners left to cut.[3]
>
> Maybe if I have four potatoes I will fry them and give them all to go around. Sometimes we don't eat. When the check comes I don't have maybe $3 left. With those $3 we have to eat. Sometimes we eat and sometimes we look at each other.[4]
>
> I don't have enough to buy food. That is the reason why I am sick today with high blood pressure, heart trouble, because I don't have money to buy the kind of food that I am supposed to have.[5]

---

[1] Witness before Commission, Seattle, Washington.
[2] Witness before Commission, Quincy, Florida.
[3] Witness before Commission, St. Joseph, Louisiana.
[4] Witness before Commission, Tucson, Arizona.
[5] Witness before Commission, Tucson, Arizona.

Medical Care

Because the poor often are isolated or without transportation, they have restricted access to proper medical attention. The care they do receive is often too late and of low quality. Yet the relative need for health care is greatest among those groups — infants, expectant mothers, and the elderly — which form a disproportionate share of the population in poverty.

Although the most advanced medical techniques in the world are available in the United States, the poor receive little advantage from them. For example, this country ranks thirteenth in the world in infant mortality and at least that low in maternal mortality. These relatively low rankings are explained in part by the uneven distribution of health services in the United States which results in a greater incidence of poor health among low-income groups.

Poor nutrition during pregnancy can hinder fetal brain development and increase the probability of premature birth. Protein deficiencies in early childhood can retard brain growth. This early damage — perhaps followed by frequent illness, further malnutrition, crowded and unsanitary living conditions — is exacerbated by lack of regular medical attention and may affect the adult's ability to obtain adequate employment. Health limitations are particularly likely to result in unemployment or underemployment among those whose skill levels are low, because jobs open to them are usually physically demanding.

The health problems of the poor are not invisible. The glazed eyes of children, legs that never grew straight, misshapen feet, sallow complexions, lack-luster hair, are easily recognized by even an untrained observer. Other physical limitations, such as low energy levels, are quite real to poor children in school and adults trying to hold down jobs, but these limitations may be misconstrued by teachers and employers.

Most of the poor cannot afford private medical care and are not covered by insurance. And many cannot afford the transportation to free medical facilities, which are often miles and hours away. Or, there may be no medical charity — public or private — available to them. Their plight is suggested in incidents related to the Commission:

> It took me nine months . . . to get a man in the nursing home. He fell and broke his hip and injured his foot. He was ninety-two years old. When we finally got an opening . . . he (had) died because the foot had already become infected, gangrenous, and it was too late.[6]
>
> I can't get a dentist appointment for my two children anywhere. "We do not take welfare patients" — and these (are) people that the Welfare recommended. As far as eyeglasses, I waited three months to have my son's eyes checked. . . .[7]

[6] Witness before Commission, Breathitt County, Kentucky (community worker).
[7] Witness before Commission, Seattle, Washington.

> . . . a couple of weeks ago she (her daughter) fell again . . . I called the doctor and I said as I am holding her, bleeding in my arms, "I's bringing my daughter," and he said, "I'm going home to dinner early this evening. You will have to find somebody else." And I said, "I don't know how to get to find anybody else. I have no way." And he said, "Well, I guess you're just going to have to find a neighbor. . . ."[8]
>
> I went in (to the County Hospital) and told the head nurse about it (his son hit by a car), she said, "Well, we can't take him." Of course he was in pain. His leg was just smashed all to pieces where the bumper hit him.[9]
>
> The only place we can refer for charity hospitalization is the University Medical Center in Little Rock (150 miles away). But even then, they are so crowded that the doctors always have to make prior appointments and make sure space is available.[10]

Housing

Millions of the poor live in substandard, squalid housing. The shanties and shacks found in rural areas often look like remnants from an earlier era. One rural resident who lives with her daughter and eight grandchildren in a small shack described her housing to the Commission:

> It is a four-room house and another little room out the house, and it rains into it. Have to get up at night and put a dishpan to keep the rain off the children. I told the owner. He told me I would have to have the house fixed up myself.[11]

The barrenness of housing of the urban poor sometimes is hidden behind the facade of ordinary looking row houses. Yet the interior may reveal serious decay — falling plaster, holes in the wall, gaps in window frames, rats and roaches, and deteriorated plumbing. One mother told the Commission:

> The house is in bad condition and every time it rains the water comes in. I've called public housing many times and they just tell you over the phone, "What am I to do about this?" And the roof leaks, and the water comes through the windows. This is a contaminated condition and a health hazard. My children get sore throats and they are sick all the time.[12]

The physical condition of the homes and neighborhoods in which the poor live and the crowding that often occurs have severe effects on health, as well as on social and behavioral patterns. The struggle to meet basic

---

[8] Witness before Commission, Seattle, Washington.
[9] Witness before Commission, Mississippi County, Arkansas.
[10] Witness before Commission, Mississippi County, Arkansas County Welfare Director).
[11] Witness before Commission, St. Joseph, Louisiana.
[12] Witness before Commission, Philadelphia, Pennsylvania.

physical needs under depressing and frustrating living conditions undermines attempts to escape from poverty.

> The people have an apathy about cleaning a place that is about to fall down on their heads. Believe me, if you lived in a house that had a leaky roof, and the paper's off the wall, rats and roaches, no matter how you clean. The front steps fall down; the back steps fall down. Half the steps in the house are broken, the pipes leak, the toilet is broken. Well, I could mention anything else, but you get the general idea. Do you blame a person for not wanting to clean a place like this?[13]

The Quality of Life

A recent study of a group of AFDC families indicated that the surveyed families spent "five-eighths as much on food as the 'average' western United States family of the same size (five members), less than five-eighths as much on housing and related costs, one-sixth as much on clothing, one-eighth as much on transportation, one-ninth as much on consumer durables, and a barely discernible amount . . . on recreation, personal care, and other such pleasures that people find in life."

In establishing the criteria for a *moderate* budget the Bureau of Labor Statistics assumes that "maintenance of health and social well-being, the nurture of children, and participation in community activities are both desirable and necessary social goals for all families." The limitations inherent in the poverty budget make these goals unattainable for poor families. Although the poor family may not starve, and although it has a roof over its head, its lack of buying power in a world where expenditures are a part of all social relationships subjects the poor family to social, if not physical, starvation. A recent study of life patterns of welfare recipients pointed out that:

> To go to school costs money — books, notebooks, pencils, gym shoes, and ice cream with the other kids. Without these the child begins to be an outcast.
>
> To go to church costs money — some Sunday clothes, carfare to get there, a little offering. Without these one cannot go.
>
> To belong to the Boy Scouts costs money — uniforms, occasional dues, shared costs of a picnic. Without these, no Scouts.
>
> To have friends into the house costs money — for a bit of food, a drink.
>
> To visit relatives costs money — for travel, a gift for the kids. These people cannot afford to visit their relatives.
>
> For a teen-ager to join his friends on the corner he must have some money — for a coke, a show.

[13] Witness before Commission, Philadelphia, Pennsylvania.

How does a fellow take a girl out on a date without some money? And how does a girl pretty herself for a fellow without some money?

How do you join a club? Buy a book, a magazine, a newspaper?

Poverty settles like an impenetrable cell over the lives of the very poor, shutting them off from every social contact, killing the spirit, casting them out from the community of human life.

It is clear both from research data, and from listening to the testimony of many poor Americans, that coping with such deprivation exerts severe personal strains on individuals and families. A resulting loss of physical and mental health exacts significant costs from all of society as well as the poor themselves.

Almost every facet of daily life is affected by the interaction of low income and social isolation. Poor urban families pay higher food prices in neighborhood independent stores because there are few suburban-type chain stores in inner city areas. Low-income neighborhoods frequently do not receive city services considered routine in most neighborhoods. In poor neighborhoods we have seen overflowing garbage pails resulting in garbage-strewn streets, while in affluent areas of the same city garbage is picked up regularly. Many low-income neighborhoods are poorly protected against crime. There are severe barriers to educational and occupational achievement:

> ... you have the situation where one member of the family is in school today and the other member isn't: and when one asks, "where is your brother today?" (he is told) "It's not his turn to wear the shoes today."[14]
>
> I keep one of them (her six children) to stay home (to babysit while she works). I figure it's bad but it's the only way for me to make a living. I keep one out; that is the only way I have to do it.[15]

Students from schools in low-income areas are often poorly educated and unprepared for adequate employment. Moreover, many suitable job opportunities are located in areas remote from the inner city and are, therefore, inaccessible to many ghetto residents.

The social problems of the urban slum intrude on family life. Parental control of children is challenged by powerful influences outside the family. The dangers of juvenile delinquency, alcoholism, drug addiction, and premarital pregnancy are real and frightening. A great proportion of crime affects the meager possessions and physical safety of the poorest in our cities.

It is often difficult even for middle-class residents of middle-class communities to escape the neighborhood's influence on themselves and on their children. How much more difficult it is for the urban poor.

[14] Witness before Commission, Manchester, New Hampshire (Mayor).
[15] Witness before Commission, Quincy, Florida.

> (My daughter asked) "Why is all them doctors out in the hallway?" I said "Doctors?" She said, "Yeah, they all got needles in their hands." . . . there's junkies, dope addicts, and the rats — don't mention them. They are going hungry now because I ain't got no food.[16]

The rural poor may be safe from some of the hazards of urban slum life, but being poor in rural America imposes severe isolation. Public transportation is virtually nonexistent, and automobiles are expensive. Few public services of high quality are available. Rural educational institutions are generally inferior and have few resources. Many counties have no physicians or hospitals. Recreational facilities are meager.

CONCLUSION

The poor inhabit a different world than the affluent, primarily because they lack money. Often they live an isolated existence in rural and urban pockets of poverty. But most of the poor do not live apart from the larger society in terms of their hopes and aspirations. Through television, magazines, and newspapers, they become aware of what others have. Their aspirations for education and achievement often differ from those of the middle class only in the possibility for realization:

> And I want to say someone ought to start doing something to show that there is emotion in disadvantaged people. They bleed like anybody else. It is not distant and strange. They do bleed. They might not get enough to eat and might not get enough sleep but they do these things. They think that you are born distant, you have no feelings, that you were born to tear up, burn up, corrupt and whatever. You have to stop telling him, gee, I know you feel bad, look at your house, look at the holes in your shoes, and things of this sort. Showing a man how really down he is, is not going to help him.[17]
>
> You know when you have a bunch of kids out here and don't have a steady job, just part-time, you think about them. You look around at yourself when the bills start coming in and the children want to eat and need clothes to wear to go to school. You can imagine how you feel.[18]

The poor are living poorly and are aware of it. They are generally unhappy with their circumstances and would like to be unpoor. Many Americans wonder why the poor do not escape from poverty. The answer to this question is clear to us: They usually cannot, because most are already doing as much as can reasonably be expected of them to change their conditions.

[16] Witness before Commission, New York City, New York.
[17] Witness before Commission, Denver, Colorado.
[18] Witness before Commission, St. Joseph, Louisiana.

28. Hunger and Malnutrition in the United States

Clark Subcommittee, U.S. Senate

In 1967 the affluent society began to hear of a vast world of malnutrition, hunger, and even starvation within its borders. Nationwide investigations by the Citizens Board of Inquiry into Hunger and Malnutrition, a group of private citizens without legislative power, revealed that millions of Americans wake up hungry, spend their day hungry, and go to bed hungry. The Board documented the high human cost of malnutrition: deformed bodies, physical illnesses, mental retardation, and early death. Subsequent trips throughout the nation by Senators confirmed these shocking findings.

These excerpts from the U.S. Senate Hearings on Hunger and Malnutrition, held in 1968, consist of the testimony of investigators and victims of hunger and malnutrition.

Widespread publicity led to loud cries from some quarters for national action to end hunger and malnutrition immediately and completely. Such action was not taken. Federal expenditures on food programs did increase, but not enough. More people are helped today than in 1967, but many of the poor are without benefit from the programs. So the job remains only half done. In 1971, ten to fifteen million poor were still hungry in America and there were still children with bloated bellies.

PREPARED STATEMENT OF LESLIE W. DUNBAR, COCHAIRMAN, CITIZENS BOARD OF INQUIRY INTO HUNGER AND MALNUTRITION; EXECUTIVE DIRECTOR, FIELD FOUNDATION

Testifying before this subcommittee on the subject of hunger and malnutrition is indeed to carry coals to Newcastle. You yourselves established the urgency of this topic by your inspection in Mississippi. That was slightly more than a year ago, however, and since then, by a multitude of witnesses, including physicians, reporters, photographers, and officials of the Depart-

From *Hearings Before the Subcommittee on Employment, Manpower, and Poverty of the Committee on Labor and Public Welfare*, U.S. Senate, 90th Congress, 2nd Session, on S. Res. 281 (May–June 1968).

ment of Agriculture, your observations have been confirmed and cogently re-stated.

Dr. Benjamin Mays and I were asked to head a committee of private citizens who, without power or prerogative, looked into these same conditions. So here we are, you as public leaders and we as private persons, each having seen much of the same thing and each having similarly resolved that this should not abide in America. You have office and authority, as we have none. Yet you have as yet been nearly as helpless as we.

I wonder if, behind and beyond even the worst of our problems, we do not have to confront the brute fact that our political processes all too frequently stand as barriers to needed reform, nor as its agents. There is no lesson more clear than that today people who have real grievances that institutions will not recognize or remedy will themselves not recognize the legitimacy of those institutions.

We dealt, as did you last year, with that most elemental and unarguable of all human grievances: hunger. We made field trips into east Kentucky, the San Antonio area, and Mississippi; to the Navaho reservation and to the Havasupai of Arizona, and to the Indian country of South Dakota; into migrant labor camps of south Florida; and into the slums of Boston, New York, and Washington. We held public hearings in Hazard (Ky.), San Antonio (Texas), Columbia (S.C.), and Birmingham (Ala.). We examined every piece of printed information we could find, and we communicated with dozens of authorities. On April 22 we published a report, copies of which you have, titled *Hunger U.S.A.* The principal conclusions of that report are, I believe, the following:

1. "In the United States in 1967, there were 8,876,700 families — including one person households — in poverty. These households . . . comprise approximately 29,900,000 persons at a level recognized by our Federal Government as impoverished. This is 15 percent of the United States population. The number of persons in households now receiving surplus commodities is 3.2 million and the number of persons in households now receiving food stamps is 2.2 million. This represents 5.4 million persons, or 18 percent of the 29,000,000 poor. Recognizing that studies have shown that food assistance programs, as presently administered, do not improve a person's diet appreciably, it is likely that as many as 33 percent of the 5.4 million individuals receiving either commodities or stamps continue to have what USDA defines as a "poor" diet (i.e. two-thirds the daily Recommended Dietary Allowance of the National Research Council). We cannot assume that any of the remaining poor — those on neither program — are getting food. According to the 1965 National Survey of the USDA, the results of which are just now being

published, approximately 10,764,000 Americans in poverty are eating what USDA regards as a "poor" diet. Moreover, 66.6 percent of the poor or 19,943,300 people are not maintaining a "satisfactory" diet (i.e. are receiving less than the full daily Recommended Dietary Allowance of the National Research Council). These people are not receiving the minimum nutrition because they cannot afford the costs and because the government has not provided adequate assistance.

"The above figures do not include the school food programs. In 1967 there were approximately 50 million children of school age. Approximately 6 million of these children come from poor families. Only 2 million of these children received free lunches in 1967. Thus, 4 million children, or two-thirds of all school age children in poverty, either paid for their lunch or went without. . . .

"Neither food stamp programs nor commodity programs exist in over one-third of our poorest counties. And where they do operate, they reach an average of only 12 percent of the poor in any county. In the South, the highest percentage of a state's poor participating in any food program — is 42.3 percent and that is in Mississippi. . . . Furthermore, welfare payments reach only a quarter of the poor."

2. Neither our hospitals nor our public health services are focused on the detection of malnutrition. Such indices as anemia and post neo-natal mortality suggest that only the barest tip of a deeply submerged iceberg of malnutrition is actually identified.

3. Malnutrition causes incalculable physical and mental hurt to those 10 million Americans. There is increasing, and now hardly disputed, evidence that lack of protein in the diet of youngsters can cause severe and irreversible brain damage. Malnutrition causes moreover, a lowering of resistance to infection and is consequently a prime cause of infant mortality after viruses, bacterial diseases, listlessness and apathy.

4. The federal food programs do not work. They reach too few people. Moreover, neither the commodities program nor the food stamp program provides the possibility of adequate nutrition. To repeat what was said above, although by the federal government's own finding there are at least 29,900,000 persons below the poverty line, there are only about 5.4 million persons on federal food programs. Furthermore, to our knowledge only two studies have been made of the nutritional benefits derived from the federal food program. One was made in the Mississippi Delta in 1967 under the Department of Agriculture's own sponsorship, and one late last year in two counties of South Carolina by Dr. John Lease of the University of South Carolina: both studies reported only slight nutritional improvements provided by the programs.

5. Food programs are, for the poor, but one more twisting and turning

of a welfare system that grinds away mercilessly and ceaselessly at their self respect and at their realistic ambition to attain self-reliance.

6. The food programs themselves are primarily administered by the Department of Agriculture. It is not appropriate that this should be so. The food programs are welfare programs, and should not be administered by a department which has as its key purpose the maximizing of income for producers of major crops.

7. Equally as bad is the fact that local option is the rule for determining whether there will be any federal food program at all. This is the Department of Agriculture's practice, despite the well established fact that it is precisely those localities with the greatest proportions of poor in which the poor are least likely to be represented or their interests protected.

These are our principal conclusions. We presented also 14 recommendations. The primary thrust of these is toward a largely self administered program providing a nutritionally sufficient diet.

We have suggested that there be free food stamps issued by right to all those qualified by low income, dependents, and medical expenses. We have further suggested that these be issued in the manner of a negative income tax payment, and in quantity fully large enough to enable recipients to have a good diet.

We think these and the other recommendations we have offered would, as we said in the Foreword to *Hunger U.S.A.*, go far "toward freeing the poor . . . from the special and often oppressively undignified guardianship of any bureaucracies. We think those who are poor can be safely assumed to have a concern for their own and their children's best interests and can, therefore, be trusted to look after themselves. The principal recommendation of this Board is, therefore, a free food stamp program keyed to need and to the objective of a completely adequate diet, and one which would be administered with minimum controls."

In conclusion, it is often to be observed, in situations such as I now find myself, that the speaker hints at awful consequences, such as demonstrations and riots, though prudently not predicting them. I won't do that. I won't do that, not only because I believe there are terrible disorders ahead — and I do believe that — but because we must all by now be tired of playing games. Every morning's newspaper confirms anew that this is a deeply troubled and seething world, and that the United States is itself in turmoil. If we owe no other duty to each other in such days as these, we do owe the duty of speaking as clearly and honestly as we can.

We confess often that we are an over-indulgent nation, and now we are even over-indulged on shock and tragedy. We have lived through so many ghastly events the last 13 or 14 years that we now seem surfeited. Our emotions are so battered and mauled that another assault on them — say, the murder of a Martin Luther King — is something we take in our national stride, as a child gets over the whooping cough or the chicken pox.

We 25 private persons who served on this Board of Inquiry learned nothing so important as the hard fact that the anxiety and the anger of the poor and hungry are both real, and that they permeate the country. If we do not heed the just needs of the poor, they will shake the walls of the republic.

So though we bring coals to Newcastle we also come back to say that you who started us on our inquiry were right. There is, as you said there was, hunger and the despair that hunger brings in this nation of ours. May you find the power to end it. We endorse Senate Resolution 281, but if you pass it and it is carried out it will at best serve only emergency needs.

STATEMENT OF GILBERT ORTIZ, M.D., OBSTETRICIAN CHAIRMAN, ASPIRA, BRONX, NEW YORK

Dr. Ortiz: Although much of the attention generated in recent weeks over the problems of hunger and malnutrition in the United States through the efforts of this distinguished committee and those of the Board of Inquiry has been directed toward rural and migrant populations, these problems are no less real in the urban areas. As a member of the Board of Inquiry I made field trips to the poverty sections of San Antonio, Tex., our Nation's 15th largest city. I saw unmistakable evidence of hunger and malnutrition there. I spoke with a pregnant mother who had had nothing to eat that day but a potato borrowed from a relative, and in whose tiny, tidy home there was no food at all, or means to prepare it.

In the Florida migrant camps I examined malnourished children suffering from parasitic infestation and was informed by a local physician that a diagnosis of anemia was routine for the majority of his patients. Such experiences were repeated for members of the Board of Inquiry everywhere we went. And this included our largest cities, such as Boston and Washington, D.C., and New York City. I did not take part, personally, in the Boston or Washington visits, but from my own practice in New York City and our field trip and staff investigations of conditions in New York documented serious problems.

At hospitals and health centers in such areas as the Bronx, hunger may be seen in patients. Malnutrition is manifested in iron deficiency anemia and a susceptibility to infection not present in the well-nourished. The children are the most often affected. Cases of rickets are still found, and there are others categorized as "failure to thrive," all related to insufficient caloric intake. These are caught in a cycle of low intake, diarrhea and further insufficient caloric intake. Gastrointestinal diseases may become a vicious debilitating cycle and are often caused by some degree of malnutrition and lead in turn to further malnutrition.

There are many reasons for hunger and malnutrition in our urban ghettos and barrios. Lack of money to buy food is the most common.

STATEMENT OF MRS. MATTIE GRINELL, NEW TOWN, NORTH DAKOTA

Mrs. Grinell: Gentlemen, I came over here to Washington, D.C. I am old enough to stay home and rest. But the councilmen over there at home don't try to do anything for us. [Mrs. Grinell was then 101 years old. She is an Indian.]

My people, they was coming over here and I came along with them to explain all these things to President Johnson.

I didn't go much to school. I didn't have much schooling. So, I can't talk very good, and I don't hardly understand much, too. Anyway, I am talking.

The people over there in my reservation, we had a hard time. All my people are having a hard time. We are poor. The councilmen don't help us. They don't try to help us. So, we had a hard time.

In my young days, we had a good time. We got lots of game going on, buffaloes and deer and antelopes and prairie chicken and fish and everything else which comes handy. So, we never starved or anything.

Our boys go and bring all kinds of fresh meat or things like that. That is the only food we used to have, the meat and corn. Now the white people came on our reservation and killed off all our buffalo and all these game here so we have nothing to eat and we are starving half the time. The white people killed all our buffaloes out and they gave us commodities, which was just cornmeal, oats, and rice and all that; that is not really our food. But we have to eat that. Most of it is all wormy; that is what we always say; it is wormy. It has worms in it. But we have a hard time to sift them and cook them and eat. That is what I was trying to explain to President Johnson, and I came.

I don't see why our President Johnson is not trying to stop that war. All our boys, he sent them to war and they fight and kill the American boys. I feel sorry for them poor boys. I have been praying for them all the time but President Johnson always sends our boys out all the time. I wonder if he has a son or grandson to go over there and see what it feels like.

Senator Nelson. What reservation are you from, Mrs. Grinell?

Mrs. Grinell. My reservation is Fort Berthold, N. Dak.

29. The Other America Revisited

Michael Harrington

More than any other book of the 1960's, Michael Harrington's The Other America *spotlighted attention on domestic poverty and brought an impassioned message about the poor to those affluent Americans who would listen. Reportedly, President John F. Kennedy was one of them.*

Seven years after the book's publication in 1962 Harrington revisited "the other America" to assess the gains of "the war against poverty." In this selection, written in 1969, he acknowledges some reduction in poverty and unemployment but finds some disquieting elements, in particular, the dim prospects for the black and the young poor and the possibility that a recession might wipe away newly won employment gains. (Harrington's anxiety was well grounded. By 1971 the unemployment rate had soared to 6 percent.)

The American poor are more militant than they were in 1962. But because they are still a minority of the population Harrington does not believe they alone can transform society. He hopes for a political coalition of the poor and nonpoor to abolish poverty. As Chairman of the Socialist Party, Harrington believes that socialism is the best way to end poverty in America, a view he presents in Reading 61.

The Other America was published in March, 1962. Now, almost seven years later, the condition that book described is objectively not quite as evil as it was; politically and morally, it is worse than ever. For despite a long, federally induced boom and an "unconditional" war on poverty, tens of millions of Americans still live in a social underworld and an even larger number are only one recession, one illness, one accident removed from it.

Ironically, perhaps the most dramatic single breakthrough of the government's anti-poverty effort is the increase in our official knowledge of the needless suffering that we tolerate. President Johnson's program did not achieve full employment for all nor provide impoverished children and aging people with an income but it did generate a tremendous amount of research, seminars, discussions, and even mass-media reports. So, since the

From Michael Harrington, "The Other America Revisited," *The Center Magazine*, 2:1 (January 1969). Reprinted with permission from *The Center Magazine*, a publication of the Center for the Study of Democratic Institutions. Revised with permission.

poor have become less invisible, for we know they are there, the society has become even more guilty; now it knows its callousness.

Revisiting the other America in 1969 is easier than going there in the late fifties and early sixties. Now Washington has produced some revealing maps of misery. In general, the official figures show some progress in eliminating poverty, but the accomplishment is so modest that one economic downturn would annul it — and the powerful voices urging a calculated increase in unemployment so that the price stability of the affluent can be protected would bring just such a downturn. . . .

There is no point in denying that there has been some progress. We are now in the seventh year of an unprecedented prosperity which was purchased, in considerable measure, with a twenty-billion-dollar tax subsidy that disproportionately favored the rich individuals and corporations. At the same time, the official unemployment figures have been reduced to under four per cent — but have not gone down to the three per cent goal that John F. Kennedy set as the mark of "full employment" when he became President. The first several years of this boom did not aid the unskilled workers and the hard-core unemployed, although eventually a few of the crumbs of good times trickled down to them.

By 1966, the poverty line had risen to $3,335.[1] (While this index went up by nine per cent, the average income of four-person families in America had increased by thirty-seven per cent, so the new criterion meant that the poor had even less of a share of affluence.) As a result, 17.8 per cent of the people were under the line in 1966 as compared to twenty-four per cent in 1959. This statistic allows the celebrators of America to claim that the other America is disappearing at a reasonable rate. It is that claim which I want to challenge here.

Pride, in short, must be somewhat restrained. The poverty line is, after all, an artificial, if extremely useful, construct. Miss Orshansky [Mollie Orshansky of the Department of Health, Education, and Welfare, a student of the poverty line] herself has pointed out that millions hover just above the definition (Daniel Patrick Moynihan calls them the "at risk" population). In 1966, there were more than three million families with incomes between $3,000 and $4,000; most of them were not officially classified as poor but all of them were in danger of becoming so with one bad break in the national economy or in their private lives. . . .

In two particularly tragic cases it is not necessary to speculate about the numbers. The children and the blacks among the poor are worse off than when the war on poverty began. "All told," writes Mollie Orshansky, "even in 1966, after a continued run of prosperity and steadily rising family

---

[1] [The poverty line is obtained by constructing an imaginary budget around the core of the USDA's low-cost and "economy" plans for diet (22¢ per meal per person in January, 1964). — Ed.]

income, one-fourth of the nation's children were in families living in poverty or hovering just above the poverty line." This fact, of course, has the most disturbing and dangerous implications for the future. On the one hand, poverty more and more becomes a fate because the educational, economic, and social disadvantages of life at the bottom become progressively more damaging; and, on the other hand, the poor still have more children than any other group. Present evidence points to the melancholy conclusion that the twenty-five per cent of the young who are poor, or near-poor, will have large families very much like the ones of which they are now members. If this is true, the current incidence of poverty among children will guarantee that, short of radical political decisions, the next generation in the other America will be even more numerous than this one.

With Negroes, the problem is more a relative position than an absolute increase in indignity, but this is still a politically explosive fact. In 1959 the Social Security Administration fixed the black percentage of the other Americans at twenty-five per cent; by 1966, the proportion had risen to thirty-three per cent. This, of course, still shows that the scandal of poverty actually afflicts more whites than blacks, but it also indicates that discrimination even applies to the rate at which people escape from beneath the poverty line. During these years of prosperity even the worst off of the white Americans have had a special advantage, compared to the Negroes. . . .

To sum up — by courtesy of the government's card file (and computer tapes) on outrages in this nation — there has been modest progress in the official figures: a drop in the poverty population from twenty-five per cent to around eighteen per cent. Nevertheless, those who crossed the line are still very close to the world of hunger and hovels. There are signs that the present-day children of the poor will become the parents of even poorer children in the immediate future. Black Americans are falling further and further behind the whites. And the subemployment statistics indicate a depression while the official jobless rates are cited to show that there is full employment.

What of the quality of life among the poor? Here, I think, the reality is more optimistic, but it is very easy to visualize a reversal of the positive trends.

The war on poverty was never more than a skirmish and the provisions for "maximum feasible participation of the poor" were quickly subverted by hysterical mayors. In theory, the country wants the disadvantaged to stand up and fight for their rights as all the immigrant groups did; in practice, we have knocked people down for taking that pious myth seriously. And yet, there has been a significant growth in local insurgency. It was given an impetus, a public legitimacy, by the anti-poverty efforts of recent years. To a degree, then, the other America has become less passive and defeated, more assertive. This is an enormous gain, for it is the psychological precondition for political and economic advance. . . .

Once this crucial point is understood, the militancy of recent years becomes important. In the South, the dramatic struggles of a mass movement in the street have led to the registration of more than a million new black voters. In the ghettos of the North, where the enemies of Negro freedom are more subtle than Governor Wallace and the disintegrative power of poverty more compelling, there have been urban *Jacqueries,* spontaneous, unplanned riots, and the emergence among the ghetto young of a new pride of race. . . .

The Negroes are not alone in their insurgency. In California, some Mexican-Americans have organized economically in unions and exercised powerful political impact during the 1968 Democratic primary. In New York, Puerto Ricans have provided a mass base for unions in hospitals and public employment, and so have Negroes. Throughout the country, there are organizations of mothers on welfare demanding an end to the bureaucratic humiliations that are carefully structured into public assistance in America. And in Appalachia, poor whites have even had some limited success in the struggle against strip mining.

Yet, as I argued at some length in the book, *Toward a Democratic Left,* even if these rebellious movements grow in size and cohesion, even if they reach out to a majority of the poor, they will not be able to transform the society by themselves. Therefore the future of activism in the other America depends, in a considerable measure, upon what the non-poor do. This is certainly true if one thinks in terms of the need to create a vast majority coalition, for only such a movement would be capable of initiating the radical changes that are required if poverty is to be abolished in America. Paradoxically, the more fundamental and thoroughgoing an economic and social program, the more heterogeneous and inclusive must its supporters be. . . . Even more immediately, insurgency among the poor is profoundly affected by the movement of the national economy. This fact leads to some larger generalizations about the dynamic of the other America in 1969.

When the Kennedy Administration began, the poor, with the exception of some Southern Negroes, were largely passive and pessimistic. This was partly a reflection of the daily life of the Eisenhower years: chronic unemployment and recession, official indifference, the invisibility of forty to fifty million people. The blacks made the first breakthrough below the Mason-Dixon line, and under the leadership of Martin Luther King, Jr., a general climate of hope developed. There was even the governmental policy of having the poor participate in the anti-poverty program. The economic and political upswing and the success of the black freedom movement in the South created the base for the beginning of a new spirit in the other America.

But, as that spirit expressed itself in various forms of militant protest, a new period began in 1965. The war in Vietnam began to dominate American domestic politics and the thirty billion dollars or more invested annually in that tragedy precluded any serious attempt at an "unconditional" war on poverty. The modest impact of the new economics was felt at the bottom of the American economy but in every way the tax cut was inversely — and perversely — related to need; the rich got the most benefit and profit, the poor the least. So the demands for change did not end. There was a great danger in this situation and it came to the fore in the Wallace campaign of 1968. When the struggle against poverty was part of a broad strategy of domestic economic expansion, white workers and members of the lower middle class had a certain common interest with blacks and the rest of the other America, even if they did not lose their prejudices. But when, because of Vietnam, the fight against want seemed to take on the aspect of a competition between the have-nots and the have-littles for scarce private and public goods, there were backlashers who feared that their own jobs, homes, and public places were being threatened.

. . . It is not difficult to imagine how certain changes in government policy would affect the other America. If there is an economic downturn, the new activism of the poor — those tentative essays in hope which we have seen — will be turned into despair, most of it passive, some of it dangerously angry. If the talk of "trading off" a little unemployment in return for increased price stability becomes more than talk, and joblessness, as a result, rises to five or six per cent, the extremely modest employment gains of our recent efforts would be abolished and the nation would return to the *status quo ante,* or worse. Up to now, when the private sector has hired marginal workers, even with federal inducements, it has done so only because a relatively tight labor market had made it economically feasible to take a few — a very few — risks on the hard-core jobless; the moment the official unemployment rate hits five per cent it will become economically imperative for corporations to fire those men and women.

This would drastically affect the quality of life in the other America. It would deprive the poor of part of their already meager economic resources (the richer a union, or a community organization, the longer it can strike). It would confirm the suspicion, which is never dispelled in the minds of the poor, that the political order of the larger society is systematically rigged against those in it who are the worst off. And most terrible of all, it would teach those who had dared to be hopeful that America was only kidding and that cynicism is the better part of valor. Under such circumstances, a few would become even more militant; the many would sink back into apathy. . . .

The scenario need not be written this way. It is possible to make the massive planned social investments that would create the setting in which the poor would become more organized and determined to control their own political and economic destiny. But, as 1968 came to an end, the happy beginning was still not very imminent. It is not just that the statistical progress in abolishing poverty has been so modest or that the position of the "at risk" population of impoverished children and of blacks is so precarious and even explosive. It is more than that: there is a very real possibility that the spiritual gains of the poor — their new sense of dignity, their awareness that they need not forever be excluded from the democratic political process — are in danger. Looking back to the other America of 1962, it may be that in the years that have passed since then we have raised up the hopes of the most abused people of this land only in order to knock them down.

30. Capitalism and Persistent Poverty

Paul A. Baran and Paul M. Sweezy

Two of America's most prominent Marxian economists, the late Paul A. Baran (1910–1964), who was professor of economics at Standford University, and Paul M. Sweezy, who formerly taught economics at Harvard University and is now editor of Monthly Review, *believe that American poverty is more extensive than usually admitted and that it cannot be eradicated under capitalism. They argue that orthodox economists had to "rediscover" poverty in America because of their misinterpretation of ameliorative trends in the post–World War II economy. According to Baran and Sweezy, these were only temporary deviations that masked the more basic long-run tendency of our economy to generate high levels of unemployment and poverty.*

In Monopoly Capital, *from which this piece is taken, Baran and Sweezy recognize that capitalism has changed a great deal since Marx, but they insist that the system still generates both wealth and poverty.*

. . . It will be useful to ask how it happened that poverty which only a few years ago had been written off as practically a thing of the past, suddenly came to occupy the center of the political stage.

There are, we believe, two parts to the explanation. First, as Marx

From Paul A. Baran and Paul M. Sweezy, *Monopoly Capital* (New York: Monthly Review Press, 1966), pp. 285–289. Reprinted by permission of the Monthly Review Press. Copyright © 1966 by Paul M. Sweezy. Editor's title, by permission.

pointed out in *Capital* and as the experience of the subsequent century of capitalist development has confirmed again and again, capitalism everywhere generates wealth at one pole and poverty at the other. This law of capitalist development, which is equally applicable to the most advanced metropolis and the most backward colony, has of course never been recognized by bourgeois economists. They have rather propagated the apologetic notion that a levelling-up tendency is inherent in capitalism.

This is where the second part of the explanation becomes relevant. At the root of capitalist poverty one always finds unemployment and underemployment — what Marx called the industrial reserve army — which directly deprive their victims of income and undermine the security and bargaining power of those with whom the unemployed compete for scarce jobs. Now during the Second World War, unemployment was really wiped out for a few years. While more than ten million men in the most productive age groups were being mobilized into the armed forces, total production was being expanded by two thirds or more. Under these circumstances, every physically able person, regardless of color, age, or sex, could get a job; and overtime became the rule rather than the exception. With several members of each family employed, family incomes in the lower-income brackets increased sharply. It would of course be wrong to say that poverty was eliminated during the war, but the improvement of living standards of poor people all over the country was nothing short of dramatic. And these favorable conditions for the underprivileged and disadvantaged continued, though in a weakened form, through the aftermath boom and the prosperity of the early 1950's, rooted in the Korean War and the huge military budgets which accompanied and followed it. For more than a decade, poverty in the United States receded and then was held at bay, while the economy as a whole expanded under the extraordinary demands of wars, hot and cold.

Bourgeois ideologists, wearing the blinkers provided by orthodox economic theory, naturally misinterpreted these developments completely. Here at last, they exulted, was capitalism behaving as they expected it to. The past was forgotten, especially the recent past of the Great Depression; the lessons of more than a century were ignored; the future was charted as an extrapolation of the wholly untypical years surrounding the greatest war in history. Hence the American Celebration, with its complacent assurance that poverty in this most affluent of societies would soon be no more than an unpleasant memory.

But capitalism's basic law of motion, temporarily thwarted, soon resumed its sway. Unemployment crept steadily upward, and the character of the new technologies of the postwar period sharply accentuated the disadvantages of unskilled and semi-skilled workers. Those at the bottom of the economic ladder who had been, in relative terms, the chief beneficiaries of wartime full employment now found themselves doubly hard hit.

By the end of the 1950's the real state of affairs could no longer be concealed: it was impossible to continue to believe in the existence of a meliorative trend which, given time, would result in the automatic liquidation of poverty. Not only was poverty still with us, as it always had been; there was evidence on all sides, but especially in the decaying centers of the big cities, that it was spreading and deepening. Affluence began to appear for what it is — not the cure for poverty but its Siamese twin.

A changed view of, and attitude toward, poverty now became inevitable. From being a passing nuisance, it suddenly became once again, as it had been before the war, a problem. The first fruit of this change was the new literature of poverty, the second its reappearance on the political stage. Johnson's "war on poverty" is in truth but a variation on a familiar theme. Herbert Hoover, running in 1928 as the Republican candidate for the presidency, declared that "we shall soon with the help of God be within sight of the day when poverty will be banished from this nation." And his successor, Franklin D. Roosevelt, vowed to change the situation in which "one third of a nation" was ill housed, ill clad, and ill fed.

We now know that neither God nor FDR managed to turn the trick, and there is little reason to assume that Lyndon Johnson can do better. In the meantime, however, we can ask what are the dimensions of the problem his "war on poverty" is intended to cope with.

To answer this question we must of course first define poverty. Bourgeois theorists frequently throw up their hands at this point. Poverty, they say, is a relative matter, and everyone is entitled to define it as he sees fit. Some even go so far as to argue that since the poorest American — say, an unemployable living on public welfare in Mississippi — undoubtedly disposes over more income than an average worker or peasant in many underdeveloped countries, there really is no poverty in the United States. To a Marxist, however, such subjective judgments are at best meaningless and at worst deliberately misleading. Every society has its own standards for measuring poverty; and though these standards may not be precisely quantifiable, they are nevertheless real, objective facts. What is involved here is essentially the concept of the conventional subsistence minimum which plays such an important part in Marx's theory of wages and surplus value. Unlike the classical economists, Marx did not think of the subsistence minimum as being physiologically determined. The worker's "natural wants, such as food, clothing, fuel, and housing vary according to the climatic and other physical conditions of his country," he wrote. "On the other hand the number and extent of his so-called necessary wants . . . are themselves the product of historical development and depend, therefore, to a great extent on the degree of civilization of a country." The subsistence minimum thus varies historically, but at any given time and place it can be identified and approximately measured. From this flows logically the definition of poverty as the condition in which those members of a society live whose incomes are insufficient to cover what is for that society and at that time the subsistence minimum.

It is evidently reasoning like this — though obviously not derived from Marx — which underlies the work of the Bureau of Labor Statistics in defining "modest but adequate" budgets for working-class families. If we equate these budgets with the conventional subsistence minimum, we can say that all whose incomes fall below the levels so delimited are living in poverty.

By this criterion, how much poverty was there in the United States in 1959, the year to which the latest census data apply?

In that year a "modest but adequate" level of living cost a family between $5,370 (Houston) and $6,567 (Chicago) in 20 large American cities. At the same time, 20 percent of the families in the country had incomes of less than $2,800 a year; another 20 percent had incomes between $2,800 and $4,800; and still another 20 percent had incomes between $4,800 and $6,500.[1]

How can we avoid the conclusion that, *by the standards of American capitalist society itself,* close to half the people are living in poverty?

31. A View of the Poverty Program

Tom Hayden

In the early 1960's, certain antiwar, antipoverty, and civil rights activists started to call themselves the New Left. The term New Left is not easily defined. New Leftists are a diverse group. They share no common ideology. Nor do they agree on tactics. Many who are now New Leftists originally worked through the establishment. This tactic failed and now New Leftists thoroughly distrust the established order and its institutions. They are disenchanted with liberals. The liberal

---

[1] [In 1970, the Bureau of Labor Statistics's "moderate" budget (equivalent to the "modest but adequate" budget of 1959) averaged $10,666 for an urban family of four. In that year, according to the U.S. Department of Commerce, median family income in the United States was $9,867 for all families, $10,005 for nonfarm families, and $6,772 for farm families. Data are also available on median income by family size. The median income was $11,167 for all families of four; $11,288 for nonfarm families of four; and $8,007 for farm families of four. However interpreted, these figures indicate that a substantial portion of the American population is still unable to maintain a moderate standard of living as defined by the U.S. Bureau of Labor Statistics. — Ed.]

solution to the poverty problem is seen as a failure because of its emphasis on reform rather than structural change.

Tom Hayden, author of this selection, is a well-known New Leftist. Hayden, a defendant in the Chicago Conspiracy Trial of 1969, began his activist career as a civil rights worker in the South. Disillusioned by his experiences, he became a founder of Students for a Democratic Society (SDS) in 1961.

In 1964 Hayden organized an SDS-sponsored community organization project in the Newark ghetto. He participated in letter and petition campaigns, picket lines, rent strikes and political campaigns. He struggled against slumlords, the welfare system, and other establishment agencies. These experiences made him even more pessimistic about the success potential of the government's strategy of community action, an integral part of the War Against Poverty. The community action program was designed to involve the hard-core poor in the war against poverty.

In the passage Hayden sees no harmony of interests between the poor and their oppressors. Hence, government-sponsored community action programs cannot solve the problems of the ghettos. Hayden speculates that conflicts too deep to be negotiated might result in violence. Then the establishment will respond by sending more police to the ghettos rather than by sharing political and economic power.

This is what happened in 1967, a year after this piece was written, when Newark and ghettos throughout the nation erupted.

Most Americans feel that our society is being improved constantly in the fields of civil rights and economic welfare. But the evidence does not necessarily point to durable improvements in people's lives since the New Deal "revolution." For Negroes, Puerto Ricans, Mexicans, Indians, Appalachian miners and many Southern whites, as well as for many industrial workers, the reforms of the last thirty years are token, illusory, or meaningless.

The Wagner Act, for instance, was supposed to lead to the unionization of workers; but today barely half of the working class is unionized, the union base in mass-production industry is declining, and national authorities rarely have acted to stop the leaks, such as the right-to-work laws, through which the meaning of the act is drained and lost. The Social Security laws, too, were supposed to serve people in distress, but today those with coverage can barely make ends meet, while the law leaves millions of people still uncovered.

From Tom Hayden, *A View of the Poverty Program: "When It's Dry You Can't Crack It with a Pick"* (July 1966). Reprinted by permission of the Center for the Study of Unemployed Youth, Graduate School of Social Work, New York University.

The 1946 Employment Act is still another case: it was supposed to ensure government action to provide a living for every American in need, but it is widely known today that the major corporations prefer a state of managed unemployment to keep their costs low and their bargaining strength high when they negotiate labor contracts. The 1949 Housing Act was to create 800,000 low-cost units by 1953, but today less than half that number are constructed and most of them are beyond the budgets of the poor. It is possible to make the same comments about the rest of our government's social programs in the areas of medical care and public health, education, urban renewal, civil rights, and simple urban services. Amidst these failures there has been established a new and explicitly public kind of authoritarianism which is growing under the name of the welfare state. Public relief clients and public housing tenants, for example, have no organization of their own with even the strength of a union local in a factory. Existing associations of welfare clients or tenants are little more than vehicles by which authorities strengthen their position. This leaves the poor fully vulnerable to the caprice of supervisors, investigators and local machine politicians. Urban renewal programs, to extend the example, mostly serve as major domestic outlets for investment capital and, consciously or not, as a means of demoralizing and politically fragmenting the poor. With its labor, welfare, and civil rights legislation, the national government gradually becomes the chief force for stabilizing the private economy and for managing social crisis. Whose welfare does this program serve? Not that of the poor, unless by accident.

I make these comments sharply because I think it is time to foresake the view that each step towards "more of the welfare state" is also a step towards greater freedom and security for the majority of the American people. Without denying the fact that solid changes have occurred, changes which lifted a large number of American workers out of conditions of brutal starvation, it is crucial to expose the uglier side of the New Deal "revolution." Those who gained security in the thirties are threatened still by the decline in union power, and the continuing possibility of unemployment and stagnation. As for those who, by the President's own definition, are poor — they remain unhelped, unrewarded and unrepresented.

The general failure of all these programs is receiving wide attention because domestic problems are becoming urgent again after the long moratorium of the forties and fifties. The decline of semi-skilled and unskilled jobs at the time of population boom among the young; the movement of industry away from urban areas; the growing concentration of the poor in the cities; the breakdown of all services and administration to the ghetto poor; the bitterness of the Negro poor and the anxiety of the whites perched slightly above them in the economy — these are the constantly restated problems which form the modern American crisis. The poverty program is the latest step taken to meet this crisis. It declares traditional ways of approaching poverty inadequate, and defines new programs to coordinate old services and also attempts to aid the so-called "unreachable" or "hard-core" poor. The program adds a community action emphasis to welfare programs.

The amount of money allocated for the poverty program is barely more than enough to consolidate existing bureaucracies. Most of it is going to local politicians, school boards, welfare agencies, housing authorities, professional personnel and even to the police; its main effect is to shore up organizational machinery of local power groups — not to shift the distribution of influence or income towards the poor. In reality, the poor only flavor the program. A few are brought into it, induced by its prestige and high salaries, but they come only as atomized individuals, separated by their choice from the great mass of people in the ghetto. The poor do not have independent organizational strength within the program, as do the political machines and social agencies.

Some of the more sophisticated poverty planners believe that the involvement of the poor is essential to effective programs; thus the heavy emphasis on, and debate about, the need for "maximum feasible participation" of the poor. What this policy concept rests upon is the observation that the modern poor cannot be socialized upward and into the mainstream of American life in the tradition of the earlier immigrants. The modern poor, according to this view, lack the tight-knit culture, the economic skills, and the expanding market opportunities which were so common in the life of the immigrants.

In the particular case of the Negro poor, it is said, the male has been robbed of his dignity, first by the slave system and later by the exploitative economy. The result is the breakdown of the family, at least in its function of preparing the young to take their places in the slots offered by the established industrial machine. Though it is not put this way, the poverty program thus becomes a parent substitute more than a meal ticket, an agency of socialization more than of welfare. Not only is this the conception which underlies the Job Corps camps and the new batteries of "psychological service" counsellors, but it underlies the community action program as well. Self-organization, the development of skills, helping oneself through social action — these are supposedly the steps by which the ghetto residents will be rehabilitated. The amount and kind of conscious stress on this process varies from city to city. A "pure" example of it is evident in testimony recently given to a Congressional subcommittee by Denton Brooks, Director of the Chicago Anti-poverty Program. Asked whether rent strikes might be necessary to make progress, his answer was negative for this reason:

> Once you get the interaction of all groups, once you have a policy that something should be done for the poor, once this becomes a

national policy, then you work on a problem and you find a positive solution. Then the need for protest is eliminated. . . .

Many of the poverty planners believe that this process [self-help by social action] will require some element of conflict instead of being a simple matter of painless assimilation. The feeling is that change can be accomplished through a "dialog" between the poor and the powerful, in which the poor assert their needs as clearly as necessary. . . .

It is expected that quite an orderly adjustment of interests can be arranged through such a process.

The planners' faith lies in the idea that all interests are negotiable. But suppose that some are not. Suppose that enabling the poor to participate means attacking the status and privileges of professional agencies. Next suppose that strengthening the political power of the poor means alienating large groups of middle class voters. Then suppose that Negro militancy causes a backlash among those same white groups. Then there would arise situations which planners cannot negotiate, because the conflicts are too serious and deep to be adjusted. It is realistic to view the ghetto as a kind of American-style colony, controlled almost completely from the outside, a place which no one can leave unless he can fit into the patterns of the colonisers. That most of the "natives" identify in part with the colonisers does not change the actual exploitative relationship. Because of the colonial relationship, the "native's" way of life is organized outside of, and against, the ruling system: the life of black youth, of welfare women, of public housing tenants, the styles of attacking white people while appearing to agree with them, the sense of "soul" and separateness, the widespread sympathy with nationalism. Finally, there is violence, an inevitable part of the protest against a system that has used, and therefore taught the uses of, violence as a means of control.

Seen in this perspective, the purposes of American domestic and foreign policy are the same: 1. to keep the poor dependent on the power structure while using them as cheap labor and promising eventual equal rights; 2. to cultivate a group of the "loyal natives" to administer the colony; 3. when disruption occur, to use military power both to suppress it and serve a warning to others that it will never work.

> It is no wonder that John McCone chaired the Commission that studied the Watts riots; he merely applied his experience with revolution abroad to the American scene. As with the pacification program aimed at Vietnamese peasants, the Watts Report blames "hotheads" and "criminal elements" in the Negro community for the disturbance, then recommends greater police efficiency, more counselling and economic aid administered by government-picked officials. The military is the strong backbone of the program, though our officials say that "winning the people's confidence" is most important. In

Vietnam and Watts, the "natives" are left with more police surrounding them — but no more political or economic power than before.

The poverty program, then, is a liberal administrative response to a colonial crisis. It cannot be successful if it supposes a harmony of interests where there are deep divisions. If it cannot admit and participate in the obvious conflicts between the poor and their assorted oppressors, then the poverty program must side finally with the colonisers. In so doing, it will only deepen the crisis by demonstrating to the natives once again that the present government does not represent them.

Chapter Eight

On Being Poor

32. Facts and Fictions About the Poor

Elizabeth Herzog

> *Is there a distinct "culture of poverty"? Some anthropologists and sociologists believe that behavior patterns and values of the poor differ significantly from those of the rest of society and form a way of life that is handed down from generation to generation. Family instability, apathy, and poor school performance are among the attributes said to be part of the culture of poverty. In this selection Elizabeth Herzog of the U.S. Children's Bureau scrutinizes the notion of a culture of poverty and offers considerable evidence that the characteristics often associated with poverty represent responses to harsh reality rather than cherished norms.*
>
> *The earlier views of Malthus, Ricardo, and Spencer shifted blame for poverty back to the poor. Similarly, whether intentionally or unintentionally, the culture-of-poverty approach tends to blame the poor for their poverty and focuses on changing the poor rather than changing society. The affluent do not have to ask uncomfortable questions about whether economic inequalities are built into our society. Perhaps that explains the concept's popularity.*

Anyone who tries to ferret out and report facts about the poor — to tell it like it is — encounters some statements that are simply not true and some that are true and not true at the same time. They may be true as far as they

From Elizabeth Herzog, "Facts and Fictions About the Poor," *Monthly Labor Review*, 92:2 (February 1969), pp. 42–49.

go but misleading if viewed out of context, or partly true but distorted into falsehood by oversimplification. . . .

THE "CULTURE OF POVERTY"

A prime example of what is partly true and partly not true is the "culture of poverty." It is also an example of the dangers inherent in setting up a half-true label and then mistaking it for an explanation or using it as a substitute for thought.

The culture-of-poverty concept provides a reminder that, in some ways, different groups live in different worlds and respond to different imperatives. Perhaps this should not have been necessary, but it was. Disraeli thrust such a reminder upon the attention of his fellow countrymen when a character in his novel, *Sybil,* declared that Queen Victoria was reigning over not one Nation, but two: ". . . two nations between whom there is no intercourse and no sympathy; who are as ignorant of each other's habits, thoughts, and feelings as if they were dwellers in different zones or inhabitants of different planets; who are formed by a different breeding, are fed by a different food, are ordered by different manners, and are not governed by the same law — The Rich and The Poor." Michael Harrington, more than a century later, was referring to that conversation when he called his book *The Other America,* and called the last chapter "The Two Nations." And Oscar Lewis [in *The Children of Sanchez*], at about the same time, expressed a similar, though by no means identical, idea in referring to the culture of poverty.

The culture-of-poverty idea, for the short time in which it was being looked at with new eyes, did set up a ripple of fresh comprehension, and this is a contribution to be respected. What is to be deplored about the concept lies less in its original thoughtful formulation than in the way it has been applied by others.

Lewis pointed out that in some ways the poor of any industrialized country resemble each other more than they resemble the prosperous in their own society. He mentioned, for example, a number of economic traits, including "the constant struggle for survival, unemployment and underemployment, low wages, a miscellany of unskilled occupations, . . . the absence of savings, a chronic shortage of cash, the absence of food reserves in the home, the pattern of frequent buying of small quantities of food as need arises, the pawning of personal goods, borrowing from local money lenders at usurious rates of interest, spontaneous informal credit devices . . . organized by neighbors, and the use of second-hand clothing and furniture."

He also mentioned a number of social and psychological characteristics, including: ". . . living in crowded quarters, a lack of privacy, gregariousness, a high incidence of alcoholism, frequent use of physical violence in the training of children, wife beating, early initiation into sex, free unions or consensual marriages, a relatively high incidence of the abandonment of mothers and children, a trend toward mother-centered families and a much greater knowledge of maternal relatives, the predominance of the nuclear family, a strong predisposition to authoritarianism, and a great emphasis on family solidarity — an ideal only rarely achieved. Other traits include . . . a sense of resignation and fatalism based upon the realities of their difficult life situation, a belief in male superiority which reaches its crystallization in *machismo* or the cult of masculinity, a corresponding martyr complex among women, and finally, a high tolerance for psychological pathology of all sorts."

Much of what he said has been documented as a description of traits commonly found among the poor in any industrialized society. A few points have been sharply challenged. But the basic question is whether this much similarity of traits does indeed constitute a culture; and the basic problem lies in the applications and implications that others have derived from assuming that it does. Before grappling with the concept in general, a few examples are in order of the specifics that make the idea of a culture of poverty difficult either to accept or to reject without reservation.

With regard to economic patterns and the social habits derived from them, one may question whether these patterns and habits are culture traits or merely pragmatic responses to real life exigencies. If the latter, then they are not necessarily culture traits — that is, learned ways of life, transmitted from generation to generation — but rather responses of each generation to the circumstances in which it grows up. Some psychosocial characteristics often attributed to the culture of poverty can also be viewed as a response to reality, ready to change if reality fosters or at least permits change. It can be argued further that certain psychological attitudes commonly attributed to the poor are in fact the products of physical reality; and that some ascribed attitudes and values are erroneously ascribed.

For example, some psychological attributes often attributed to the culture of poverty are intertwined with the effects of hunger and malnutrition in such a way that they operate both as cause and as effect. The most familiar effects of extreme malnutrition are loss of weight, weakness, and anemia. In addition, according to one authority [Norman Jolliffe], various functional changes occur that are often mistaken for neurasthenic manifestations, including "excessive fatigueability, disturbances in sleep, inability to concentrate." Other symptoms cited [by Alvin Schorr] in connection with prolonged malnutrition are "depression, loss of ambition, apathy, lethargy, impotence, and a sensation of being old." Obviously, some characteristics that nutritional experts attribute to diet deficiency are the same ones often ascribed to the culture of poverty.

SCHOOL ACHIEVEMENT

Poor school performance by children of the slums is often attributed to the low esteem in which book learning is held by the culture of poverty, and the consequent lack of interest by parents in the schooling of their children. That inadequate diet can contribute to poor school performance has been established by systematic studies as well as by unsystematic observation.

Poor school performance is also promoted by lack of sleep, a deficiency which is caused in some instances by staying up late to watch television, but often is the result of overcrowded housing. To raise the subject of housing leads into an array of traits often associated with the culture of poverty, yet often produced by physical condition. Among those that have been described are pessimism and passivity, stress to which the individual cannot adapt, a state of dissatisfaction, pleasure in company but not in solitude, difficulty in household management and child rearing, and relationships that tend to spread out in the neighborhood rather than deeply into the family. The effects of poor housing on physical health have been widely discussed, including safety, respiratory and skin diseases, lead poisoning, and rat bites.

Because school achievement has been so important a focus of poverty problems and of efforts to solve them, it is especially appropriate for illustrating the possibility that features often ascribe to the culture of poverty may in fact be reflections of middle class behavior and attitudes. One such attitude, namely, the expectation of the teacher with regard to the child's ability to learn, has had some attention and is likely to receive more.

Scattered evidence is piling up in support of Kenneth Clark's thesis that ghetto children do poorly in school because the teachers expect them to do poorly. In Washington, D.C., for example, the academic average in the public schools has been reported as far below the national norm. However, one school in a very poor neighborhood stood out far above the average for the city. According to newspaper accounts, the difference was that the school principal would not accept the proposition that ghetto children could not learn, and would not allow the teachers in her school to accept it. And the children did learn, as attested by the academic scores. This kind of evidence was reinforced by an experiment in another city, where teachers in a very poor neighborhood were told that — on the basis of psychological tests — certain children in their classes were likely to show remarkable intellectual gains. The children, in fact, had been selected at random. Nevertheless, during the year those particular children did make gains significantly greater than those of their classmates. Apparently, because the teachers expected them to learn, they did learn.[1]

Another characteristic often attributed to the culture of poverty is lack of motivation. But motivation is a product of multiple ingredients and not a unitary trait. Moreover, it is a response as well as an attribute and is affected, as we have just seen, by nutrition, general health level, and other life circumstances that influence energy and ability to concentrate. It includes, also, aspiration and expectation, and the stronger of these is expectation. If expectation is very low, aspiration can be crippled. At one time, it was assumed that ghetto parents had very low educational aspirations for their children. A number of studies have made it clear, however, that the educational aspirations of very low-income parents for their children are often as high as, or higher than, those of the affluent. Their expectations, on the other hand, had not been high. Nor have they seen themselves as playing any role in helping their children to actual educational achievement. A great deal of the effort to involve parents in school and preschool activities has been directed toward convincing them that home and parents play a vital part in a child's school performance, and in demonstrating to them ways of making their part constructive.

FAMILY NORMS AND FORMS

Of all the features ascribed to the culture of poverty, perhaps the most deplored is family instability with all its concomitants — including female-headed families, illegitimacy, and dependence on public assistance, especially Aid to Families of Dependent Children (AFDC). Our census data assure us that family instability does characterize the poor in this country: Divorce and separation are on the whole inversely correlated with income. Yet there is abundant evidence that the norms of stable family life are preferred by the poor as well as by the prosperous.

This point embodies and illustrates one of the chief problems about the culture of poverty concept. To be acceptable at all, the culutre of poverty must be viewed, not as a culture but as a "subculture," a culture within a culture, existing within and as part of our prevailing culture of the middle class. With regard to family norms and forms especially, there is ample and increasing evidence that stable marriage and family life are accepted as a preferred ideal by most poor people, white and nonwhite. Such evidence was offered by Hylan Lewis's study of childrearing practices among low-income families, has been supported by the investigations of Hyman Rodman, by numerous reports and studies of AFDC clients — including

[1] [Details of this experiment are found on page 267. — Ed.]

that conducted by Greenleigh Associates, and has recently been reinforced in a number of research and demonstration projects conducted under grants from the Department of Health, Education, and Welfare.

According to these and other reports, middle class standards of sex and family life do not rank as high on the value pyramid of the poor as on that of the prosperous. But they are preferred as luxuries one would gladly be able to afford — just as certain business men prefer certain forms of honesty, while considering them unrealistic for practice in daily life. This ability to believe in one set of values while practicing a different set is by no means unique to the poor. Many of us experience something like it occasionally or frequently. However, like the mote in the eye, or the spot in the middle of the forehead, it's easier to see on the other fellow.

The exigencies that prompt the poor to depart from preferred norms of family life and sex behavior include, among many things, early marriage, lack of education, employment problems, and welfare regulations. The man who is not a provider loses status in the eyes of the community, his family, and himself. He may leave because of this or because his family cannot obtain public assistance while he is present.

The vicious cycle is aggravated by the fact that the poor have larger families than the nonpoor. Not because large families are their choice. Overall, the preferred American family size is about the same at all economic levels, about three children. However, the nonpoor have greater access to means of limiting the family and of averting extramarital pregnancy. It is by now a familiar fact that large families are more likely to be poor than small families, and that families which are both large and nonwhite run double risk of poverty.

Illegitimacy is more frequent among the poor than the nonpoor. But the preferred norms include birth in wedlock for poor and nonpoor, white and nonwhite. On this point also, evidence piles up from many sources, and sometimes it is very poignant evidence. We hear of a child taunted by classmates for not knowing who his father is, punished by a teacher for reporting as reality his fantasies about a nonexistent father, sidling up to a strange man on the street in the hope of being called "Son." The evidence also indicates, however, that at different economic levels, birth status occupies a different rank in the value hierarchy.

The different ranking of values is illustrated by Hylan Lewis' study, which was conducted in the District of Columbia. The mothers in his sample, white and nonwhite, dreaded unmarried motherhood for their daughters, prayed that it might not happen, and were devastated if it did. Yet they were equally emphatic, all of them, that if it did happen they would not try to persaude the young couple to marry — not unless they really loved each other. A good marriage they viewed as one of life's chief blessings and certainly one of its rarest blessings; but a bad marriage, in their eyes, was worse than none. A study of the Detroit area reports greater readiness of white girls than of Negro girls to marry because of pregnancy. It does not, however, report the economic status of the girls who were pregnant before marriage. Therefore, once again, a question remains, whether differences in illegitimacy rates are associated primarily with socioeconomic status or with color.

It is unfortunate that the white-nonwhite category is so much easier to apply than a socioeconomic classification, since it has led to reporting some figures (such as illegitimacy) only in terms of age and color. This habit of reporting, in turn, leads to overrating of ethnic factors and underrating of other factors. It has been estimated that if illegitimacy statistics could be controlled for income, the difference between white and nonwhite illegitimacy rates would dwindle dramatically.

THE SLAVERY HERITAGE

In other respects also, the habit of reporting by color rather than by income fosters the habit of attributing to ethnic background differences that may in fact derive chiefly from socioeconomic status. For example, the differences in family life patterns between nonwhites and whites in poverty are dwarfed by the resemblances, if comparisons are made within specified income levels. Myron Lefcowitz, among others, has shown that differences by income are more striking than differences by color, when controlled even very roughly by income; and that when Negro and white children with similar family incomes are compared, differences between them in educational achievement diminish and differences by class appear more striking than differences by color. Description of families in northern white slums could easily be mistaken for descriptions of families in the Harlem ghetto, whether one reads Lloyd Warner (1941), Hollingshead (1949) or Walter Miller (1959).

This leads to a paradox: The culture of poverty concept bumps against the thesis that low-income Negro patterns of family life and sex behavior are primarily the heritage of the slavery years. The patterns so often described as a cultural legacy of slavery are to a large extent the patterns ascribed to the culture of poverty among people who have never been slaves. Yet those who invoke the slavery-specific thesis use it to document differences between Negroes and whites, and offer it as *the* explanation of behavior patterns among low-income Negroes.

With regard to the features ascribed — for example, family instability, woman-based households, overt sex antagonism, illegitimacy, large families, interpersonal violence, depression, apathy, sense of lacking control over one's own fate — no inconsistency is involved. Slavery, in fact, can be viewed — for some slaves and to some extent — as an extreme version of poverty with a few repulsive additions. The inconsistency lies in attributing to the heritage of slavery the same behavior patterns that, for other groups, are attributed to poverty, and then assuming that the slavery, heritage, in itself, accounts for those behavior patterns when they occur among Negroes.

The point has been made that the differences between very low-income whites and Negroes are dwarfed by the similarities, with regard to characteristics so far investigated. This is not to argue against the existence of differences. It is also arguable, however, that such differences could be attributable to a century of prejudice, discrimination, and persecution as much as or more than to the preceding years of slavery.

The argument is complicated by the fact that, in our society, economic status to a large extent determines culture, so that it is very difficult to disentangle what we mean by culture and what we mean by class. This intertwining is, of course, built into the culture-of-poverty concept.

SUBCULTURE OR CULTURE

The various specifics mentioned illustrate considerations that point to two conclusions concerning "the culture of poverty": If the concept is to be useful at all, it must be explicitly recognized as a subculture rather than a culture; but under any name, poverty lacks the essential elements of a culture.

With regard to the first point, the poor, like the nonpoor, on the whole accept the norms and standards of what has come to be called the mainstream culture. Any subculture coexists and competes with a number of other subcultures. Most citizens of the United States are members of a good many subcultures: Family, peers, colleagues, organizations, and so forth, each with its own norms and imperatives. Which set wins out at any given moment depends on the personal makeup and history of the individual, on the nature of the situation and on coincidental circumstances. The complexity of this mixture makes doubly inappropriate what I have called the "cookie-cutter concept of culture" — the idea that a culture produces individuals as identical as cookies cut from the same mold.

A subculture of poverty, to the extent that it exists, can explain relatively little about a specific individual at a specific moment. It can, however, offer a pat phrase: "It's the culture," as a substitute for thought and for action. To the extent that this substitute is accepted, the concept jeopardizes both thought and action. "It's the culture," can mean "they don't mind, that's the way they like it, and anyway it's built-in, so you can't do anything about it."

The second point is that, under any name, poverty lacks some essential elements of a culture. The chief one is a matter of identification. Members of a culture, or a subculture, have a sense of belonging to a culture entity with institutions, patterns, and shared beliefs. Committed members have a sense of allegiance as well as of identity. Even those who want to break away have the feeling that they are separating themselves from an entity that exists and claims them as members. Corollary to this is the sense of participating in the life of a broad group, sharing in a system of beliefs and practices. This positive aspect of culture, the sense of belonging, with its corollary elements of sharing and of participating, has not characterized the people who served as models for the culture of poverty concept.

On the contrary, some of the closest students of slum life emphasize the unincorporated quality of life in the slums. There are gangs and cliques, but their subculture is the gang or the clique. The neighborhoods consist of people who happen to live near each other. A salient characteristic of AFDC mothers and of many other slum dwellers is their social isolation. The lack of worldly goods, according to these observers of large city slums, does not create a sense of community, of common institutions and customs, practices and beliefs. The life-ways of the slum dwellers represent, not a system of culturally evolved patterns, but rather a series of adjustments to exigencies perceived as unpredictable and uncontrollable.

It may be asked, is a culture of poverty evolving from the civil rights movement and the Poor People's Campaign? If so, it is by no means what has been meant hitherto by the culture of poverty. Some salient traits of the movements now on the march represent the most conspicuous lacks in the so-called culture of poverty: Commitment, energetic motivation, hope. It may well be that these movements will shoulder aside preoccupation with and arguments about the culture of poverty. What they produce to supersede it remains to be seen. But no development will free us of the need to subject simple and easy generalizations to cautious and continuous checking against available evidence.

33. The Welfare System

*President's Commission
on Income Maintenance Programs*

Relief recipients are the most scorned members of American society. And welfare is the most controversial program for the poor. Yet discussions about welfare too often ignore the real root of the problem: an economy that does not provide enough decent-paying jobs automatically condemns part of the population to poverty. One of the biggest causes of this poverty was and is America's response to its agricultural revolution. Farm workers and their families, replaced by farm machinery and rejected by society, faced an American version of the enclosures. In the short span from 1940 to 1970, tens of millions of people — including many southern blacks — streamed into cities seeking new and better lives. Some did find them, but many others found only the misery of unemployment or poverty wages. And even those who found work lost their jobs through automation and the relocation of industry in white suburbs. Rural poverty became urban poverty and relief simply spelled survival at the end of a bleak road.

Ironically, the Elizabethan Poor Laws, the original model for American relief, were enacted in an earlier era of enclosures when mass destitution among uprooted and landless peasants threatened the stability of seventeenth century England. Vestiges of Poor Law thinking still abound: miserly payments, humiliation of recipients, attempts to impose residency requirements, means tests, and the 1971 work-test requirement for welfare. Another vestige is the denial of relief to the working poor and to most of the able-bodied unemployed. This practice encourages family disintegration, for a family may be better off financially if the father deserts it.

A convincing explanation of the contradictions that are built into the welfare system is offered by Frances Fox Piven and Richard A. Cloward in Regulating the Poor (1971). They claim that for more than three centuries the true function of relief has not been to eliminate poverty but to provide just enough aid to stave off rebellion among the poor, while maintaining a supply of cheap labor. The latter is accomplished by outright exclusion of able-bodied men from relief and also by degrading, punitive treatment of those on welfare — treatment designed to instill a fear of relief among persons for whom the only alternative is to work at the most menial, low-wage jobs. Needless to say, such practices also hold down the cost of relief to taxpayers.

Today, everyone agrees that the present system of public assistance needs revamping, but differs greatly on what needs changing. Conservatives assert that recipients are coddled and overpaid, whereas liberals, radicals, and the poor feel that current payments are inadequate and that the system chains the poor to poverty.

Are there less degrading alternatives to welfare? A guaranteed income is one possibility. But whether such a guarantee would perpetuate or eliminate poverty depends on how much income is guaranteed. In 1970, the government's own poverty line was set at about $4,000 for a family of four whereas the U.S. Bureau of Labor Statistics claimed that an urban family of four required $6,960 to maintain a "lower" living standard and about $10,666 to maintain a "modest" but adequate living standard. So the question remains: how much income should be guaranteed? The Family Assistance Plan proposed as a welfare reform measure by President Nixon in 1969, although not really a guaranteed income, suggested a basic minimum of $1,600 annually for a family of four without other income, with subsidy payments to the working poor on a decreasing scale until earnings reach $3,920 a year. That plan would not eliminate poverty. Some would be helped but millions would still be destitute. A modest proposal that would do much to eliminate the desperate poverty of millions of citizens is the $6,500 minimum for an urban family of four advocated in 1971 by the National Welfare Rights Organization. That figure, based on the Bureau of Labor Statistics "lower" living standard, seems politically unattainable. Taxpayers are unwilling to pay the price and, with centuries of the work ethic embedded in their psyches, staunchly resist the idea that people who do not work should get as much as those who do.

Not only is society unwilling to guarantee income, but it also will not guarantee jobs. Contrary to a middle class myth, the poor also believe in the work ethic and prefer work to welfare. So it is especially ironic and cruel that society will not guarantee a job at a living wage for all who wish to work, hence eliminating much of the need for welfare and permitting the unemployed and working poor to enter the mainstream of American life. Resistance to guaranteed income and jobs is heightened by racism. Blacks are a substantial portion (though a minority) of those on welfare, a fact that partly explains why so many whites oppose income and job guarantees.

Despite much fanfare, ignorance beclouds public thinking about welfare. The following passage, a description of public assistance programs and recipients from a report of the President's Commission on Income Maintenance Programs, helps to remove the veil of myth around welfare. Whatever rumors there may be to the contrary, a life on relief is still a life of misery.

PUBLIC ASSISTANCE

Public Assistance is the major cash income support program aimed specifically at the poor. The basic components of current Public Assistance programs were enacted in the midst of the Depression in 1935, along with Old Age and Survivors Insurance and Unemployment Insurance. Aid was granted only to certain categories of the needy: the blind (Aid to the Blind), the aged (Old Age Assistance), and mothers with dependent

From *Poverty amid Plenty: The American Paradox. The Report of the President's Commission on Income Maintenance Programs* (Washington, D.C.: U.S. Government Printing Office, November 1969).

children (Aid to Families with Dependent Children). Membership in one of these categories was accepted as proof of nonemployability. In later years a program for the disabled (Aid to the Permanently and Totally Disabled) was added, and an Unemployed Father (AFDC–UF) provision was added to AFDC to assist families with an unemployed father in the home. These Federally supported programs cover the bulk of Public Assistance, but there are also State and local programs of General Assistance in which the Federal Government has no part. The General Assistance programs are not necessarily restricted to any categorical group and are small in scope. In February 1969 more than 10 million Americans were receiving aid from all Assistance programs, including General Assistance.

Although the programs are financed jointly by Federal, State, and local governments, they are administered at the State and local level. The aggregate expenditure for cash assistance benefits in 1968 was $5 billion, of which the Federal share was $3.1 billion. Table 1 shows the expenditures by program for calendar 1968, and the number of recipients aided by each program at some point during the year.

Table 1. *Number of Recipients of Public Assistance and Money Payments to Recipients by Program, 1968*

Program	Number of recipients[a] (millions)	Benefits (millions)	
		Total	Federal
Old Age Assistance (OAA)	2.3	$1,673	$1,135
Aid to Blind (AB)	.1	88	50
Aid to the Permanently and Totally Disabled (APTD)	.9	655	389
Aid to Families with Dependent Children (AFDC) (Includes unemployed father provision AFDC-UF)	8.0	2,824	1,540
Total	11.3	$5,240	$3,114

Source: U.S. Department of Health, Education, and Welfare, National Center for Social Statistics.
[a] Aided any time during calendar 1968. The number of persons receiving aid at any particular time is somewhat lower.

Local General Assistance programs provided another $0.4 billion to 800,000 recipients.

THE FEDERAL ROLE IN ADMINISTRATION

Because these are grants-in-aid to States to support their programs, individual States have great latitude in shaping their own programs and, indeed, in deciding whether or not to operate any program. No program is mandatory for any State. To be eligible for Federal matching funds, a State must meet only a small number of Federal requirements. While most States have elected to join all programs, they did not do so all at once. Only twenty-five States, for example, have instituted AFDC-Unemployed Father programs to aid families with an unemployed father in the home, as authorized under a 1961 Amendment to the Social Security Act. Nevada has never adopted a program of Aid to the Permanently and Totally Disabled. Similarly, there is no Federal power to set payment standards or to require States to pay benefits equal to the need standards which they have determined themselves. Adequacy of grants in a State depends entirely on the will and the priorities of the State Government. If a State does not have the funds or chooses not to spend them on Public Assistance, the Federal Government has little recourse.

The most important mechanism for control that the Federal Government has at its disposal is the power to reject a State plan on the basis of noncompliance with Federal law, and to cut off funds completely. In no case has a State been discontinued. At any given time, many State programs are not in compliance with one or another provision of the Federal regulations, but the administering agency is hesitant to cut off funds, since those hurt will be the poor, not the State.

Thus, there are, in effect, fifty different cash assistance programs each of OAA, AFDC, and AB, twenty-five programs of AFDC–UF, and forty-nine programs of APTD (exclusive of programs in the District of Columbia, Guam, Puerto Rico, and the Virgin Islands). There are then over 300 separate programs of cash Public Assistance receiving Federal funds, covering different categories of the population under widely varying standards.

Clearly, it is impossible to describe welfare as a monolithic structure. Complete and accurate knowledge of the actual operations of State and local programs is not available at the Federal level. New administrative guidelines may be issued by the Federal Government with comparatively little information on how they will be interpreted and instituted below this level. Changes can be implemented locally without the knowledge of Federal policymakers. The multiplicity of governments involved has made effective policy coordination nearly impossible.

ELIGIBILITY DETERMINATION

Less than two-fifths of the poor receive aid from any of these assistance programs. Because programs are restricted to specific categories, many poor persons are excluded entirely. Poor working men and their families are ineligible for Federal programs, and only a few States supplement earnings through local programs. Eligibility is determined by an income which falls below a minimum standard set by the State of residence, membership in an aid category, and a variety of nonfinancial tests. The nonfinancial tests seem to keep many low-income persons in eligible categories of the population from receiving benefits.

Membership in an aid category is determined as follows: for OAA, one must be 65 years old or more; for AB, one must have less than 20/200 vision in the better eye with correcting lens; for APTD, one must be certified medically as permanently and totally disabled and usually one must need the care and support of another person; and for AFDC, there must be a child who is deprived of the care and support of at least one parent due to absence, incapacity, death, or unemployment.

In ascertaining the income of potential aid recipients, the cash value of assets generally is considered as income, so that they must be liquidated by would-be recipients. An exception is frequently made for property used as a home, but a limit is placed on its value. In 31 States, liens are taken on the homes of recipients.

Nonfinancial eligibility tests vary widely among the States, and within each State for the different categories of assistance. Factors which have been commonly used by States include:

requirements that applicants be U.S. citizens;

requirements that applicants have resided in the State for some period up to five years;

requirements that anything in excess of small amounts of assets, or insurance policies be disposed of to be eligible;

requirements that a woman maintain a "suitable home" to be eligible for AFDC. Under this provision official scrutiny of morals is encouraged; and

requirements that relatives' income be taken into account in determining eligibility, despite the fact that some relatives (e.g., grandparents) have no legal responsibility to provide support, and regardless of whether any support is, in fact, provided.

States have been free to apply these and other criteria so as to restrict eligibility and minimize welfare expenditures, despite the fact that most of the programs' cost are paid by the Federal Government. Many of these regulations have operated to treat welfare recipients as a class apart; they have imposed restrictions on recipients that would not be enforceable if applied to the general public under civil law.

In recent years, many of the rules established by State legislatures and welfare departments have been overturned by the courts on constitutional grounds. Residence requirements were held unconstitutional by the Supreme Court in a decision handed down in April 1969. "Suitable home" provisions also were overturned. The number of cases in which well-established State regulations have been found to be unconstitutional is particularly disturbing in view of the number of years that those regulations have been applied to applicants for and recipients of Public Assistance.

BUDGET DETERMINATION

The income level which is needed to sustain a poor individual or family is determined by States in accord with periodic budget studies. The amount of budgeted need varies by program and with family size and composition. The budget levels set are often many years out of date, since they are adjusted infrequently. These budget levels are not necessarily the amount which the State will pay in benefits.

The amount States set as needed for an AFDC family of four ranged from $144 in North Carolina to $332 in New Jersey and $419 in Alaska in 1968. For an aged woman living alone, the "need" ranged from $82 in South Carolina to $182 in Nebraska and $262 in Alaska in the same year. The average budgeted need for a family of four on AFDC was $238 in April of 1968, or slightly below $60 per month per person. For a single elderly person the average budgeted need at the same time came to $124. Thus, it is clear that budget standards vary considerably for individuals, depending on the program for which they are eligible.

. . . The variation in allowable rent and in the food budget among programs seems unrealistic: It is unlikely that the food requirements of an active adult female raising children are less than those of an aged person, yet the AFDC mother is allotted $26.50 for food per month against $39 for a recipient of Old Age Assistance.

BENEFIT AMOUNTS

Not only are budget standards generally inadequate, but most States do not pay the full amounts that they have set as minimum requirements. Twenty-six States make payments that fall short of their own minimum standards in AFDC and sixteen in OAA. The reduced payments are determined by applying reduction formulas and imposing legislative ceilings on payments to cases. . . . Thus, Alabama which has a cost standard of $177 for a family of four on AFDC pays only $89. Rarely do payments approach the poverty level.

The reduction formulas lead to wide variations among States in *average* payments to recipients. In January 1969 AFDC recipients received an average of $9.50 in Mississippi and $65.50 in Massachusetts. . . .

Public Assistance payments raise recipients' living standards more than no payments at all, but clearly do not provide enough income to facilitate long-range planning or to ease short-run problems substantially. Requirements that assets must be exhausted or signed over to the welfare department reduce financial resources to the lowest level, and make it almost impossible for recipients to accumulate any savings.

The failure to provide enough income to maintain the health of potentially employable persons, to cover costs of training or searching for jobs, or to provide adequate nourishment and clothing for children is inconsistent with a desire to provide recipients with hope for the future. In New York City where AFDC grants are among the highest in the Nation, 30 percent of the welfare mothers with children in school in one survey said that, at times, the children stayed home from school because they did not have the necessary shoes or clothes. Twenty percent reported that they sometimes kept their children home from school because they were ashamed of the way the children were dressed.

Indications come from a variety of sources that many assistance recipients are hungry, due to a need to juggle the food budgets to meet other needs. Allocations for rent are substantially underbudgeted in most areas of the country, and recipients must make up the difference from funds allotted for other purposes. Witnesses at Commission hearings stated that often the money must be taken out of the food budget.

Testimony elicited at field hearings bore witness to the hardships — physical, emotional, psychological, and social — worked on recipients. Several witnesses hinted at engaging in illegal activities to supplement their welfare checks in order to survive. The reactions of these and other recipient witnesses ranged from gratitude for aid but hope for more, to resignation to low living standards, to professed lack of understanding as to why levels were so low, to anger and bitterness and professed knowledge that "the system" is designed to keep them "down."

The following figures from a survey of the AFDC caseload conducted by the Department of Health, Education, and Welfare in 1967, indicated low living standards borne by AFDC families:

- 11.2% had no private use of a kitchen;
- 24.0% had no hot and cold running water;
- 22.5% had no private use of a flush toilet;
- 22.4% had no private use of a bathroom with shower or tub;
- 30.1% had not enough beds for all family members;
- 24.8% had not enough furniture so that everyone could sit down while eating;
- 45.8% had no milk for the children sometime in the past six months because of lack of money; and
- 17.4% had children who stayed home from school sometime in the past six months due to lack of shoes or clothes.

Clearly, recipients of aid are in very poor condition, despite the existence of Public Assistance. Public Assistance generally enables recipients barely to continue to exist.

CHARACTERISTICS OF RECIPIENTS

Old Age Assistance recipients have a median age of 76.6 years, 4.1 years higher than the median for the group of all persons 65 and over. Women make up two-thirds of the caseload and 66 percent of them are widows. Because of physical or mental conditions, 17 percent of OAA recipients are confined to their homes and 8 percent are confined to their beds. Over 54 percent live in nonmetropolitan areas, and over 35 percent of all recipients live alone.

About half of the APTD recipients are disabled by the chronic diseases usually associated with old age, and one-fourth are disabled by mental diseases and disorders. The recipients are concentrated in older age groups and tend to live in nonmetropolitan areas. Many of them have never been married. Their educational level is extremely low. Of those who worked, most men were laborers and most women were domestic servants. In spite of permanent and total disablement, one-fourth of all APTD recipients live alone. One in twenty live in a hotel or boarding house.

Blind recipients are divided about equally between metropolitan and nonmetropolitan areas. Their median age is 61.3 years, and almost 75 percent are 50 or over. The recipients are divided about equally between men and women, and a large proportion never have been married. Eighteen percent live alone. Their educational level is generally very low. Of the men, 42 percent have not worked in the last ten years.

In almost three-fourths of AFDC cases the father is absent due to divorce, separation, desertion, imprisonment, or other reasons. Most AFDC recipients are urban residents. Most children are quite young, with the median age estimated at about 7.4 years; almost 75 percent are under 13. Although many families are large, almost two-thirds of the families have three or fewer children. In a typical family there is only one adult — the mother — and she is unemployed and probably unemployable in the short-run. Although her educational level is high compared to that of persons in the adult programs, she still tends to be under-educated. Over 40 percent have not completed grade school.

GROWTH IN WELFARE

At the time of their enactment, the Public Assistance programs were expected to wither away as the social insurance programs matured and developed. Instead they have grown at an accelerating rate. For . . . social insurance programs can provide adequate income only to persons or families with long labor force attachments at high earnings. Despite 33 years of maturing of the OASDI system, for example, one million beneficiaries of Old Age Insurance have incomes low enough to receive Old Age Assistance supplementation.

Most of the rapid growth in Public Assistance is accounted for by the AFDC program. The adult programs have remained fairly stable. The number of AFDC recipients has risen from 3 million in December 1960 to 6.5 million in December 1969. Costs have risen from $994 million in 1960 to an estimated $3.5 billion in 1969. Continued growth is projected.

Factors accounting for the recent growth cannot be isolated precisely, but the following seem to account for most of the increase:

Eligibility requirements have been broadened. Federal legislation since 1961 has enabled States to extend aid to families headed by unemployed parents, to a second adult in the family, to older children if attending school, and to a few other groups.

Rejection of residency requirements, the "suitable home" provision, and the "man in the house" rule by the Supreme Court has increased the number of families who are eligible.

States have increased their budget standards, thereby increasing the number of potentially eligible people. A recent study attributes much of the growth in New York City to this factor.

An increase in the proportion of poor families applying for welfare. The poverty program and recently organized welfare rights groups have reduced the stigma attached to welfare and encouraged families to apply.

A rise in the proportion of applicants who are accepted. Welfare departments and individual caseworkers have considerable discretion in determining eligibility and payments. They have become more liberal in exercising this discretion, either as a conscious policy or as a response to a changed political climate.

A change in the composition of poor families headed by women. While there has been no increase in the total number of poor families headed by women, there are indications that these families who remain poor are more in need of and more likely to receive welfare because of factors such as large family size.

Increasing urbanization of the population. The great migration from rural to urban areas since World War II has brought more poor people to the city, where a cash income is required for survival, and reduced the number of poor farmers subsisting on crops and in-kind income.

EMPLOYMENT AND WELFARE

Many assistance recipients have worked in the past, despite the fact that there was little profit in it. Originally, every dollar earned by an aid recipient reduced the payment by a dollar, in effect imposing a 100 percent tax on earnings. In 1962 recipients were allowed to deduct costs of employment, such as bus fare, from total earnings. Thus, if a fatherless family consisting of a mother and three children were entitled to benefits of $160 per month and if the woman earned $60, benefits were reduced by $60, minus costs of employment. The mother's total net income — $160 — was no greater than if she had not worked. Her children may have been left unattended, her own housework neglected, and her income unchanged. Yet in November 1967, 18 percent of AFDC cases had some income from earnings. Average monthly earnings of the workers in these families were $138. Of the mothers who worked, the average gross earnings received were $138 per month. In the absence of these earnings, AFDC payments could have been $200 million higher in that year.

In an effort to provide some financial incentive for finding work, the Social Security Act was amended in late 1967 to allow assistance recipients to retain more of their earnings. Currently, they may keep the first $30 and one-third of the remainder of their monthly earnings in addition to their assistance benefits. This change, which imposes a 67 percent marginal tax rate on earnings, is unlikely to reduce either the costs or the number of recipients. In order to get off the program, many would have to earn more than their skills allow. In New York City, the adult in a family of four would have to earn $2.54 per hour for a full year in order to become ineligible for any welfare benefits. Because benefits are based on family size, heads of larger families would have to earn even higher wages before income from wages alone exceeded welfare benefits plus one-third of wages. Yet many people are receiving welfare precisely because their lack of education and marketable skills keeps them from jobs paying adequate salaries.

Assistance recipients commonly remain out of the labor force due to lack of suitable child care facilities at reasonable cost. Despite availability of Federal funds to provide day care, States have been unable to develop facilities.

34. Nigger

Dick Gregory

Economists, sociologists, and social workers have written tomes about welfare, almost always as outsiders looking in. Consequently, their books too often ignore the recipients' humanity and aspirations.
Here Dick Gregory, black civil rights leader and a foremost Ameri-

can humorist, draws from his own experience to paint a picture of life on welfare. What emerges is a vivid portrait of his mother that bears little resemblance to the stereotype of a woman on welfare. Like untold welfare mothers who today inhabit Watts, Harlem, and Hough, Mrs. Gregory was hard-working, proud, and loved her children. But she knew that poverty doomed them to inadequate housing, food, and medical care. Their very survival depended on her accepting the humiliation of the system that forced her to become a "welfare cheater."

Like a lot of Negro kids, we never would have made it without our Momma. When there was no fatback to go with the beans, no socks to go with the shoes, no hope to go with tomorrow, she'd smile and say: "We ain't poor, we're just broke." Poor is a state of mind you never grow out of, but being broke is just a temporary condition. She always had a big smile, even when her legs and feet swelled from high blood pressure and she collapsed across the table with sugar diabetes. You have to smile twenty-four hours a day, Momma would say. If you walk through life showing the aggravation you've gone through, people will feel sorry for you, and they'll never respect you. She taught us that man has two ways out in life — laughing or crying. There's more hope in laughing. A man can fall down the stairs and lie there in such pain and horror that his own wife will collapse and faint at the sight. But if he can just hold back his pain for a minute she might be able to collect herself and call the doctor. It might mean the difference between his living to laugh again or dying there on the spot. . . .

But I wonder about my Momma sometimes, and all the other Negro mothers who got up at 6 A.M. to go to the white man's house with sacks over their shoes because it was so wet and cold. I wonder how they made it. They worked very hard for the man, they made his breakfast and they scrubbed his floors and they diapered his babies. They didn't have too much time for us.

I wonder about my Momma, who walked out of a white woman's clean house at midnight and came back to her own where the lights had been out for three months, and the pipes were frozen and the wind came in through the cracks. She'd have to make deals with the rats: leave some food out for them so they wouldn't gnaw on the doors or bite the babies. The roaches, they were just like part of the family.

I wonder how she felt telling those white kids she took care of to brush

From *Nigger: An Autobiography* by Dick Gregory with Robert Lipsyte. Copyright © 1964 by Dick Gregory Enterprises, Inc. Published by E. P. Dutton and Company, Inc. Reprinted with permission of E. P. Dutton and Company, Inc., and of George Allen and Unwin Ltd.

their teeth after they ate, to wash their hands after they peed. She could never tell her own kids because there wasn't soap or water back home.

    I wonder how my Momma felt when we came home from school with a list of vitamins and pills and cod liver oils the school nurse said we had to have. Momma would cry all night, and then go out and spend most of the rent money for pills. A week later the white man would come for his eighteen dollars rent and Momma would plead with him to wait until tomorrow. She had lost her pocketbook. The relief check was coming. The white folks had some money for her. Tomorrow. I'd be hiding in the coal closet because there was only supposed to be two kids in the flat, and I could hear the rent man curse my Momma and call her a liar. And when he finally went away, Momma put the sacks on her shoes and went off to the rich white folks' house to dress the rich white kids so their mother could take them to a special baby doctor. . . .

    I wonder how my Momma stayed so good and beautiful in her soul when she worked seven days a week on swollen legs and feet, how she kept teaching us to smile and laugh when the house was dark and cold and she never knew when one of her hungry kids was going to ask about Daddy.

    I wonder how she kept from teaching us hate when the social worker came around. She was a nasty bitch with a pinched face who said: "We have reason to suspect you are working, Miss Gregory, and you can be sure I'm going to check on you. We don't stand for welfare cheaters."

    Momma, a welfare cheater. A criminal who couldn't stand to see her kids go hungry, or grow up in slums and end up mugging people in dark corners. I guess the system didn't want her to get off relief, the way it kept sending social workers around to be sure Momma wasn't trying to make things better.

    I remember how that social worker would poke around the house, wrinkling her nose at the coal dust on the chilly linoleum floor, shaking her head at the bugs crawling over the dirty dishes in the sink. My Momma would have to stand there and make like she was too lazy to keep her own house clean. She could never let on that she spent all day cleaning another woman's house for two dollars and carfare. She would have to follow that nasty bitch around those drafty three rooms, keeping her fingers crossed that the telephone hidden in the closet wouldn't ring. Welfare cases weren't supposed to have telephones.

    But Momma figured that some day the Gregory kids were going to get off North Taylor Street and into a world where they would have to compete with kids who grew up with telephones in their houses. She didn't want us to be at a disadvantage. She couldn't explain that to the social worker. And she couldn't explain that while she was out spoon-feeding somebody else's kids, she was worrying about her own kids, that she could rest her mind by picking up the telephone and calling us — to find out if we had bread for our baloney or baloney for our bread, to see if any of us had gotten run over by the streetcar while we played in the gutter, to make sure the house hadn't burnt down from the papers and magazines we stuffed in the stove when the coal ran out.

35. Why the Poor Remain Poor

President's Commission on Income Maintenance Programs

Many of America's affluent middle class still cling to the myth of Horatio Alger: If only the poor would work harder, they could rise out of their poverty.

Not so, claims the President's Commission on Income Maintenance Programs. Our economic and social structure virtually guarantees poverty for millions. The Commission then shows why, with few bootstraps available, the poor are doomed to remain poor — unless society aids them.

The Commission's conclusions, reached after a 22-month study, are particularly noteworthy considering the establishment backgrounds of its members: mainly board chairmen and presidents of banking, insurance, and manufacturing firms and prominent persons from the legal, academic, political, and labor worlds.

The paradox of poverty in the midst of plenty causes many to ask why some people remain poor when so many of their fellow Americans have successfully joined the ranks of the affluent. It is often assumed that anyone who wishes to live well can achieve that objective by seeking and accepting work. It is often argued that the poor are to blame for their own circumstances and should be expected to lift themselves from poverty.

The Commission has concluded that these assertions are incorrect. Our economic and social structure virtually guarantees poverty for millions of Americans. Unemployment and underemployment are basic facts of American life. The risks of poverty are common to millions more who depend on earnings for their income. We all grow old. We all can fall victim to unemployment caused by technological change or industrial relocation. Any of us could become sick or disabled. And becoming

From *Poverty amid Plenty: The American Paradox. The Report of the President's Commission on Income Maintenance Programs* (Washington, D.C.: U.S. Government Printing Office, November 1969).

unpoor is extraordinarily difficult. What does a disabled man, an elderly couple, or a child *do* to escape poverty? How does a woman with six children survive while she is hunting work or being trained? How does an unskilled, middle-aged laborer adjust to the loss of a job?

The simple fact is that most of the poor remain poor because access to income through work is currently beyond their reach.

THE AGED

Old age is usually a period of nonemployment. Society neither expects nor assists the aged to work. Retirement at age 65 is common in both industry and government, and discrimination in hiring against the aged and aging is common among employers.

The aged possess limited earning potential. They generally are expected to live on pensions, savings, and Social Security benefits. Too frequently, savings and pensions deemed adequate at an earlier time become insufficient as inflation raises the cost of living. Millions of hardworking Americans, accustomed all their lives to paying their way, find themselves becoming unalterably and unavoidably poor in old age.

In 1966, 6.4 million aged persons and their dependents were in poverty. Over a million of these persons lived in families where the family head worked for at least part of the year, and almost half a million lived in families where the head worked 50–52 weeks. The average family income was more than $600 below the poverty line; this gap was about equal for low-income aged families whether the head worked or not. Average family income for poor households headed by the aged was below $1,200.

In 1966, 65 percent of the aged were over 70. Half of those over age 65 were 73 or older. The older a person is in the aged population, the less his total income is likely to be. Earning opportunities decline because advancing age often brings increasing infirmity. Moreover, the older a person is, the greater the likelihood that he has not earned high Social Security benefits or accumulated benefits in one of the newer private pension plans, and that he has exhausted his assets.

The poor will remain poor once they retire, and others who retire may become poor in their old age. Opportunities for the aged poor to make any improvement in their own lives are remote and unrealistic. Only public programs can make a difference in their incomes.

THE NONAGED

While the aged apparently can do little about their poverty, what about the 24.6 million *nonaged* persons who were poor in 1966? Six percent of these people were in families headed by aged poor persons, so their poverty can be linked to the elderly family heads on whom they depended. What possibilities do the remaining nonaged persons have to escape poverty through their own efforts? The unpleasant truth is that these possibilities are extraordinarily limited.

The work experience of the 4.5 million nonaged heads of poor families provides dramatic documentation of their limited ability to change substantially their circumstances on their own. In all, the heads of 1.9 million poor families — 42 percent of the total — worked full-time for more than 40 weeks of the year. Most of the remaining heads of families did some work:

Of the 4.5 million nonaged heads of poor families, 3.3 million or 73 percent worked for some period of time during 1966; 1.2 million did not work at all.

Of the 3.3 million who worked, nearly 60 percent worked full-time for most of the year. The rest worked either less than 40 weeks a year or less than 35 hours a week, because of illness, family responsibilities, inability to find sufficient work, or other reasons.

. . . More than 70 percent of the nonaged heads of poor families worked for some period, yet remained in poverty. The Commission considers the fact that 42 percent of the nonaged heads of poor families worked full-time for most of the year to be as significant in understanding poverty as the fact that 58 percent worked less than that, or did not work at all.

The different degrees of participation in the labor force among the poor seem due to chance more than to motivation or other factors. Unemployment or underemployment among the poor are often due to forces that cannot be controlled by the poor themselves. There are not two distinct categories of poor — those who can work and those who can not. Nor can the poor be divided into those who will work and those who will not. For many, the desire to work is strong, but the opportunities are not readily available. The opening or closing of a factory, ill health of the breadwinner, inability to find transportation, loss of a babysitter, weather conditions, and similar factors greatly affect employment opportunities.

Of the 1.2 million poor nonaged family heads who did not work at all in 1966:

Nearly half were women with responsibilities for young children.

Another third were unable to perform any work because of illness or disability.

Of the remaining 230,000, 40 percent were unable to work because they were attending school, and about 15 percent reported that they were simply unable to find any work.

A residual group of about 100,000 remains. It includes those who did not work at all during the year for reasons other than those listed.

Thus, less than three percent of the nonaged heads of poor families might have freely chosen not to work at all. But many in this residual group actually may have had little choice between work and poverty. For example, many poor individuals do not work because of disabilities which ordinarily are not recognized in official statistics, particularly disabilities of a mental, rather than a physical nature.

FACTORS INHIBITING PROGRESS

Clearly, the experience of the poor indicates that work alone is no guarantee of escaping poverty. Why is it that employment — the basic source of income for most Americans — fails the poor?

Several factors account for this. Family size is relevant; the costs of supporting a large number of children can result in poverty for workers with even relatively high earnings. Low wages and/or lack of sufficient hours and weeks of work can account for a good deal of poverty. Disabilities prevent many from working. Poor preparation for working careers and discrimination affect many others. And, for large numbers of people, work is simply not available. Let us examine the impact of these factors more closely.

An Economy at Less than 100 Percent Employment

There is some unemployment even in the best of times, and it is not evenly distributed over the economy. A desire to avoid accelerating inflation has led policymakers to accept some unemployment. But it must be recognized that this policy has much to do with explaining poverty for many families. A 4 percent unemployment rate — considered by many to be the lowest feasible, long-term unemployment rate — means that not everyone can work who wants to work. It also means that wages will be lower than they would be if there were greater competition for workers. It means that young people without work experience, people with low educational attainments, and members of minority groups subject to discrimination will be particularly handicapped in their search for employment. Moreover, official unemployment statistics do not reflect the number of persons who have withdrawn completely from the labor force because of long-term inability to find jobs.

Obviously, the state of the American economy and the consequent structure of opportunities at the local level can enhance or impede employability greatly. A fully employed person, earning good wages one day, can find himself suddenly unemployed and locally unemployable due to a work force reduction or plant closing. In the absence of strong aggregate demand, even well-planned efforts to find jobs can be ineffective.

> We were very much concerned with the fact that young people wanted to work and needed jobs; 2,782 screened applicants were approved. My Committee had a task of contacting private employers to try to develop jobs. We contacted all of the churches of the communities; we contacted approximately 350 private employers. We had the Governor of the State of Iowa coming in to kick it off by announcement. We had good radio, local press, and television coverage. We sent out a letter signed by the mayors of three central cities inviting people to get involved. The end result was that we got nine job offers. The amount of money that we realized from the nine jobs wouldn't pay for the postage and printing costs.[1]

The demand for labor also will affect the outcome of training programs. Many witnesses at Commission hearings expressed frustration at going through training programs which were not geared to jobs currently available or to the skills of the trainees.

> For instance, the Job Opportunity Center which was very effective, listened to some technician who had no feeling for the programs at all and trained 40 teacher's aides. But nobody alerted the school board or got any consideration from them as to whether they would hire them. So these people are right back on the streets where they are more frustrated than ever because they know now that they have some training.[2]

> The program put me into them (three different types of training for jobs). What I was wondering is if they could put somebody in there who has been through the mill like I have and talk to the people, tell them what kind of a job they could get and what they would like. . . . Because they sent me to Lowrey Field for sheet metal. Well, they say it pays pretty good but it takes four years to learn the trade and then $400 to join the union. And then you have to know too much math and algebra and all that.[3]

> I have been trained . . . I was trained with my cane (for the blind). Training people for what, for sitting in the corner? They have given me the training of a king or queen and today I still sit in my corner with my knitting in my hand. . . . I have been trained to take dictaphone dictation and I have been trained to do answering services and I have been trained to do sewing. . . . And what am I doing today? Sitting in my corner, waiting for the world to call me a leech. I am not willing to give any more time for any more training, thank you.[4]

---

[1] Witness before Commission, Waterloo, Iowa.
[2] Witness before Commission, Denver, Colorado.
[3] Witness before Commission, Denver, Colorado.
[4] Witness before Commission, Albuquerque, New Mexico.

> Well . . . back in 1965, I went to the Bureau of Indian Affairs school . . . and they accepted me and I received my training in Chicago. The trouble was that I went out for welding and somehow when I got up there they had me down as a barber. (After completing barbering courses and finally receiving training as a welder) I tried to get a job and they throw the bit up to me about "Do you have any tools?" or "Do you have any experience?" And I say no. And I can't get no job, they won't hire me. I might as well go out and dig a ditch for Tom or Joe . . . because I am sick and tired of going to trade school.[5]
>
> The whole system is bad . . . you start them on training full of hope and what guarantee? What job is there after the end of that training? Nothing but a waiting list.[6]
>
> People are training for the jobs that they originally were hopeful of getting. But the problem has been that we haven't been able to locate them a job with industry because of the fact, as you probably are aware by now, there are no jobs in Albuquerque, New Mexico.[7]

When there are no jobs for the head of the family, then other members of the family may have to help support the family. One witness told the Commission:

> A poor family cannot put his child to work according to age, he puts him to work according to the need of his family.[8]

In 1966 at least 160,000 male family heads were forced to work less than they desired because of an inability to find more steady employment. More than a million others were working part-time hours at low-paying marginal tasks.

One witness heard by the Commission, for example, spends part of the year raising cotton on a ten-acre plot in return for a share of the product. After paying all the costs associated with raising the crop, his net income from sharecropping is $400 annually. In addition, he earns $5.00 daily as a tractor operator when that work is available. During the winter, he sells firewood to supplement his income. He testified:

> Nine people live off of it. Just figure how could you do it with nine people; just one biscuit a day. A man with $5.00 can hardly cover that. And I only receive that through the summer. Winter time there ain't nothing to do. They give us a little something to do around and pay up what we owe; you don't get through paying what you

---

[5] Witnesses before Commission, Isleta Indian Pueblo, near Albuquerque, New Mexico.
[6] Witness before Commission, Los Angeles, California.
[7] Witness before Commission, Albuquerque, New Mexico (director of a training program).
[8] Witness before Commission, Quincy, Florida.

owe. And if there were something to do, I would sure appreciate doing it. I wouldn't back off from no work.[9]

Low Earnings

Full-time employment at the current Federal minimum wage of $1.60 an hour will provide a family of four or more with an annual income below the poverty line. In 1966, 3.1 million men working full-time, two-thirds of whom were family heads, earned less than $1.60 an hour. In 1967, almost half of the Nation's labor force was employed in occupations or industries not covered by the minimum wage provisions of the Fair Labor Standards Act. Many of the families of such workers are poor.

The sources of low wages can be found on both the demand and the supply sides of the labor market. The spread of complex automated industrial technology continually reduces the relative demand for workers in low-skilled occupations. Emigration from the agricultural sector, the growing number of youth, and increased participation of middle-aged women in the labor force add to the supply of low-wage job candidates.

In certain instances, however, low earnings reflect a breakdown in the market itself, either because of immobility of labor and capital resources or because of discrimination in hiring. There is overwhelming evidence that the employment opportunities of nonwhite workers and female workers are more limited in number and lower in quality than those open to white male workers.

The fact that so many workers accept employment at very low wages indicates the basic strength of the work ethic in the economy. Although their jobs are often unpleasant and physically demanding, many workers have remained ready and willing to work for wages which cannot keep their families out of poverty.

Large Families

Large families need substantial incomes just to avoid poverty. According to the Social Security Administration's poverty index for 1968, a nonfarm family composed of two parents and five children would need at least $5,789 to maintain even the most basic standard of living. If the head worked full-time year-round, he would have to earn nearly $3.00 per hour to achieve this target. In 1966 over 40 percent of the poor families with children headed by employed men under age 65 had more than three children to support. With an average family size of 4.6 persons, many working family heads are financially handicapped even when earning a relatively good annual income.

---

[9] Witness before Commission, St. Joseph, Louisiana.

Poverty and Education

The association between education and income is a familiar one. Formal education not only enhances the quality of one's life, it also pays a high dividend in material rewards. Those with little education are at a disadvantage in the labor market. The heads of nearly three-quarters of all poor families in 1966 did not graduate from high school. Indeed, nearly one in five of the poor nonaged male and female family heads had completed less than six years of formal schooling — a level barely above functional illiteracy.

Limited education does not guarantee a life of poverty, but the income distribution is highly skewed in favor of the more educated. One fourth of those with less than eight years of schooling earned less than $3,000 while only 6 percent of high school graduates had earnings that low. In 1967, the median income of families whose heads had completed less than eight years of schooling was about one-third that of families headed by college graduates. The gap between their median incomes was about $8,000.

With a high proportion of the poor uneducated, it is unrealistic to expect great upward mobility in terms of income. Those with low education levels receive the low-paying jobs that offer little opportunity for advancement. Once family responsibilities are acquired, this handicap is imposed on the entire family.

The effects of limited education are quite pervasive. For many of the undereducated, the most routine job-seeking activities may be difficult. People who are embarrassed by their inability to speak correctly, or to understand questions and the reasons behind them, or to fill out detailed forms quickly, or to grasp instructions, are particularly disadvantaged in securing a job. When a job opportunity is extended some of the uneducated do not take it because of their conviction that they cannot compete effectively. At an earlier point in our economic history, brawn and willingness to work would have been sufficient, but increasingly even menial jobs require high school diplomas. Many persons have been left out of the job market, not because they cannot do the work, but because employers would rather hire "over-educated" workers. One able-bodied male who did heavy manual farm work during the season testified that he could not move to the city and do more steady factory work because "Most jobs like that won't hire a guy without an education (who) can't fill out a form."[10]

Poverty and Location

Two-thirds of the poor lived in urban areas in 1966. However, the risk of being poor was greater for those who resided in rural areas, whether they

---

[10] Witness before Commission, Mississippi County, Arkansas.

lived on or off the farm. Almost 20 percent of the rural population was poor, compared with about 14 percent for the urban population. Opportunities for earning are fewer in rural than urban areas, and work is more often seasonal.

The poor are somewhat concentrated geographically. Twenty percent of Southern families were poor in 1966, while only 9 percent of non-Southern families were poor. Half of all poor families lived in the South. Although nearly two-thirds of all poor nonwhite families lived in the South in 1966, Southern poverty was by no means confined to nonwhites. Close to 2 million white families — 42 percent of all poor white families — were residents of Southern States. The conditions that are conducive to poverty — low wages, low average education, seasonal employment, and declining opportunities for the unskilled — are especially prevalent in the South. These factors cross racial lines, although nonwhites are particularly affected.

Another focal point for poverty is the inner core of major cities, from which it is often difficult, time consuming, and expensive to reach well-paying jobs in outlying areas.

> We have one new employer who will employ 1600 people. A great many of these women will be trained by the employer. It is not essential that they have previous experience. But there is no transportation to this particular employer's place of business.[11]
>
> In your core city, the jobs that are available will not pay a sustaining wage. They run from 80 cents per hour probably up to $1.30. A person who has a family to support cannot do it on this wage scale. . . . Another thing is that jobs that do pay a sustaining wage are located in your suburban areas. There is no way of getting transportation to get to them. Transportation in Denver is inadequate. They don't run adequate buses to job sites. Most of the people don't have cars.[12]

In many American cities, the story is the same: There are no jobs where the poor live, the poor cannot afford — or are not allowed — to live where the jobs are opening up, and there is no transportation between these two places.

Poverty and the Female-Headed Family

The employment opportunities for women heading poor families are more limited than those for men. Because of their family responsibilities, women may be severely restricted from holding down even a part-time job. One in every two women heading poor families did not work in 1966.

---

[11] Witness before Commission, Atlanta, Georgia.
[12] Witness before Commission, Denver, Colorado.

Getting and keeping a job imposes certain conditions that are especially burdensome for women heading poor families. Working requires either that all children be old enough to care for themselves or that some day care provisions be made for the children. There are few such facilities available, even for those who can afford to pay. Many women heading families with children can work only at the expense of their family responsibilities.

> I would like to state . . . that I do have a high school education; I have one year of college. I have ten years working experience behind me. The reason I am not employed at the present and am having to take AFDC is because of inadequate child care for my children.[13]

Many of the jobs available do not pay enough to cover the cost of child care and other employment expenses. Jobs for which the majority of female heads of households qualify are at the lower end of the pay scale. In 1966 almost 50 percent of all employed white women heading poor families and 75 percent of nonwhite women heading poor families worked in service occupations, one of the lowest paid groups. For many such women, Public Assistance offers a more secure existence. It has been estimated that 70 percent of mothers receiving Aid to Families with Dependent Children could not earn more money by working than they receive in assistance payments because of their low skill and educational levels. One witness told the Commission:

> I said that I was a New Careerist in the CEP, Concentrated Employment Program. I earn $1.60 an hour and I take home $242.22 every month for the support of myself and three children. My rent is $75 a month. The cost of my being employed far exceeds my income. . . . By this I mean that it would be to my advantage to be on welfare. I am one of those people that are motivated, but is it worth it? I sometimes wonder.[14]

Discrimination and Poverty

At first glance it seems that poverty is a white problem — two-thirds of the poor are white, while one-third are nonwhite. However, 12 percent of the white population is poor while over 40 percent of the much smaller nonwhite population is poor.

The greater incidence of poverty among nonwhites reflects several factors: larger family size, lower average earnings, a greater proportion of female-headed families, lower educational levels, and the greater proportion of nonwhites living in the South. Yet, holding each of these factors

---

[13] Witness before Commission, Seattle, Washington.
[14] Witness before Commission, Albuquerque, New Mexico.

constant and comparing across racial lines, nonwhites remain at a disadvantage.

Much of this differential is a result of direct or indirect discrimination. Many employers still are unwilling to hire members of minority groups. Others will employ them only in the most menial jobs. Some minority group members find themselves unable to compete for jobs because discrimination in public programs has provided them with inferior education or training.

> Our (Negro high) school is not up to the (white) standard. I remember a few days ago I visited our school and to my surprise—and this has been existing for several years—there were five classes in the gym going on at the same time, and one of these classes was a music class.[15]
>
> My check will run about $120 and his (a white) will run two something. . . . He probably might be cleaning up. He is not doing the type of (heavy) work that I am doing.[16]
>
> Ability testing is done in English. I would like to take all these English-speaking teachers and give them a test in Spanish and see how their ability is going to run. Terminology and pictures with which the child is not familiar are used. The Puerto Ricans have never seen a sleigh, because we never had snow.[17]

MOBILITY AMONG THE POOR

The little that is known about changes in income status over time is not heartening. Poverty persists in families headed by year-round, full-time workers. It persists in multiple-earner families. And it persists, to varying degrees, among the aged and nonaged, among families headed by men and women, and among blacks and whites.

Between 1965 and 1966, the number of households classified as poor declined by almost 3 percent. This net change, however, obscures considerable movement of households into and out of poverty. Some 36 percent of those households classified as poor in 1965 had, for one reason or another, left poverty by 1966. Of those classified as poor in 1966, 34 percent were not poor in the previous year. These flows indicate that the risk of poverty is considerably more pervasive than has been imagined.

Finally, the 64 percent remaining in poverty were disproportionately comprised of nonwhites, female-headed families, those in the South, and those families headed by a person with less than a high school education. For these groups, poverty is not a way station, it is a dead end.

---

[15] Witness before Commission, St. Joseph, Louisiana.
[16] Witness before Commission, St. Joseph, Louisiana.
[17] Witness before a Commission, Philadelphia, Pennsylvania.

Determinants of Poverty Flows

A move across the poverty line — in either direction — can be the consequence of a variety of uncontrollable changes in the household's circumstances. The addition or loss of an earner, a change in the size or composition of the family, a fluctuation in the wage level or hours worked by family members — all bear heavily on the probability that a family will experience a change in its economic status. Certain influences, however, stand out in bold relief.

Work, when available, can contribute significantly to a family's success in avoiding poverty. Over the 1965–1966 period, the rate of escape from poverty for families headed by a full-year worker was nearly twice as large as that for families whose head worked part-year or not at all. Conversely, the rate of entrance into poverty for the latter group was over seven times that of the former. The greater the amount of time the head spent working, the more likely the family was to have left or not to have entered poverty. This was true of whites and nonwhites, for male and female-headed families, and for the young and old. Indeed, in almost every conceivable comparison, those who worked fared better than those who did not.

More striking than the recorded successes are the failures. Of those families classified as poor in 1965 which were headed by a full-time, year-round worker, 43 percent failed to escape poverty during the following year. In terms of absolute numbers there were nearly as many families leaving poverty whose heads worked less than 48 weeks as families whose heads worked 48 or more weeks. Clearly, work alone is no guarantee of leaving poverty.

Extent of Income Mobility

Despite the way statistical indices are often used, poverty is not an either/or state. There are shades of poverty just as there are shades of wealth. This distinction is particularly important in discussing movements across a fixed poverty line. A person whose income is slightly below the poverty line can statistically move out of poverty by increasing his income by a small amount, but his standard of living will remain unchanged and he still will feel poor.

Of those persons who moved out of poverty between 1965 and 1966, a large number did not move far: one-eighth remained within $200 of the poverty line and one-quarter remained within $500 of the poverty line. For families such as these, it might be questioned whether the recorded change was significant. Of those falling into poverty, almost one-fifth fell less than $200 below the line and nearly half were within $500 of the line. Thus much of the movement into and out of poverty is really movement close to the line.

CONCLUSION

The persistence of poverty and the extensive movements into and out of poverty testify to the fact that problems of income inadequacy and income insecurity are common to large segments of the population. Age and disability, loss of employment for technological or personal reasons, large family size, and poorly paid employment, pose potential risks to all who depend on wages. And, in our society, 80 percent of the population receive the major portion of their income from wages. The wage earner's income is highly vulnerable to the chance circumstances of life. Few families, for example, could weather long-term illness of the earner without serious financial problems, even if they possessed savings, health insurance, or accumulated sick leave. Few families could afford the retraining of a laid-off primary worker without great difficulty. The living standard of most families would be seriously jeopardized, and some would become poor.

For most of those who are currently poor, changes in economic status are largely beyond their control. Generally, they are doing what they can considering their age, health status, social circumstances, location, education, and opportunities for employment. Poverty is not a chosen way of life. Both the statistical data and personal observations by members of this Commission have made it clear to us that most of the poor are poor because affluence is beyond their grasp. The aged poor have made their contribution as workers and now many are dependent on inadequate retirement incomes. The disabled are similarly handicapped. The working poor are attempting to be productive and still are poor.

With so many working at jobs that are both unpleasant and financially unrewarding, one wonders how the stereotype of the malingering poor can be sustained. It is wrong that so much attention is focused on the few laggards. Among the poor are a small number who will be very successful in escaping from poverty on their own, and a majority who will work hard but remain poor. Very few of those capable of self-help seem to be doing nothing.

For the bulk of the poor, both young and old, unemployed and working, urban and rural, there are few bootstraps available by which they can pull themselves out of poverty. As individuals, some of our poor fellow citizens can overcome the limitations imposed by chronic significant levels of unemployment and underemployment, various forms of discrimination, and an opportunity system which — while perhaps unparalleled in the world — needs to be improved. But as a group they cannot. Society must aid them or they will remain poor.

36. Congress and the Rats

*U.S. Civil Rights Commission
and Congressional Record*

For the urban poor the rat symbolizes the living hell of slum life. Psychologists have found that ghetto children fear rats more than anything else. And with good reason. About 14,000 Americans are bitten by rats each year. Rats are a serious health menace in ghettos, where they chew walls, attack children, and spread disease and terror.

Yet less than two weeks after the start of the Newark riots of 1967, Congress defeated the Rat Extermination Bill of 1967, which would have appropriated $40 million to local governments for a three-year rat control program.

In the first selection a Cleveland slum dweller tells the U.S. Civil Rights Commission what it's like to live with rats. The next three pieces are from the debate on the Rat Extermination Bill. Congresswoman Griffiths testifies in support of the bill, followed by Congressman Devine in opposition and Congressman Kupferman in support of the bill.

Rat control funds were eventually approved by Congress, but the national response to this daily scourge of slums is a reminder that the pleas of the poor often fall on hostile and callous ears, like those of Congressman Devine and his many colleagues who ridiculed and voted against the original bill.

HATTIE MAE DUGAN, CLEVELAND SLUM DWELLER, TO THE CIVIL RIGHTS COMMISSION

Mrs. Dugan was asked whether rats were a problem in her neighborhood. "Yes, they are. I was living in one apartment, the rats got in bed with me and my sister is still living in the same building and the rats are jumping up and down. The kids they play with rats like a child would play with a dog or something. They chase them around the house and things like this."

The testimony of Hattie Mae Dugan is from the U.S. Civil Rights Commission, *A Time to Listen . . . A Time to Act: Voices from the Ghettos of the Nation's Cities* (Washington, D.C.: U.S. Government Printing Office, November 1967). The statements made before the House of Representatives are from the *Congressional Record* (July 20, 1967).

MARTHA GRIFFITHS (D.-MICH.)
TO THE HOUSE OF REPRESENTATIVES

Mr. Speaker, I thank the chairman.

Before this bill becomes too funny, I would like to say a few words for it. I am in support of this bill, Mr. Speaker. When I first came to this Congress I asked the Library of Congress how much money this Nation had spent on defense in its history. They put some Ph.D.'s to work on the subject, and after 3 months replied that at that time — 13 years ago — we had spent more than $1 trillion on defense. I observed the other day, when we had the Defense appropriation bill — which as I recall was for more than $75 billion — there was only one person who voted "No."

I would like to point out to those who may not be aware of it or to those who may have forgotten it, that rats are Johnny-come-latelys to recorded history. They were unknown in the ancient cities of the world. They came in out of the Arabian deserts about the 12th century, and from that day to this they have killed more human beings than all of the generals in the world combined. They have made Genghis Khan, Hitler, and all the other men look like pikers. Man has attempted to kill them and he has won a few battles, but he has lost the war.

The only enemy that has ever really killed rats is other rats.

For the benefit of those who may not know it, the average rat lives 3 years. It has a rootless tooth that grows 29½ inches in those 3 years. They have been known to cut through 4 feet of reinforced concrete.

All of the methods that one could possibly use cannot conceivably kill off more than 98 percent of the rats in one block. If there are left two males and 10 females, there will be 3,000 rats in 1 year to replace those that have been killed.

Perhaps Members think it does not make any real difference, and perhaps they think this is really a local problem, that it is a family problem, and why not get some rat poison and kill the rats in the household?

I should like to remind the Members who sit here in this body that they eat in restaurants night after night after night, and that all that can be done in this Capitol cannot control the rat population.

Rats are a living cargo of death. Their tails swish through sewers and over that food we eat. Their stomachs are filled with tularemia, amebic dysentery. They carry the most deadly diseases, and some think it is funny. Some do not want to spend $40 million.

Mr. Speaker, if we are going to spend $79 billion to try to kill off a few Vietcong, believe me I would spend $40 million to kill off the most devastating enemy man has ever had.

SAMUEL DEVINE (R.-OHIO)
TO THE HOUSE OF REPRESENTATIVES

The committee report claims "many children" are attacked, "maimed and even killed by rats, as an everyday occurrence." Come, now, let us have some supporting information. I am sure if rats were killing children every day, all of us would have heard something about it. The report goes on to say Philadelphia, St. Louis, and Cleveland have all recently averaged over 50 ratbites per year. Golly, almost one a week — so, spend $40 million. . . .

Inquiry through local dealers indicates rattraps — not mousetraps — sell for $3.30 per dozen or about 28 cents each. A pretty fair brand of cheese costs 49 cents per pound and would bait 35 traps. So, for an extremely small personal investment, nearly every citizen could cooperate and eliminate this problem, and at the same time, save their Government $40 million. Would not this seem to be a wise step, particularly when the President and his advisers are calling on all Americans for more taxes to pay for the costs of Government?

Finally, one of our respected colleagues tells me he has about 23 cats in and around his barns, all of which he will make available to HUD, without charge. These feline ratcatchers are most effective, particularly since they are led by a highly respected tomcat called Cotton that has earned a most enviable reputation in the ratcatching department.

Seriously, here is an excellent opportunity for the President, the administration, the Congress, to do more than pay lipservice to reducing Federal spending, and I urge my colleagues to vote against this bill known as H.R. 11000.

THEODORE KUPFERMAN (D.-N.Y.)
TO THE HOUSE OF REPRESENTATIVES

Mr. Speaker, I was shocked and chagrined at the vote just now. I say this to those who voted "aye" overwhelmingly on the antiriot bill yesterday, that seldom can one find such inconsistency in such a short period of time.

Mr. Speaker, we asserted yesterday Federal supremacy on a local problem to suppress violent dissent, but today we vote to invite violent dissent.

Mr. Speaker, I have seen rat-infested areas and buildings in the slums of the city of New York. Adjoining the congressional district which it is my honor to represent, is the congressional district represented by Adam Clayton Powell. One might say that I am serving as the interim voluntary Congressman for that area.

Mr. Speaker, I have seen some of the conditions which exist there.

If you were a hard-working father coming home from work to find one of young children bitten by a rat, you might very well start a small riot yourself.

Mr. Speaker, I am ashamed of the vote today on this question.

Chapter Nine

The Invisible Poor: Far away or Forgotten

37. Red Man's Heritage: The Lagoon of Excrement

Robert G. Sherrill

> *For three centuries the American Indian has faced systematic destruction of his life and culture. He was defeated by the white man and robbed of his best lands. The growth and affluence of white America is mirrored in the decline and poverty of the Indian, who today has an average life span of only forty-four years. He desperately needs employment, housing and self-sustaining agriculture and industry. But lacking money for equipment, necessity often forces him to lease land to whites at bargain rates.*
>
> *The Indian was "rediscovered" along with poverty in America. But has "rediscovery" made his life any different? Political reporter Robert Sherrill wanted to learn what changes had been made on an Oglala Sioux reservation several years after a much-heralded visit by the late Senator Robert Kennedy. In the following article, Sherrill sadly concludes that an indifferent government has initiated few improvements.*

When important politicians pass through the land of the Oglala Sioux, local Bureau of Indian Affairs officials sometimes persuade Charlie Red Cloud to put on his feathered regalia and come into the reservation's main com-

From Robert G. Sherrill, "Red Man's Heritage: The Lagoon of Excrement," *The Nation*, 209:16 (November 10, 1969), pp. 500–503. Reprinted by permission.

munity, Pine Ridge [South Dakota], to have his picture taken shaking hands with the visiting dignitaries.

Such are the erosions of custom that Charlie is only a ceremonial chief, but he has impeccable credentials, being descended from the "original" Red Cloud, who in the pantheon of Sioux heroes probably ranks just below Sitting Bull, the spoiler of General Custer. A hundred years ago Red Cloud whipped the U.S. Army and forced a treaty on his own terms regarding the penetration of the Sioux hunting domain by white travelers.

So politicians should be proud to shake the hand of Charlie Red Cloud. Yet he is always asked to come to them. They never go out to his home for the ceremonial handshake and photo. And the reasons are obvious. For one thing, they might never make it. In the rainy season the road to Charlie's home, though it is just outside town, is a bog. And to get there the visitor must pass between the city dump on the left and, on the right, a shiny pond into which the community of Pine Ridge poured its raw sewage for several years. From Chief Red Cloud's residence, one has a perfect view of both the dump and the lagoon of excrement.

Another reason why the old chieftain's home may be avoided by visiting politicians is that it is an embarrassment to behold, being, from a distance, almost indistinguishable in size and shape from its outhouse. Charlie has no electricity, no plumbing. In the new democracy of this impoverished reservation, that's the way ceremonial chiefs must live — like just about everybody else.

Because the white man's government feared the original Red Cloud as much as it hated him, it built the old chief a handsome two-story home on the reservation, hoping that that would keep him happy and out of mischief. But since the white man's government today neither fears nor hates Charlie Red Cloud, but is completely indifferent to him, he gets nothing.

No minority group in this country is as poor as the 380,000 or so Indians who live on reservations. The average family income for Indians is said to be about $1,500, but the average on-reservation income is much lower. Unemployment ranges from 45 per cent to 98 per cent, the latter being the winter rate on some of the Dakota reservations. The Bureau of Indian Affairs estimates that 71 per cent of reservation Indians live in inadequate housing, but a more accurate estimate — 90 per cent — is given by Alvin M. Josephy, Jr., in his recent *The Indian Heritage of America*.

These national figures readily apply to the Oglala Sioux. A couple of years ago Robert Kennedy visited the Pine Ridge Reservation. Because he promised to help them, the residents remember him with affection, and they enjoy pointing out the very cabin at which Senator Kennedy began his tour of the town. (It is a one-room cabin which, in fact, looks better than most of the other dwellings.)

Recently, for *The Nation,* I backtracked over Kennedy's path to see what improvements had been made — not by him, since he had no time to make good on his promises, but by others who might have been goaded into action by the national notoriety Kennedy gave to Pine Ridge.

There were a few improvements, but even some of these few seemed to have been made in a mood of black humor. For instance, the Pine Ridge Reservation has a brand-new landing strip. It is long enough to accommodate jetliners, but as far as I could discover, no Indian on this reservation owns even a Piper Cub. Most could not afford a kite.

The Bureau of Indian Affairs disclaims responsibility for this "improvement." They say it was contracted for by the tribe's own politicians and paid for out of the tribe's budget. If that is true, it would support what some of the Indians say — that when the BIA doesn't get to them, their own venal politicians do.

For more than ninety years many of the Oglala Sioux have made every effort to go along with the white man's programs. They have lived in peace, but they have been almost totally unproductive because they have been given nothing to work with. They have no capital base on which to build.

The Pine Ridge Reservation has no bank. It has no dry goods store, no department store, no hotel or motel, no dime store, no theatre, no drugstore worth mentioning, none of the usual outlets for "comfort commerce." Neither does it have a hardware store, a feed store or a farm equipment agency.

The government spent $10,000 on a study of the prospects for building a profitable motel on the reservation, and the study showed that it would work. But the Small Business Administration turned down the application for construction money. Off-reservation banks display the usual coolness to Indian enterprise. It is reportedly easy for an Indian to get a loan to buy a car, but difficult for him to get a loan to buy a tractor.

Aside from the highways that pass through the community of Pine Ridge, there is only one paved street on the "Indian side" of town (on the other side, where the U.S. Public Health Service and Bureau of Indian Affairs bureaucrats live, many of the streets are paved). This one paved street leads to what is locally known, with the wry humor in which these Indians excel, as "the industrial square." There is no industry on industrial square. The only building is a warehouse holding the U.S. Government commodities (flour, meal, etc.) that are given to the Indians to keep them from literally starving to death. The only industry on the reservation is a moccasin factory that hires about thirty Indians. There used to be a couple of fishhook factories, but these died when wholesalers found that the work could be done more cheaply by Swedes and Japanese.

In housing, employment and life style, the 10,000 to 12,000 Sioux (I got differing estimates of the population) on the Pine Ridge Reservation are still untouched by the benevolence of Washington. A few families are living in abandoned auto bodies. Some families live in tents, some in abandoned chicken coops. Many families (possibly as many as 50 per cent, conservative observers say) will spend this winter and the rest of their lives in minuscule huts with dirt floors. At least 75 per cent of the dwellings on this reservation have no plumbing.

At least two-thirds of the working-age men have no steady employment. Their families subsist on welfare checks and commodity handouts. The tribe leases out thousands of acres of farming and grazing land to white men at bargain rates (because most of the Indians can't raise enough money to buy herds or farming equipment themselves), and some of this lease money is distributed. But it is easy to find Indians who get virtually nothing from this communism. One woman said she received $1.20 as her share last year; another said she received $13 for the year.

One old woman, Grandma Tobacco they called her, said she would have received $392 last year from lease money, but that the Bureau of Indian Affairs had given her some food during the winter and deducted the cost of that from the payments. She also accused the BIA of deducting the cost of her son's funeral. Because she was supposed to get $392, Grandma Tobacco said, she couldn't receive regular welfare payments. When we visited Grandma Tobacco, she was patching her hut with mud in preparation for the bitter cold South Dakota winter ahead, and on the radiator of an abandoned car (it seems that the white car dealers in the towns surrounding the reservation have succeeded in unloading all their junk cars on the Indians) she was drying the hooves and anklebones from a cow. There was no meat on the bones, but she said she would boil the hooves and bones and a few strips of hide and make soup from them later this winter. There was no plumbing in her hut. She carries water from a creek, a mile and a half down the hill. She is 77.

When the military establishment at Igloo, S.D., closed down, it wiped out the town, and a few of the small frame buildings were shipped to the reservation and sold to the Indians for houses. Sally Little Flower (that isn't her real name), her husband and nine children moved into one of them. It was quite a step up from her previous home, which was 9 by 12 feet in floor span — about the size of an ordinary living room rug. In that box of a home they had slept and eaten — except in the summer, when the children slept in two car hulls outside. In the winter the nine children slept on the floor.

In their previous home, Sally's family bathed one at a time; and when that one person was bathing, the other ten persons stayed outside to permit some privacy. In their new home, despite its small size (too small to permit all to eat at one sitting even if they use the kitchen and living room for it), there is a bathroom. The only trouble is: there is no plumbing. The U.S. Public Health Service has the responsibility for installing the plumbing in reservation homes, and for two years it has claimed that it lacked the money to install the pipes.

So Sally's family hauls water in two milk cans. They have been getting it at the Sun Dance grounds (a kind of public fair grounds) a couple of miles away, but now their car has broken down and they aren't sure where they will get their water. Still, they are among the luckier ones. Some Indians who live in the back-country part of the reservation must haul water for 12 miles.

Nobody knows for sure how many need housing on the Pine Ridge Reservation, but Eugene Rooks, a member of the tribe and director of its housing program, told me that, assuming there are 3,000 families, at least 2,500 are in critical need of new shelter.

The government has made virtually no effort to fill this need. Before 1960 it did nothing at all; since then it has built about 200 houses to rent and to sell. There is some talk that fifty or so houses will be started next May.

But the requirements for buying these new houses would be uniquely discriminatory against just about everyone. Under federal standards, to be eligible to buy a two-bedroom home one would have to earn at least $2,805 a year. The average annual income on the Pine Ridge Reservation is well below half that amount. Also, houses won't be built for Indians who live more than one-quarter mile from an all-weather road. According to Rooks that automatically eliminates 95 per cent of the Indians on the reservation.

In an effort to meet the paving requirements, at least in the community of Pine Ridge, Rooks applied to the regional office of the Urban Renewal Agency in Chicago for money to build streets and sewers. Agency officials replied: "We don't do that sort of thing. You don't understand the purpose of urban renewal. We will inform you as to the projects available under urban renewal if you wish. We'll send you a handbook."

But no handbook was sent, and when Rooks wrote again requesting it, the regional office replied: "The Urban Renewal Handbook is not distributed through the regional office. Your subscription for the handbook should be ordered from the Superintendent of Documents in Washington, D.C. The price is $14. If we can be of further assistance, please contact us." This kind of maddening federal shuffle is the normal reception to applications from the tribal government.

It isn't that the federal government is ignorant of Indian needs. The BIA admits that about 5,000 new homes are needed by South Dakota Indians and that 2,300 of those now standing are in desperate need of repair. As Rooks explained: "We have been surveyed to death. Every cotton-picking college, large or small, that gets a grant to study the Indians descends on us. We've got surveys gathering dust for a hundred years in the BIA office. This whole thing is awfully humorous, but it is tragic, too."

Oddly enough, the situation at Pine Ridge is not altogether hopeless. It is quite true that the BIA and the various housing and economic development agencies of the federal government have given every indication of wanting to ignore Pine Ridge for another 100 years. The Farmers Home Administration, for example, has shown much more interest in building swimming pools and golf courses for the rural wealthy than in putting up homes for the rural poor, including Indians.

Nevertheless, some grass-roots efforts are being made on the Indians' behalf. The help is coming, of all places, from electric cooperative associations. Although in recent years most rural electric cooperatives have seemed more bent on making money than on upgrading life in their areas, the Dakota co-ops — largely through the leadership of Harlan Severson, top official with the East River Electric Power Cooperative of South Dakota — still adhere to many of the enthusiasms of Midwest radicals.

Recently, some of these co-ops held a rural low-cost housing conference in Sioux Falls. It had to be pitched — and properly so — to improving housing for both whites and Indians, since whites in that area don't get very excited about helping Indians alone. The case for both races was made dramatic enough by Dr. George Rucker, research director for the Rural Housing Alliance, who told the conference that, at the present rate of construction, the 53,000 housing units needed by Dakota families won't be completed until the year 2016.

If the co-ops, which have some political leverage even under Republican administrations, can get the construction started, Chief Red Cloud's folks just might be able to sneak a few houses for themselves into the program.

And if the co-ops fail, there is always reason to place confidence in youth. More than 50 per cent of the inhabitants of the dreary Pine Ridge Reservation are under the age of 16. They are becoming more vocal, more militant all the time. The movement so far is not sufficiently organized to disturb Washington, and the older Indians give no encouragement to the militancy. Few of the older ones would even talk about their troubles. As one ancient said angrily, "It is nobody's business how the Indian lives." But the younger members of the tribe, especially those who have wandered off for a time to Milwaukee and Minneapolis and Los Angeles, are beginning to talk about forcing Washington to pay attention. What Pine Ridge perhaps needs most is some convincing war paint on the young braves' clubhouses.

38. Mississippi

Leon Howell

In Mississippi extreme poverty and violent racism walk hand in hand. Leon Howell shows how blacks have been systematically disenfranchised, terrorized, and pauperized in the state with the nation's lowest per capita income. What emerges is a stark account of the connection between agricultural progress, politics, racism, and deprivation. For Howell, Mississippi is part of a larger sickness in America. He feels that our unconcern for the destruction of human beings in the South now haunts us in the festering cities of the North, to which millions of downtrodden southern blacks have fled.

. . . What there is to see in Mississippi gives the lie to much of what we have assumed about our own country. In stark intensity, it reveals more than we would wish to know about our own sickness.

But one certainty emerges; the agonies of our cities, the crises which literally can rip this nation apart, will not so easily be ignored. Our unconcern for the systematic destruction of human beings in Mississippi and other parts of the South has come back to haunt us as the portent of our national destruction. It is America's failure; it is only most easily detected in the Mississippi Delta.

The Delta, shrouded in myth, refers specifically to that portion of the level, rich "black-belt" stretching from Virginia into Arkansas, which runs through the northwestern corner of Mississippi. It is, more precisely, the flat alluvial plain, with topsoil thirty-five feet deep in places, which runs 200 miles long and about sixty-five miles wide; it is defined by the two major river systems almost surrounding it, the lower Mississippi and the Coldwater-Tallahatchie-Yazoo. Created by countless floods, the six million acres contain some of the richest land in America.

William Faulkner wrote once that cotton there "grows man-tall in the very cracks of the sidewalk." Cotton has been king here and remains so; but the fragile fiber has often been a cantankerous despot. Ironically an outsider — an Egyptian intruder — it has made dictatorial demands on the organization of life. Delicate and demanding, cotton requires constant pro-

From Leon Howell, *Freedom City* (Richmond, Va.: John Knox Press, 1969), pp. 16–23. © M. E. Bratcher 1969. Reprinted by permission.

tection from beetles and weeds; water causes it to rot and a drought burns it out. The soil which nourishes it is soon exhausted. But the Mississippi planter has, with the great assistance of his much cursed national government, turned on his tyrant, and, if he is not in complete control, he has worked out something of an entente. Mechanical pickers, long unattractive to the planter (in 1953 only fourteen percent of the Delta's crop was picked by machine), have almost completely taken over the role of the human picker. As much as ninety-five percent of the 1967 crop was machine picked.

Chemicals, in large part developed with federal funds, likewise have replaced the cotton chopper. Improved fertilizers, new cultivation theories, and the increased efficiency of the machines have more than doubled the yield per acre. Man hours per acre once averaged 165 for men and mules; last year machines cut that to thirty-five, and it is dropping.

There have been two results. In large part because of federal pressure to reduce the amount of land planted, less than half the 2,554,000 acres cultivated in 1953 were needed fifteen years later to produce more cotton. And in 1966, the government not only paid people not to grow cotton but had bought enough of what was produced to have a surplus of more than 14,000,000 bales.

Also, there is no longer any need for the seasonal worker. Over the past decade, more than 100,000 people have been thrown out of work, such as it was.

The calumny of America stands exposed to itself and the world in these statistics. For the federal government not only produced most of the momentum for the technological advances which started the revolution in the Delta, it also has worked very skillfully to protect the growers affected by it. We have, that is, a federal "welfare" program for the wealthy plantation owner. But the federal government has done nothing significant at all for the people affected by this revolution, and the state of Mississippi has done even less.

What little that gets done through anti-poverty programs remains almost exclusively in the hands of those who use it to manipulate and manage the lives of those they are supposedly helping. And in the midst of it all, people have the gall to spout hackneyed phrases about "I got what I got on my own. They could too if they weren't sorry."

Item: The anti-poverty program in Clarksdale received about two million dollars last year. Half the members of its twenty-eight-member board, all white conservatives, quit, complaining that too much money was being wasted and that the government was attempting to make a spectacle out of them. Twenty-seven farming units in the same county received two million dollars, the same figure almost exactly, not to plant cotton. If there were complaints about federal wastefulness, no one has recorded them.

The result over the past few years, as surely all know by now, has been a flood of "refugees" out of the state and along the bus routes, highways, and rail lines to St. Louis and Chicago and other points north. (One million from Mississippi in Chicago alone.) The result has been to pour the fuel of discontent and brokenness onto the already volatile and overcrowded ghettos, suffering their own deprivation.

Overwhelming evidence confirms that official Mississippi views this exodus as its own "final solution," though it vehemently denies it for the record. Yet the primary reason for keeping industry out of the Delta has been precisely this. In an interview on Public Broadcasting Laboratory, Mr. Sims Lockett, a Clarksdale lawyer who speaks for the conservatives in Mississippi, said:

> I don't think that there is any true future for the Negro in this community or the white persons in this community . . . unless and until we change the racial ratio.
>
> If we had — if half the Negroes in this community left tomorrow, the ones that are left behind would benefit immensely . . . We've got to distribute the Negroes more evenly throughout the country. I do not think that the cities can survive where the Negroes become dominant insofar as numbers are concerned. Nor do I think that the South can survive if we continue with the ratio that we have at the present time.

In other words, we in Mississippi wash our hands of it all; we can't worry about people we no longer need.

This bit of casuistry simply won't do it, not for a country which claims to have a social conscience, especially not for a people that identifies itself as Christian.

One historical example should be an adequate illustration of why such a position is intolerable.

There were 189,884 Negro registered voters in Mississippi in 1890, one of the least-known facts of Mississippi history. Mississippi was conditionally readmitted to the Union in 1870; one of the specifications was that it would never "amend or change [the Constitution of Mississippi of 1869] as to deprive any citizen or class of citizens of the United States of the right to vote who are entitled to vote by the constitution herein recognized." The Constitution of 1869 said that the right to vote went to all male inhabitants twenty-one or over who had resided in Mississippi for six months and were not insane. From 1890, when there were 70,000 more registered Negro voters than white, intense pressure and discrimination reduced that number to 23,801 in 1961.

There are those who contend that the endemic violence of Mississippi over the past eighty years springs precisely from this massive drive for disenfranchisement. That, certainly, was the ingredient which set off the chain of horror of the summer of 1964.

Professor James W. Silver, in his brilliant exploration of the double captivity of black and white in Mississippi in *Mississippi: The Closed Society* (must reading for any real understanding of Mississippi), states:

> Violence and the threat of violence have confirmed and enforced the image of unanimity.
>
> This, then, is the essence of the closed society. For whatever reason, the community sets up the orthodox view. Its people are constantly indoctrinated. . . . When there is no effective challenge to the code, a mild toleration of dissent is evident, provided the nonconformist is tactful and does not go far. But with a substantial challenge from the outside — to slavery in the 1850's and to segregation in the 1950's — the society tightly closes its ranks, becomes inflexible and stubborn, and lets no scruple, legal or ethical, stand in the way of the enforcement of the orthodoxy. The voice of reason is stilled and the moderate either goes along or is eliminated.

A whole people has been systematically disenfranchised, exploited, deprived, manipulated, and broken, in the name of the orthodoxy and for the sake of the needs of the cotton-dominated economy. And now these destroyed people, no longer needed, increasingly a burden and a growing threat to the unanimity of the society, and, indeed, to the physical safety of its people, will be turned loose to exist in desperate poverty or to journey to a new location, unprepared, lost, and vulnerable. Violence, direct and indirect, has driven them from their native land.

There are, of course, large numbers of moderates in Mississippi who blanch at the thought of overt violence. Yet through fear, and more precisely, through the lack of concern that grips our whole society — now severely indicted in the Kerner Commission report as "white racist" — these moderates have not moved to close off either the physical violence of the nightrider or the more subtle violence of the poverty of the lives of those they have used and discarded. [Robert Sherrill, in *Gothic Politics in the Deep South,* says:]

> Peckerwoods ride by and shoot into Negro shanties at night; good people refuse to distribute federal surplus food to hungry Negroes in the winter, thus insuring their eager return to the fields at $3 a day come spring (it is not unheard of for Delta Negroes to die from cold and malnutrition in the winter). It is the difference between those who, merrily sucking a jawful of Red Man tobacco, are willing to work and sweat to dig a grave in the night to hide their murder, and that smaller group whom Hodding Carter called "the uptown Ku Klux Klan" — men of substance who would not

think of night riding, either to kill or to catch a killer; they are the Rotary Club of Indianola who did their civic duty by buying more riot guns for the local police when the SNCC youngsters came to town, not the farmers who later burned down the Freedom Labor Union's headquarters.

As the young and able and the bright have left the state, those left behind are often the very young and the very old. Most poignant are the children. "The Negro children of Mississippi are its deepest tragedy. Beyond the violence and the obvious planned manipulation of a people is the awful knowledge that here are thousands and thousands of children who will not ever be free in any real sense. They were marked in the womb, debased in infancy, and face a life already circumscribed by their stunted bodies and minds. I am chilled by that memory."

These words, spoken slowly and with difficulty by Rev. David Barnes, came from a year he spent in Mississippi as a volunteer for the Delta Ministry of the National Council of Churches. He said them a year before the terrible "hungry children report" of the Southern Regional Council. Six doctors of national reputation made a study of children in the Delta and reported:

> In sum, we saw children who are hungry and who are sick — children for whom hunger is a daily fact of life and sickness, in many forms, an inevitability. We do not want to quibble over words but "malnutrition" is not quite what we found; the boys and girls we saw were hungry — weak, in pain, sick; their lives are being shortened; they are, in fact, visibly and predictably losing their health, their energy, their spirits. They are suffering from hunger and disease and directly or indirectly they are dying from them — which is exactly what "starvation" means.

If the crime rests directly on the heads of those who have perpetuated the dehumanizing system in Mississippi, all America stands indicted for its "uptown KKK" silence. The history of federal involvement in Mississippi has been one of compromise, often in the name of political realities, with practices and conditions unconscionable for any nation, much less one which claims to be just.

It began in early days and implicates us today. One illustration will, again, serve as mirror of the whole.

In January, 1965, the remarkable Mrs. Fannie Lou Hamer contested the right of Representative Jamie L. Whitten to represent the Second Congressional District. Her charges were simple and direct: Whitten did not have the right to represent that district because 52.45 percent of the adult population was black but only 2.97 percent was allowed to register to vote, both because of planned intimidation and the long history cited earlier of systematic denial of the vote to Negroes. Two other women challenged their representative on the same grounds.

In Congress on January 4, 1965, all other members were sworn in to decide how to handle the challenge. Confronted with this evidence, Congress had the opportunity to refuse the seats until the case was settled; almost surely with the backing of the administration, Speaker John McCormick and Rep. Carl Albert managed to get the delegation seated until the challenge was decided (by a vote of 276–149). Rep. James Roosevelt of California had prepared a speech he was never able to deliver: "We dare not let men pretend to a seat in this honorable House who have been chosen by a closed vote in a closed society. If we do, we betray this House and the people of the United States and the Constitution they wrote for us."

After the seating of the representatives, the challenge was simply not recognized again. Political expediency at the highest levels demanded that the powerful southern bloc not be riled. . . .

. . . There may be some value in the intimations urgently offered by a concerned observer, one haunted by the knowledge that in Mississippi as indeed in India and Harlem and Guatemala and on Oklahoma Indian reservations, there are people who are hungry, who are sick, who are homeless, who are imprisoned by their society; haunted by that sure knowledge that the rationalizations of the middle class — "I got where I am because I worked for it" — are completely untenable in the face of the proof we now have that a baby in the womb whose mother has a protein deficiency is already crippled, that a child starving at two will never be able to catch up physically, mentally, or emotionally; haunted by the riches of a nation that makes the building of superhighways and going to the moon priorities over feeding our hungry, releasing our captives; haunted by the pious protestations of national morality in the face of such sure evidence of our corruption; and haunted by the words of warning in the Bible that we each have a final report to make, and, whatever judgment day means in our secular age, that we must face the seering biblical warning:

> ". . . for I was hungry and you gave me no food, I was thirsty and you gave me no drink, I was a stranger and you did not welcome me, naked and you did not clothe me, sick and in prison and you did not visit me." Then they also will answer, "Lord, when did we see thee hungry or thirsty or a stranger or naked or sick or in prison, and did not minister to thee?" Then he will answer them, "Truly, I say to you, as you did it not to one of the least of these, you did it not to me." And they will go away into eternal punishment . . . (Matt. 25:42–46).

39. Appalachia: The Corporate Fiefdom

Harry M. Caudill

Appalachia is an ecological and human disaster. The wanton exploitation of natural resources and people are built into the region's economy. The deprivation of its population and the rape of the land are well-known facts. Harry Caudill, a Kentucky lawyer and former state legislator with centuries-old roots in Appalachia, here relates the less publicized tale of how the area enriches some of America's largest corporations. Caudill shows the interrelatedness of absentee ownership, politics, poverty, the dole, and the physical destruction of miners. Appalachia is a bleak reminder that affluence for some may be at the price of poverty for others.

Bubbling with enthusiasm and filled with grand visions of the impending Great Society, Hubert Humphrey declared during the 1964 campaign that poverty would be driven from America in ten years, and when he signed into law the Appalachian Regional Development Act of 1965, Lyndon Johnson grandiloquently told the 15,000,000 inhabitants of long stagnant Appalachia to take hope. "The dole," he effervesced, "is dead!"

In the last four years life has improved a little for most people in the poverty-plagued Appalachian highlands. Construction of a network of semi-modern highways has been commenced and a string of new vocational schools has been opened for unskilled mountain youths. In Kentucky and West Virginia, poorly supervised work programs — the "happy pappies" — brought some money to empty pockets and new color to the shallow cheeks of many children. Since the advent of medicaid and medicare health standards have improved markedly for thousands of elderly, disabled and dependent people (gains which have been accompanied by many abuses and some shocking debasements of medical ethics).

But in resource-rich Appalachia the dole is not dead and poverty still grips the isolated farms, remote hamlets and shabby towns. The flicker of hope that came in 1964 has died and the old patterns of life continue: the able and discerning flee to the cities and the rest sink into deepening apathy and resignation. And well they may, for the forces that rule their homeland

From Harry M. Caudill, "The Corporate Fiefdom," *Commonweal*, 89:16 (January 24, 1969). Reprinted by permission of Commonweal Publishing Co., Inc.

are too powerful and cunning to be resisted. Amid the misery of Appalachian poverty those forces find the meat of prosperity and riches.

The opening words of the report by the President's Appalachian Regional Commission (1964) provide an insight into the territory's vast potential: "Appalachia has natural advantages which might normally have been the base for a thriving industrial and commercial complex. Below its surface lie some of the nation's richest mineral deposits, including the seams which have provided almost two-thirds of the nation's coal supply. The region receives an annual rainfall substantially above the national average. More than three-fifths of the land is heavily forested. Its mountains offer some of the most beautiful landscapes in eastern America, readily lending themselves to tourism and recreation."

Nevertheless Appalachia has enjoyed no normal development of its gargantuan stores of natural wealth. More than 90 percent of its mineral reserves are absentee-owned — held in fee by oil, gas, steel and coal corporations whose principal offices are nearly always outside the mountains. Bought for a pittance in the nineteenth century from ignorant and impoverished highlanders, Appalachian fuels and ores have provided much of America's industrial and military muscle. In the last 85 years, half a trillion dollars worth of raw wealth — coal, oil, gas, limestone, marble, cement rock, copper, iron ore, timber — has been hauled out in a process that brought enormous benefits to the rest of the nation and ever-deepening crisis to Appalachia itself. Today, the huge mineral fields remain in economic and political bondage — fiefdoms of a few score corporations in Pittsburgh, Philadelphia, Baltimore and New York. The extractive industries are practically the only private employers in dozens of counties and, by judicious use of political muscle, manage to control the public payrolls as well.

Eastern Kentucky, the sickest part of sick Appalachia, illustrates with grim clarity the horrible cancer fastened on much of the region and its people by a combination of absentee exploitation and venal government. The map of this once magnificent corner of America is sprinkled with the names of such industrial giants as Ford, International Harvester, U.S. Steel, Republic Steel, Bethlehem Steel, Occidental Petroleum and Columbia Gas. Less famous entities include American Associates, Ltd., Elkhorn Coal Corporation, The Big Sandy Corporation, Virginia Iron, Coal and Coke Company, the Penn-Virginia Company and the Kentucky River Coal Corporation. The two latter companies are almost certainly the most profitable investor-owned corporations in America, retaining as net profit *after taxes* some 61% of gross receipts and paying about 45% of gross receipts to their shareholders.

Great or small, these firms are the masters of Appalachia and their hold on Kentucky is especially tight. The state house and court houses reflect their policies. Governors appoint their officers and friends to the governing and advisory boards of state colleges and to the agencies that manage most of the state's affairs. County Judges appoint their representatives to local taxing bodies — a practice that keeps revenues so low that Perry County is currently paying only 5% of the cost of operating its schools. Well-heeled lobbies dominate legislative corridors so completely that Kentucky's tax structure is a medieval nightmare, totally unbelievable in its oppression of the numerous poor for the benefit of the robber barons. The state levies a 5 percent sales tax on food, clothing, medicines, fuel, building materials, coffins — on every item the ordinary citizen uses between the cradle and the grave. But it exempts diesel oil for locomotives, concrete blocks for oil and gas, and all coal burned in the colossal steam plants operated by T.V.A. and electric power corporations and co-ops! Thus it shamelessly taxes bread for little children and exempts coal for big power plants. It applies to family automobiles and farm trucks but exempts bull-dozers, power-shovels, augers and "continuous miners" used by the coal industry, some of which sell for hundreds of thousands of dollars. The Kentucky tax-collector's net was woven with immense ingenuity to catch the little fish and let the big ones swim safely through its meshes.

Senator Lee Metcalf of Montana has introduced a bill that would correct many of the grotesque tax inequities that have plagued Appalachia for so long. The measure would levy a federal severance tax on all minerals mined in America with full credit allowed the taxpayer for severance taxes paid to the states. Since each state would surely impose severance taxes under these circumstances, the legislation offers a huge windfall to Appalachia. Under it, for example, West Virginia would collect about $45,000,000 annually and Kentucky would receive about $25,000,000. But the governors and U.S. Senators of these states have said no word in support of the proposal.

Eastern Kentucky is still the domain of laissez faire where nineteenth century indifference to human welfare reigns unchecked and, apparently, uncheckable. Profits are habitually placed above lives — a concept that has strewn the land with widows and orphans and made the funeral business a lucrative one indeed. . . .

Explosions are dramatic and deadly but the great enemy of miners is silent and hidden. It is dust from coal, sandstone and shale — dust that can coat a man's lungs with mortar-hard deposits, etch them with scars, pit them with sores and turn them a ghastly black. Mining dust produces silicosis and pneumoconiosis (black lung) and turns men into choking, wheezing, agony-wracked relics. There are between 80,000 and 100,000 of such disabled men in Appalachia and twelve thousand or more of them live in Kentucky. This scandal of American industry is all the worse because so little has been done to prevent it. . . .

... The toll is terrible. Dr. I. E. Buff, a cardiologist of Charleston, West Virginia, believes that at least 50 percent of the nation's miners suffer disability from this industrial scourge. Dr. Jan Lieben, formerly Director of the Pennsylvania Division of Occupational Health, has expressed the opinion that a thousand miners are dying of black lung each year in Pennsylvania alone. . . .

Once contracted, these dust diseases have no cure and virtually any degree can be totally incapacitating. Only prevention offers any hope at present. Yet neither the rich mining industry, the miners Union (with more than $83,000,000 in its treasury and another $185,000,000 in its Health and Welfare Fund) nor any agency of State or Federal Government has made any serious, sustained investment in research in this vital field. Little Belgium is currently spending much more money than the U.S. investigating prevention and treatment of miners' lung diseases, Great Britain and the Common Market countries combined are devoting fifteen times as much capital to the problem.

It is certain that miners close to the dusty coal face ought to wear airtight helmets similar to those used by divers, with air pumped to them from safe areas. But as the coal fields fill with dying men and the welfare rolls balloon to support them and their families, H. N. Kirkpatrick, a mine operator who is also Commissioner of Kentucky's Department of Mines and Minerals, spoke for the industry when he told a mine safety conference in Washington . . . "Present laws are basically sound." He heaped fulsome praise on mining companies and urged that no hasty steps be taken for fear of their "economically destructive" impact on the industry. Apparently dying miners are quite acceptable, but lessened profit sheets are altogether unbearable.

In eight years as head of the Department of the Interior, whose Bureau of Mines enforces federal safety laws, Stewart Udall witnessed the ruin of thousands of soft-coal-miners. As uncertain a lance as ever entered the lists, he finally, in the last months of his administration, recommended some tightening of the 1952 U.S. Coal Mine Safety Act. . . .

The United States now claims an ever-growing share of the world's coal market while other countries close mines in order to divert their workmen to more desirable tasks. Much of this cheap coal comes from the Appalachian hills in a half dozen states. There the ghastly bill for this industrial and commercial "success story" mounts inexorably. It is manifest in worn, crippled men on canes and crutches, their pale pinched faces peering from the windows of sagging shacks. It stares out of the vacant eyes of hundreds of people lined up at the first of each month to cash welfare checks and receive "food stamps." It springs from regional statistics that chart declining school enrollments, dwindling birth rates and sustained out-migration.

... It rattles in the convulsed coughing of derelicts who only yesterday were diggers of America's coal.

In America, governments have become big business indeed, but not nearly big enough to divorce themselves from an unholy alliance with the mining industries they are sworn to regulate and police. And until they are big enough and determined enough to assure justice and safety to miners and their communities both, poverty and the dole will remain integral parts of Appalachian life while many administrations come and go.

40. The Economics of Aging

Special Committee on Aging,
U.S. Senate

Science has added years to life, but old age often means ill-health and loneliness. For millions of Americans it is also a time of poverty. Three out of ten persons sixty-five years and older are officially poor. But the aged poor do not riot. As occupants of old apartments, decaying houses, furnished rooms, and nursing homes, they are scarcely visible to the young.

What portends for the future? The Senate Special Committee on Aging explains the economics of aging and shows why, despite the existence of Social Security and private pensions, the poverty of old age can be expected to increase, unless our youth-oriented society acts now to share its abundance with the elderly.

THE TASK FORCE REPORT IN BRIEF

1. Americans living in retirement are suffering from an income gap in relation to younger people. And as the gap widens, low income continues to be the Number One problem facing most of our 20 million persons 65 years or older, as well as other millions just a few years younger.

From *Hearings Before the Special Committee on Aging,* U.S. Senate, 91st Congress, 1st Session, Part 1, Survey Hearings (Washington, D.C.: U.S. Government Printing Office, April 1969), appendix 1, pp. 155–158.

The "gap" is widening: Median income of families with an aged head was 51 percent of that for younger families in 1961, but only 46 percent in 1967.

Three out of 10 people 65 and older — in contrast to one in nine younger people — were living in poverty in 1966, yet *many of these aged people did not become poor until they became old.*

An additional one-tenth of our aged population was on the poverty borderline.

About five in 10 families with an aged head had less than $4,000 income in 1967; about one in five was below $2,000.

Of older people living alone or with nonrelatives in 1967, half had incomes below $1,480, and one-fourth had $1,000 or less.

Even the level of living set by the Bureau of Labor Statistics in its Retired Couple's Budget is well beyond the means of most older people, especially for those who retired years ago. The average social security benefit of a couple retiring in 1950 met half the BLS budget cost then, but today it meets less than one-third.

Unemployment and early retirement among the 60 to 64 population are creating problems that demand much the same attention as that required by the population aged 65 and over.

2. More Americans are spending more years in retirement periods of indeterminate length and uncertain needs, causing a mounting strain on resources they had when they began retirement. For an ever-rising proportion of women — most of them widows — the problem is especially severe.

Half of all people now 65 and over are about 73 or older. In the years ahead, the increase will be particularly great at the oldest ages. With the population 65 and older projected to rise 50 percent between 1960–85, the population 85 and older may double.

Increasingly, the rising population of widows is attempting to live independently, even if independence is purchased at the price of poverty.

Our "retirement revolution" reflects two trends: at one end an increase in the number of very old aged; at the other, earlier departure from the labor force.

3. Unless positive action is taken, the economic position of persons now old will deteriorate markedly in the years ahead.

National economic growth, while putting added dollars into pockets of the working group, increases pressures on the retiree. A rise in earnings of 4 percent annually — a not unrealistic assumption in view of recent performance — means consumption levels would approximately double in two decades, placing those on fixed income at a seriously deepening disadvantage in the marketplace.

Earnings drop as advanced age further curtails already limited earnings opportunities. (In comparison to the age group 65–72, only half as many men 73 and over and a third as many women worked in 1962, and the earnings of the oldest workers were significantly lower.)

Assets are reduced — in some cases, exhausted. Homeownership — the most important asset of the elderly — becomes especially difficult to maintain with advanced age, mounting taxes and other rising costs.

Medical needs and the costs of meeting these needs rise with declining health. The rise in these costs is only partly met by Medicare, which covered 35 percent of health costs of the aged in 1967.

Inflation erodes already inadequate incomes over longer retirement periods. (An annual rise of only 2 percent will reduce the purchasing power of fixed incomes by 18 percent after one decade and by 33 percent after two decades.)

4. Today's inadequacies in retirement income — and the policies and trends that perpetuate them — should be of direct concern not only to our population of aged and aging Americans, but also to those in middle age or younger. Most parents today face a common problem: How can they allocate earnings to meet current obligations to their family and still have something left over for retirement?

The margin for saving — the excess of income over consumption expenditures — has been small for most families during most years of the worklife, especially for workers in the less skilled occupations.

In addition, with an outlook for sustained economic growth, how realistic is it to expect today's workers voluntarily to forego consumption in order to save for the years ahead when this requires that they *significantly reduce their present standard of living to provide adequately for an uncertain and "distant" old age?*

5. Projections and various studies indicate that Social Security, private pensions, and other forms of retirement income are not improving fast enough to reverse or significantly counter present economic trends.

The overwhelming proportion of people retiring today receive total pension income from both public and private pensions — which is only 20 to 40 percent of their average earnings in the years prior to retirement.

Of families retiring in the next decade and a half, it has been projected that almost 60 percent of those with preretirement earnings between $4,000 to $8,000 will receive pension income of less than half these earnings.

Projections to 1980 indicate that about half the couples and more than three-fourths of the unmarried retirees will receive $3,000 or less in pension income. And these projections use relatively liberal assumptions with respect to increases in private and public benefit levels.

The same projection found that more than two-thirds of retired couples could be expected to receive less than $3,000 in social security benefits in 1980.

Even under earlier projections, now known to be too optimistic, only a third to two-fifths of all aged persons in 1980 were expected to have income from private group pensions.

In addition, private pensions cover less than half the work force and this coverage is concentrated among higher paid workers; those in the greatest need in old age will be least likely to receive these pensions.

Early retirement is a developing trend that could seriously impede attempts to improve the income position of future aged populations. (In recent years, more than half of the men retiring have done so before age 65.)

Among the proposed methods of raising the incomes of the aged population are various proposals for improved pensions, constant purchasing bonds, tax relief, increased public services, and improved welfare payments. No single proposal, however, can be expected to have a significant impact unless tied to broad policy decisions.

6. Facing what must be recognized as a worsening retirement income crisis, the Nation must take positive, comprehensive actions going far beyond those taken within recent years. The Nation faces these basic policy issues:

What is an adequate level of income for retired persons?

What part in attaining this level should be played by governmental programs, by voluntary group action, and by individual effort?

Is the economic problem of aging a temporary problem that requires a different solution or a different "mix" of solutions for today's aged than for those reaching old age in the future?

CONCLUSIONS

The task force has not attempted to enumerate and evaluate the many policy alternatives that have been recommended to deal with the economic problems of the aged. There are, however, a number of important conclusions which we feel are supported by the statistics summarized here and discussed more fully in the Report [of the Special Committee Task Force].

Low income in old age is not a transitional problem that, given present trends, will solve itself.

Unless action is taken now, most aged will not have sufficient income to provide in retirement "A healthful, self-respecting manner of living which allows normal participation in community life."

The Social Security system has failed to keep up with the rising income needs of the aged.

To a large extent social security benefit increases in the past have resulted, not from legislation with the purposeful intent of tapping a greater part of the rising national product for old people, but rather as a secondary result of attempts to deal with the severe and potentially explosive hardship problems facing many older people. In consequence, these past efforts have been aimed primarily at maintaining the economic status of the aged at some minimal standard or subsistence level in the face of rising prices.

Sufficient evidence now exists to spotlight certain special economic problems of the aged which compound the general problem of low income. Among the areas identified for immediate congressional attention are:

(a) Income maintenance of widows — a particularly disadvantaged group.
(b) Health needs and rising medical costs.
(c) Problems associated with homeownership and taxation.
(d) Employment opportunities in old age.
(e) Implications of early retirement trends.

Simultaneously, congressional attention should be directed to (1) the various techniques for measuring and projecting the income needs of the aged population and to their use in decision making and (2) the appropriateness of methods now used or proposed for use in the adjustment of retirement benefits to changing conditions.

A reasonable definition of adequacy demands that the aged population, both now and in the future, be assured *a share in the growth of the economy.*

If old age is to be more than a period when people decline and die, some way must be found whereby the aged, who have helped in the past to provide the basis for rising living standards, are guaranteed a share in some of the "harvested fruits." What this requires is a substantial transfer of income from the working to the retired population in order to improve the *relative* economic status of the aged.

Such assurance can best *be provided, or can* only *be provided, through governmental programs, particularly the social insurance system of*

OASDHI, which carry commitments for future older Americans — the workers of today — as well as for this generation of the aged.

The financial soundness of the Social Security system depends, essentially, on the Government's taxing powers which, in a vigorously growing economy, permit great flexibility to meet changing retirement needs. And retirement needs *are* changing as expectations rise and as American families increasingly begin to evaluate the adequacy of their retirement income in relation to their standard of living prior to retirement.

Private group pensions and personal savings — tailored as they are to individual needs, preferences, and financing ability — will continue to be essential supplements to basic social security benefits in the future. The Government should explore and lend support to various methods of promoting and encouraging such supplementary sources of retirement income.

Chapter Ten

A Harvest of Shame

41. The Condition of Farm Workers and Small Farmers

National Sharecroppers Fund

The efficiency of American agriculture has achieved worldwide fame, but brought few benefits to those who toil in the fields. The Reports of the National Sharecroppers Fund discuss the relationship between the impoverished condition of farm workers and small farmers and trends in technology, corporate farming and government programs.

Most farm workers are unorganized and mired in poverty. In 1970, they averaged $1.42 an hour — low enough, but the seasonality of the work reduced their annual income even more, to about $1,500. Despite their destitution they are scarcely touched by social legislation, while government agricultural programs heap millions of dollars in subsidies on large owners, including huge corporate farms.

The 1969 Report expects mechanization to have as great an impact on fruit and vegetable harvesting in the coming decades as it did on cotton harvesting in the 1960's. If this prediction is correct, we can foresee grim consequences: the countryside will disgorge more of its redundant unskilled workers into urban slums, where unemployment is already rampant. Is this inevitable or are there alternatives? The answer depends on whether society accepts full responsibility for the displaced. Judging from the past record, in the absence of a large-scale social movement to force the society to assume the responsibility, there is little cause for optimism.

THE YEAR IN BRIEF

1970 was the year in which many Americans examined anew the costs of achieving efficiency in agriculture through bigness. In the name of "the most efficient agriculture in the world," federal policy for thirty years had abetted through sumptuous subsidies the growth of bigger and richer farms. Millions of small operators had been driven off the land, as much the victims of government policy as of competition. With little education or hope, they had crowded into the great urban centers, adding to the crisis of poverty and racism, social tension and violence, pollution and deteriorating services. Now, Americans learned that the race towards bigness was also depleting and polluting the soil, water, atmosphere, and food through excessive use of hazardous pesticides and fertilizers.

Survival demanded both an ecologically balanced system of production and the revitalization of rural life, but neither was on the government's agenda. The rural poor continued to suffer from the meagerest diets, the lowest incomes, the worst unemployment, the most dilapidated housing, the least adequate medical care, and the most blatant racial discrimination. Almost every government attempt to help had been transmuted into a device either to make the rich richer and the poor poorer or to regulate and pacify the poor with token assistance.

Progress came primarily from the efforts of the poor themselves in organizing small farm cooperatives, self-help projects, and unions. NSF's experience in the field gives ample evidence that rural people want to stay where they have roots and that, if given the chance to live with dignity, will work hard to succeed. The victory won this year by California's grape pickers in the United Farm Workers Organizing Committee raised the hopes of many struggling to overcome rural poverty and deprivation. These gains represented significant steps toward a livable environment for all.

IS THE SMALL FARMER OBSOLETE?

The exodus of small farmers continues, while government agricultural policy remains attuned to the interests of large farmers. More than 2.7 million farmers, nearly all of them small operators, have abandoned farming or sold out to bigger competitors since 1950. Only about 2 million small farms are left now. Between 1950 and 1970, the total number of farm residents has declined from 23 million to 9.7 million people.

The Department of Agriculture (USDA) keeps growing bigger as farm population dwindles. Between 1950 and 1970, USDA appropriations rose

From James M. Pierce, *The Condition of Farm Workers and Small Farmers in 1970*. Report to the National Board of the National Sharecroppers Fund (New York, 1971).

from $2.3 billion to $7.5 billion and its staff grew from 84,000 to 125,000. Most of USDA's money and time are devoted to expanding and improving the operations of the one million farmers with gross sales of $10,000 or more whom its officials consider serious commercial producers.

SUBSIDIES

USDA acreage reduction and price support programs bestow the biggest subsidies on the largest farmers. In 1970, the top 137,000 farmers, or less than 5 percent of all farmers, received 46 percent of the $3.7 billion in subsidy payments. A California cotton producer led with $4.4 million, eight other operations received $1 million or more, and 23 got $500,000 or more.

The prosperity of big farmers has also been financed by USDA research programs through their development of new crops, fertilizers, pest controls, irrigation techniques, and labor-saving machinery suitable primarily for large-scale agriculture. Big operators have enjoyed a host of other government subsidies, many of them hidden. Large landowners, especially in the West, have reaped windfalls in land appreciation from federally-financed irrigation systems and a vast network of dams and canals built by the federal government. In many cases, the government has helped landowners make new lands fertile while at the same time paying them not to grow crops. The most significant hidden subsidy to big farms is a labor subsidy: exclusion of farm workers from the protections that apply to other workers, such as workmen's compensation, unemployment insurance, and collective bargaining, has kept their labor costs among the lowest in the nation.

RICH FARMERS BENEFIT

This multiplicity of subsidies has hastened the penetration of the farm economy by ever-larger units and the growth of corporate farming. Twenty years ago the average farm size was 215 acres; today it is estimated to be 387 acres. The nation's 40,000 largest farms — less than one percent of all farms — accounted for at least one-third of all agricultural production. Farm prices in 1970 fell to 67 percent of parity, the lowest since the Depression, but many farms of this size still earned a 10 percent return on investment — the average in farming is 3 percent — comparable to the profits of major industrial corporations.

The Agriculture Act of 1970 leaves farm policy basically unchanged. The new legislation sets limits of $55,000 per crop on subsidies in wheat, feed grains, and cotton (sugar is not affected). But it still rests on a system of planned scarcity and a subsidization process that widens the gap between big and small operators. Already large cotton growers are resorting to a variety of legal maneuvers — such as splitting their holdings among family members so each can get a check — to keep on qualifying for maximum payments. Total expenditures for subsidy programs are expected to continue at the present rate.

THE MOVEMENT OF CORPORATIONS INTO FARMING*

Factory-like farm operations became an increasing reality in 1969 as giant corporations continued to move into agriculture. An estimated 90 percent of all broiler chickens produced in the U.S. came from highly automated farms; 13 corporations, including Ralston Purina, Pillsbury, and Swift & Company, produced about 40 percent. About 31 percent of the farmland in Florida was cultivated by corporations; large canners such as Minute Maid (owned by Coca Cola) and Libby, McNeill and Libby owned an estimated 20 percent of Florida's citrus groves, up from one percent in 1960. Large diversified corporations, not previously identified with farming, such as Purex and AMK (through its newly acquired subsidiary United Fruit Company) were rapidly moving into large-scale vegetable growing.

The real threat of conglomerate farming lies not only in the amount of land the corporations possess but in their ability to control and use the market structure to squeeze out smaller producers. It is almost impossible for small farmers to compete against large conglomerates that are integrated in production, processing, marketing, and even retailing. Moreover, the large conglomerates have an advantage over small farmers in their ability to take farming losses over a period of years, writing them off against taxable income from other enterprises.

The continued development of corporation farming also has serious implications for farm labor. The corporation farms are in a better position to take advantage of technological advances that reduce the need for farm workers. And large diversified corporations are in a better position to thwart the efforts of farm worker unions seeking improved wages and working conditions. . . .

MECHANIZATION AND THE FUTURE OF FARM WORKERS AND SMALL FARMERS

Mechanization has probably been the most important single factor in the declining need for farm workers and in forcing small farmers out of agriculture. Whereas in the 1960's mechanization probably had its greatest impact on cotton farming in the South, in the next decade it should have its

* From Fay Bennett, *The Condition of Farm Workers and Small Farmers in 1969.* Report to the National Board of the National Sharecroppers Fund (New York, 1971).

greatest impact on the harvesting of fruits and vegetables. In 1969 an estimated 58 percent of the total vegetable harvest was mechanized, and this figure is expected to increase to about 73 percent by 1975. By 1980, 90 to 100 percent of all fruits and vegetables will probably be mechanically harvested.

The mechanical harvest of fruits and vegetables could ultimately mean the loss of about 450,000 jobs for seasonal farm workers. The greatest impact would be on the 56,000 farm workers, many of them migrants, whose main employment during the year is farm work but who work at it fewer than 150 days per year.

DISCRIMINATION IN FARM PROGRAMS*

All small farmers have suffered from government policy, but black farmers have been the chief victims. In 1950, there were 560,000 black-operated farms; today there are only 98,000. In the same period, the total black farm population fell from 3,158,000 to 938,000; the average annual loss was 10.5 percent compared to 3.9 percent among whites.

USDA has been repeatedly found guilty of discriminating against blacks. The worst rights offender among USDA-assisted programs is the Cooperative Extension Service (CES). A recent audit of the operation of the Alabama CES conducted by the Inspector General's Office of USDA found the situation unimproved since the passage of the Civil Rights Act of 1965. Black county agents are assigned work on a racial basis, are subordinate to white agents, and often have heavier work loads in areas with large black populations. Deprived of adequate services, black farmers remain handicapped by outmoded techniques and low productivity.

Blacks are still virtually unrepresented on the Agricultural Stabilization and Conservation Service's locally elected farmer committees which determine crop allotments and price support payments. There are only three black members among the 4,100 county-level committeemen in the South, less than one-tenth of one percent in a region where blacks are from 10 to 20 percent or more of the farm operators and where they comprise a majority in 58 counties.

The Farmers Home Administration (FmHA), USDA's credit agency for low-income rural people, has steadily improved black representation on its county committees and has noticeably increased black participation in its low-interest loan programs. Yet the help that it does provide black farmers is unequal to that given whites who are similarly impoverished. In 1969, the average size of operating loans received by black borrowers was $2,226, while loans to whites averaged $5,928. The average size of economic opportunity loans was $1,319 to blacks, $2,281 to whites.

* From James M. Pierce, *The Condition of Farm Workers and Small Farmers in 1970.* Report to the National Board of the National Sharecroppers Fund (New York, 1971).

BLACK MIGRATION PERSISTS

The migration of blacks out of the South continued during the last decade at nearly the same pace as in the 1940s and 1950s. The 1970 census estimates show a net migration from the 16 Southern states of 1.4 million blacks in the 1960s, as compared with 1.5 million in each of the previous decades. Migration — primarily to California and Northern urban states — was at an annual rate of 140,000. Earlier predictions that the movement out of the rural South had diminished assumed that black Southerners were finding more jobs in their own region as a result of economic growth and federal equal employment laws. The new data suggest that blacks have not been able to break through job barriers in significant numbers.

HIRED FARM WORKERS

Agriculture is still one of the nation's largest employers. About 2.5 million persons did some hired farm work in 1970, a decrease of 4 percent from the 2.6 million in 1969. Of these, about 1.1 million were casual laborers, who worked less than 25 days, and 1.4 million were noncasual workers. The number of migrant workers ranged from the government's low estimate of 196,000 to half a million estimated by the United Farm Workers Organizing Committee. (Migrants are not counted in any official census.)

For an average of 80 days of farm work, hired farm workers earned $887 in cash wages. The 1.4 million noncasual workers (those working 25 days or more) averaged 137 days and earned $1,519 from all sources. Domestic migratory workers averaged 123 days and earned $1,697. Nearly 1.5 million persons did farm work only, averaging 102 days and earning $1,083. Approximately 555,000 farm workers are now covered by the $1.30 minimum wage. The annual composite hourly farm worker's wage rose to $1.42 in 1970 from $1.33 in 1969, yet was only 42 percent of the average factory worker's wage. Despite the establishment of a federal minimum wage for farm workers, their relative wage position has not improved appreciably during the last twenty years.

ACCIDENTS

Farm work remains one of the most hazardous occupations. Agriculture ranked third, behind only mining and construction, in work-related deaths in 1970. Even with the phasing out of DDT, chemical pesticides are still a major danger to farm workers and their families. In California alone, one in every six farm workers annually suffers injuries due to pesticides. Parathion, a nerve gas derivative, and other organo-phosphates endanger the health of workers in and around Florida's citrus groves.

FARM LABOR ORGANIZING

In July 1970, when the United Farm Workers Organizing Committee (UFWOC) signed contracts with most of California's table grape growers, the event climaxed nearly a century of efforts to organize the people who harvest the nation's crops. Farm workers were either too poor to strike or too itinerant to organize. And when they protested, vigilantes, often joined by the law, beat them down. A combination of factors made the UFWOC breakthrough possible: skillful organization and leadership, the ability to link economic demands with the broader movement for dignity and social justice, and wide support of the two-year grape boycott by labor, church, civic, and civil rights organizations. The contracts, which cover about 10,000 vineyard workers, call for an hourly wage of $1.80 in 1970 and increases to $1.95 in 1971 and $2.05 in 1972. In addition, they provide for incentive payments of 20 cents for each box of grapes picked, grower contributions of 10 cents an hour to the union's health and welfare plan, and 2 cents for each box to the economic development fund (used chiefly to build housing for retired field workers). Jobs are assigned through the union hiring hall, thus eliminating the need for labor contractors and crew leaders. The contracts also set up joint worker-grower committees to regulate the use of dangerous pesticides and guarantee that delivered produce will contain no more than tolerance levels of pesticides.

Even as the grape contracts were being signed, UFWOC was getting involved in another major battle. In August, 7,000 workers walked off the Salinas Valley lettuce fields after growers refused to hold secret union elections and signed backdoor agreements with the Teamsters Union. Following a court injunction against all strike activity in the Salinas area, UFWOC leader Cesar Chavez announced a nationwide boycott of nonunion lettuce grown in California and Arizona. By the end of the year, four large lettuce companies — Inter Harvest (United Fruit), Fresh Pict (Purex), Pic 'n Pac (S. S. Pierce Co.), and D'Arrigo Bros. — had rescinded their contracts with the Teamsters and signed with UFWOC.

While farm workers in California are making significant progress, the great majority of farm workers are still unorganized. UFWOC's organizing successes in the West will need to be duplicated in states like Texas and Florida before farm unionism wields the bargaining power necessary to inaugurate a truly new era in American agriculture.

CHILD LABOR

A substantial segment of agriculture still depends on child labor: one-fourth of farm wage workers, or as many as 800,000, are under 16 —

some as young as 6 years of age. In Aroostook County, Maine, 35 percent of the potato acreage was harvested largely by children. In the Willamette Valley of Oregon, 75 percent of the strawberry and bean harvesters were children. An investigation by the American Friends Service Committee of child labor abuse found conditions reminiscent of sweatshops of the 1930s, with children stooping and crawling through fields sprayed with DDT in 100-degree heat for 10 hours a day to harvest crops.

Most children of farm worker families suffer serious educational disadvantages. The impact of the federal education program for migrant children, according to a study by the National Committee on the Education of Migrant Children, has "not dented indifference to and neglect of migrants on the part of cities and states." While children went hungry and untreated medically, $17 million of budgeted federal funds were turned back unused by the states.

MIGRANTS AND FEDERAL PROGRAMS

Poor health, squalid housing, and powerlessness continue to be the lot of migrant workers. Federal programs designed to help lack adequate funding and are administered by state and local bodies often unresponsive to migrant needs.

The migrant's life expectancy of 49, twenty years less than the average, reflects the gap between the medical care he gets and that received by most Americans. While the average person now pays about $300 per year for health services, only $15 is expended for each migrant under the government's Migrant Health Program. Bad and unsanitary housing adds to the misery of migrants. Since 1962 the Migrant Housing Program has produced 7,300 units which meet only 2 percent of the total need, and has used only 30 percent of the funds available.

Major federal programs to aid poor people also serve migrants poorly, if at all. A 1969 study of food assistance programs showed only 16 percent of the migrants in Texas participating, less than 2 percent in Michigan, and less than .001 percent in Wisconsin. The Farm Labor Service, originally created to help farm workers get the best jobs available, often assists in their exploitation. A suit brought by California Rural Legal Assistance (CRLA) charges that the Farm Labor Service offices in that state serve to depress wages and working conditions, primarily through the device of referring a surplus of workers to growers who violate minimum wage and health laws. CRLA, one of the few federally funded efforts that have advanced the interests of farm workers, was in grave danger in 1970 as the big growers and Governor Ronald Reagan of California pressured a wavering Administration in Washington to cancel the program.

LEGISLATION AND GOVERNMENT HEARINGS

Congress voted to extend unemployment compensation coverage to an additional 4.8 million workers, but refused once again to include farm workers. Meanwhile, big grower spokesmen continued to oppose meaningful coverage of farm workers under the National Labor Relations Act. While the AFL-CIO continues to press for their inclusion, UFWOC believes such coverage would weaken its power because the present NLRA outlaws secondary boycotts. The operations that employ most of the workers in agriculture are too big and diversified to be brought under effective economic pressure by the strike tactics allowed by the NLRA. Instead, UFWOC favors a return to the original Wagner Act which set up the NLRA in 1935 and under which organized labor gained most of its current strength.

Senator Edward Kennedy introduced a bill to curb continuing and widespread employment of illegal entrants, mostly from Mexico, by making farmers who hire them subject to prosecution. Alien workers, willing to accept lower rates of pay than residents, still constitute a serious problem: in the twelve months ending June 30, 1970, over 58,000 aliens working in agriculture were deported. Because of a lack of public interest, hearings on this bill have not been held. Hearings held by Senator Walter Mondale's Subcommittee on Migratory Labor, following the nationwide showing of NBC-TV's "Migrant," represented an important attempt to make giant corporations in agriculture accountable for their treatment of farm workers. Exposure of substandard working and living conditions in its Florida citrus groves forced the Coca-Cola Company to announce a program of improvements.

Senator George McGovern's Select Committee on Nutrition and Human Needs held a series of hearings that underscored the shocking housing conditions in rural areas. One improvement came in the 1970 Housing Act, which provides for an increase in the maximum grant for construction of farm labor housing from 66⅔ percent to 90 percent.

POVERTY CENSUS RISES

For the first time since 1959, the number of Americans living in poverty increased. In 1970 the poverty census climbed to 25.5 million, up 1.2 million from 1969, according to federal figures. Conditions for the rural poor are getting worse — especially for the blacks who, as a group, are falling farther behind whites. Not only are more black people poor — one black in three compared to one white in ten — but they now represent 31.5 percent of the poor compared to 27.9 percent in 1959. They are also poorer, on the average, than their white counterparts: the typical poor black family's income was $1,300 below the poverty line; the average poor white's was $1,000 below.

42. Farm Labor

G. C. Henry

Should agricultural workers continue to be excluded from labor laws? Yes, says G. C. Henry, who argues that minimum wage laws, unemployment insurance, and collective bargaining rights covering most industrial workers should continue to exclude farm workers. Henry's anti–farm workers stance is not surprising. He is Employment and Labor Relations Manager of the California Packing Corporation, and his views are typical of business interests in the agricultural industry. The core of his reasoning is that agriculture is a special case of an industry in which unions and strikes could be ruinous. Henry also reasons that agriculture requires workers who move with the crops. Thus he feels that all impediments to labor mobility have negative consequences. Even compulsory school attendance for children of farm workers is an impediment, since families concerned about education might be reluctant to be continually on the move. Henry's solution to the problem is to import more temporary foreign agricultural workers. But he ignores experience showing how that practice depresses farm wages and working conditions. Behind his arguments is the fact that agricultural interests oppose whatever stands in the way of maximizing profits.

Speaking for farm workers, Cesar Chavez said, "God knows that we are not beasts of burden, agricultural implements or rented slaves; we are men." God may know. But so far the continued exemption of farm workers from most social legislation is a measure of the widespread support for Henry's view in the body politic.

It is fashionable these days to propose that our farm labor problems would disappear if only the social legislation applicable to industrial workers could be applied to farm workers. Three of the areas of industrial social

From G. C. Henry, "Farm Labor," in *Rural Poverty and Regional Progress in an Urban Society* (1969), Task Force on Economic Growth and Opportunity, Chamber of Commerce of the United States. Reprinted by permission.

legislation most commonly referred to for application to farming are minimum wages, unemployment insurance and collective bargaining.

It seems obvious that the minimum wage will have the long-term effect of driving the social misfits out of the farm labor market consigning them to the role of welfare recipients, much as it has done in industry. The professional farm laborer will not be directly affected by any minimum wage since his earnings are usually in excess of any minimum established in our industrial society and very often he has earnings far in excess of present industrial minimums. The chief effect of the minimum wage would be to raise the earnings of some of the newer, local, seasonal workers whose primary interest in agriculture is vacation work or supplementary income.

Unemployment compensation, as we know it today, could have little or great impact on agriculture depending on how the industrial laws were interpreted for farming. If its interpretation produces any significant unemployment income however, it appears that it would have the effect of taking more people out of the migrant labor stream. . . .

Further, there is a most difficult problem related to these higher minimum wages and unemployment compensation on the farms. If adopted in any sense which produces significant income for farm workers, these would have the effect of encouraging farmers to switch from high labor usage crops to lower labor usage crops with corresponding losses to the fresh fruit and vegetable packinghouse workers, frozen food industry workers, and the canning industry workers, and the workers in such related occupations as can making, carton making, trucking, banking, and others.

. . . Collective bargaining, if applied in agriculture as we see it in industry, would require leadership of such quality as to be found only in the heavens. Strikes are not unknown in the industrial segments of our society, and it must be admitted that a strike in an industrial situation is seldom fatal. A strike on a farm could only occur when there are people employed. Since significant numbers of people are employed on farms only at the most vital times of the farmer's growing and harvesting season, a strike of even a few days means the total destruction of the farmer at practically no loss to the worker. . . .

Collective bargaining — as we know it in industry — is not for agriculture without peril to very large segments of our society.

Let us examine some of our other forms of social legislation.

This country, which started as an agricultural economy, gradually has changed so that today we are known as the greatest industrial nation on earth. In adopting programs to solve many of the social problems incident to an industrial society, we have adopted programs with which few would argue. No one today would argue against compulsory school attendance; few, if any, would be unfavorable to our federal and state laws encouraging home ownership through such devices as the FHA, veterans' home loans, and favorable treatment of mortgage interest for income tax purposes. No one would seriously question the basic purpose of our welfare and unemployment laws. Few would question the seniority systems developed through collective bargaining in our large industries and supplemental unemployment benefits and similar measures. Yet, when all of these are examined, we find that they are peculiarly adapted to factory life where the factory remains in a fixed location and workers are relatively frozen in their locations.

To clarify this situation: Compulsory school attendance means that families are reluctant to move from place to place because the changing school situation does a disservice to their children's education. Measures to encourage home ownership mean that people are less free to move from place to place. Welfare and unemployment insurance administration presupposes that there is a government agent who knows the recipient and knows of his efforts to secure employment which would make him ineligible for such assistance. This freezes people at a given location where they can receive such supervision. Seniority systems and supplemental unemployment benefits presuppose that the worker has a tie to a given factory or employer and is thus less free to move from job to job.

This is the vital point. For the kind of laborer we are considering for agriculture, the very essence of the work requires that he move about from place to place. Some find an analogy in the building trades where workers move from one short job to another. The essential difference, however, is that in the building trades, except for relatively long-term commitments on large projects, most movement is confined to relatively small geographical areas. In other words, our city carpenter returns to his home each evening. The movement from job to job in agriculture essentially requires much larger distances for short-term employment. The migratory patterns in farm labor are dictated by the crops which ripen in the winter and early spring in the South, and progressively ripen later as one proceeds to more northerly locations.

All of these considerations are not to say that nothing can or should be done to seek out better solutions to social problems of farm workers. It does mean, however, that the solutions found for the social problems of an industrial society are seldom applicable in an agricultural society. We must look for different solutions. . . .

It seems inevitable to me that eventually this nation will find this is the solution to our agricultural labor supply program. Obviously, the temporary importation of foreign, supplemental farm labor must be accomplished in a manner which does not deprive our own citizens from either the opportunity to work or for a decent wage and proper working conditions. Nevertheless, by permitting shortages of labor to be filled by temporary, foreign supplemental labor — labor which can be sent home as soon as the seasonal need has subsided — then we will not have recreated for some future generation the social problems that past generations have handed to us. In other words, if during the past 100 years this country had been willing and able to import seasonal farm labor for temporary need and had sent them home each year when the need was over, much of the social problems we believe we see on the farm would not exist, and much of our industrial slums would not exist either.

43. Letter from Delano

Cesar Chavez

Bitter labor strife in the 1930's and the protection of the National Labor Relations Act brought union representation to millions of poorly paid industrial workers. For most this meant higher wages, greater security, and more dignity. But the lowest-wage sectors of our economy remained unorganized and unprotected by federal labor relations legislation. "Organize the unorganized," the rallying cry of the youthful and idealistic Congress of Industrial Organization (CIO) in the 1930's, had a hollow ring by the 1950's. Rhetoric replaced action as the labor movement sought respectability, not social responsibility toward their still-oppressed brethren. There was no great drive by established unions to reach out to poverty-stricken workers such as those in agriculture.

Farm workers today still lack the legal rights long since acquired by most other workers. Their earnings are incredibly low, averaging about $1,500 per year. They are almost entirely unorganized. But there are signs of change. In 1965, Cesar Chavez, farm worker and union organizer of agricultural laborers in California, gained national prominence as the cry of "huelga" (strike) echoed through the Delano vineyards. Grape pickers were embarking on a battle to end their poverty.

Chavez is a Mexican-American whose background parallels that of many migrants. Child labor is rampant in agriculture; about 800,000 children under sixteen, some only six years old, toil in America's fields. And only one out of three farm laborers has completed more than eight years of school. Chavez was ten years old when he first worked in Delano. After attending more than thirty schools, he was forced to drop out completely in the eighth grade to help support his family.

The statement by Chavez reproduced below was issued on Good

Friday, 1969. It is in the form of an open letter to the head of a growers organization which opposed the unionization of grape pickers. Chavez is a deeply religious man who has been profoundly influenced by Gandhi's philosophy of nonviolent struggle. The letter is an impassioned defense of such tactics and explains why masses of farm workers are so determined to engage in nonviolent battles for their freedom and humanity.

After five years of struggle which included strikes and a nationwide boycott of grapes, all the Delano workers gained union recognition.

The road away from poverty is long and slippery. So far only the first step has been taken. But Chavez has already started the arduous task of organizing other agricultural workers.

Good Friday 1969.

E. L. Barr, Jr., President
California Grape and Tree Fruit League
717 Market St.
San Francisco, California

Dear Mr. Barr:

I am sad to hear about your accusations in the press that our union movement and table grape boycott have been successful because we have used violence and terror tactics. If what you say is true, I have been a failure and should withdraw from the struggle; but you are left with the awesome moral responsibility, before God and man, to come forward with whatever information you have so that corrective action can begin at once. If for any reason you fail to come forth to substantiate your charges, then you must be held responsible for committing violence against us, albeit violence of the tongue. I am convinced that you as a human being did not mean what you said but rather acted hastily under pressure from the public relations firm that has been hired to try to counteract the tremendous moral force of our movement. How many times we ourselves have felt the need to lash out in anger and bitterness.

Today on Good Friday 1969 we remember the life and the sacrifice of Martin Luther King, Jr., who gave himself totally to the nonviolent struggle for peace and justice. In his "Letter from Birmingham Jail" Dr. King describes better than I could our hopes for the strike and boycott: "Injustice must be exposed, with all the tension its exposure creates, to the light of human conscience and the air of national opinion before it can be

From Cesar E. Chavez, "Letter from Delano." Copyright 1969 Christian Century Foundation. Reprinted by permission from the April 23, 1969, issue of *The Christian Century.*

cured." For our part I admit that we have seized upon every tactic and strategy consistent with the morality of our cause to expose that injustice and thus to heighten the sensitivity of the American conscience so that farm workers will have without bloodshed their own union and the dignity of bargaining with their agribusiness employers. By lying about the nature of our movement, Mr. Barr, you are working against nonviolent social change. Unwittingly perhaps, you may unleash that other force which our union by discipline and deed, censure and education has sought to avoid, that panacean shortcut: that senseless violence which honors no color, class or neighborhood.

You must understand — I must make you understand — that our membership and the hopes and aspirations of the hundreds of thousands of the poor and dispossessed that have been raised on our account are, above all, human beings, no better and no worse than any other cross-section of human society; we are not saints because we are poor, but by the same measure neither are we immoral. We are men and women who have suffered and endured much, and not only because of our abject poverty but because we have been kept poor. The colors of our skins, the languages of our cultural and native origins, the lack of formal education, the exclusion from the democratic process, the numbers of our slain in recent wars — all these burdens generation after generation have sought to demoralize us, to break our human spirit. But God knows that we are not beasts of burden, agricultural implements or rented slaves; we are men. And mark this well, Mr. Barr, we are men locked in a death struggle against man's inhumanity to man in the industry that you represent. And this struggle itself gives meaning to our life and ennobles our dying.

As your industry has experienced, our strikers here in Delano and those who represent us throughout the world are well trained for this struggle. They have been under the gun, they have been kicked and beaten and herded by dogs, they have been cursed and ridiculed, they have been stripped and chained and jailed, they have been sprayed with the poisons used in vineyards; but they have been taught not to lie down and die nor to flee in shame, but to resist with every ounce of human endurance and spirit. To resist not with retaliation in kind but to overcome with love and compassion, with ingenuity and creativity, with hard work and longer hours, with stamina and patient tenacity, with truth and public appeal, with friends and allies, with mobility and discipline, with politics and law, and with prayer and fasting. They were not trained in a month or even a year; after all, this new harvest season will mark our fourth full year of strike and even now we continue to plan and prepare for the years to come. Time accomplishes for the poor what money does for the rich.

This is not to pretend that we have everywhere been successful enough or that we have not made mistakes. And while we do not belittle or underestimate our adversaries — for they are the rich and the powerful and they possess the land — we are not afraid nor do we cringe from the confrontation. We welcome it! We have planned for it. We know that our cause is just, that history is a story of social revolution, and that the poor shall inherit the land.

Once again, I appeal to you as the representative of your industry and as a man. I ask you to recognize and bargain with our union before the economic pressure of the boycott and strike takes an irrevocable toll; but if not, I ask you to at least sit down with us to discuss the safeguards necessary to keep our historical struggle free of violence. I make this appeal because as one of the leaders of our nonviolent movement, I know and accept my responsibility for preventing, if possible, the destruction of human life and property. For these reasons and knowing of Gandhi's admonition that fasting is the last resort in place of the sword, during a most critical time in our movement last February 1968 I undertook a 25-day fast. I repeat to you the principle enunciated to the membership at the start of the fast: if to build our union required the deliberate taking of life, either the life of a grower or his child, or the life of a farm worker or his child, then I choose not to see the union built.

Mr. Barr, let me be painfully honest with you. You must understand these things. We advocate militant nonviolence as our means for social revolution and to achieve justice for our people, but we are not blind or deaf to the desperate and moody winds of human frustration, impatience and rage that blow among us. Gandhi himself admitted that if his only choice were cowardice or violence, he would choose violence. Men are not angels, and time and tide wait for no man. Precisely because of these powerful human emotions, we have tried to involve masses of people in their own struggle. Participation and self-determination remain the best experience of freedom, and free men instinctively prefer democratic change and even protect the rights guaranteed to seek it. Only the enslaved in despair have need of violent overthrow.

This letter does not express all that is in my heart, Mr. Barr. But if it says nothing else it says that we do not hate you or rejoice to see your industry destroyed; we hate the agribusiness system that seeks to keep us enslaved, and we shall overcome and change it not by retaliation or bloodshed but by a determined nonviolent struggle carried on by those masses of farm workers who intend to be free and human.

Sincerely yours,
CESAR E. CHAVEZ.

United Farm Workers Organizing Committee, A.F.L.-C.I.O. Delano, California.

Chapter Eleven

Racism, Black Poverty, and Ghettos

44. How the Federal Government Builds Ghettos

National Committee Against Discrimination in Housing

Segregation in American cities and suburbs is so widespread and so deeply imbedded in the national psyche that many regard it as natural. The National Committee Against Discrimination in Housing, however, presents evidence showing that the federal government, through its various housing policies, has been the nation's prime ghetto-builder. Now, with the problem so huge, only massive federal housing programs and policies against discrimination can reverse the pattern.

Unfortunately, there is little evidence that the federal government is about to initiate a program that would integrate America's cities and suburbs.

A U.S. SEAL ON THE GHETTO

. . . From the moment the Government entered the housing business, back in the early thirties, it also entered the segregation business. In 1938 the official FHA *Underwriting Manual* cautioned home-buyers: "If a neighborhood is to retain stability, it is necessary that properties shall continue to be occupied by the same social and racial group." The manual recom-

---

From *How the Federal Government Builds Ghettos*, 1967. National Committee Against Discrimination in Housing, Inc. (NCDH), 1865 Broadway, New York, N.Y. 10023. Reprinted with permission.

mended use of restrictive covenants to keep out "inharmonious racial groups." And, leaving nothing to chance, it provided a model restrictive covenant for any reader who couldn't write his own.

In another manual, not revised until 1949, FHA urged its mortgage valuators to consider whether "effective restrictive covenants against the entire tract are recorded, since these provide the surest protection against undesirable encroachment. . . ." It warned valuators to beware of "adverse influences," such as "the infiltration of business and industrial uses, lower-class occupancy and inharmonious racial groups."

Other Federal agencies at the time were equally racist. The Federal Home Loan Bank Board, created in 1932, expressly favored racial segregation in residential neighborhoods. So did the Home Owners Loan Corporation, organized in 1933 to buy up and refinance delinquent mortgages. The corporation sold houses *only* to members of the dominant race in a given neighborhood. As for the public housing program, it early established a policy of "racial equity" — a polite way of saying separate but equal housing — and to this day most local housing authorities operate on this old, comfortable basis.

In the forties Federal race relations advisors (now known as intergroup relations specialists) counted it a victory if they could persuade local builders and politicians to build *any* housing for Negroes. Only a few mentioned integrated housing. Thus, in a speech in 1947, Congressman Frank Buchanan of Pennsylvania lauded race relations advisors for encouraging Negro housing in such cities as Englewood, N.J., Miami and Atlanta — cities which in the sixties have been scenes of racial turmoil precisely because they are segregated.

The Government did its work well. It fixed white racist patterns in thousands of new suburbs, where 80 per cent of all new housing is now being built. As Edward Rutledge, NCDH executive director, pointed out in a Senate hearing last year, "the Federal Housing Administration, through its insuring and underwriting programs, and the Federal highway agencies, through their road-building activities, jointly underwrote and made possible the growth of the lily-white suburbs. Negroes who were able to afford suburban housing were restricted to all-Negro subdivisions; the mass of low-income Negroes and other minorities, the urban poor, were left to pile up in the central cities."

FHA and the Veterans Administration together have financed more than $120 billion-worth of new housing since World War II. Less than two per cent of it has been available to nonwhite families, and much of that on a strictly segregated basis. "It is one thing," declared Gunnar Myrdal in *The American Dilemma,* "when private tenants, property owners and financial institutions maintain and extend the pattern of racial segregation in housing. It is quite another matter when a Federal agency chooses to side with the segregationists."

In 1948 the U.S. Supreme Court compelled a change by striking down enforcement of restrictive covenants. But it wasn't until 18 months later that FHA took notice of the decision and announced it would no longer insure loans where such covenants were imposed. By that time, however, restrictive covenants had a life of their own, having become a widely accepted technique of neighborhood segregation. To this day such covenants are included in countless property deeds, and home-buyers sign them under the false impression they are legally enforceable. As a practical matter, then, the courts have been unable to kill off a racist weed which the Federal establishment itself planted and then cultivated.

Thus the Government has spent years practicing "affirmative" segregation, and it has worked all too well. Now only an extraordinary nationwide effort — in short, affirmative *de*segregation — can effect a meaningful turnabout. And, as NCDH has continuously pointed out, only the Federal Government can mobilize such an effort: it has the money; it has the power; and it has the unanswerable moral obligation to undo the mischief it has sown.

GALLOPING SEGREGATION

Thanks to Federal largesse, white Americans have separated themselves from Negro Americans. This process continues today without pause and without much thought, as Negroes are jammed into the central city and white families flee to newer, "safer" locales. In consequence, the racial ghetto has become a national institution, casting a fixed shadow on the social landscape and on our collective imagination. So natural a part of the landscape does it seem, that many Americans have difficulty imagining another kind of world — a world, that is, in which Negroes and whites live in the same neighborhoods, attend the same churches, shop in the same stores, use the same playgrounds and send their children to the same schools. Note, for example, that a large proportion of the public looks upon integrated neighborhoods in disbelief and prefers to call them "transitional." Also, Negro families who move into white neighborhoods are called "pioneers," which is to say they have gone forth to do battle with nature. In a society led by the blind, the man with eyesight is something of a freak.

The ghetto is self-perpetuating, for by separating the white child from the Negro child we hand on to both our own dear delusions of race. We are now trapped in a situation where we must push for a miscellany of tortuous techniques, from pairing to busing, designed to integrate schools which serve segregated neighborhoods, both black and white. These schools must pretend that Americans live in one world and not two, but the children know better because they know their neighborhoods. The bus from the Negro ghetto in Evanston, Illinois, comes every morning to Lincolnwood elementary school, and the white children on the playground shout, "Here comes the colored bus!"

Neighborhood segregation is thus the sour grape that sets each new generation's teeth on edge. Right now we are creating another generation of Americans committed in their bones to segregation, not because we are formally teaching it (in many homes and schools we are *teaching* just the opposite), but because we are *living* it.

A few years ago in a Chicago suburb about eighty-five frightened people met to protest the presence of the town's first Negro family. "I moved out here so my kids could have grass and trees and sunshine," a young father shouted. "And now look what's happening!" We have created a world in which it is possible for intelligent people to believe that Negroes blot out the sun.

Thanks to sociologist Karl E. Taeuber's segregation index, we now have a statistical measure of our madness. Using 1960 census figures, Taeuber analyzed the degree of racial separation in 207 cities, placing them on a scale from zero (no segregation) to 100 (complete segregation). The *least* segregated city — San Jose, California — had an index of 60.4. Half the cities had segregation ratings above 87 and a quarter exceeded 91. Only eight cities had ratings below 70.

As Taeuber observes, "No elaborate analysis is necessary to conclude from these figures that a high degree of residential segregation based on race is a universal characteristic of American cities. This segregation is found in the cities of the North and West as well as of the South; in large cities as well as small; in nonindustrial cities as well as industrial; in cities with hundreds of thousands of Negro residents as well as those with only a few thousand. . . ."

Apart from the scandal of apartheid, the figures point to enormous needless suffering by millions of Americans, simply because they are Negroes. For example, nearly two-thirds of the dwelling units occupied by Negro families in urban areas are substandard, compared to less than one-fifth of the units occupied by whites. In many cities the incidence of overcrowding among Negroes runs eight or nine times higher than that of whites.

The lower incomes of many Negro families are, of course, a factor here. But the critical factor is racial discrimination. In Chicago, almost half the Negro families earning $7,000 or more live in substandard dwellings; for white families with comparable incomes the figure is only six per cent. Similarly, in New York City, about one-third of the Negro families earning $7,000 or more live in overcrowded dwellings, compared with 10 per cent of whites with comparable incomes. And a recent study in Washington, D.C. indicates that even among Negro households with incomes exceeding $10,000, the incidence of overcrowding is more than 25 per cent!

The conclusion is inescapable that Negroes live in the impacted racial ghettos neither by choice nor by income, but by compulsion. In effect, galloping segregation creates "artificial" slums — rundown, overcrowded neighborhoods which are less a product of economic law than of white stupidity. That is one reason why our current war against poverty is so plainly ineffectual, especially in our cities. Instead of breaking up the ghettos, it merely aims to make them habitable. The war against poverty is pouring millions of dollars into Watts but it is not helping Negroes to get out of Watts.

Further, the poverty war relies on education and on job training and placement as its major weapons, and these programs are increasingly meaningless in the face of widespread ghettoism. Our slum schools may not be all they should be, but even if they were, they could not redress the damage ghettos inflict on children. Results of the Head Start program suggest that the child's home and neighborhood have at least as much to do with what he learns — and what he does not learn — as the school. The effects of Head Start on pre-school children have been found to be very positive — and very temporary.

As for jobs, a recent U.S. Labor Department study notes that more than half of all new industrial and mercantile buildings during the past ten years were constructed *outside* America's central cities — precisely where most Negroes are not. "This reveals a long term tendency for major sources of employment to be located quite a distance from the residence of workers with a very high incidence of unemployment and poverty," observed Secretary of Labor Willard Wirtz. All of which underscores the Negro's dilemma: locked up within the central city, he finds that the jobs are moving to the suburbs as fast as the whites.

In sum, the ghetto *is* poverty; and a "war" that proposes to eliminate the one while leaving the other intact is not a war at all — it is a cruel pretense. . . .

Most of the evidence indicates that we are losing the struggle. In 1910, 73 per cent of the Negro population lived in rural areas; today 73 per cent of the Negro population lives in urban areas. Washington, D.C. is already more than 60 per cent Negro, and most other cities are headed in this direction. In a special Federal census taken in Los Angeles after the summer riots of 1965, segregation was found to be *increasing* in each of the seven neighborhoods that make up the Negro ghetto of South Los Angeles. In the Green Meadows section alone, nonwhite occupancy rose from 58.9 per cent of all dwelling units in 1960 to 79 per cent in 1965 — this despite more than 100,000 housing vacancies in greater Los Angeles!

Meanwhile, white families, free to live where they please, continue to seek "trees and grass and sunshine" in the white suburbs. A recent survey of population movements in New York City, for example, reveals that

400,000 whites, mostly of child-rearing age, left the city during the years 1960 through 1964.

Thus, we continue to transform the inner city and suburbia into one-class, one-race sepulchres — tombs for the American promise of democracy. . . .

THE FEDERAL RESPONSIBILITY

In its Bill of Particulars . . . the National Committee Against Discrimination in Housing lists 17 specific ways in which the Federal Government builds ghettos, and calls for as many remedies. The charges and the remedies spring from the single assumption that the Federal Government is the country's master builder. In the war against segregation in housing no one can remain neutral, least of all the Government of the United States. Every decision it makes, and every decision it fails to make, has an impact for good or evil upon the lives of every American, black and white. "The only thing necessary for the triumph of evil," said Edmund Burke, "is for good men to do nothing." There is still time for our Federal leaders to act. It is one minute before midnight.

45. The Impact of Housing Patterns on Job Opportunities

National Committee Against Discrimination in Housing

Residential segregation in the United States has existed for many decades, but in recent years metropolitan areas have become more racially polarized than ever. Increasingly, the central cities have become poverty-stricken ghettos and the affluent whites have fled to the suburbs. Now, according to the National Committee Against Discrimination in Housing, segregation based on race and income have themselves become factors in the perpetuation of nonwhite unemployment and poverty. The reason is that job openings have declined in central cities but grown rapidly in suburban areas that are inaccessible to ghetto-dwellers. Thus, plentiful, low-cost, nondiscriminatory housing is urgently needed in the suburbs. Otherwise there seems little likelihood of significantly reducing unemployment among urban blacks.

A SUMMARY OF MAJOR FINDINGS OF THIS STUDY

The primary conclusion to be drawn from this preliminary study of where people live and where the jobs are is that residents of the nation's racial ghettos are severely handicapped in their search for employment by housing market conditions and discriminatory practices. Nonwhites and other minorities increasingly are contained in circumscribed areas of central cities; employment opportunities increasingly are locating in outlying sections and suburban communities where Negroes are denied access to living accommodations. In short, jobs are moving beyond the geographic reach of those who need them most.

As a consequence, the cities — more and more the habitat of the elderly, the black, and the poor — are plagued by a multiplicity of problems not the least of which is the social dynamite bred by extreme poverty, deprivation and racial discrimination. The economic and operational problems of city governments, business interests, and community institutions are pyramiding, and the people of the city are ever more stripped of essential services.

Where People Live

The proportion of the nation's Negro population living in rural areas and urban areas has undergone a *total reversal* during the last 50 years: 73 per cent rural in 1910 to 73 per cent urban in 1960.

Eighty per cent of all Negroes living in urban (metropolitan) areas in 1960 lived in central cities, contrasted with less than 50 per cent of the urban white population.

Between 1960 and 1966, the white population in central cities declined by 900,000, despite an increase of over 10 million whites living in metropolitan areas.

By 1966, only 27 per cent of the nation's white population lived in central cities, compared with 55 per cent of the total Negro population.

The increasing color separation between center city and suburbia is exemplified by the counter movement of population in metropolitan Baltimore. Between 1940 and 1960, the center city nonwhite population grew from 19.4 to 35.0 per cent. During the same period, while the white population in Baltimore's suburban ring grew by 196.8 per cent (from 247,171 to 733,592), the nonwhite proportion of the suburban population shrank from 11.9 to 6.9 per cent.

From *The Impact of Housing Patterns on Job Opportunities,* 1968. National Committee Against Discrimination in Housing, Inc. (NCDH), 1865 Broadway, New York, N.Y. 10023. Reprinted with permission.

Unemployment and Under-employment[1]

For almost 20 years nonwhite unemployment rates have fluctuated between 1½ and 2½ times those for whites.

In *non-poverty* areas recently surveyed, unemployment for nonwhites was 7.2 per cent compared with 3.6 per cent for whites.

In *poverty* areas, the unemployment rate for nonwhites was 9.4 per cent, contrasted with 6.0 per cent for whites.

Figures from the U.S. Labor Department's new index of "sub-employment" are even more staggering. This index includes the unemployed, heads of households earning less than poverty-level wages, part-time workers, etc. Average sub-employment was found to be *34.6 per cent* in ghetto areas recently surveyed in eight cities over the nation, while the conventional unemployment rate in these areas had been shown as 10 per cent.

The unemployment rate for nonwhite males from 14 to 19 years of age was 31 per cent; for females in this age group, 46 per cent.

If nonwhites continue to hold the same proportion of jobs in each occupation, by 1975 the unemployment rate for Negroes will be more than five times that for the labor force as a whole.

Where the Jobs Are[2]

The overwhelming proportion of new jobs created in recent years have been located outside the center cities in areas where Negroes are denied housing either by overt discrimination or lack of moderate-cost accommodations.

A recent Bureau of Labor Statistics study shows that from 1960 to 1965 at least 62 per cent of valuation permits for new industrial buildings and 52 per cent of those for mercantile establishments were for construction in the suburbs.

The actual number of jobs has declined in many major cities. For example, from 1951 to 1965, St. Louis City lost 62,000 jobs; Philadelphia lost 49,000. Even in cities where slight gains have been made in clerical and white collar employment, there has been a loss in semi-skilled and unskilled jobs. Manufacturing jobs in New York City dropped by almost 50,000 from 1962 to 1965, with an additional decline of some 6,400 jobs in trade; San Francisco lost 4,400 jobs in manufacturing, and 1,100 in trade.

In the five cities covered by this study (Baltimore, New York, Philadelphia, St. Louis and San Francisco), from 1951 to 1965 manufacturing employment decreased by some 360,000 jobs.

[1] [See Appendix, Tables 3, 4, and 5. — Ed.]
[2] [See Appendix, Table 6. — Ed.]

Commutation is not a practical solution for reducing the disparity between job location and the housing location of minorities: it is prohibitively expensive; excessively time-consuming; and the ghetto poor are in no position to maintain the automobiles necessary for most commutes. For instance, to commute from Hunter's Point in San Francisco to a job in suburban Contra Costa County in the East Bay area would cost $3.00 per day, consume four to five hours in daily travel time, and would involve three or four transfers. In many cases, public transportation is not available from center cities to suburban plant locations.

Disparities in Training

Unpublished figures for enrollment in Government training programs indicate that nonwhites, particularly young Negroes, are being seriously shortchanged.

The majority of Negro participants are being trained for those jobs which are the lowest paid and offer the least chance for advancement.

Those in most critical need of training are Negro males; the largest percentage of Negro enrollees are females.

Most of the Negro enrollment in manpower training programs is for vocational courses under the Institutional programs, with Negro males comprising about 31 per cent of total male enrollment and Negro females accounting for 42 per cent. Under this program, the enrollee must still search for a job when the training is completed.

Those enrolled in On-the-Job Training programs are salaried while they learn and generally have a job when they complete the course. Under OJT, 98 per cent of the Negro trainees (96 per cent of the whites) obtained work related to their training. Yet Negroes comprise only 13.8 per cent of all OJT trainees, whereas they make up 35.9 per cent of the less advantageous Institutional program enrollment.

The racial disparity in Government training programs becomes even greater when examined by occupational breakdown. Negroes training under the Institutional program for metal-working jobs make up 25 per cent of the enrollment; but Negroes are only 10 per cent of all metal-working trainees in the On-the-Job program. In building trades, Negroes are 26 per cent of the Institutional trainees; but only 18 per cent of the OJT enrollees. For lower paying jobs in hospitals, hotels and restaurants, nonwhites make up 40 per cent of the Institutional trainee enrollment and 34 per cent of the enrollment for OJT.

The types of industry which are locating in the suburbs are precisely those most amenable to OJT programs. Therefore, exclusionary housing patterns must be recognized as a likely deterrent to Negro participation in this most advantageous of the manpower training programs.

Toward a Rational Solution

Present programs, public and pirvate, to deal with the problems of minorities and the poor are diffuse, confused, piecemeal, and totally uncoordinated. As a result, little is being accomplished in lifting the burden of unemployment and under-employment from the backs of Negroes, other minorities, and poor whites as well.

The only rational solution lies in comprehensive, metropolitan-wide planning and programming which embraces all of the economic, social and political factors affecting community life: housing, education, training, employment, health, transportation, cultural amenities, economic development, and — above all — human dignity and freedom.

46. Menial Jobs and Black Poverty

*National Advisory Commission
on Civil Disorders*

Today black youths are increasingly rejecting the menial jobs our society has traditionally offered them. And with good reason. As the National Commission on Civil Disorders (the Kerner Commission) found, jobs alone are no guarantee against poverty. Appointed by President Johnson to investigate the causes of the ghetto riots of 1967, the Commission says that nonwhite men lost $4.8 billion in wages (1966) because they were working in lower-paying occupational categories than all men in the labor force. However, even that sum does not represent the full cost of the distorted occupational distribution to the nonwhite community. For instance the Commission's estimate does not include the loss of earnings of nonwhite women who are forced to work at menial jobs, nor the loss of earnings caused by the well-known clustering of nonwhites in lower-paying jobs within each broad occupational category.

The distortions created by generations of discrimination by employers and unions and government, by separate and inferior schools, and by apartheid-like housing cannot be wished away. The present black revolution has a strong economic motivation. The fight for better jobs, urgently needed upgrading on the job, real educational opportunity, and the struggle against every form of racism and discrimination are all part of a battle against black poverty. Some individuals have already benefited, but progress has been too slow and white resistance too great to have altered significantly the depressed condition of the black people as a whole.

Even more important perhaps than unemployment is the related problem of the undesirable nature of many jobs open to Negroes. Negro workers are concentrated in the lowest-skilled and lowest-paying occupations. These jobs often involve substandard wages, great instability and uncertainty of tenure, extremely low status in the eyes of both employer and employee, little or no chance for meaningful advancement, and unpleasant or exhausting duties. Negro men in particular are more than twice as likely as whites to be in unskilled or service jobs which pay far less than most:

Type of Occupation	Percentage of Male Workers in Each Type of Occupation —1966		Median Earnings of All Male Civilians in Each Occupation —1965
	White	Nonwhite	
Professional, technical, managerial	27%	9%	$7,603
Clerical and sales	14	9	$5,532
Craftsmen and foremen	20	12	$6,270
Operatives	20	27	$5,046
Service Workers	6	16	$3,436
Nonfarm laborers	6	20	$2,410
Farmers and farm workers	7	8	$1,699

This concentration in the least desirable jobs can be viewed another way by calculating the changes which would occur if Negro men were employed in various occupations in the same proportions as the male labor force as a whole (*not* solely the white labor force).

Thus, upgrading the employment of Negro men to make their occupational distribution identical with that of the labor force as a whole would have an immense impact upon the nature of their occupations. About 1.3 million nonwhite men — or 28 percent of those employed in 1966 — would move up the employment ladder into one of the higher-status and higher-paying categories. The effect of such a shift upon the incomes of Negro men would be very great. Using the 1966 job distribution, the shift indicated above would produce about $4.8 billion more earned income for nonwhite men alone if they received the 1965 median income in each occupation. This would be a rise of approximately 30 percent in the earn-

From *Report of the National Advisory Commission on Civil Disorders* (Washington, D.C.: U.S. Government Printing Office, March 1968).

	Number of Male Nonwhite Workers — 1966			
Type of Occupation	As Actually Distributed	If Distributed the Same as All Male Workers	Difference	
			No.	Percent
Professional, technical, managerial	415,000	1,173,000	+758,000	+183%
Clerical and sales	415,000	628,000	+213,000	+ 51%
Craftsmen and foremen	553,000	894,000	+341,000	+ 62%
Operatives	1,244,000	964,000	−280,000	− 23%
Service workers	737,000	326,000	−411,000	− 56%
Nonfarm laborers	922,000	340,000	−582,000	− 63%
Farmers and farm workers	369,000	330,000	− 39,000	− 11%

ings actually received by all nonwhite men in 1965 (not counting any sources of income other than wages and salaries).

Of course, the kind of "instant upgrading" visualized in these calculations does not represent a practical alternative for national policy. The economy cannot drastically reduce the total number of low-status jobs it now contains, or shift large numbers of people upward in occupation in any short period. Therefore, major upgrading in the employment status of Negro men must come through a faster relative expansion of higher-level jobs than lower-level jobs (which has been occurring for several decades), an improvement in the skills of nonwhite workers so they can obtain a higher proportion of those added better jobs, and a drastic reduction of discriminatory hiring and promotion practices in all enterprises, both private and public.

Nevertheless, this hypothetical example clearly shows that the concentration of male Negro employment at the lowest end of the occupational scale is greatly depressing the incomes of United States Negroes in general. In fact, this is the single most important source of poverty among Negroes. It is even more important than unemployment, as can be shown by a second hypothetical calculation. In 1966, there were about 702,000 unemployed nonwhites in the United States on the average, including adults and teenagers, and allowing for the Census Bureau undercount of Negroes. If every one of these persons had been employed and had received the median amount earned by nonwhite males in 1966 ($3,864), this would have added a total of $2.7 billion to nonwhite income as a whole. If only enough of these persons had been employed at that wage to reduce nonwhite unemployment from 7.3 to 3.3 percent — the rate among whites in 1966 — then the income gain for nonwhites would have totaled about $1.5 billion. But if nonwhite unemployment remained at 7.3 percent, and nonwhite men were upgraded so that they had the same occupational distribution and incomes as all men in the labor force considered together, this would have produced about $4.8 billion in additional income, as noted above (using 1965 earnings for calculation). Thus the potential income gains from upgrading the male nonwhite labor force are much larger than those from reducing nonwhite unemployment.

This conclusion underlines the difficulty of really improving the economic status of Negro men. It is far easier to create new jobs than either to create new jobs with relatively high status and earning power, or to upgrade existing employed or partly-employed workers into such better-quality employment. Yet only such upgrading will eliminate the fundamental basis of poverty and deprivation among Negro families.

47. For Sam Smith, Hospital Orderly: A Battle Whose Time Has Come

John M. McClintock

The organization of unskilled hospital workers is the urban counterpart of Cesar Chavez's drive to unionize farm workers. The hospital industry is one of the nation's largest low-wage employers. In many cities, blacks and other minority group workers comprise the bulk of the unskilled hospital worker force. For the most part, they are unorganized. But this, too, is beginning to change. Large-scale organization began in hospitals in New York City with the struggles and victories of Local 1199 in the late 1950's and 1960's. Now the movement is spreading to other cities, including some in the South.

Hospital unions represent an exception to the deteriorated relations between blacks and organized labor caused by the racially exclusionary policies of craft unions. Battles for higher pay and union recognition on the part of hospital workers have been closely identified with the civil rights movement.

John M. McClintock's report tells what happens when low-wage hospital workers in Baltimore try to end their poverty by unionizing.

"We was making 40 cents an hour, working 12 hours at a stretch. And, man, I couldn't cut it. I couldn't make it with four kids."

The frail 58-year-old Negro was talking the other day about his job in a Baltimore nursing home in 1962. The workers had organized a strike, only

From John M. McClintock, "For Sam Smith, Hospital Orderly: A Battle Whose Time Has Come," *Baltimore Sun* (December 7, 1969). Reprinted by permission.

to return to their jobs a few days later. Nobody had enough money to stay out.

"We had nothing. We got nothing. We was nothing," he said.

The worker's comment is typical of the plight of the nation's 2.5 million hospital and nursing home employees. And it partially explains the civil rights fervor that has characterized the recent union organizing drives at hospitals in [Baltimore]. The workers are the dishwashers, nurses' aides, cooks, attendants and so-called "menials" whom one sees but never really recognizes.

The television soap operas do not thrill us with the exploits of Sam Smith, hospital orderly. The romance and fire is reserved for doctors and nurses.

The orderlies and dishwashers are essential only to the unromantic, unmentionable processes of health care: the dirty linen, the bed pans, the scraping of plates, the pushing of wheelchairs. These are the lowest jobs, jobs that attract workers from the lowest rung of the socio-economic ladder — the Negroes, the Puerto Ricans, the Mexican-Americans.

When the Johns Hopkins Hospital talks about its workers as "employees whom we will continue to treat with dignity and respect," everyone knows they are talking about Negroes. And when New York-based Local 1199E of the Hospital and Nursing Home Employees Union (AFL-CIO) began its Baltimore drive last April, everyone knew that its appeal was to Negroes.

The union was then in one of the greatest battles of the American labor movement. It had confronted two public hospitals in Charleston, S.C., with a strike by Negro women hospital workers. The strike, which lasted 113 days, involved the Southern Christian Leadership Conference, and for months television screens in the nation were filled with pictures of Mrs. Martin Luther King, Jr., and the Rev. Ralph David Abernathy marching in support of the workers.

It was not a labor battle in the traditional sense. The union was challenging racism in the home state of Strom Thurmond and Mendel Rivers.

If the union could win there, it could win anywhere. The same conditions — perhaps to a lesser degree — prevailed in nearly every metropolitan hospital in the country. At stake were the allegiances of the nation's health-care workers who, for the most part, had never been unionized. These 2.5 million workers are greater in number than the workers in the country's basic steel industry.

The union victory in Charleston inextricably identified it with the civil rights movement of Martin Luther King, Jr. The union had won a series of tough strikes before in New York city, but this strike — with its curfews and National Guard troops — had the flavor of Selma, Ala., of the white establishment beating down on an oppressed minority.

The effect on the organizing drive in Baltimore has been spectacular. In the past eight months, the union has achieved recognition at 5 major hospitals, including the Hopkins, and 14 nursing homes. With 6,000 members, it already has become one of the largest in the state; there are about 11,000 hospital workers in the Baltimore area. The union membership figure also includes nursing home employees whose total number is not known. The four other hospitals that have recognized the union are Lutheran, Maryland General, Franklin Square and Sinai. An election is to be held next week at the Greater Baltimore Medical Center and at the John F. Kennedy Institute for retarded children.

The victories at the hospitals were especially impressive since such non-profit institutions are exempted from federal collective bargaining laws and they were not required to hold representative elections.

But the Charleston message had been unmistakably clear. No one wanted a Charleston in Baltimore. The union was granted its elections.

And in the key election at the Hopkins — the largest, most prestigious hospital in the state — Mrs. King was flown to Baltimore to rally support. The workers subsequently voted overwhelmingly for the union. The handwriting of Martin Luther King, Jr., was on the wall. In only one case, that of tiny North Charles General Hospital, was the union defeated in an election here.

Charleston had been the kickoff to a national organizing campaign that went successively to Baltimore, Durham, N.C., Pittsburgh, Philadelphia-Harrisburg and Dayton, Ohio. Only in Baltimore, however, has the union achieved such open recognition. . . .

While much of the union appeal is oriented to minority groups, the union demand for such things as a $100-a-week minimum, improved fringe benefits and job mobility has an equally great appeal. A typical Baltimore hospital worker's starting wage is about $72 a week — or about $3,744 a year, which is barely above the federal poverty line for a non-farm family of four.

The 22 metropolitan hospitals in the Baltimore area have estimated that the union demands would push up labor costs by $37 million. Hospital officials, though, are not worried so much by the $100 minimum as by the escalator effect it will have in pushing up the wages of other employees.

As a result, for example, the Johns Hopkins Hospital has estimated the rate for a semi-private room would be raised from $51 to $69 a day. The union counters the cost argument with the statement that the workers "are not philanthropists." The union also says that higher wages insure against a hospital's normal high rate of turnover among nonprofessional employees and thus reduce training costs. . . .

Local 1199 has enjoyed a spectacular growth since its beginning in 1958. In 11 years its membership has increased from 5,500 to 42,500. The local is actually a division of the Retail, Wholesale Drugstore Union which was founded in 1932 by seven Jewish pharmacists in New York. The president of the union is Leon J. Davis, one of the founders.

The drug union, started during the Depression, was instrumental in breaking the color-line for many Negro pharmacists in Harlem, where stores were owned by whites.

The union also opened up to Negroes positions in drugstores that had hitherto been for white only. Negroes were usually hired as porters.

The hospital division was formed in 1958 after the union's first victory at Montefiore Hospital in the Bronx.

After two key 1199 strikes, in 1963 and 1965, the New York State Legislature smoothed the way when it granted unions the right to organize hospital workers who were previously exempted from collective bargaining laws.

48. Blame the Negro Child

Doxey A. Wilkerson

Lack of education and lack of money have long been partners. Lack of education, however, is only one of many causes of black poverty. Racism may be an even more significant factor in reducing the income of black people, since blacks reap much lower monetary rewards from education than whites. For instance, the median income of black males with 12 years of schooling is less than for whites with 8 years of schooling. (See Appendix, Table 6.) Despite such dismal evidence, education is usually regarded as a crucial — though not sufficient — weapon against poverty. In many cities the poor have been involved in struggles to gain influence or control of the schools that educate their children. Traditionally, poor parents have had no say over the educational establishment and now they accuse the schools of failing their children. But why do children from impoverished backgrounds so often fail in school?

Doxey Wilkerson, a prominent black educator who is a professor of education at the Ferkhauf Graduate School of Yeshiva University, claims that schools reflect the class and racial biases of society and don't really expect black or poor children to learn. So they don't learn. But educators then develop theories that blame the children instead of the schools.

Wilkerson offers concrete evidence that children from impoverished

> backgrounds can learn. And he feels that some individual educators are sincerely striving to overcome the stultifying practices of slum schools. But Wilkerson feels that schools mirror society's values and probably won't make the massive changes that are needed until and unless true democratic values prevail in our society.

Throughout the history of class society, the exploiters of men have been prone to blame their victims for the degradation imposed upon them, developing self-serving theories to cloak oppression. As with the black man in this country, for example: he was enslaved "because" he was inferior. He is oppressed in the urban ghetto today "because" the nuclear family unit is broken. This pattern of up-side-down rationalizing extends into many areas of our national life. The concern here is for its manifestations in the education of Negro children in the public schools.

When I was coming along in college during the 1920's, the psychologists of our land were still enthralled with the big intelligence-testing spree initiated during World War I; and, in all seriousness, we were taught that Negroes were "poorly endowed by nature." Their low academic performance in school was evidence of their innate intellectual inferiority. Successive generations of teachers were brought up on this doctrine, and its impact in our profession is still pronounced. If the children fail in school, they — or perhaps their progenitors — are to blame; certainly not their teachers!

During the 1940's and 1950's, however, this racist doctrine lost academic respectability. The once immutable IQ, supposedly set by the genes, was exposed as an unstable function of cultural experience. More fundamentally, even the concept of genetically-determined "potential" for learning was undermined by the theoretical work of [Jean] Piaget, [J. Mc. V.] Hunt and others. Most reputable behavioral scientists now embrace the interaction theory of the development of intellectual function, emphasizing the decisive influence of the organism's encounters with its environment.

It is anachronistic, therefore, for a senior staff member [Roger A. Freeman] of the conservative Hoover Institution at Stanford University to assert in 1968 that psychological tests "permit us to determine with a high degree of accuracy and reliability the innate capacity of children," and on that basis to propose part-time schooling and apprenticeship as the proper education for the children of the poor. More consistent with modern behavioral-science theory — and also with the democratic professions of our society — is the well-documented conclusion of [Milton] Schwebel's schol-

From Doxey A. Wilkerson, "Blame the Negro Child," *Freedomways*, 4th qtr. (1968). Reprinted by permission.

arly new book: Although we do not yet know how to cope with the learning problems of the tiny proportion of children who are neurologically impaired, "for all the rest of our children, there is no known reason to believe that they will be unable to do the work of an academic high school or college. . . . Who can be educated? *Everyman*."

If black children — and poor children generally — have the same "native endowment" as children of any other race or social class, then the educational profession would seem to be confronted with the challenge: Teach them or admit your own failure. But no; our ideological resources for escaping that trap are by no means exhausted.

During the early 1960's when the civil rights movement was united around the demand for school integration, the grossly sub-standard achievement levels that prevail in segregated Negro schools were dramatized throughout the country. Sending black children to white schools was advocated as a means to equalize educational opportunity. But public officials found it politically inexpedient to integrate the schools, and they countered with plans for large-scale improvement of the separate Negro schools.

During the past five or six years, special new programs of school improvement have proliferated across the land, mainly — but not exclusively — in the urban Negro ghetto. Generally called "compensatory education," they include developments on all educational levels — Head Start and other preschool programs, a wide range of remedial and enrichment programs within the regular grades, dropout prevention and reclamation programs, Upward Bound and similar programs to facilitate college entrance, and many more. Very large sums of money from philanthropic and federal sources have gone to support these new programs of compensatory education.

Paralleling this development, there emerged a vast literature on "the education of disadvantaged children"; and its dominant theoretical premise carries a new rationalization for the failure of our schools to educate Negro and other children of the poor. It is commonly held that the substandard academic performance generally found among disadvantaged children is mainly — if not exclusively — a function of negative influences in the environment where they were nurtured. It is said that because of conditions of poverty and discrimination in home and community, these children enter school with deficiencies in auditory and visual perception, retarded language development, poor self-concept, low academic motivation, and seriously limited experiential background. These and other socially-induced "deficits" are said to account for the high incidence of school failures and dropouts among children of the ghetto.

Thus, the profession is again off the hook. Whereas two decades ago we could point to "these children's" IQ's in the 80's, now we say they are "culturally deprived" — and this, let it be noted, carries no derogatory implications about their ancestry.

There is no doubt that a large proportion of the children from the ghetto do enter school less advanced educationally than more privileged children. There is no clear evidence, however, that primary socialization under conditions of poverty and discrimination *precludes* effective learning in school. This is the crucial question; and there is considerable evidence that, given appropriate learning experiences, disadvantaged children do, indeed, learn effectively. . . .

Further illustrative of the educability of the poor are the results achieved by [Moshe] Smilansky and his associates working with Middle Eastern Jews in Israel. Their "social disadvantages" and associated academic retardation are strikingly similar to those of children in our urban ghettos. Smilansky and his co-workers operate on the premise that poor children, too, can learn; and through imaginative educational programs they commonly raise these children's IQ's by twenty points on the preschool level, and by ten points in adolescence. Such results, incidentally, are frequently achieved in experimental programs in our own country, especially among preschool children.

It is generally found in our schools — as in [Martin] Deutsch's work at the Institute for Developmental Studies — that the achievement differences between lower-class Negro children and middle-class white children are minimal at grade one, but increase progressively as children move through the grades. Thus, the Negro children become more and more retarded while they are in school. Could it be that what happens to them there has some causal relationship to their increasing retardation?

I have examined the cumulative records of children in ghetto schools, noting what teachers recorded about the same children in successive grades; and a striking pattern tends to emerge. In a substantial majority of cases, youngsters who were characterized as "bright" and "cooperative" and "delightful" in first and second grade tend to be described as "apathetic" and "failing" and "behavior problems" by fourth grade and after. Is this metamorphosis to be explained solely — or even primarily — in terms of their social background? Could it be that negative school experiences had something to do with the change?

Several summers ago, [Kenneth B.] Clark and his associates at the Northside Center for Child Development brought in a number of disadvantaged children from Harlem — all from impoverished homes, all seriously retarded in school — and undertook to teach them to read. They worked with them one hour a day, five days a week, for four weeks. Standard tests showed that the average child gained eight months in reading achievement during this period, and the smallest gain made by any child was four months in reading achievement. In the fall, these children returned to their regular schools; and after nine months they were tested again. The average gain in reading for the whole school year was zero! Are these findings to be explained in terms of the children's "culturally deprived" backgrounds, or must they be explained in terms of differences in the appropriateness of their learning experiences at the Northside Center and in their regular schools?

This recital need not be extended. Suffice it to say that evidence mounts to prove that the "cultural deprivation" hypothesis is bankrupt. Like its predecessor, the doctrine of "genetic inferiority," it is untenable as an explanation for the prevailing academic retardation among children from the ghetto. When provided with learning experiences appropriate to their developmental needs, these children, despite their impoverished background, do learn effectively. Their academic failures must be attributed in large measure to inappropriate learning experiences.

It is not difficult to identify such inappropriate learning experiences in schools serving Negro children in the urban ghetto, including most of our schools with the new programs of compensatory education.

We start out with stereotypic ideas about what "these children" are like, conjuring up the whole array of negative characteristics listed over and over again in the literature on the education of disadvantaged children. Overlooked is the important pedagogical fact that the children of the ghetto, like all children, are wondrously varied human beings — in background experiences, academic ability, self-concept, aspiration, motivation, and interpersonal relations. They do not come from a common mold.

We assume that these children have been so scarred by their early experiences in home and community that whatever potential they once had for effective learning has been irreparably damaged. We really do not expect them to learn.

We confront them in school with prepackaged curricular materials and tasks developed for children from a different subculture; and when they fail, we find confirmation of our prior judgment that they lack the experiential background for cognitive growth. Rarely do we accept these children at whatever may be their current stages of development, and then devise materials and methods which serve their needs at that point.

Our whole professional posture tends to be defensive. Prevailing school practice is assumed to be sound; and if the children from the ghetto do not fit into our program, the fault is theirs, not the school's.

Not long ago, [Robert] Rosenthal and [Lenore] Jacobson conducted an experiment on the West Coast that is highly relevant to the defeatist approach of our schools to the education of black children from the ghetto.

They told teachers that some new tests indicated that particular children in their several classes should be expected to show spurts in academic achievement during the year. This was completely untrue; there was no such evidence; and nothing more was said about it after the initial announcements. The teachers went about their work as usual, with no suggestion that anything special be done with the children designated as incipient "bloomers." Yet, tests at the end of the year revealed that these particular children did, indeed, show dramatic spurts in achievement. Apparently the only explanation is that the teachers were led, through deception, to *expect* the children to show rapid gains.

The experimenters comment that one reason the disadvantaged "child does poorly in school is because that is what is expected of him. In other words his shortcomings may originate not in his different ethnic, cultural and economic background but in his teachers' response to that background."

There is no doubt that much of the academic retardation so prevalent among Negro children is a function of negative attitudes and inept practices among the professionals who run the schools. My experience suggests, however, that only a small proportion of these teachers and supervisors are consciously motivated by indifference toward their pupils or a desire to hold them back. Quite the contrary! Most of them really do not know how to teach children from impoverished backgrounds, and they assuage their professional conscience through recourse to pseudo-scientific theories about why their pupils "cannot" learn. Blame the victim!

Here and there about the country, there are many institutions and educators who are fighting hard to combat the stultifying ideology and stodgy practices which prevail among schools serving the Negro poor, and they are getting some results. I believe, however, that a major turn in educational practice will require massive intervention from without.

Our profession is now responding to the undemocratic social-class and racist values which are currently dominant in the culture, values which can be changed only through substantial restructuring of the society and the school system it supports. The profession will respond differently when the democratic movement achieves sufficient power to place the education of the poor much higher than it now is on our nation's list of priorities.

49. Comparing the Immigrant and the Negro Experience

National Advisory Commission on Civil Disorders

Why don't blacks escape poverty like our European immigrants? That question puzzles many white students. Some answers are provided by the National Commission on Civil Disorders as it examines problems urban blacks faced that did not confront the foreign-born.

Unlike European immigrants, when blacks arrived in the cities they encountered all-pervasive discrimination, a declining need for unskilled labor, and few political opportunities; some cultural factors were also more favorable to immigrants — for instance, the foreign-born could run stores for their non–English-speaking countrymen.

The ease and speed of the immigrants' rise from poverty is sometimes overstated. But even so, there were avenues of escape, and all the traditional routes are now closed to blacks. So the popular analogy between the immigrants and the black experience is patently untrue. Furthermore it is particularly dangerous, as it diverts attention from the Commission's exhortation to develop new exits for the poor who are trapped in today's ghettos.

We have in the preceding chapters surveyed the historical background of racial discrimination and traced its effects on Negro employment, on the social structure of the ghetto community, and on the conditions of life that surround the urban Negro poor. Here we address a fundamental question that many white Americans are asking today: why has the Negro been unable to escape from poverty and the ghetto like the European immigrants?

THE MATURING ECONOMY

The changing nature of the American economy is one major reason. When the European immigrants were arriving in large numbers, America was becoming an urban-industrial society. To build its major cities and industries, America needed great pools of unskilled labor. The immigrants

From *Report of the National Advisory Commission on Civil Disorders* (Washington, D.C.: U.S. Government Printing Office, March 1968).

provided the labor, gained an economic foothold, and thereby enabled their children and grandchildren to move up to skilled, white collar, and professional employment.

Since World War II, especially, America's urban-industrial society has matured; unskilled labor is far less essential than before, and blue-collar jobs of all kinds are decreasing in number and importance as a source of new employment. The Negroes who migrated to the great urban centers lacked the skills essential to the new economy; and the schools of the ghetto have been unable to provide the education that can qualify them for decent jobs. The Negro migrant, unlike the immigrant, found little opportunity in the city; he had arrived too late, and the unskilled labor he had to offer was no longer needed.

THE DISABILITY OF RACE

Racial discrimination is undoubtedly the second major reason why the Negro has been unable to escape from poverty. The structure of discrimination has persistently narrowed his opportunities and restricted his prospects. Well before the high tide of immigration from overseas, Negroes were already relegated to the poorly paid, low status occupations. Had it not been for racial discrimination, the North might well have recruited Southern Negroes after the Civil War to provide the labor for building the burgoning urban-industrial economy. Instead, Northern employers looked to Europe for their sources of unskilled labor. Upon the arrival of the immigrants, the Negroes were dislodged from the few urban occupations they had dominated. Not until World War II were Negroes generally hired for industrial jobs, and by that time the decline in the need for unskilled labor had already begun. European immigrants, too, suffered from discrimination, but never was it so pervasive as the prejudice against color in America, which has formed a bar to advancement, unlike any other.

ENTRY INTO THE POLITICAL SYSTEM

Political opportunities also played an important role in enabling the European immigrants to escape from poverty. The immigrants settled for the most part in rapidly growing cities that had powerful and expanding political machines, which gave them economic advantages in exchange for political support. The political machines were decentralized; and ward-level grievance machinery, as well as personal representation, enabled the immigrant to make his voice heard and his power felt. Since the local political organizations exercised considerable influence over public building in the cities, they provided employment in construction jobs for their immigrant voters. Ethnic groups often dominated one or more of the municipal services — police and fire protection, sanitation, and even public education.

By the time the Negroes arrived, the situation had altered dramatically. The great wave of public building had virtually come to an end; reform groups were beginning to attack the political machines; the machines were no longer so powerful or so well equipped to provide jobs and other favors.

Although the political machines retained their hold over the areas settled by Negroes, the scarcity of patronage jobs made them unwilling to share with the Negroes the political positions they had created in these neighborhoods. For example, Harlem was dominated by white politicians for many years after it had become a Negro ghetto; even today, New York's Lower East Side, which is now predominantly Puerto Rican, is strongly influenced by politicians of the older immigrant groups.

This pattern exists in many other American cities. Negroes are still underrepresented in city councils and in most agencies.

Segregation played a role here too. The immigrants and their descendants felt threatened by the arrival of the Negro and prevented a Negro-immigrant coalition that might have saved the old political machines. Reform groups, nominally more liberal on the race issue, were often dominated by businessmen and middle-class city residents who usually opposed coalition with any low-income group, white or black.

CULTURAL FACTORS

Cultural factors also made it easier for the immigrants to escape from poverty. They came to America from much poorer societies, with a low standard of living, and they came at a time when job aspirations were low. When most jobs in the American economy were unskilled, they sensed little deprivation in being forced to take the dirty and poorly paid jobs. Moreover, their families were large, and many breadwinners, some of whom never married, contributed to the total family income. As a result, family units managed to live even from the lowest paid jobs and still put some money aside for savings or investment, for example, to purchase a house or tenement, or to open a store or factory. Since the immigrants spoke little English and had their own ethnic culture, they needed stores to supply them with ethnic foods and other services. Since their family structures were patriarchal, men found satisfactions in family life that helped compensate for the bad jobs they had to take and the hard work they had to endure.

Negroes came to the city under quite different circumstances. Generally relegated to jobs that others would not take, they were paid too little to be able to put money in savings for new enterprises. Since they spoke English, they had no need for their own stores; besides, the areas they occupied were already filled with stores. In addition, Negroes lacked the extended family characteristic of certain European groups — each household usually had only one or two breadwinners. Moreover, Negro men had fewer cultural incentives to work in a dirty job for the sake of the family. As a result of slavery and of long periods of male unemployment afterwards, the Negro family structure had become matriarchal; the man played a secondary and marginal role in his family. For many Negro men, then, there were few of the cultural and psychological rewards of family life. A marginal figure in the family, particularly when unemployed, Negro men were often rejected by their wives or often abandoned their homes because they felt themselves useless to their families.

Although most Negro men worked as hard as the immigrants to support their families, their rewards were less. The jobs did not pay enough to enable them to support their families, for prices and living standards had risen since the immigrants had come, and the entrepreneurial opportunities that had allowed some immigrants to become independent, even rich, had vanished. Above all, Negroes suffered from segregation, which denied them access to the good jobs and the right unions, and which deprived them of the opportunity to buy real estate or obtain business loans or move out of the ghetto and bring up their children in middle-class neighborhoods. Immigrants were able to leave their ghettos as soon as they had the money; segregation has denied Negroes the opportunity to live elsewhere.

THE VITAL ELEMENT OF TIME

Finally, nostalgia makes it easy to exaggerate the ease of escape of the white immigrants from the ghettos. When the immigrants were immersed in poverty, they too lived in slums, and these neighborhoods exhibited fearfully high rates of alcoholism, desertion, illegitimacy, and the other pathologies associated with poverty. Just as some Negro men desert their families when they are unemployed and their wives can get jobs, so did the men of other ethnic groups, even though time and affluence have clouded white memories of the past.

Today, whites tend to exaggerate how well and how quickly they escaped from poverty, and contrast their experience with poverty-stricken Negroes. The fact is, among many of the Southern and Eastern Europeans who came to America in the last great wave of immigration, those who came already urbanized were the first to escape from poverty. The others who came to America from rural backgrounds, as Negroes did, are only now, after three generations, in the final stages of escaping from poverty. Until the last 10 years or so, most of these were employed in blue-collar jobs, and only a small proportion of their children were able or willing to attend college. In other words, only the third, and in many cases, only the fourth generation has been able to achieve the kind of middle-class income and status that allows it to send its children to college. Because of favorable economic and political conditions, these ethnic groups were able to escape from lower-class status to working class and lower middle-class status, but it has taken them three generations.

Negroes have been concentrated in the city for only two generations, and they have been there under much less favorable conditions. Moreover, their escape from poverty has been blocked in part by the resistance of the European ethnic groups; they have been unable to enter some unions and to move into some neighborhoods outside the ghetto because descendants of the European immigrants who control these unions and neighborhoods have not yet abandoned them for middle-class occupations and areas.

Even so, some Negroes have escaped poverty, and they have done so in only two generations; their success is less visible than that of the immigrants in many cases, for residential segregation has forced them to remain in the ghetto. Still, the proportion of nonwhites employed in white-collar, technical, and professional jobs has risen from 10.2 percent in 1950 to 20.8 percent in 1966, and the proportion attending college has risen an equal amount. Indeed, the development of a small but steadily increasing Negro middle class while the greater part of the Negro population is stagnating economically is creating a growing gap between Negro haves and have-nots.

This gap, as well as the awareness of its existence by those left behind, undoubtedly adds to the feelings of desperation and anger which breed civil disorders. Low-income Negroes realize that segregation and lack of job opportunities have made it possible for only a small proportion of all Negroes to escape poverty and the summer disorders are at least in part a protest against being left behind and left out.

The immigrant who labored long hours at hard and often menial work had the hope of a better future, if not for himself then for his children. This was the promise of the "American dream" — the society offered to all a future that was open-ended; with hard work and perseverance, a man and his family could in time achieve not only material well-being but "position" and status.

For the Negro family in the urban ghetto, there is a different vision — the future seems to lead only to a dead-end.

What the American economy of the late 19th and early 20th century was able to do to help the European immigrants escape from poverty is now largely impossible. New methods of escape must be found for the majority of today's poor.

Chapter Twelve

Poverty, Inequality, and Unemployment

50. Poverty, Income Inequality, and Privilege

Robert L. Heilbroner

Through his numerous books, Robert L. Heilbroner, professor of economics at the New School for Social Research, has helped to dispel the notion that economics is dull. In The Worldly Philosophers, The Making of Economic Society, *and other works, he stresses the relationship among economic, social, and political forces.*

In this selection from an article entitled "The Future of Capitalism," Heilbroner lays bare some crucial but seldom-discussed underpinnings of poverty. He reminds us that capitalism is a system of privilege whose core institutions, revolving around private profits from private property, result in the unequal distribution of wealth and income.

Heilbroner argues that absolute poverty — extremely low living standards — can disappear under capitalism in America in three or four decades or sooner, without altering our basic institutions. This can occur through future economic growth and the gradual shift from military to social expenditures. But to reduce the concentration of income and wealth would require basic institutional change and would be resisted by those with privilege, money, and power. Hence, Heilbroner foresees a longer future for the inequality of income and wealth in America than for poverty.

This article first appeared in 1966. Much has happened since then to weaken the case for Heilbroner's limited optimism. There is greater resistance to shifting funds from military to social uses than he anticipated. But riots and other events make more questionable his assumption that the elimination of absolute poverty can be postponed for three or four decades.

. . . Why do societies resist change? A full explanation of social inertia must reach deep into the psychological and technical underpinnings of the human community. But in the process of gradual social adjustment it is clear enough where to look for the main sources of the resistance to change. They are to be found in the structure of privilege inherent in all social systems.

Privilege is not an attribute we are accustomed to stress when we consider the construction of *our* social order. When pressed, we are, of course, aware of its core institution in capitalism — the right to reap private benefits from the use of the means of production and the right to utilize the dynamic forces of the marketplace for private enrichment. The element of privilege in these institutions, however — that is, their operative result in favoring certain individuals and classes — is usually passed over in silence in favor of their purely functional aspects. Thus, private property is ordinarily explained as being no more than a convenient instrumentality for the efficient operation of an economic system, or the market elements of Land, Labor, and Capital as purely neutral "factors of production."

Now these institutions and relationships do indeed fulfill the purposes for which they are advertised. But this is not the only use they have. Land, Labor, and Capital are not just functional parts of a mechanism but are categories of social existence that bring vast differences in life chances with them. It is not just Labor on the one hand, and Land or Capital on the other; it is the Bronx on the one hand and Park Avenue on the other. Similarly, private property is not merely a pragmatic arrangement devised for the facilitation of production, but a social institution that brings to some members of the community a style of life qualitatively different from that afforded to the rest. In a word, the operation of capitalism as a *functional* system results in a structure of wealth and income characteristic of capitalism as a *system of privilege* — a structure in which the top two per cent of American families own between two-thirds and three-quarters of all corporate stock, and enjoy incomes roughly ten times larger than the average received within the nation as a whole.

From Robert L. Heilbroner, "The Future of Capitalism," *Commentary* (April 1966). Reprinted from *Commentary* by permission; copyright © 1966 by the American Jewish Committee. Editor's title, by permission.

The mere presence of these concentrations of wealth or large disparities of income does not in itself differentiate the system of privilege under capitalism from those of most other societies in history. Rather, what marks off our system is that wealth and income within capitalism are not mainly derived from non-economic activity, such as war, plunder, extortionate taxation, etc., but arise from the activity of marketers or the use of property by its owners.

This mixture of the functional and the privileged aspects of capitalism has a curious but important political consequence. It is that privilege under capitalism is much less "visible," especially to the favored groups, than privilege under other systems. The upper classes in feudalism were keenly alive to the gulf that separated them from the lower classes, and perfectly open about the need for preserving it. The upper groups under capitalism, on the other hand, are typically unaware that the advantages accruing to them from following the paths of the market economy constitute in any sense or fashion a privilege.

This lack of self-awareness is rendered even more acute by virtue of another differentiating characteristic of privilege under capitalism. It is that privilege is limited to the advantages inherent in the economic structure of society. That is, the same civil and criminal law, the same duties in war and peace, apply to both economically privileged and unprivileged. It would be a mistake to concentrate on obvious differences in the application of the law as being of the essence. Rather, one must contrast the single system of law and obligation under capitalism — however one-sidedly administered — with the *differing* systems that apply to privileged and unprivileged in other societies.

The divorce of economic from political or social privilege brings up the obvious fact that, at least in democratic societies like America, the privileged distribution of economic rewards is exposed to the corrective efforts of the democratic electorate. The question is, however, why the structure of privilege has remained relatively intact, despite so long an exposure to the potentially leveling influences of the majority.

In part, we can trace the answer to the very "invisibility" of privilege we have just described. Furthermore, in all stable societies the structure of privilege appears to the general public not as a special dispensation, but as the natural order of things, with which their own interests and sentiments are identified. This is especially true under capitalism, where the privileges of wealth are open, at least in theory, and to some extent in practice, to all comers. Finally, the overall results of capitalism, particularly in America during the entire 20th century and recently in Europe as well, have been sufficiently rewarding to hold anticapitalist sentiment to a relatively small segment of the population.

That the defense of privilege is the active source of resistance to social and economic change may appear so obvious as scarcely to be worth emphasizing. Obvious or not, it is a fact too often passed over in silence. It seems to me impossible to analyze the nature of the opposition to change without stressing the vulgar but central fact that every person who is rich under capitalism is a beneficiary of its inherent privileges. Taking the American system as it now exists, it seems fair to assert that the chance to own and acquire wealth constitutes a primary — perhaps even a dominating — social motivation for most men, and that those who enjoy or aspire to these privileges will not readily acquiesce in changes that will substantially lessen their chances of maintaining or gaining them.

The touchstone of privilege provides an indispensable key when we now return to our main theme. If it does not give us an exact calculus by which to compute what changes will and will not be acceptable, it does give us an angle of entry, a point of view, without which attempts to cope with the problem of social change are apt to have no relevance at all.

Take, for example, the problem of the poverty that now afflicts some 30 or 40 million Americans. Our alleged cause of this poverty has always directly stressed the privileges of capitalism. This is the view that poverty under capitalism is largely ascribable to wage exploitation. There is clearly an element of truth here, in that the affluence of the favored groups in capitalism does indeed stem from institutions that divert income from the community at large into the channels of dividends, interest, rent, monopoly returns, etc. It is by no means clear, however, that the amount of this diversion, if redistributed among the masses, would spell the difference between their poverty and their well-being. On the contrary, it is now generally acknowledged that the level of wages reflects workers' productivity more than any other single factor, and that this productivity in turn is primarily determined by the quantity and the quality of the capital equipment of the economic system.

Certainly, the productivity of the great mass of workers under capitalism has steadily increased, and so have their real wages. Today, for example, industrial workers in America cannot be classified as "poor" by prevailing absolute standards, if we take $4,000 a year as defining a level of minimum adequacy for a small family. Although wage poverty is clearly present in capitalism, it is primarily restricted to the agricultural areas and to the lowest categories of skills in the service trades. No small part of it is accounted for by discrimination against Negroes, and by the really shocking levels of income of Negro farm and service labor. On the other hand, the proportion of the labor force that is afflicted with this poverty is steadily diminishing. Farmers, farm managers, and farm laborers together will probably constitute only 5 per cent of the labor force within a decade. The low-paid non-farm common laborer, who constituted over 12 per cent of the working force in 1900, makes up only 5 per cent of it today and will be a smaller percentage tomorrow.

There remains, nevertheless, the question of how much the existing level of wages could be increased if the categories of capitalist privilege did not exist. Since it is difficult to estimate accurately the total amount of "privileged" income under capitalism, let us take as its convenient representation the sum total of all corporate profits before tax. In the mid 1960's, these profits exceeded $70 billion a year. If this sum were distributed equally among the 70 million members of the work force, the average share would be $1,000. For the lowest-paid workers, such as migrant farm laborers, this would represent an increase in annual incomes of 100 per cent or more — an immense gain. For the average industrial worker, however, the gain would be in the neighborhood of 20–25 per cent, certainly a large increase but not one that would fundamentally alter his living standards.

Thus, insofar as the institutions of capitalism constitute a drain upon non-privileged groups, it can be fairly said that they are only marginally responsible for any inadequacy in the prevailing general level of income. Individual companies may indeed be capable of vastly improving the lot of their workers — General Motors makes nearly as much gross profit on a car as it pays out in wages, and "could," therefore, virtually double its wages. But for the economy as a whole, no such large margin of redistribution is possible. So long, then, as the defense of these privileges does not result in substantially *increasing* the share of national income accruing to the privileged elements of the nation, it seems fair to conclude that the level of material well-being under capitalism is limited mainly by the levels of productivity it can reach. If the trend of growth of the past century is continued, the average level of real wages for industrial labor should double in another two to three decades. This would bring average earnings to a level of about $10,000 and would effectively spell the abolition of wage poverty, under any definition.

This conclusion does not close our investigation into the relationship between poverty and privilege, but rather directs it toward what is now revealed as the principal cause of poverty. This is the fact that large groups within the population — the aged, the handicapped, the sick, the unemployed, the castaways in rural backwaters — have no active tie into the market economy and must therefore subsist at the very meager levels to which non-participants in the work process are consigned. There is only one way that their condition can be quickly alleviated, but that one way would be very effective indeed. This is to redistribute to them enough income earned or received by more favored members of the community to bring them to levels of economic decency. A program with this objective would require some $10- to $12 billion above the public assistance that the poor now receive in this country. Such a sum would amount to approximately a seventh of corporate profits before tax. Alternatively, shared among the 11- or 12 million consumer units who constitute the top 20 per cent of the nation's income receivers, it would require an average additional tax of roughly $1,000 on incomes that average $16,000.

In both cases, in other words, a program to eliminate sheer need among the poor would constitute a sizable incursion into the incomes enjoyed by favored groups, although hardly such an invasion as to constitute the elimination of these privileges. Thus, the failure to carry out such a program cannot be laid to the "objective" or functional difference that such a redistribution would entail, but simply to the general unwillingness of those who enjoy higher incomes to share their good fortune with those who do not. As Adam Walinsky has very aptly put it, "The middle class knows that the economists are right when they say that poverty would be eliminated if we only will it; they simply do not will it."

To what extent does that conclusion, then, lead to the prospect of alleviating poverty within the next generation or so? In the short run the outlook is not very hopeful. Given the temptations of luxury consumption and the general lack of deep concern in a nation lulled by middle-class images of itself, it is doubtful that very effective programs of social rescue can be launched within the next decade or two. Yet, of all the problems confronting capitalism, poverty seems the least likely to be blocked permanently by the resistance of privilege. Tax receipts are now growing at the rate of some $6 billion a year simply as a consequence of the growth of the level of output, and this flow of funds to the government will increase over the future. It may be that these receipts will be used for larger arms expenditures for some years, but assuming that full-scale war will be averted, sooner or later the arms budget must level off. Thereafter the funds will become available for use either in the form of tax reductions — an operation which normally favors the well-to-do — or as the wherewithal for a major assault on the slums, etc. In this choice between the claims of privilege and those of social reform, the balance is apt to be tipped by the emerging new national elites, especially from government. In addition, a gradual liberalization of the prevailing business ideology is likely to ease opposition to measures that clearly promise to improve the quality of society without substantially affecting its basic institutions of privilege.

It is idle to predict when Harlem will be reconstructed and Appalachia reborn, since so much depends on the turn of events in the international arena. Yet it seems to me that the general dimensions of the problem make it possible to envisage the substantial alleviation — perhaps even the virtual elimination — of massive poverty within the limits of capitalism three or four decades hence, or possibly even sooner.

The elimination of poverty is, however, only part of a larger problem within capitalism — the problem of income distribution. Hence, we might now look to the chances that capitalism will alter the moral anomalies of wealth as well as those of poverty.

Here it is not so easy to foresee a change in the operational results of the system of privilege. Since the 1930's, the political intent of the public has clearly been to bring about some lessening of the concentration of income that goes to the very rich, and some diminution of the enclaves of family wealth that have passed intact from one generation to the next. Thus, we have seen the introduction of estate taxes that levy imposts of about one-third on net estates of only $1 million, and of fully half on net estates of $5 million; and these rates have been supplemented by measures to prevent the tax-free passage of wealth before death by gift.

Since the enactment of these taxes, a full generation has passed, and we would therefore expect to see some impact of the legislation in a significant lowering of the concentration of wealth among the top families. Instead, we find that the share held by the top families has decreased only slightly — from 33 per cent of all personal wealth in 1922, to 29 per cent in 1953 (the last year for which such calculations exist). Concentration of stock — the single most important medium for the investment of large wealth — has shown no tendency to decline since 1922. Equally recalcitrant before egalitarian measures is the flow of income to topmost groups. Legal tax rates on top incomes have risen from 54 per cent under President Hoover to over 90 per cent in the 1940's and early 1950's, and to 72 per cent in the mid 1960's. The presumed higher incidence of taxes at the peak of the income pyramid has, however, been subverted by innumerable stratagems of trusts, family sharing of income, capital gains, deferred compensation, or other means of tax avoidance or outright tax evasion.

There is no indication that this resistive capacity of the system of privilege is likely to weaken, at least within the time span of a generation. Nor is there any sign that the "natural workings" of the system will lessen the flow of income to the top. The statistics of income distribution clearly show a slow but regular drift of income *toward* the upper end of the spectrum. Three per cent of all income was received by income receivers in the $15,000-and-up brackets in 1947; in 1963, in terms of constant dollars, this fraction had grown to eight. This determined self-perpetuation of large concentrations of private wealth is likely to continue — afflicting the social order with that peculiar irresponsibility that is the unhappy hallmark of the system. The power of wealth is by no means the only source of power in America and may, in fact, be expected to decline. But the voice of money still speaks very loudly, and the capacity of wealth to surmount the half-acquiescent opposition of a democratic political system promises that it will continue to resound in America for a long while to come.

The Relationship Between Liberty and Equality

51. Liberalism and Egalitarianism

Milton Friedman

> *Is there a conflict between liberty and equality? That question is often asked, especially when steps are being contemplated to reduce inequality.*
>
> *Milton Friedman of the University of Chicago, a past president of the American Economic Association, is a leading contemporary exponent of laissez-faire. He argues that equality comes sharply into conflict with freedom when state power is used to redistribute income to achieve "justice," but in Reading 52, R. H. Tawney argues the opposite.*

The heart of the liberal philosophy is a belief in the dignity of the individual, in his freedom to make the most of his capacities and opportunities according to his own lights, subject only to the proviso that he not interfere with the freedom of other individuals to do the same. This implies a belief in the equality of men in one sense; in their inequality in another. Each man has an equal right to freedom. This is an important and fundamental right precisely because men are different, because one man will want to do different things with his freedom than another, and in the process can contribute more than another to the general culture of the society in which many men live.

The liberal will therefore distinguish sharply between equality of rights and equality of opportunity, on the one hand, and material equality or equality of outcome on the other. He may welcome the fact that a free society in fact tends toward greater material equality than any other yet tried. But he will regard this as a desirable by-product of a free society, not its major justification. He will welcome measures that promote both freedom and equality — such as measures to eliminate monopoly power and to improve the operation of the market. He will regard private charity directed at helping the less fortunate as an example of the proper use of

From Milton Friedman, *Capitalism and Freedom*. © 1962 by The University of Chicago. Reprinted by permission of the publisher and author.

freedom. And he may approve state action toward ameliorating poverty as a more effective way in which the great bulk of the community can achieve a common objective. He will do so with regret, however, at having to substitute compulsory for voluntary action.

The egalitarian will go this far, too. But he will want to go further. He will defend taking from some to give to others, not as a more effective means whereby the "some" can achieve an objective they want to achieve, but on grounds of "justice." At this point, equality comes sharply into conflict with freedom; one must choose. One cannot be both an egalitarian, in this sense, and a liberal.

52. Equality and Liberty

R. H. Tawney

Is there a conflict between liberty and equality? Answering in the negative, the late R. H. Tawney (1880–1962), an eminent British economic historian and socialist philosopher, presents a viewpoint that differs radically from that of Milton Friedman in Reading 51. Tawney claims that the real question is: freedom for whom? He asserts that what remains when the state refrains from intervening is often tyranny, not liberty.

Freedom for the strong is oppression for the weak; and oppression . . . is not less oppressive when its strength is derived from superior wealth, than when it relies on a preponderance of physical force. Hence, when steps to diminish inequality are denounced as infringements of freedom, the first question to be answered is one not always asked. It is: freedom for whom? There is no such thing as freedom in the abstract, divorced from the realities of a particular time and place. Whatever else the conception may imply, it involves a power of choice between alternatives, a choice which is real, not merely nominal, between alternatives which exist in fact, not only on paper. Because a man is most a man when he thinks, wills and acts, freedom deserves the sublime things which poets have said about it; but, as part of the prose of everyday life, it is quite practical and realistic. It means the ability to do, or to refrain from doing, definite things, at a definite moment, in definite circumstances, or it means nothing at all. The second

From R. H. Tawney, *Equality*, 4th rev. ed. (London: George Allen and Unwin, Ltd., 1952). Reprinted by permission.

question which arises, therefore, is not less simple. It is whether the range of alternatives open to ordinary men, and the capacity of the latter to follow their own preferences in choosing between them, have or have not been increased by measures correcting inequalities or neutralizing their effects. If an affirmative reply be given, liberty and equality can live as friends; if a negative one, they are condemned to be foes.

A verdict upon these issues can not be stated in general terms. It depends upon the varying degrees to which, before the reforms in question, liberty, in the sense defined, was in practice enjoyed by different sections of the population. Nor, since the problems presented by great concentrations of economic power are not identical with those caused by inequalities in the distribution of income, can the effects on liberty of the different policies employed to cope with each be described by a formula covering both. There are societies — to consider the former topic first — in which economic power, if it can be said to exist, is dispersed in fragments among a multitude of petty proprietors, peasant farmers, small masters and traders, and in which, therefore, except at a few key points, such as credit and marketing, it presents no crucial problem. In such conditions private enterprise is private in fact, as well as in name, and action to control or supersede it, though attempted by authoritarian governments both in previous centuries and our own, is, if desirable at all, a matter of secondary concern. In industrial civilizations, the practical realities, which determine the content of political terms, are obviously different. Even in them, it is still often assumed by privileged classes that, when the State refrains from intervening, the condition which remains, as a result of its inaction, is liberty. In reality, what not infrequently remains is, not liberty, but tyranny.

The Trade-off Between Unemployment and Inflation

53. Analytical Aspects of Unemployment

Walter Galenson

> *Full employment is necessary but not sufficient to end poverty. The job market cannot be used to end poverty when there are not enough jobs to go around. If experienced workers are being laid off, the inexperienced will not be hired. Nor will the unskilled be upgraded. And job training programs for the poor become meaningless.*

Yet some economists believe that we should not even try to get below 4 percent unemployment. Why? And why do governments sometimes deliberately try to increase unemployment?

In Reading 53, Walter Galenson, a Cornell University labor economist, explains and critically evaluates the theory held by most economists that there is a trade-off between unemployment and inflation.

Those who consider 4 percent unemployment "full employment" obviously are more concerned about price stability than about the unemployed. But in recent years, the relationship between inflation and unemployment has been more complex. Increased government spending for the Vietnam war without offsetting tax increases led to inflation. In order to curb inflation the new Nixon administration decided (1969) to increase unemployment by tightening the money supply. Unemployment did rise — to 6 percent. But the inflation remained. So then it was not either inflation or unemployment, but both at the same time.

Galenson's economic analysis is complemented by Art Buchwald's satirical analysis in Reading 54.

An average unemployment rate of 4 percent is frequently cited as the lowest that is consistent with a stable economy in the United States. The Council of Economic Advisers terms this an "interim target," but others go further and warn that anything lower would inevitably lead to inflation.

Much of the current reasoning is based on the work of A. W. Phillips, a British economist who conducted a statistical investigation into the relationship between wage changes and unemployment in Great Britain between 1861 and 1957. Phillips concluded that if unemployment stood at 5 percent, money wages remained stable; but that when unemployment fell to 2½ percent, money wages rose between 2 and 3 percent a year.

Phillips' statistics and his methodology have come in for severe criticism. Other analyses of the British experience have not yielded nearly such conclusive results. Attempts to find similar relationships for the United States have not been successful for recent years, and only partly so for earlier periods. It has been pointed out that profits, business expectations, and industrial concentration may yield equally good results in explaining wage changes. Most important of all, the observed relationships between wages and unemployment are not sufficiently precise to permit firm policy conclusions to be drawn from them.

Nevertheless, the idea continues to attract attention. Two eminent American economists, Paul Samuelson and Robert Solow, have stated their belief that under current conditions in the United States unemployment would

From *A Primer on Employment and Wages,* by Walter Galenson. Copyright © 1966 by Random House, Inc. Reprinted by permission.

have to be as high as 5–6 percent to prevent wages from rising by more than 2½ percent a year (this is about the long-run annual growth in productivity), while a 3 percent unemployment rate would result in prices rising on the order of 4–5 percent a year as a result of wage increases. They point out, however, that changes in labor-market institutions could result in modification of the suggested relationship between wages and unemployment.

We have already pointed out in the chapter dealing with trade unionism that labor leaders are less likely to demand substantial wage increases when a good many workers are idle than when labor is scarce. Employers are less apt to bid wages up when a pool of unemployed workers from which they can hire is available. But this is not at all the same thing as the assertion that there exists a fixed, predictable relationship between wages or prices and unemployment, so that if we lower unemployment to rate x, we can confidently expect wages or prices to rise at rate y.

It is instructive to examine the experience of nations other than the United States in this respect. . . . In general terms, low unemployment and some price inflation went hand in hand. However, the relationships shown are by no means precise; for example, Belgium had a much higher rate of unemployment than the United States and still experienced some price rise, while Germany managed to contain price inflation despite relatively low unemployment.

Great caution must be exercised in drawing inferences from simple comparisons of this nature. Nations differ in many respects, and their economies operate in very diverse ways. All that one can say is that several advanced nations, Great Britain, Sweden, and Germany among them, were able to maintain low unemployment levels without running into politically impossible degrees of price inflation. One cannot predict from these data how much inflation the United States would have experienced at, say, British levels of unemployment, but the experience of Western Europe at least suggests that, contrary to the Samuelson-Solow predictions, the trade-off between unemployment and price change may be well within the bounds of acceptability.

Professor Stanley Lebergott, a prominent student of American unemployment, has proposed that a maximum of 3.5 percent unemployment be set as a national policy goal. With respect to the possible effect on prices, he says: "American experience suggests that within likely peacetime unemployment ranges the conflict is not as great as might appear. Recent studies indicate that postwar wage changes are largely accounted for by factors other than the unemployment rate."

My own reaction is that this goal is too modest, if anything. There is no reason why we should not aim at a level consonant with the postwar experience of the major European nations. One argument often advanced against our ever being able to achieve, say, a 2 percent unemployment rate

Table 1. Unemployment and Cost of Living in Western Europe and the United States, 1953-1961

	Average Annual Unemployment (as a percentage of the labor force)		Percent Increase in Cost of Living	
	1953-1961	1956-1961	1953-1961	1956-1961
France	1.1	0.9	38	34
Netherlands	1.6	1.4	23	14
Great Britain	1.6	1.7	25	12
Sweden	2.1	1.8	28	17
Germany	3.9	2.5	14	10
United States	5.1	5.4	12	10
Italy	6.7*	6.2	18	8
Belgium	8.3	7.4	11	7

Source: United Nations, Compendium of Social Statistics, 1963.
* 1954-1961.

is that our economy is so diverse and dynamic as to require more labor mobility, and hence more unemployment. But this is an assertion that has never been proved. Europe is also experiencing a great deal of labor mobility, with men and women in large numbers crossing the barriers of nationality and language in search of work. The question may at least be raised, for example, whether the difficulty and time lost in moving from New York to Chicago are really greater than in the move from London to Manchester, from Stuttgart to Hamburg, from Stockholm to Gothenburg — to say nothing of Naples to Bremen.

The real problem may lie in attitudes rather than in the character of the economic environment. The late principal economist [Jack Downie] of the Organization for Economic Cooperation and Development, whose job it was to make comparisons among Western nations, put the matter very aptly:

> . . . it is hard to avoid the conclusion that the contrast between European and American price history from 1956 to 1962 is an accurate index of a contrast in attitudes. Much has been said in Europe about the importance of price stability. But nowhere, — not even in Germany, supposedly the classic example of inflation neurosis — have countries been prepared in the event to arrest their growth and create unemployment simply in order to stop prices from rising.
>
> . . . When prices start rising, the more cautious governmental advisers, usually associated with the Treasury Department and the Federal Reserve System, will counsel restraint, even at the expense of halting the boom. Those whose eyes are fixed on the elimination of unemployment are likely to argue that prices should be permitted to rise. Whether the brakes should

be applied by raising interest rates, increasing bank reserve requirements, raising taxes, or in some other manner, will be decided in the realm of politics, not economics. The Eisenhower administration was inclined to be cautious, while the Kennedy and Johnson administrations have been more venturesome, though it must be added that no real test for them has thus far been posed.

The issue boils down to whether we are willing to risk a measure of price inflation in order to achieve full employment. What we do not know, as should be evident from the previous discussion of the Phillips theory, is the precise trade-off between price change and unemployment. No one wants a Latin American type of galloping inflation in order to achieve a European level of employment. But suppose unemployment could be lowered to 2.5 percent on the basis of a 2 percent annual price rise? Or a 3 percent price rise?

It is not inconceivable that with proper management of the economy, full employment can be attained together with price stability. The experience of the years 1961–1965 is hopeful, though not conclusive. However, an unchanging price level is not necessarily the equivalent of a sound economy. Price stability may be too high a price to pay for substantial unused resources of men and machines.

54. The No-Job Corps

Art Buchwald

> *In Reading 53, economist Walter Galenson gives a technical explanation of the trade-off between unemployment and inflation. But here, Art Buchwald, one of America's leading satirists, tells what happens to a worker when theory is put into practice and he is notified that he has become a front-line soldier in the president's fight against inflation.*

Washington

There has been a great deal of discussion by the government concerning unemployment. No one likes to be without a job, but it seems to me that if you explain it to someone in terms that he can understand, the unemployed person will be willing to go along with it.

From Art Buchwald, "The No-Job Corps," (February 24, 1970). Copyright, Los Angeles Times/Washington Post News Service. Reprinted by permission.

"I beg your pardon. Is that a pink slip in your hand?"

"Yeh."

"Well, congratulations. You can consider yourself a front-line soldier in the President's fight against inflation."

"I can?"

"Yes, sir. And under government regulations you are entitled to a complete explanation as to why you find yourself in what we refer to as the 'unemployment rate zone.' Incidentally, you will be happy to know that your being laid off came as no surprise to us."

"It didn't?"

"No, sir. Your government predicted that given high interest rates and a tight money situation, you would be out of work by February. Here it is, right on the graph."

"I'll be darned. You guys really know your stuff. But what do I tell my family?"

"You can tell them that although they will have to put up with a certain amount of inconvenience, the upward spiral in unemployment — to which I might say you've made such a valuable contribution — will have a very definite effect on the stabilization of prices."

"They'll be happy to hear that."

"If it weren't for people like you, I'm afraid the economy would have kept overheating and your dollars would have lost their purchasing power. But if we can raise the unemployment level to a reasonable figure, say 4.5%, without putting the country into a recession, we can bring prices down by 1975."

"It makes sense to me, but I would like to ask you a question. Am I better off reversing inflation by being unemployed, or am I better off working and earning dollars that have less value?"

"That's the kind of question that we in the government resent. I would say in the short run you might be better off earning inflationary dollars. But if you're truly concerned about the economy of the country, then you should be willing to be part of the 4.5% of the population that we need on our unemployment rolls."

"But why me?"

"Everyone says, 'why me?' It has to be *somebody*. If we are to take strong anti-inflation measures, we have to have a citizenry ready to make financial sacrifices. All we're asking of you is to stay unemployed until the economy cools off."

"How long will that be?"

"We're projecting 18 months, but I'd count on two years to be on the safe side."

"What am I supposed to do in the meantime?"

"This is a Certificate of Unemployment which you can hang on the wall.

It attests to the fact that your government appreciates all you are doing to keep the economy from spiraling sky-high."

"Gosh, it's beautiful."

"I might mention that only the elite of the labor force in this country are entitled to this certificate. You can be very proud that you are among the chosen few."

"Wait until my family sees it. Is there anything else that I can do to help fight inflation?"

"Just stay off the streets. And don't call us. We'll call you."

Chapter Thirteen

The Paths from Poverty

55. The Alleviation of Poverty

Milton Friedman

Is there an alternative to welfare? In recent years, support has been mounting for a guaranteed annual income based on a negative income tax. The proposals differ significantly but the seminal idea for the negative income tax, which influenced President Nixon's Family Assistance Plan, stems from University of Chicago economist Milton Friedman.

Friedman's approach is simple. Set a floor under income and have the government pay the difference between family income and that minimum in the form of a subsidy or negative income tax. If there is other income, continue partial payments until total earnings rise to a stated level above the minimum.

In contrast to some negative income tax plans, Friedman's presentation is essentially conservative. Friedman candidly admits that he devised the negative income tax as a cheap substitute for the "rag bag" of already existing government programs. Most proponents feel that the negative income tax should replace the welfare system and Friedman concurs. But the negative income tax is just the beginning for Friedman. As a staunch advocate of laissez-faire, he would also abolish social security, minimum wage laws, labor laws, public housing and all other government programs which might help low income people.

What would be the consequence of his plan? Some of the poor in the South would benefit from larger cash payments than they now receive from welfare. But poverty would not be eliminated. In fact, many people would be made poorer through implementation of his proposal. Deprivation would increase among those recipients of social security and welfare who already receive larger payments than Friedman advocates. And to make matters worse, nonmonetary assistance would vanish. There would be no help for the aged. No help for children. No school lunches. No housing programs. Instead of expanding, these admittedly inadequate social welfare programs would contract and die. A family of four with no other income would receive $1,200 ($300 a person in 1961)[1] and would then be left on its own, still impoverished.

The extraordinary economic growth experienced by Western countries during the past two centuries and the wide distribution of the benefits of free enterprise have enormously reduced the extent of poverty in any absolute sense in the capitalistic countries of the West. But poverty is in part a relative matter, and even in these countries, there are clearly many people living under conditions that the rest of us label as poverty.

One recourse, and in many ways the most desirable, is private charity. It is noteworthy that the heyday of laissez-faire, the middle and late nineteenth century in Britain and the United States, saw an extraordinary proliferation of private eleemosynary organizations and institutions. One of the major costs of the extension of governmental welfare activities has been the corresponding decline in private charitable activities.

It can be argued that private charity is insufficient because the benefits from it accrue to people other than those who make the gifts — again, a neighborhood effect. I am distressed by the sight of poverty; I am benefited by its alleviation; but I am benefited equally whether I or someone else pays for its alleviation; the benefits of other people's charity therefore partly accrue to me. To put it differently, we might all of us be willing to contribute to the relief of poverty, *provided* everyone else did. We might not be willing to contribute the same amount without such assurance. In small communities, public pressure can suffice to realize the proviso even with private charity. In the large impersonal communities that are increasingly coming to dominate our society, it is much more difficult for it to do so.

Suppose one accepts, as I do, this line of reasoning as justifying governmental action to alleviate poverty; to set, as it were, a floor under the standard of life of every person in the community. There remain the questions, how much and how. I see no way of deciding "how much" except in

From Milton Friedman, *Capitalism and Freedom*, pp. 190–195. © 1962 by The University of Chicago. Reprinted by permission of the publisher and author.

[1] Even if Friedman would allow a somewhat higher figure today, much the same would hold true.

terms of the amount of taxes we — by which I mean the great bulk of us — are willing to impose on ourselves for the purpose. The question, "how," affords more room for speculation.

Two things seem clear. First, if the objective is to alleviate poverty, we should have a program directed at helping the poor. There is every reason to help the poor man who happens to be a farmer, not because he is a farmer but because he is poor. The program, that is, should be designed to help people as people not as members of particular occupational groups or age groups or wage-rate groups or labor organizations or industries. This is a defect of farm programs, general old-age benefits, minimum-wage laws, pro-union legislation, tariffs, licensing provisions of crafts or professions, and so on in seemingly endless profusion. Second, so far as possible the program should, while operating through the market, not distort the market or impede its functioning. This is a defect of price supports, minimum-wage laws, tariffs and the like.

The arrangement that recommends itself on purely mechanical grounds is a negative income tax. We now have an exemption of $600 per person under the federal income tax (plus a minimum 10 per cent flat deduction). If an individual receives $100 taxable income, i.e., an income of $100 in excess of the exemption and deductions, he pays a tax. Under the proposal, if his taxable income [were] minus $100, i.e., $100 less than the exemption plus deductions, he would pay a negative tax, i.e., receive a subsidy. If the rate of subsidy were, say, 50 per cent, he would receive $50. If he had no income at all, and, for simplicity, no deductions, and the rate were constant, he would receive $300. He might receive more than this if he had deductions, for example, for medical expenses, so that his income less deductions, was negative even before subtracting the exemption. The rates of subsidy could, of course, be graduated just as the rates of tax above the exemption are. In this way, it would be possible to set a floor below which no man's net income (defined now to include the subsidy) could fall — in the simple example $300 per person. The precise floor set would depend on what the community could afford.

The advantages of this arrangement are clear. It is directed specifically at the problem of poverty. It gives help in the form most useful to the individual, namely, cash. It is general and could be substituted for the host of special measures now in effect. It makes explicit the cost borne by society. It operates outside the market. Like any other measures to alleviate poverty, it reduces the incentives of those helped to help themselves, but it does not eliminate that incentive entirely, as a system of supplementing incomes up to some fixed minimum would. An extra dollar earned always means more money available for expenditure.

No doubt there would be problems of administration, but these seem to me a minor disadvantage, if they be a disadvantage at all. The system would fit directly into our current income tax system and could be administered along with it. The present tax system covers the bulk of income recipients and the necessity of covering all would have the by-product of improving the operation of the present income tax. More important, if enacted as a substitute for the present rag bag of measures directed at the same end, the total administrative burden would surely be reduced.

A few brief calculations suggest also that this proposal could be far less costly in money, let alone in the degree of governmental intervention involved, than our present collection of welfare measures. Alternatively, these calculations can be regarded as showing how wasteful our present measures are, judged as measures for helping the poor.

In 1961, government [expenditures] amounted to something like $33 billion (federal, state, and local) on direct welfare payments and programs of all kinds: old age assistance, social security benefit payments, aid to dependent children, general assistance, farm price support programs, public housing, etc.[1] I have excluded veterans' benefits in making this calculation. I have also made no allowance for the direct and indirect costs of such measures as minimum-wage laws, tariffs, licensing provisions, and so on, or for the costs of public health activities, state and local expenditures on hospitals, mental institutions, and the like.

There are approximately 57 million consumer units (unattached individuals and families) in the United States. The 1961 expenditures of $33 billion would have financed outright cash grants of nearly $6,000 per consumer unit to the 10 per cent with the lowest incomes. Such grants would have raised their incomes above the average for all units in the United States. Alternatively, these expenditures would have financed grants of nearly $3,000 per consumer unit to the 20 per cent with the lowest incomes. Even if one went so far as that one-third whom New Dealers were fond of calling ill-fed, ill-housed, and ill-clothed, 1961 expenditures would have financed grants of nearly $2,000 per consumer unit, roughly the sum which, after allowing for the change in the level of prices, was the income which separated the lower one-third in the middle 1930's from the upper two-thirds. Today, fewer than one-eighth of consumer units have an income, adjusted for the change in the level of prices, as low as that of the lowest third in the middle 1930's.

Clearly, these are all far more extravagant programs than can be justified

[1] This figure is equal to government transfer payments ($31.1 billion) less veterans' benefits ($4.8 billion), both from the Department of Commerce national income accounts, plus federal expenditures on the agricultural program ($5.5 billion) plus federal expenditures on public housing and other aids to housing ($0.5 billion), both for year ending June 30, 1961 from Treasury accounts, plus a rough allowance of $0.7 billion to raise it to even billions and to allow for administrative costs of federal programs, omitted state and local programs, and miscellaneous items. My guess is that this figure is a substantial underestimate.

to "alleviate poverty" even by a rather generous interpretation of that term. A program which *supplemented* the incomes of the 20 per cent of the consumer units with the lowest incomes so as to raise them to the lowest income of the rest would cost less than half of what we are now spending.

The major disadvantage of the proposed negative income tax is its political implications. It establishes a system under which taxes are imposed on some to pay subsidies to others. And presumably, these others have a vote. There is always the danger that instead of being an arrangement under which the great majority tax themselves willingly to help an unfortunate minority, it will be converted into one under which a majority imposes taxes for its own benefit on an unwilling minority. Because this proposal makes the process so explicit, the danger is perhaps greater than with other measures. I see no solution to this problem except to rely on the self-restraint and good will of the electorate.

Writing about a corresponding problem — British old-age pensions — in 1914, Dicey said, "Surely a sensible and a benevolent man may well ask himself whether England as a whole will gain by enacting that the receipt of poor relief, in the shape of a pension, shall be consistent with the pensioner's retaining the right to join in the election of a Member of Parliament."

The verdict of experience in Britain on Dicey's question must as yet be regarded as mixed. England did move to universal suffrage without the disfranchisement of either pensioners or other recipients of state aid. And there has been an enormous expansion of taxation of some for the benefit of others, which must surely be regarded as having retarded Britain's growth, and so may not even have benefited most of those who regard themselves as on the receiving end. But these measures have not destroyed, at least as yet, Britain's liberties or its predominantly capitalistic system. And, more important, there have been some signs of a turning of the tide and of the exercise of self-restraint on the part of the electorate.

56. A "Freedom Budget"

A. Philip Randolph Institute

Can poverty and deprivation in America be abolished within a decade? The Freedom Budget is a comprehensive plan that shows how to accomplish that ambitious goal. Endorsed by A. Philip Randolph, the late Ralph Bunche, the late Martin Luther King, Jr., Michael Harrington, John Kenneth Galbraith, and several hundred other prominent black and white citizens in 1966, the Budget calls for a national plan with target dates for attaining various objectives.

The federal government would play the key role. A crucial assumption of the Budget is that the American economy normally operates at less than full capacity. If our economy utilized all its resources and grew by 4½ to 5 percent annually instead of our more usual 3 percent, the decade's total output would be $2.3 trillion larger than with the usual lower growth rate. Part of that extra "economic growth dividend" could finance a panoply of unmet needs.

The plan is a liberal reform approach to poverty. Massive government expenditures are proposed, but not socialism or the end of private enterprise. The Freedom Budget assumes that poverty can be eliminated effortlessly and without class conflict since rich and poor alike can make absolute gains from the larger pie.

Is the Freedom Budget realistic? A national plan put men on the moon. The Freedom Budget was proposed in 1966, but there is still no national plan to end poverty.

THE "FREEDOM BUDGET" IN BRIEF

Basic Principles

The "Freedom Budget" stems from seven basic principles:

1. Freedom on the American scene must include what Franklin D. Roosevelt called "freedom from want." This can be achieved, not by the power of any one group, but by the power of a fully-employed U.S. economy plus the power of the aroused conscience of the American people;

2. "Freedom from want" for an increasing majority of our citizens is not good enough; it must embrace all. Our economy is rich enough, and should be just enough, to reject as intolerable the ghetto within stone's throw of the duplex apartment; the alien worlds of slums and suburbs; the unemployment rate four times as high in some localities as in the nation at large; the millions receiving substandard wages despite many thousands of millionaires; the low-income farmers despite luxury restaurants; the poverty among 34 million and the deprivation among another 28 million, in a land where median family income is now close to $7,000, and where the families in the top income fifth have about eight times as much income as the families in the lowest income fifth. We have already received tragic warning that there is no prospect for domestic tranquility in a nation divided between the affluent and the desperately poor;

From *A "Freedom Budget" for All Americans* (1966). Reprinted by permission of the A. Philip Randolph Institute, New York.

3. The U.S. economy has the productive power to abolish "freedom from want" by 1975, not by pulling down those at the top but by lifting those at the bottom, if we start *now* and do our best. What we have the power to do, we will in fact do, if we *care* enough about doing it. The real issue is neither economic nor financial, but moral;

4. Our economy is now too abundant for the poverty or deprivation still afflicting almost a third of a nation to be explained mainly by the personal characteristics of the victims. True, personal deficiencies have a bearing upon the economic condition of many individuals. But it is even more true that deficiencies in nationwide policies and programs, evidencing a default in the national conscience, spawn and perpetuate these personal deficiencies. Just as malaria has been stamped out more by clearing swamps than by injecting quinine, the main attack upon poverty and deprivation must deal more with the nationwide environment than with the individual. Beyond this, the modern technology has advanced to the point where every American should enjoy "freedom from want," regardless of personal characteristics;

5. While "freedom from want" by 1975 will require action at all levels, private and public, the leadership role must be taken by our Federal Government. It alone represents all the people. Its policies and programs exert the most powerful single influence upon economic performance and social thinking. We accept this principle without question during a total war against external enemies. A *"war* against poverty" establishes the same principle on the domestic front;

6. A war against want cannot be won with declarations of intent. It cannot be won with token or inadequate programs which identify areas of need, but apply policies and programs which only scratch the surface. It demands specific quantitative goals, fully responsive to the need, and commitment to their attainment;

7. This war against want must be color blind. Negroes will benefit most relative to their numbers because, for reasons not of their making, want is most heavily concentrated among them. But in absolute numbers, the vast majority of those yearning for release from want are white. And those already free from want, both white and nonwhite, cannot enjoy fully the benefits of economic progress and the blessings of democracy until "freedom from want" becomes universal throughout the land.

Basic Objectives

Founded upon these principles, the seven basic objectives of the "Freedom Budget" are these:

1. *To restore full employment as rapidly as possible,* and to maintain it thereafter, for all able and willing to work, and for all whom adequate

training and education would make able and willing. This means an unemployment rate below 3 percent by early 1968, and preferably 2 percent. Full 40 percent of all U.S. poverty is due directly to inadequate employment opportunity, and involuntary unemployment is corrosive of the human spirit;

2. *To assure adequate incomes for those employed.* . . .

3. *To guarantee a minimum adequacy level of income to all those who cannot or should not be gainfully employed.* . . .

4. *To wipe out the slum ghettos, and provide a decent home for every American family, within a decade.*

5. *To provide, for all Americans, modern medical care and educational opportunity up to the limits of their abilities and ambitions, at costs within their means.*

6. *To overcome other manifestations of neglect in the public sector, by purifying our airs and waters, and bringing our transportation systems and natural resource development into line with the needs of a growing population and an expanding economy.*

7. *To unite sustained full employment with sustained full production and high economic growth.*

The Key Role of Our Federal Government

The "Freedom Budget" sets forth the above seven basic objectives in specific and quantitative terms. It sets time schedules for their accomplishment. It establishes their feasibility by means of a balance sheet of all of our needs and resources, with due allowance for all of our other private and public undertakings and aspirations as a nation and a people.

In this way, the "Freedom Budget" is a call to action. But the response to this call must take the form of national programs and policies, with the Federal Government exercising that leadership role which is consistent with our history, our institutions, and our needs. The six prime elements in this Federal responsibility are now set forth.

1. Beginning with 1967, the President's Economic Reports should embody the equivalent of a "Freedom Budget." These Reports should quantify ten-year goals for full employment and full production, for the practical liquidation of U.S. poverty by 1975, for wiping out the slum ghettos, and indeed for each of the seven basic objectives set forth in the "Freedom Budget." With due allowance for private and public performance at other levels, but with a firm determination by our Federal Government to close the gaps, all major Federal economic, financial, and social policies — including the Federal Budget — should be geared to attainment of these ten-year goals, starting at once in realistic magnitudes;

2. The bedrock civilized responsibility rests with our Federal Govern-

A. Philip Randolph Institute

ment to guarantee sustained full employment. The Government should at once and continuously lead in organizing and financing enough job-creating activities to close the gap between full employment and employment provided at other public and private levels. None of these Federally-created jobs need to be made-work, because our unmet needs in the public sector are large enough to absorb beneficially this Federal effort. Training programs, to be effective, must be synchronized with job creation;

3. The Federal Government should exert the full weight of its authority toward immediate enactment of a Federal minimum wage of $2.00 an hour, with coverage extended to the uppermost constitutional limits of Federal power. This would be a moderate start toward eradication of substandard living standards among millions of those employed;

4. A new farm program, with accent upon incomes rather than prices, should focus upon parity of income for farmers and liquidation of farm poverty by 1975. More than 43 percent of all farm families now live in poverty, contrasted with only 13 percent of all nonfarm families;

5. To lift out of poverty and also above deprivation those who cannot or should not be employed, there should be a Federally-initiated and supported guaranteed annual income, to supplement rather than to supplant a sustained full-employment policy at decent pay. The antipoverty goal alone involves lifting almost all multiple-person families above $3,130 by 1975. Pending this, there should be immediate and vast improvements in all Social Security and welfare programs, with greatly enlarged Federal contributions to all of them, including old-age insurance and assistance, general public assistance, special-purpose public assistance, unemployment insurance, and workmen's compensation;

6. Fiscal and monetary policies should be readjusted to place far more weight upon distributive justice. The massive Federal tax reductions in recent years tended to redistribute income with undue concern for those high up in the income structure, and inadequate concern for those lower down. State and local taxes and indirect taxes are so regressive — they bear with such excessive weight upon low-income people — that we should make the Federal income tax much more progressive than now. The decision to rely so heavily upon tax reduction and so little upon increased domestic spending to stimulate the economy was undesirable; it lowered our capacity to serve some of the greatest priorities of our national needs which depend upon public spending and are hardly helped by tax reduction. The current monetary policy does little to curb the excesses in the economy, and places a severe handicap upon activities of utmost urgency, especially housing. The sharply rising interest rates help those most who need help least, and hurt those most who need help most, because it is the lower income people who depend most upon borrowing. We cannot afford to neglect equity and social considerations in fiscal and monetary policies

which transfer billions of dollars every year from some to others. Improved income distribution also helps the whole economy.

The "Economic Growth Dividend" in the "Freedom Budget": Uses of This Dividend

We cannot enjoy what we do not produce. The "Freedom Budget" recognizes that all of the goals which it sets must be supported by the output of the U.S. economy. This output should grow greatly from year to year, under policies designed to assure sustained maximum employment, production, and purchasing power in accord with the objectives of the Employment Act of 1946.

With such policies, our total national production (measured in 1964 dollars) should rise from about 663 billion in 1965 to 1,085–1,120 billion by 1975. This would mean, for the ten years 1966–1975 inclusive, a level of total national production *averaging annually* 231.5–244.2 billion dollars higher, and *aggregating* over the ten years 2,315–2,442 billion dollars higher, than if total production remained during these ten years at the 1965 rate. This aggregate ten-year figure of 2,315–2,442 billion dollars is the "economic growth dividend" upon which the "Freedom Budget" draws to fulfill its purposes.

The "Freedom Budget" does not contemplate that this "economic growth dividend" be achieved by revolutionary nor even drastic changes in the division of responsibility between private enterprise and government under our free institutions. To illustrate, in 1965, 63.7 percent of our total national production was in the form of private consumer outlays, 16.5 percent in the form of private investment, and 19.8 percent in the form of public outlays at all levels for goods and services. Under the "higher" goals in the "Freedom Budget," these relationships in 1975 would be 63.5 percent, 16.9 percent, and 19.6 percent.

But while the "Freedom Budget" will not be regarded as socialistic, it is indeed socially-minded. It insists that we must make deliberate efforts to assure that, through combined private and public efforts, a large enough proportion of this "economic growth dividend" shall be directed toward the great priorities of our national needs: liquidation of private poverty, restoration of our cities, abolition of the slum ghettos, improvement of rural life, and removal of the glaring deficiencies in facilities and services in "the public sector" of our economy. The "Freedom Budget" thus has moral as well as materialistic purposes.

The use of only a fair and moderate portion of this "economic growth dividend" to support the great priority purposes in the "Freedom Budget" makes it clear that even those who are already affluent or wealthy would not be penalized in any way in order to accomplish these great priority purposes. Entirely to the contrary, they would continue to enjoy what they have now, and also share largely and directly in the "economic growth dividend" itself. They would also benefit indirectly in multiple ways by the portions of the "economic growth dividend" used to support these great national priorities.

57. Recommendations for National Action

*National Advisory Commission
on Civil Disorders*

Two centuries ago Tom Paine observed: "Whatever the apparent cause of any riots may be, the real one is always want of happiness." Not surprisingly, the report of the Kerner Commission, set up to investigate the causes of the 1967 riots, documented the unrelieved misery that envelops ghetto life.

The Commission made recommendations for national action. These aimed to create a single nation from our two separate and unequal Americas and centered around employment, education, welfare, and housing.

One major suggestion was to create 2 million new jobs in three years to absorb the hard-core unemployed and reduce unemployment. Three years later a depression had created 1.7 million additional unemployed. Another suggestion was for a uniform national welfare standard of at least $3,335 per year for a family of four, to be primarily federally financed. President Nixon's plan (not yet adopted) called for a $1,600 minimum plus food stamps. Other dreary tales could be recited. For, despite minor changes, the nation's response has been perilously inadequate and far from the total commitment called for by the Commission. And the want of happiness in the ghettos has not receded.

No American — white or black — can escape the consequences of the continuing social and economic decay of our major cities.

Only a commitment to national action on an unprecedented scale can shape a future compatible with the historic ideals of American society.

The great productivity of our economy, and a federal revenue system

From *Report of the National Advisory Commission on Civil Disorders* (Washington, D.C.: U.S. Government Printing Office, March 1968).

which is highly responsive to economic growth, can provide the resources.

The major need is to generate new will — the will to tax ourselves to the extent necessary to meet the vital needs of the nation.

We have set forth goals and proposed strategies to reach those goals. We discuss and recommend programs not to commit each of us to specific parts of such programs but to illustrate the type and dimension of action needed.

The major goal is the creation of a true union — a single society and a single American identity. Toward that goal, we propose the following objectives for national action:

> Opening up opportunities to those who are restricted by racial segregation and discrimination, and eliminating all barriers to their choice of jobs, education and housing.
> Removing the frustration of powerlessness among the disadvantaged by providing the means for them to deal with the problems that affect their own lives and by increasing the capacity of our public and private institutions to respond to these problems.
> Increasing communication across racial lines to destroy stereotypes, to halt polarization, end distrust and hostility, and create common ground for efforts toward public order and social justice.

We propose these aims to fulfill our pledge of equality and to meet the fundamental needs of a democratic and civilized society — domestic peace and social justice.

EMPLOYMENT

Pervasive unemployment and underemployment are the most persistent and serious grievances in minority areas. They are inextricably linked to the problem of civil disorder.

Despite growing federal expenditures for manpower development and training programs, and sustained general economic prosperity and increasing demands for skilled workers, about two million — white and nonwhite — are permanently unemployed. About ten million are underemployed, of whom 6.5 million work full time for wages below the poverty line.

The 500,000 "hard-core" unemployed in the central cities who lack a basic education and are unable to hold a steady job are made up in large part of Negro males between the ages of 18 and 25. In the riot cities which we surveyed, Negroes were three times as likely as whites to hold unskilled jobs, which are often part time, seasonal, low-paying and "dead end."

Negro males between the ages of 15 and 25 predominated among the rioters. More than 20 percent of the rioters were unemployed, and many who were employed held intermittent, low status, unskilled jobs which they regarded as below their education and ability.

The Commission recommends that the federal government:

> Undertake joint efforts with cities and states to consolidate existing manpower programs to avoid fragmentation and duplication.
>
> Take immediate action to create 2,000,000 new jobs over the next three years — one million in the public sector and one million in the private sector — to absorb the hard-core unemployed and materially reduce the level of underemployment for all workers, black and white. We propose 250,000 public sector and 300,000 private sector jobs in the first year.
>
> Provide on-the-job training by both public and private employers with reimbursement to private employers for the extra costs of training the hard-core unemployed, by contract or by tax credits.
>
> Provide tax and other incentives to investment in rural as well as urban poverty areas in order to offer to the rural poor an alternative to migration to urban centers.
>
> Take new and vigorous action to remove artificial barriers to employment and promotion, including not only racial discrimination but, in certain cases, arrest records or lack of a high school diploma. Strengthen those agencies such as the Equal Employment Opportunity Commission, charged with eliminating discriminatory practices, and provide full support for Title VI of the 1964 Civil Rights Act allowing federal grant-in-aid funds to be withheld from activities which discriminate on grounds of color or race.

The Commission commends the recent public commitment of the National Council of the Building and Construction Trades Unions, AFL-CIO, to encourage and recruit Negro membership in apprenticeship programs. This commitment should be intensified and implemented.

EDUCATION

Education in a democratic society must equip children to develop their potential and to participate fully in American life. For the community at large, the schools have discharged this responsibility well. But for many minorities, and particularly for the children of the ghetto, the schools have failed to provide the educational experience which could overcome the effects of discrimination and deprivation.

This failure is one of the persistent sources of grievance and resentment within the Negro community. The hostility of Negro parents and students toward the school system is generating increasing conflict and causing disruption within many city school districts. But the most dramatic evidence of the relationship between educational practices and civil disorders lies in the high incidence of riot participation by ghetto youth who have not completed high school.

The bleak record of public education for ghetto children is growing worse. In the critical skills — verbal and reading ability — Negro students are falling further behind whites with each year of school completed. The high unemployment and underemployment rate for Negro youth is evidence, in part, of the growing educational crisis.

We support integration as the priority education strategy; it is essential to the future of American society. In this last summer's disorders we have seen the consequences of racial isolation at all levels, and of attitudes toward race, on both sides, produced by three centuries of myth, ignorance, and bias. It is indispensable that opportunities for interaction between the races be expanded.

We recognize that the growing dominance of pupils from disadvantaged minorities in city school populations will not soon be reversed. No matter how great the effort toward desegregation, many children of the ghetto will not, within their school careers, attend integrated schools.

If existing disadvantages are not to be perpetuated, we must drastically improve the quality of ghetto education. Equality of results with all-white schools must be the goal.

To implement these strategies, the Commission recommends:

> Sharply increased efforts to eliminate de facto segregation in our schools through substantial federal aid to school systems seeking to desegregate either within the system or in cooperation with neighboring school systems.
>
> Elimination of racial discrimination in Northern as well as Southern schools by vigorous application of Title VI of the Civil Rights Act of 1964.
>
> Extension of quality early childhood education to every disadvantaged child in the country.
>
> Efforts to improve dramatically schools serving disadvantaged children through substantial federal funding of year-round compensatory education programs, improved teaching, and expanded experimentation and research.
>
> Elimination of illiteracy through greater federal support for adult basic education.
>
> Enlarged opportunities for parent and community participation in the public schools.
>
> Reoriented vocational education emphasizing work-experience training and the involvement of business and industry.
>
> Expanded opportunities for higher education through increased federal assistance to disadvantaged students.
>
> Revision of state aid formulas to assure more per student aid to

districts having a high proportion of disadvantaged school-age children.

THE WELFARE SYSTEM

Our present system of public welfare is designed to save money instead of people, and tragically ends up doing neither. This system has two critical deficiencies:

First, it excludes large numbers of persons who are in great need, and who, if provided a decent level of support, might be able to become more productive and self-sufficient. No federal funds are available for millions of men and women who are needy but neither aged, handicapped nor the parents of minor children.

Second, for those included, the system provides assistance well below the minimum necessary for a decent level of existence, and imposes restrictions that encourage continued dependency on welfare and undermine self-respect.

A welter of statutory requirements and administrative practices and regulations operate to remind recipients that they are considered untrustworthy, promiscuous and lazy. Residence requirements prevent assistance to people in need who are newly arrived in the state. Regular searches of recipients' homes violate privacy. Inadequate social services compound the problems.

The Commission recommends that the federal government, acting with state and local governments where necessary, reform the existing welfare system to:

> Establish uniform national standards of assistance at least as high as the annual "poverty level" of income, now set by the Social Security Administration at $3,335 per year for an urban family of four.
>
> Require that all states receiving federal welfare contributions participate in the Aid to Families with Dependent Children — Unemployed Parents program (AFDC-UP) that permits assistance to families with both father and mother in the home, thus aiding the family while it is still intact.
>
> Bear a substantially greater portion of all welfare costs — at least 90 percent of total payments.
>
> Increase incentives for seeking employment and job training, but remove restrictions recently enacted by the Congress that would compel mothers of young children to work.
>
> Provide more adequate social services through neighborhood centers and family-planning programs.
>
> **Remove the freeze** placed by the 1967 welfare amendments on the

percentage of children in a state that can be covered by federal assistance.

Eliminate residence requirements.

As a long-range goal, the Commission recommends that the federal government seek to develop a national system of income supplementation based strictly on need with two broad and basic purposes:

> To provide, for those who can work or who do work, any necessary supplements in such a way as to develop incentives for fuller employment;
>
> To provide, for those who cannot work and for mothers who decide to remain with their children, a minimum standard of decent living, and to aid in the saving of children from the prison of poverty that has held their parents.

A broad system of supplementation would involve substantially greater federal expenditures than anything now contemplated. The cost will range widely depending on the standard of need accepted as the "basic allowance" to individuals and families, and on the rate at which additional income above this level is taxed. Yet if the deepening cycle of poverty and dependence on welfare can be broken, if the children of the poor can be given the opportunity to scale the wall that now separates them from the rest of society, the return on this investment will be great indeed.

HOUSING

After more than three decades of fragmented and grossly underfunded federal housing programs, nearly six million substandard housing units remain occupied in the United States.

The housing problem is particularly acute in the minority ghettos. Nearly two-thirds of all non-white families living in the central cities today live in neighborhoods marked with substandard housing and general urban blight. Two major factors are responsible.

First: Many ghetto residents simply cannot pay the rent necessary to support decent housing. In Detroit, for example, over 40 percent of the non-white occupied units in 1960 required rent of over 35 percent of the tenants' income.

Second: Discrimination prevents access to many non-slum areas, particularly the suburbs, where good housing exists. In addition, by creating a "back pressure" in the racial ghettos, it makes it possible for landlords to break up apartments for denser occupancy, and keeps prices and rents of deteriorated ghetto housing higher than they would be in a truly free market.

To date, federal programs have been able to do comparatively little to provide housing for the disadvantaged. In the 31-year history of subsidized federal housing, only about 800,000 units have been constructed, with recent production averaging about 50,000 units a year. By comparison, over a period only three years longer, FHA insurance guarantees have made possible the construction of over ten million middle and upper-income units.

Two points are fundamental to the Commission's recommendations:

First: Federal housing programs must be given a new thrust aimed at overcoming the prevailing patterns of racial segregation. If this is not done, those programs will continue to concentrate the most impoverished and dependent segments of the population into the central-city ghettos where there is already a critical gap between the needs of the population and the public resources to deal with them.

Second: The private sector must be brought into the production and financing of low and moderate rental housing to supply the capabilities and capital necessary to meet the housing needs of the nation.

The Commission recommends that the federal government:

> Enact a comprehensive and enforceable federal open housing law to cover the sale or rental of all housing, including single family homes.
>
> Reorient federal housing programs to place more low and moderate income housing outside of ghetto areas.
>
> Bring within the reach of low and moderate income families within the next five years six million new and existing units of decent housing, beginning with 600,000 units in the next year.

To reach this goal we recommend:

> Expansion and modification of the rent supplement program to permit use of supplements for existing housing, thus greatly increasing the reach of the program.
>
> Expansion and modification of the below-market interest rate program to enlarge the interest subsidy to all sponsors and provide interest-free loans to nonprofit sponsors to cover pre-construction costs, and permit sale of projects to nonprofit corporations, cooperatives, or condominiums.
>
> Creation of an ownership supplement program similar to present rent supplements, to make home ownership possible for low-income families.
>
> Federal writedown of interest rates on loans to private builders constructing moderate-rent housing.
>
> Expansion of the public housing program, with emphasis on small units on scattered sites, and leasing and "turnkey" programs.
>
> Expansion of the Model Cities program.
>
> Expansion and reorientation of the urban renewal program to

give priority to projects directly assisting low-income households to obtain adequate housing.

CONCLUSION

One of the first witnesses to be invited to appear before this Commission was Dr. Kenneth B. Clark, a distinguished and perceptive scholar. Referring to the reports of earlier riot commissions, he said:

> I read that report . . . of the 1919 riot in Chicago, and it is as if I were reading the report of the investigating committee on the Harlem riot of '35, the report of the investigating committee on the Harlem riot of '43, the report of the McCone Commission on the Watts riot.
>
> I must again in candor say to you members of this Commission — it is a kind of Alice in Wonderland — with the same moving picture re-shown over and over again, the same analysis, the same recommendations, and the same inaction.

These words come to our minds as we conclude this report.

We have provided an honest beginning. We have learned much. But we have uncovered no startling truths, no unique insights, no simple solutions. The destruction and the bitterness of racial disorder, the harsh polemics of black revolt and white repression have been seen and heard before in this country.

It is time now to end the destruction and the violence, not only in the streets of the ghetto but in the lives of people.

58. The Myth and Irrationality of Black Capitalism

James Boggs

Is black capitalism the answer to the economic problems of ghettos, where so many businesses are white-owned? James Boggs, an auto worker and a leading black socialist theorist, takes a negative view.

A black nationalist in the tradition of Marx, Boggs adds the perspective of economic class to his analysis of racism and black poverty. He views the decay of black communities as a natural consequence of capitalist exploitation. Black capitalism will not do, according to Boggs. It cannot help the impoverished black masses and if "success-

> *ful" would only substitute black for white exploiters. At the heart of Boggs's proposal for the economic development of the black community is a call for large-scale social ownership rather than private individual enterprise.*

It is now nearly fifteen years since the black movement started out to achieve civil rights through integration into the system. Year after year the movement has gained momentum until today millions of black people in all strata of life consider themselves part of the movement. At no other time in our 400 years on this continent have black people sustained such a long period of activity. We have had rebellions and revolts of short duration, but it is quite apparent that what we are now engaged in is not just a revolt, not just a rebellion, but a full-fledged movement driving toward full growth and maturity and therefore requiring a serious examination of the fundamental nature of the system that we are attacking and the system that we are trying to build.

It is also now quite clear that black people, who have been the chief victims of the system that is under attack, are the ones who have to make this examination; because for us it is a very concrete and not just an abstract question. We have evaded this question because in reality we recognized that to tamper with the system is to tamper with the whole society and all its institutions.

Now we cannot evade the question any longer.

When we talk about the system, we are talking about capitalism. I repeat: When we talk about the system, we are talking about capitalism. Let us not be afraid to say it. And when we talk about capitalism, we are talking about the system that has created the situation that blacks are in today! Let us be clear about that too. Black underdevelopment is a product of capitalist development. Black America is underdeveloped today because of capitalist semi-colonialism, just as Africa, Asia, and Latin America are underdeveloped today because of capitalist colonialism. We cannot look at the underdevelopment of the black community separately from capitalism any more than we can look at the development of racism separately from capitalism. . . .

Capitalism in the United States is unique because, unlike capitalism elsewhere — which first exploited its indigenous people and then fanned out through colonialism to exploit other races in other countries — it started out by dispossessing one set of people (the Indians) and then importing another set of people (the Africans) to do the work on the land.

This method of enslavement not only made blacks the first working class in the country to be exploited for their *labor* but made blacks the foundation of the capital necessary for early industrialization. . . .

Today, in an effort to protect this capitalist system, the white power structure is seeking once again to re-enslave black people by offering them black capitalism. Now, scientifically speaking, there is no such thing as a black capitalism which is different from white capitalism or capitalism of any other color. Capitalism, regardless of its color, is a system of exploitation of one set of people by another set of people. . . .

. . . In reality, black capitalism is a dream and a delusion. Blacks have no one underneath them to exploit. So black capitalism would have to exploit a black labor force which is already at the bottom of the ladder and is in no mood to change from one exploiter to another just because he is of the same color.

Nevertheless, as residents and indigenous members of the black community we recognize its need for development. Our question, therefore, is how *can* it be developed? How *should* it be developed? To answer these questions, we must clarify the nature of its underdevelopment. . . .

The economic undevelopment of a colony is the result of the fact that the colony's natural and historical process of development was interrupted and destroyed by colonialism, so that large sections of the country have been forced to become or remain pre-industrial or agricultural. For example, many of these societies once had their own handicraft industries which were destroyed by Western economic penetration. Most were turned into one-crop countries to supply raw materials or agricultural produce to the Western imperialists. In struggling for independence from imperialism, these societies are fighting for the opportunity to develop themselves industrially.

On the other hand, the physical structure of the black communities inside the United States is the direct result of industrial development, which has turned these communities into wastelands, abandoned by an industry that has undergone technological revolutions. The physical structure of black communities is like that of the abandoned mining communities in Appalachia whose original reason for existence has been destroyed by the discovery of new forms of energy or whose coal veins were exhausted by decades of mining. . . .

Secondly, the black community is not technologically backward in the same way as the majority of communities in an undeveloped nation in Asia, Africa, or Latin America are. In these countries the vast majority of people still live on the land and, until recently, had had experience in using only the most elementary agricultural tools, such as the hoe or the plough. In these countries a revolution in agriculture must accompany the industrial revolution. By contrast, the mechanization of agriculture has already taken place in the United States, forcing the black people (who were this country's first working class on the land) to move to the cities. The great majority of blacks have now lived in the city for the last generation and have been exposed to the most modern appliances and machinery. In the use or production of these appliances and machines, the blacks are no less developed than the great majority of white workers.

The undevelopment of blacks is primarily in two areas:

1. They have been systematically excluded from the supervisory, planning, and decision-making roles which would have given them practical experience and skills in organizing, planning, and administration.

2. They have been systematically excluded from the higher education which would have given them the abstract and conceptual tools necessary for research and technological innovation at *this* stage of economic development, when productivity is more dependent on imagination, knowledge, and the concepts of systems — on mental processes — than it is on manual labor.

From the preceding analysis we can propose certain fundamental guidelines for any programs aimed at developing black communities:

1. Black communities are today capitalist communities, communities which have been developed by capitalist methods. Their present stage of decay, decline, and dilapidation — their present stage of undevelopment — is a product of capitalist exploitation. They have been used and re-used to produce profit by every form of capitalist: landlords, construction industries, merchants, insurance brokers, bankers, finance companies, racketeers, and manufacturers of cars, appliances, steel, and every other kind of industrial commodity. Development for the black community means getting rid of these exploiters, *not* replacing white exploiters by black ones.

2. Any future development of the black community must start from the bottom up, not from the top down. The people at the very bottom of the black community, the chief victims of capitalist exploitation, cannot be delivered from their bottom position by black capitalist exploitation. They are the ones in the most pressing need of rapid development. They are also the fastest growing section of the black community. They are the black street force, the ADC mothers, welfare recipients, domestic servants, unskilled laborers, etc. These — not the relatively small black middle class — are the people who must be given an opportunity to exercise initiative, to make important decisions, and to get a higher education, if the black community is to be developed. . . .

3. Struggle should be built into any program of black community development in order to stimulate crisis learning and escalate and expand the sense of civic rights and responsibilities. The struggles should be on issues

related to the concrete grievances most deeply felt by the lowest layer of the black community — on issues of education, welfare, health, housing, police brutality — and should be aimed at mobilizing this layer for control of these institutions inside the black community as the only means to reverse the manifest failure of these institutions to meet the needs of black people. . . .

4. Any program for the development of the black community must provide for and encourage development at an extremely rapid, crash program, pace and not at an evolutionary or gradual pace. Otherwise, in view of the rapid growth of the black population, and particularly of its most oppressed sector, deterioration will proceed more rapidly than development. For example, in a community where there is a pressing need for at least 10,000 low-cost housing units, the building of a couple of hundred units here and there in the course of a year does not begin to fill the need for the original 10,000 units — while at the same time another thousand or more units have deteriorated far below livable level. . . .

5. The black community cannot possibly be developed by introducing into it the trivial skills and the outmoded technology of yesteryear. Proposals for funding small businesses which can only use sweatshop methods or machinery which is already or will soon become obsolete means funding businesses which are bound to fail, thereby increasing the decay in the black community. Proposals for vocational training or employment of the hard-core in black or white businesses (on the theory that what black people need most to develop the black community is the discipline of work and money in their pockets) are simply proposals for pacification and for maintaining the black community in its present stage of undevelopment. . . . The jobs for which blacks should be educated are the jobs of the future, such as aerospace engineers, recreation directors, dentists, computer programmers, mass media production workers, communications equipment experts, medical technicians, operations researchers, teachers, quality control. There can be no economic development of the black community unless black people are developed for these jobs with a bright future. . . .

. . . Any attempt to interest them in dead-end jobs or in education for dead-end jobs will only increase the decay and disorder in the black community, because rather than accept these jobs or this education, black youth will take to the streets. . . .

6. Any program for the development of the black community must be based on large-scale social ownership rather than on private individual enterprise. In this period of large-scale production and distribution, private individual enterprises (or small businesses) can only remain marginal and dependent, adding to the sense of hopelessness and powerlessness inside the black community.

The social needs of the community, consciously determined by the community, *not* the needs or interests of particular individual entrepreneurs, must be the determining fact in the allocation of resources. The philosophy that automatic progress will result for the community if enterprising individuals are allowed to pursue their private interests must be consciously rejected. Equally illusory is the idea that development of the black community can take place through the operation of "blind" or "unseen" economic forces. The black community can only be developed through community control of the public institutions, public funds, and other community resources, including land inside the black community, all of which are in fact the public property of the black community.

Massive educational programs, including programs of struggle, must be instituted inside the black community to establish clearly in the minds of black people the fact that the institutions which most directly affect the lives of the deepest layer of the black community (schools, hospitals, law-enforcement agencies, welfare agencies) are the property of the black community, paid for by our taxes, and that therefore the black community has the right to control the funds which go into the operation and administration of these institutions. This right is reinforced and made more urgent by the fact that these institutions have completely failed to meet black needs while under white control. . . .

In these campaigns special emphasis should also be placed on the question of land reform and acquisition. Over the last thirty years, the federal government has changed land tenure and agricultural technology through massive subsidies involving the plowing-under of vast areas of land, rural electrification, agricultural research, etc. But all this has been for the benefit of whites who have become millionaire farmers and landowners, at the expense of blacks who have been driven off the land altogether or have been retained as farm laborers, averaging less than $5.00 a day, or $800 a year, in wages.

In the South the black community must undertake a massive land reform movement to force the federal government to turn these plowed-under lands over to the millions of blacks still in the South, for black community organizations to develop. . . .

A similar campaign for land reform and acquisition should be organized in the urban areas of the North where the great majority of blacks are now concentrated. The concept of "eminent domain," or the acquisition of private property for public use, has already been well established in the Urban Renewal program. However, up to now "eminent domain" has been exercised only in the interest of white developers and residents, and against the interests of black homeowners and the black community. Federal subsidies have been used to expel blacks from their homes, businesses, and churches, and then to improve the areas which have then been turned over to private developers to build homes for middle-class and wealthy whites.

The principle of "eminent domain" must now be employed to acquire land for the purposes of the black community. Vacant land, land owned by whites which has been allowed to deteriorate, etc., must be acquired and turned over to black communities to plan and develop under black control and with black labor, for the purpose of creating communities which will meet the many-sided needs of black people for housing, health, education, recreation, shopping facilities, etc., and which will be a source of participation, pride, and inspiration to the black community and particularly to black youth. . . .

The application of the concept of social ownership and control by the black community is essential to the involvement of the black street force in the development of the black community. These "untouchables" have no property which they can call their own and absolutely no reason to believe that they will ever acquire any. The only future before them is in the prisons, the military, or the streets. They are the ones who have sparked the urban rebellions. Yet, up to now, after each rebellion they have been excluded from participation, while middle-class blacks have presumed to speak for them and to extract petty concessions which have uplifted these blacks but have left the "untouchables" out in the cold. . . .

7. Since pacification of these rebellious forces has been the chief purpose of all so-called development programs, it is no accident that most of these programs have been single-action, one-year, or "one hot summer" programs, without any fundamental perspective for developing new social institutions or for resolving the basic issues and grievances which affect the largest section of the black community.

On the other hand, it is obvious that any serious programs for the development of the black community must be based on comprehensive planning for at least a five-year period. Piecemeal, single-action, one-year, or "one hot summer" programs are worse than no programs at all. They constitute tokenism in the economic sphere and produce the same result as tokenism in any sphere: the increased discontent of the masses of the community.

The purpose of these five-year comprehensive programs must be the reconstruction and reorganization of all the social institutions inside the black community which have manifestly failed to meet the needs of the black community. Any programs for the development of the black community which are worth funding at all must be programs that are not just for the curing of defects. Rather they must be for the purpose of creating new types of social institutions through the mobilization of the social creativity of black youth, ADC mothers, welfare recipients, and all those in the black community who are the main victims of the systematic degradation and exploitation of American racism. Development for the black community at this stage in history means *social ownership, social change, social pioneering,* and *social reconstruction.*

The Peace Dividend: Swords into Plowshares?

59. Reorder National Priorities

National Commission on the Causes and Prevention of Violence

> *More federal money for social programs is a necessary though not sufficient ingredient in any recipe to end poverty. But over the years Pentagon priorities and budgets have received top billing.*
>
> *The war in Vietnam convinced many Americans of the incompatibility of military expansion and domestic justice. In Reading 59, the National Commission on the Causes and Prevention of Violence, headed by Milton Eisenhower, advocates a reordering of our national priorities and a $20 billion increase in federal general welfare expenditures after the termination of the Vietnam war.*
>
> *Unfortunately, there is no automatic mechanism to funnel funds released from the military budget into social uses. Nor is there universal support for the idea that the "peace dividend" should be used to reorder priorities. And the proposal conflicts with the plans of those in power who give high priority to the continuation of huge military budgets after termination of the Vietnam war, as expressed by Daniel Patrick Moynihan in Reading 60.*

For the first time in man's history, this nation is nearing the capability of releasing all citizens from the poverty and social privation that hitherto have been accepted as the inevitable lot of mankind. We have also achieved an enormous capacity to communicate: the poor, the black, and other deprived groups among us can see daily on their television sets what

From *To Establish Justice, to Insure Domestic Tranquility. Final Report of the National Commission on the Causes and Prevention of Violence* (Washington, D.C.: U.S. Government Printing Office, December 13, 1969).

they are missing, and how near their release from bondage can be. But our institutions have not yet made it possible for an expectant populace to achieve what our economy and technology are becoming capable of providing.

In our judgment, the time is upon us for a reordering of national priorities and for a greater investment of resources in the fulfillment of two basic purposes of our Constitution — to "establish justice" and to "insure domestic tranquility."

We solemnly declare our conviction that this nation is entering a period in which our people need to be as concerned by the internal dangers to our free society as by any probable combination of external threats. We recognize that substantial amounts of funds cannot be transferred from sterile war purposes to more productive ones until our participation in the Vietnam war is ended. We also recognize that to make our society essentially free of poverty and discrimination, and to make our sprawling urban areas fit to inhabit, will cost a great deal of money and will take a great length of time. We believe, however, that we can and should make a major decision now to reassess our national priorities by placing these objectives in the first rank of the nation's goals.

The decision that has the greatest effect on the level of our expenditures for these objectives is what we decide to spend on the national defense. For three decades, the national defense has ranked first by far in our scale of priorities, much of the time necessarily so. With occasional exceptions, whatever the Administration has requested for the Armed Forces has been readily granted. Since 1939 there have been a number of occasions when the Administration's budget requests for the Armed Forces have been exceeded by Congressional appropriations; for most other federal programs the opposite is true. For example, actual appropriations for the general welfare (health, labor, education, housing, pollution, and law enforcement) are currently running more than five billion dollars annually below the amounts previously authorized by the Congress.

Our Commission is not competent to recommend a specific level of national defense expenditures. We recognize that without the deterrent capability essential for security against external attack, internal freedom and security would not be possible. It is to be expected that our military leaders will, like other government officials, stress the extreme urgency of the programs under their charge. But we believe the time has come to question whether expenditures for the general welfare should continue to be subordinated to those for national defense.

Defense expenditures, stated in 1968 prices, fell from about 78 billion dollars in 1953 (at the end of the Korean War) to about 60 billion dollars in 1954 and remained at that level for the decade 1955 to 1964. But by 1968 they had risen again to the present 81 billion dollar annual level as the result of our major commitment of troops to Vietnam.

Federal expenditures for the general welfare, while they have increased substantially over the past several years, are now approximately 60 billion dollars, of which $25 billion represents social security payments.

As a first step, we should try to reverse this relationship. When our participation in the Vietnam War is concluded, we recommend increasing annual general welfare expenditures by about 20 billion dollars (stated in 1968 dollars), partly by reducing military expenditures and partly by use of increased tax revenues resulting from the growth of the Gross National Product. We suggest this only as an initial goal; as the Gross National Product and tax revenues continue to rise, we should strive to keep military expenditures level (in constant dollars), while general welfare expenditures should continue to increase until essential social goals are achieved. . . .

Whether somewhat more or less than the amounts we have indicated should be provided to overcome social ills is not the important point. What is important is that the people of this nation recognize both the possibilities and the need for choice. For an entire generation, we have necessarily been more aware of and responsive to the external dangers to our society than to the internal dangers. In this Commission's opinion, the internal dangers now demand a greater awareness and a more substantial response — one that can only be made if we face the need to reorder our priorities. It is time to balance the risks and precautions we take abroad against those we take here at home.

60. There Will Be No Peace Dividend

Daniel Patrick Moynihan

In Reading 59, the National Commission on the Causes and Prevention of Violence advocated that the nation should reorder its priorities and divert $20 billion from military expenditures to social uses after the end of the Vietnam war. But not everyone agrees that the "peace dividend" should be used as the Commission suggests. A different view of the peace dividend is given here by sociologist Daniel Patrick Moynihan. Moynihan, then President Nixon's assistant for urban affairs, tells a 1969 White House press conference that there will be no peace dividend forthcoming, claiming that these funds are "evanescent like the morning clouds around San Clemente." But the poor will not rest content with Moynihan's analysis. The struggle against bloated military budgets will be increasingly recognized as an integral part of the battle to end poverty in America.

Q: What kind of peace and growth dividends does your study anticipate?

Dr. Moynihan: This was not my study. The study was headed by Dr. Stein. He chose not to define it in those terms however. He chose simply to speak in terms of the continued growth of revenues and claims on revenues.

Q: It will be some gross dividend, if not $22.9 billion?

Dr. Moynihan: I think it is fair to say that the idea of any sudden discontinuity — I mean, you are poor one day and rich the next — I am sorry, it is not going to happen.

Q: Can you elaborate on why, after Vietnam, all this money will not be available?

Dr. Moynihan: I think the real accurate question is, "Who thought it was going to be in the first place?" The continued claims on the economy are real and the growth of the economy is fixed in certain degrees by productivity in the labor force.

Q: You estimate that some $20 billion is spent in Vietnam. What happens to that money?

Dr. Moynihan: The needs and other parts of the defense establishment are fairly clear. The amount in which we have depleted resources to maintain the effort in Vietnam seems to be much more important than people had anticipated. The simple fact is, we are not going to go through a process where one day you simply stop a process of expenditure that had been going on and suddenly all the surplus comes pouring into you.

We are going to have a growth of GNP and a growth of the Federal Government and the issue is going to be, in the next five years, how do you allocate that increase, and it is to that more realistic question that the Urban Affairs Council is addressed.

Q: Are you repudiating the earlier report and prediction?

Dr. Moynihan: Repudiate would be much too strong a word. We are proceeding on a different set of assumptions. . . .

Q: Can you say how much of the peace dividends will be used up in the defense area?

Dr. Moynihan: I think the peace dividends turned out to be evanescent, like the morning clouds around San Clemente.

From a press release of the White House press conference of Daniel Patrick Moynihan (San Clemente, Calif., August 25, 1969).

61. Why We Need Socialism in America

Michael Harrington

> *Nearly a decade after his book about poverty shocked the affluent society, Michael Harrington, whose views on the War Against Poverty appear in Reading 29, offers his diagnosis of why the world's richest country still has not eliminated poverty and inequality. Harrington, Chairman of the Socialist Party, feels that these problems cannot be solved under capitalism — not even under affluent capitalism — because sharp class divisions and the concentration of economic power perpetuate poverty and inequality and vitiate efforts to establish social justice through welfare-state reforms.*
>
> *Harrington claims a profit-oriented economy inevitably produces distorted priorities that favor the rich. But the majority are far from affluent. The Bureau of Labor Statistics estimated that in 1970 an average urban family of four required $10,666 to achieve a "moderate" living standard. But half of all American nonfarm families of four that year had incomes of less than $11,288. So Harrington proposes priorities that would benefit poorly paid workers and the lower middle class as well as the poor. He believes these could be attained only under socialism, with production for need, not profit.*
>
> *Poorly paid workers and the lower middle class, fearful of potential competition from the poor, often oppose them politically. But Harrington hopes that these and other millions of Americans will join with the poor to work for socialism and equality, from which all would benefit.*

America needs socialism. Our technology has produced unprecedented wealth, rotted great cities, threatened the very air and water, and embittered races, generations, and social classes.

Our vision of society, even when most liberal, is too conservative to resolve these contradictions, for they are aspects of a system that has a deep, even principled commitment to the wrong priorities. And while significant reforms — often socialist in inspiration — have modified some

---

From Michael Harrington, "Why We Need Socialism in America," *Dissent*, 17:3, (May–June 1970). Reprinted by permission. Much of the material presented here will be contained in Mr. Harrington's forthcoming book, *Socialism: Past, Present and Future.*

of the extreme forms of capitalist injustice, the post-Keynesian welfare state still allows huge corporations to make decisions of fundamental social importance without consulting either those who are affected or those who work for them.

But isn't it an act of leftist nostalgia to indict American society in this way? Today, one is told, the United States is the richest country in the history of mankind, and its remaining problems can be taken care of by pragmatic technicians acting within the framework of the welfare state.

It is precisely this conventional assumption about our present and future that I propose to challenge. I will show that our affluence is so misshapen that it does not even meet the needs of the majority of the people. The most humane of technocrats cannot cope with the basic causes of these antisocial policies, if only because they are located in an entrenched and possessive system of power. Only a democratic mass movement could challenge this vested interest in our current crises. And it is just possible that the "success" of American capitalism will accomplish what its sweatshops failed to do: make socialism politically relevant.

I say these things with a full knowledge of the ways in which the socialist idea has been confused, betrayed, and eviscerated during the past 150 years. Indeed, one of the aims of this essay is to try to face up to these difficulties with candor and to make the idea of socialism more precise. If that attempt is successful, what will emerge at the end of this study will not be the promise of a magical cure-all to bring complete and eternal happiness to all men but a more modest yet still audacious program for making America a good society.

IS REFORM OF THE WELFARE STATE ENOUGH?

There are three basic reasons why the reform of the welfare state will not solve our most urgent problems:

the class structure of capitalist society vitiates, or subverts, almost every such effort toward social justice;

private, corporate power cannot tolerate the comprehensive and democratic planning we desperately need;

and even if these first two obstacles to providing every citizen with a decent house, income, and job were overcome, the system still has an inherent tendency to make affluence self-destructive.

In thus documenting the limits of the welfare state it may seem that I am contemptuous of past reforms or of those liberals who do not share my conviction that there must be fundamental, structural change. Nothing could be further from the truth. The welfare state was an enormous advance over the cruelty and indifference to human suffering that characterized early capitalism. It was achieved through struggle and great sacrifice — sometimes of life itself — on the part of "ordinary" people who, even though they had usually been denied an adequate education, tutored the wealthy in some of the fundamentals of social decency. And to the extent that there is a mass "left wing" in the United States, it is composed largely of precisely those groups — trade unionists, minorities, middle-class idealists — which fought these great battles and are determined to preserve the gains they brought.

Far from being simply a matter of keeping the record straight, this point has profound political implications for the future. It is important that socialists demonstrate the inherent inability of the welfare state, based as it is upon a capitalist economy and social structure, to deal with problems that demand anticapitalist allocations of resources. But that does not mean, as some young leftists in recent times have thought, that the welfare state is to be dismissed as a "fraud" that prevents the people from coming to truly radical conclusions. For if millions of Americans are to become socialists they will do so because, in the struggle to make that welfare state respond to their immediate needs they will have discovered that they must go beyond it. If socialists were arrogantly to dismiss these battles as irrelevant, they would play no role when masses of their fellow citizens turned left.

Socialists, then, must be in the forefront of every fight to defend and extend the welfare state, even as they criticize its inability to solve fundamental problems and even as they propose alternatives to it. In this context, the following analysis of the severe limits capitalism imposes upon the welfare state is designed not to prove that liberals are foolish and deluded, but that their liberal values can only be completely realized on the basis of a socialist program.

The welfare state, for all its value, tends to provide benefits in inverse relationship to human need. And not — the point is crucial — because there is a conspiracy of the affluent, but as a "natural consequence of the division of society into unequal social classes."

Through vigorous and radical reforms it is possible to offset — though not to remove — this inherent tendency within capitalist society to distribute public benefits according to the inequalities of private wealth. Any movement that attempts to carry out such reforms will be going against the grain of the system itself. This has not kept socialists from participating in every one of these struggles, nor will it in the future. But if the gains are to be permanent, if they are not to be reversed when a period of social innovation is followed by a swing back to capitalist normality, then there must be basic, structural changes. Instead of episodic victories within an antisocial environment, there must be a concerted effort to create a new human environment.

How Inequality Is Built into the System

The class divisions of welfare capitalism which are the root cause of this problem are not, it must be stressed, simply unfair in some abstract sense. Were that the case, a sophisticated conservative argument might be persuasive; since to some extent the growth of the economy benefits everyone, even those who are worst off, there is no point in endangering these gains on behalf of a vision of egalitarianism. What really concerns the poor, this argument continues, is not the rise or fall of their *relative* share of affluence but the steady increase in their absolute standard of living. In fact, however, inequality means not merely that there are sharply unequal proportions of goods distributed among the various social sectors of the population. It also signifies a socioeconomic process, at once dynamic and destructive, which determines that public and private resources shall be spent in an increasingly antisocial way, thereby threatening the well-being of the entire society.

Housing is a crucial case in point. Even under liberal administrations, the government has been much more solicitous about the comfort of the rich than the shelter of the poor. Not only is this policy morally outrageous; it has had disastrous social consequences. Yet it must be emphasized that in thus investing billions in the creation of public problems, Washington did not act maliciously but only followed — unconsciously, automatically, "naturally" — the priorities structured into our society's class divisions. Thus:

in 1962 the value of a single tax deduction to the 20 percent of Americans with the highest incomes was worth twice as much as all the monies spent on public housing for the one-fifth who were poorest, and this figure does not even take into account the government support for below-market rates of interest to build suburbia;

in 1969, the *Wall Street Journal* reported, the $2.5 billion for urban freeways was a far greater subsidy to car owners who daily fled the central city than was the $175 million subsidy to mass transit, and Richard Nixon's 1970 Budget continued this perverse allocation of resources by providing public transportation with only 6 percent of the funds assigned to highways;

as the National Commission on Civil Disorders (the "Riot Commission" of 1968) computed the figures, during roughly the same 30-year period the government helped to construct over 10 million housing units for home builders, i.e. for the middle class and the rich, but provided only 650,000 units of low-cost housing for the poor.

Michael Harrington

Skewed Priorities and Social Consequences

It would be a mistake to think Washington discriminated only against the poor. For, as a White House Conference told President Johnson in 1966, *the entire lower half of the American population is excluded from the market for new housing,* a market that could not exist without massive federal support. This point needs special emphasis if only because many people, with the best of intentions, concluded from the rediscovery of poverty in America in the sixties that the bulk of the nation was affluent while only a minority was poor. The statistics, far from describing a simple division between the rich and the poverty-stricken, show that we have in this country a *majority* — composed of the poor, the near-poor, more than half the workers and lower-middle class — which does not even have a "moderate standard of living" as defined by the government.

When Washington used its powers to improve conditions for a wealthy elite, the poor suffered most because they had the most urgent claim on the funds thus squandered on the upper class; but a majority of the people, including tens of millions who were not poor, were also deprived of benefits that should have rightfully been theirs. Worse, in carrying out these discriminatory policies, the federal programs did positive harm to those most in need. As an American Presidential commission recently reported, ". . . over the last decades, government action through urban renewal, highway programs, demolitions on public housing sites, code enforcement, and other programs has destroyed more housing for the poor than government at all levels has built for them." But then this is a familiar injustice: "Fifty years ago," wrote Alvin Schorr in 1968, "a British Royal Commission for Inquiry into the Housing of the Working Classes observed, with dismay, that poor people rarely benefited when land was cleared and model housing erected."

In the America of the seventies these fantastically skewed priorities will have momentous social consequences. For Washington has, in effect, been aggravating the very social problems to which it points with alarm. By financing the flight of the middle class from the metropolis and helping industry locate in the suburbs, the central city has been allowed to rot — with federal encouragement. As a result such related evils as violence, bitter old age, intensified racism, the decay of the traditional centers of culture, all grew worse. A study commissioned by the government and chaired by Milton Eisenhower gave the darkest view of these trends. The National Commission on the Causes and Prevention of Violence said that, "lacking effective public action," the centers of the great American cities would be safe only in the daytime when crowds gave the individual a sense of security, and that they would be dangerous and empty at night. The big downtown apartment buildings would become "fortified cells for upper-middle and high-income populations living at prime locations in the city." The ghettos would become "places of terror with widespread crime, perhaps entirely out of police control during nighttime hours." And the suburbs would be ringed by freeways patrolled by lightly armored cars.

So the government's discriminatory social policies have done much more than to exacerbate inequality; they have helped to promote a fantastic antidesign for living. How then can we explain why sincere and dedicated men — as those who presided over these disastrous programs often were — would lavish public funds to aggravate social problems? The answer is to be found in the class character of American society and in the commercial logic which both derives from it and pervades governmental decisions.

The 1969 Report of the Council of Economic Advisers provides candid documentation of this pattern. "Investing in new housing for low-income families — particularly in big cities — is usually a losing proposition," the Council said, "Indeed the *most profitable investment* is often one that demolishes homes of low-income families to make room for business and higher-income families." (Emphasis added.) It is obvious that the criterion of profitability to which the Council refers is private since, as the gloomy projections of the Violence Commission demonstrate, the social cost of the present system is bankrupting the society. Yet precisely this private calculus is the one the government follows. As the Urban Problems Commission put it, ". . . renewal was and is too often looked upon as a federally financed gimmick to provide relatively cheap land for a miscellany of profitable or prestigious enterprises."

In a society based on class inequality and suffused with commercial values, it just doesn't "make sense" to waste resources on social uses or beauty — or anything that cannot be quantified in dollars and cents. Our legislators, drawn almost exclusively from the middle and upper classes, cannot bring themselves to forget those principles that are sacred to a private economy. To them it seems logical to invest the federal dollar in undertakings that run the lowest risk and will show the highest and most immediate return.

Housing is only one example of how the welfare state observes the priorities of maldistributed wealth even when it attempts to serve the common good. Other cases in point can be found in literally every department of government. The American welfare system in the sixties reached only a third of the poor and provided them, on a national average, with only half of what they needed. Meanwhile, in 1969, the richest one-sixth among the farmers (individuals and corporations) received two-thirds of the agricultural subsidies, or about $2.5 billion. Given the relation of social classes in this field, America's commitment to promote "agriculture" is also a commitment to help the rich at the expense of the poor. And if one considers the various deductions in the tax codes as an indirect form of government expense — by not collecting money from an individual, Washington increases his income as surely as if it had sent him a check — one will note that they total up to $50 billion, with the bulk of that sum going to oil men, home builders, stock-market speculators, and others from the top of the economic pyramid.

Education and Social Inequality

It is in education that the effect of systematic inequality is most damaging. America is becoming a "knowledge economy" in which higher and higher educational credentials are required, sometimes unnecessarily, in order to get a good job. This is one of the most important areas of socialized effort since, either through public schools or aid to private education, the state supplies the modern economy with "its decisive factor of production, which is trained manpower." Although public spending on education in the sixties increased at a rate faster than that of the Gross National Product, those Americans in the most desperate straits were not reached.

So it is that in the sixties a rather optimistic study of social mobility in the United States found that there is an "oversupply" of youth at the bottom of the economic structure: the *Manpower Report of the President, 1969,* reported that the unprecedented recent boom had clearly revealed "economic expansion alone was insufficient to employ many people who had been bypassed in the general advance because of inexperience, lack of skills, and cultural deprivation." Now it is bad enough that such a group should exist at all. What is truly intolerable is the extent to which the social class structure denies it effective access to tax-supported education and works and thereby makes it both self-perpetuating and hereditary.

For if, as Christopher Jencks and David Riesman document in *The Academic Revolution,* society is divided into blue- and white-collar groups, the high school seniors from the white-collar background are four times as likely to score in the top rather than in the bottom 10 percent, while the blue-collar students are twice as likely to be at the bottom rather than at the top. One way of coping with such depressing statistics is to argue that they reflect the "middle-class bias" of the tests used to evaluate students. There have been demands to do away with IQ tests and standard grading, to assign each racial and ethnic group a quota of admissions in state-supported colleges (the top 10 percent of Negro, Puerto Ricans, Mexican-Americans, and others would have places reserved for them, so there would be competition only within these communities but not among them or with the non-ethnics).

To those who charge that the tests are "unfair to the poor," Riesman and Jencks cogently reply, "Life is unfair to the poor. Tests are merely the results. Urban middle-class life in general and professional work in particular seem to nourish potential academic skills and interests in parents, while lower-class life does the opposite." The conclusion they come to is much more radical than that offered by people who simply denounce "educational racism" — or even propose separate but inferior college faculties for the children of the poor and the minorities. Riesman and Jencks write:

> So long as the distribution of power and privilege remains radically unequal, so long as some children are raised by adults at the bottom while others are raised by adults at the top, the children will more often than not turn out unequal. . . . We suspect that these differences account for more of the class variation in college changes than all other differences combined.

Jencks and Riesman then raise a basic psychological point. Suppose by an act of political will the schools could be transformed so as to favor the minorities while the fundamental social inequalities were left intact. That, they hold, "could be a formula for misery. A mobile, fluid society in which men move up and down is simultaneously a competitive, insecure, and invidious society." "What America needs," they conclude, "is not more mobility but more equality. So long as American life is premised on dramatic inequalities of wealth and power, *no* system for allocating social roles will be very satisfactory." Exactly!

In education, housing, and agriculture, in welfare and every other area of social life, it is therefore necessary to attack the systematic concentration of economic power in order to achieve serious reform. The fulfillment of liberal values, in short, requires structural changes in our class relationships, changes transcending the capitalist limits of today's welfare state.

Epilogue

Unfortunately, an epilogue is not an epitaph. Poverty in the United States has not died. Nor is it about to do so. For more than two decades, American society relied on economic growth, not redistribution of income, to end poverty and reduce social conflict. Growth was a solution for many, but millions of other poor did not benefit. They are still poor and still with us — some even in abject poverty. Economic growth alone is not the answer to these people's problems. One immediate solution calls for redistribution of income: a guaranteed income that would permit families to live at a reasonable standard. But the Welfare Reform Bill passed by the House of Representatives in June 1971 provides a mere $2,400 yearly income for a family of four — a far cry from the National Welfare Rights Organization's call for an income guarantee of $6,500 for an urban family of four (1971). The nation is unwilling to guarantee employment for all at a living wage, and in 1971, Nixon even vetoed a child-care bill that would have enabled working mothers to obtain sorely needed day care for their children.

The persistence of racism has further hindered the eradication of poverty, because the vastly higher incidence of poverty among blacks makes the white majority less willing to take measures that would help the poor. And, as Mitchell I. Ginsberg, dean of the Columbia University School of Social Work, has observed, attitudes toward the poor "have never been so hostile." (*New York Times* [December 15, 1971], p. 38.)

The poor lack the political strength to force the society to give them a larger share of the nation's income. But it is clear that the poor no longer accept their subservient role. As the Gross National Product of the United States soars above the $1 trillion level, crime is mounting, cities are deteriorating, and social tensions are rising. Perhaps this situation is the price of a society that has achieved wealth without equity, for, as British social critic Richard M. Titmuss has said, "History suggests that human nature is not strong enough to maintain itself in true community where great disparities of income and wealth persist." ("Poverty vs. Inequality," *The Nation* [January 8, 1965].) Because of the absence of any commitment toward major social change in America, the editor remains pessimistic about the possibility of ending poverty. But it is her hope that readers will join the poor in their struggle for a more equitable society and thereby will help disprove this dismal prophecy.

Appendix

Table 1. Median Family Income of Negroes and Other Nonwhite Races as a Percentage of White Median Family Income, 1950–1970

	Families of Negroes and Other Nonwhite Races	Families of Negroes
1950	54%	NA[1]
1951	53	NA
1952	57	NA
1953	56	NA
1954	56	NA
1955	55	NA
1956	53	NA
1957	54	NA
1958	51	NA
1959	52	NA
1960	55	NA
1961	53	NA
1962	53	NA
1963	53	NA
1964	56	54%
1965	55	54
1966	60	58
1967	62	59
1968	63	60
1969	63	61
1970	64	61

Source: U.S. Bureau of Labor Statistics and U.S. Bureau of the Census, *The Status of Negroes in the United States, 1970.* BLS Report No. 394, Current Population Reports, Series P-23, No. 38.

Note: Annual figures shown are based on the Current Population Survey.

[1] Data not available from 1950 to 1963.

Table 2. Median Income of Men by Years of School Completed, 1969

Years of School Completed by Men Aged 25–54	Negro	White	Negro Income as a Percentage of White Income
Elementary school			
Less than eight	$3,922	$5,509	71%
Eight	4,472	7,018	64
High school			
One to three	5,327	7,812	68
Four	6,192	8,829	70
College			
One to three	7,427	9,831	76
Four or more	8,669	12,354	70

Source: U.S. Bureau of Labor Statistics and U.S. Bureau of the Census, *The Social and Economic Status of Negroes in the United States, 1970*. BLS Report No. 394, Current Population Reports, Series P-23, No. 38 (July 1971).

Table 3. Unemployment Rates,[1] 1948–1970

	Negroes and Other Nonwhite Races	Whites	Ratio of Blacks and Other Races to Whites
1948	5.2%	3.2%	1.6%
1949	8.9	5.6	1.6
1950	9.0	4.9	1.8
1951	5.3	3.1	1.7
1952	5.4	2.8	1.9
1953	4.5	2.7	1.7
1954	9.9	5.0	2.0
1955	8.7	3.9	2.2
1956	8.3	3.6	2.3
1957	7.9	3.8	2.1
1958	12.6	6.1	2.1
1959	10.7	4.8	2.2
1960	10.2	4.9	2.1
1961	12.4	6.0	2.1
1962	10.9	4.9	2.2
1963	10.8	5.0	2.2
1964	9.6	4.6	2.1
1965	8.1	4.1	2.0
1966	7.3	3.3	2.2
1967	7.4	3.4	2.2
1968	6.7	3.2	2.1
1969	6.5	3.2	2.0
1970	8.2	4.5	1.8

Source: U.S. Bureau of Labor Statistics and U.S. Bureau of the Census, *Recent Trends in Social and Economic Conditions of Negroes in the United States*, BLS Report No. 347, Current Population Reports, Series P-23, No. 26 (July 1968), and *The Social and Economic Status of Negroes in the United States, 1970*, BLS Report No. 394, Current Population Reports, Series P-23, No. 38 (July 1971).

[1] The unemployment rate is the percentage of unemployed in the civilian labor force.

Appendix

Table 4. *Unemployment Rates[1] for Slum Areas and Metropolitan Areas, 1966*

Metropolitan Area and Slum Area	Slum Area, November 1966	Metropolitan Area,[2] Average for year ending August 1966
Boston: Roxbury	6.9%	3.7%
Cleveland: Hough and surrounding neighborhood	15.6	3.5
Detroit: Central Woodward	10.1	4.3
Los Angeles: South Los Angeles	12.0	6.0
New Orleans: several contiguous areas	10.0	NA[3]
New York: Harlem	8.1	
New York: East Harlem	9.0	4.6
New York: Bedford-Stuyvesant	6.2	
Philadelphia: North Philadelphia	11.0	4.3
Phoenix: Salt River Bed	13.2	NA
St. Louis: North Side	12.9	4.5
San Antonio: East and West sides	8.1	NA
San Francisco–Oakland: Mission-Fillmore	11.1	5.2
San Francisco–Oakland: Bayside	13.0	
San Juan: El Fangito	15.8	NA

Source: U.S. Department of Labor, *Manpower Report of the President* (April 1967).

[1] The unemployment rate is the percentage of unemployed in the civilian labor force.

[2] Metropolitan area data are based on special tabulations of data from the Current Population Survey. The slum data presented here relate to the cities surveyed jointly by the Department of Labor and State Employment Service agencies.

[3] Data not available.

Table 5. *Subemployment Rate[1] in Ten Slums, 1966*

Area	Subemployment Rate
Boston: Roxbury	24%
New Orleans: several contiguous areas	45
New York: Harlem	29
New York: East Harlem	33
New York: Bedford-Stuyvesant	28
Philadelphia: North Philadelphia	34
Phoenix: Salt River Bed	42
St. Louis: North Side	39
San Antonio: East and West Sides	47
San Francisco: Mission-Fillmore	25

Source: U.S. Department of Labor, *Manpower Report of the President* (April 1967).

[1] The subemployment index includes: (1) people classed as unemployed, because they were jobless and looking for work during the survey week; (2) those working only part time, though they wanted full-time work; (3) heads of households under 65 years of age who earn less than $60 a week, though working full time; also individuals under 65, not heads of households who earn less than $56 a week on a full-time job (the equivalent of $1.40 an hour for a 40-hour week); (4) half the number of "non-

Table 6. Employment Growth in Five Cities and Their Suburbs, 1951–1965

	Number of New Jobs			Percentage of Increase in New Jobs		
	City	Suburbs	Metropolitan Area	City	Suburbs	Metropolitan Area
Baltimore	1,450	86,086	87,536	1.7	98.3	20.3
New York	127,753	387,873	515,626	24.8	75.2	15.6
Philadelphia	−49,461	215,296	165,835	−29.8	129.8	14.5
St. Louis	−61,800	141,911	80,111	−77.1	177.1	13.9
San Francisco	9,346	185,742	195,089	4.8	95.2	31.1

Source: National Committee Against Discrimination in Housing, *The Impact of Housing Patterns on Job Opportunities* (1968).

participants" among men aged 20 to 64 (on the assumption that the other half are not potential workers, chiefly because of physical or mental disabilities or severe personal problems; and (5) an estimate of the male "undercount" group (based on the assumption that the number of men in the area should bear the same relation to the number of women that exists in the population generally; also that half of the unfound men are in the four groups of subemployed people just listed — the others being either employed or not potential workers).

Suggestions for Further Reading

Readers may find it helpful to consult the complete works from which the selections in this text have been taken. The literature about poverty is vast and growing, and the editor has made no attempt to compile a comprehensive bibliography. The following list excludes the works from which excerpts have been taken and merely suggests a few of the many other excellent books that are useful in analyzing the problems of poverty.

Batchelder, Alan B. *The Economics of Poverty*. 2nd ed. (New York: Wiley, 1971).

Brenner, Robert. *From the Depths: The Discovery of Poverty in the United States* (New York: New York University Press, 1956).

Cash, Edgar S., ed. *Our Brother's Keeper: The Indian in White America* (Washington, D.C.: New Community Press, 1969).

Caudill, Harry M. *Night Comes to the Cumberlands: A Biography of a Depressed Area* (Boston: Little, Brown, 1963).

Clark, Kenneth B. *Dark Ghetto: Dilemmas of Social Power* (New York: Harper and Row, Harper Torchbooks, 1967).

Coles, Robert, and Clayton, Al. *Still Hungry in America* (New York: New American Library, 1969).

Domhoff, G. William. *Who Rules America?* (Englewood Cliffs, N.J.: Prentice-Hall, Spectrum Book, 1967).

Ferman, Louis A., Kornbluh, Joyce L., and Haber, Alan. *Poverty in America: A Book of Readings*, rev. ed. (Ann Arbor, Mich.: University of Michigan Press, 1968).

Galbraith, John Kenneth. *The Affluent Society* (New York: Mentor, New American Library, 1963).

Grant, Joanne, ed. *Black Protest: History, Documents and Analyses, 1619 to the Present* (New York: Fawcett, 1968).

Hamilton, David. *A Primer on the Economics of Poverty* (New York: Random House, 1968).

Harrington, Michael. *The Other America: Poverty in the United States*, rev. ed. (Baltimore: Pelican Books, Penguin Books, 1969).

Heilbroner, Robert L. *The Worldly Philosophers: The Lives, Times and Ideas of the Great Economic Thinkers*. 3rd ed. (New York: Clarion Books, Simon and Schuster, 1968).

Henderson, William L., and Ledebur, Larry C. *Economic Disparity: Problems and Strategies for Black America* (New York: Free Press, 1970).

Hofstadter, Richard. *Social Darwinism in American Thought* (Boston: Beacon Press, 1955).

Hunter, Robert. *Poverty* (1904). Edited by Peter d'A. Jones (New York: Harper and Row, Harper Torchbooks, 1965).

Jacobson, Julius, ed. *The Negro and the American Labor Movement* (Garden City, N.Y.: Anchor Books, Doubleday, 1968).

Kershaw, Joseph A., with Courant, Paul N. *Government Against Poverty* (Chicago: Markham, 1970).

Kolko, Gabriel. *Wealth and Power in America: An Analysis of Social Class and Income Distribution* (New York: Praeger, 1962).

Lampman, Robert J. *The Share of Top Wealth Holders in National Wealth* (Princeton, N.J.: Princeton University Press, 1962).

Lens, Sidney. *Poverty: America's Enduring Paradox* (New York: Crowell, 1969).

Levitan, Sar A. *The Great Society's Poor Law: A New Approach to Poverty* (Baltimore: Johns Hopkins Press, 1969).

Mantoux, Paul. *The Industrial Revolution in the Eighteenth Century: An Outline of the Beginnings of the Modern Factory System in England* (1905). rev. ed. (New York: Harper and Row, Harper Torchbooks, 1962).

Marshall, Ray. *The Negro Worker* (New York: Random House, 1967).

Matthiessen, Peter. *Sal Si Puedes: Cesar Chavez and the New American Revolution* (New York: Delta Books, Dell, 1969).

Mencher, Samuel. *Poor Law to Poverty Program: Economic Security Policy in Britain and the United States* (Pittsburgh: University of Pittsburgh Press, 1967).

Miller, Herman. *Rich Man, Poor Man* (New York: Crowell, 1964).

Miller, S. M., and Roby, Pamela. *The Future of Inequality* (New York: Basic Books, 1970).

Myrdal, Gunnar. *Objectivity in Social Research* (New York: Pantheon, 1969).

Piven, Frances Fox, and Cloward, Richard A. *Regulating the Poor: The Function of Public Welfare* (New York: Pantheon, 1971).

Polanyi, Karl. *The Great Transformation: The Political and Economic Origins of Our Time* (Boston: Beacon Press, 1957).

Ross, Arthur M., and Hill, Herbert. *Employment, Race, and Poverty* (New York: Harcourt Brace Jovanovich, 1967).

Seligman, Ben B., ed. *Aspects of Poverty: Selected Studies of Social Problems* (New York: Crowell, 1968).

Shannon, David A. *The Great Depression* (Englewood Cliffs, N.J.: Prentice-Hall, Spectrum, 1960).

Stein, Bruno. *On Relief: The Economics of Poverty and Public Welfare* (New York: Basic Books, 1971).

Steiner, Stan. *The New Indians* (New York: Delta Books, Dell, 1968).

Tabb, William K. *The Political Economy of the Black Ghetto* (New York: Norton, 1970).

Tawney, R. H. *Religion and the Rise of Capitalism* (New York: Mentor, New American Library, 1954).

Titmuss, Richard M. *Commitment to Welfare* (New York: Pantheon, 1968).

Valentine, Charles A. *Culture and Poverty: A Critique and Counter Proposals* (Chicago: University of Chicago Press, 1968).

Wilcox, Clair. *Toward Social Welfare: An Analysis of Programs and Proposals Attacking Poverty, Insecurity and Inequality of Opportunity* (Homewood, Ill.: Irwin, 1969).

Will, Robert E., and Vatter, Harold G., eds. *Poverty in Affluence: The Social, Political, and Economic Dimensions of Poverty in the United States* (New York: Harcourt Brace Jovanovich, 1970).

Wogaman, Philip. *Guaranteed Annual Income: The Moral Issues* (Nashville, Tenn.: Abingdon Press, 1968).

Index of Authors and Titles

Alleviation of Poverty, The, 291
Analytical Aspects of Unemployment, 284
Answer to Malthus, An, 34
A. Philip Randolph Institute, 295
Appalachia: The Corporate Fiefdom, 223
Attitude of the Bourgeoisie Towards the Proletariat, The, 58

Baran, Paul A., 164
Blame the Negro Child, 264
Bloody Legislation Against Paupers, 10
Boggs, James, 308
Buchwald, Art, 288
Business Is the First to Seek Relief, 121

Capitalism and Persistent Poverty, 164
Caudill, Harry M., 223
Change the Environment and Change the Man, 44
Chavez, Cesar, 245
Clark Subcommittee, U.S. Senate, 153
Comparing the Immigrant and the Negro Experience, 270
Condition of Black People in the South, 1890, The, 80
Condition of Farm Workers and Small Farmers, The, 233
Condition of Labor (See *Rerum Novarum*)
Congress and the Rats, 207
Congressional Record, 207

Continued Progress of the Working Classes Under Capitalism, The, 102

Devine, Samuel (See *Congress and the Rats*)
Distribution of Wealth Depends on the Laws and Customs of Society, The, 50
Douglass, Frederick, 76
DuBois, W. E. Burghardt, 80
Dunbar, Leslie W. (See Clark Subcommittee)

Economics of Aging, The, 227
Eisenhower Commission (See National Commission on the Causes and Prevention of Violence)
Engels, Friedrich, 58
Equality and Liberty, 283

Facts and Fictions About the Poor, 173
Farm Labor, 242
For Sam Smith, Hospital Orderly: A Battle Whose Time Has Come, 261
"Freedom Budget," A, 295
Friedman, Milton, 282, 291

Galenson, Walter, 284
General Theory of Employment, Interest, and Money, The, 117
George, Henry, 85
Godwin, William, 34
Gregory, Dick, 191

Griffiths, Martha (See *Congress and the Rats*)
Grinnell, Mrs. Mattie (See Clark Subcommittee)

Harrington, Michael, 159, 319
Hayden, Tom, 167
Heilbroner, Robert L., 275
Heineman Commission (See President's Commission on Income Maintenance Programs)
Henry, G. C., 242
Herzog, Elizabeth, 173
High Earnings of Labor Are an Advantage to Society, The, 19
Howell, Leon, 217
How the Federal Government Builds Ghettos, 249
Hunger and Malnutrition in the United States, 153

Impact of Housing Patterns on Job Opportunities, The, 254
Innuit Indians and the London Poor, The, 96

Kerner Commission (See National Advisory Commission on Civil Disorders)
Keynes, John Maynard, 117
Kupferman, Theodore (See *Congress and the Rats*)

LaGuardia, Fiorello H., 121
Leo XIII (See Pope Leo XIII)
Letter from Delano, 245
Liberalism and Egalitarianism, 282
Life in the Slave Quarters and Life in the Big House, 76
London, Jack, 96

McClintock, John M., 261
Malthus, Thomas Robert, 30
Marshall, Alfred, 102
Marx, Karl, 10, 69
Meaning of Poverty, The, 143
Menial Jobs and Black Poverty, 258
Mill, John Stuart, 50
Mississippi, 217
Moynihan, Daniel Patrick, 317
Myth and Irrationality of Black Capitalism, The, 308

National Advisory Commission on Civil Disorders, 258, 270, 301
National Commission on the Causes and Prevention of Violence, 315
National Committee Against Discrimination in Housing, 249, 254
National Sharecroppers Fund, 233
Nigger, 191
No-Job Corps, The, 288

One-Third of a Nation, 112
Origin of the Poor Law and the Law of Settlement, The, 15
Ornati, Oscar, 140
Ortiz, Gilbert (See Clark Subcommittee)
Other America Revisited, The, 159
Owen, Robert, 44

Paine, Thomas, 24
Petty, Sir William, 12
Pigou, A. C., 108
Plan for Social Reform, A, 24
Poor Are the Unfit, The, 89
Pope Leo XIII, 92
Poverty, Income Inequality, and Privilege, 275
Poverty Is Nature's Punishment for Overpopulation, 30
President's Commission on Income Maintenance Programs, 143, 181, 194
Progress and Poverty, 85

Recommendations for National Action, 301
Red Man's Heritage: The Lagoon of Excrement, 211
Relative Surplus Population and Capital Accumulation, 69
Reorder National Priorities, 315
Rerum Novarum, 92
Ricardo, David, 38
Riis, Jacob, 98
Roosevelt, Franklin Delano, 112

Security for a People, 115
Sherrill, Robert G., 211
Should the Unemployed Be Hanged?, 12
Smith, Adam, 15, 19
Social Security Board, 115

Index

Special Committee on Aging, U.S. Senate, 227
Spencer, Herbert, 89
Sweezy, Paul M., 164

Tawney, R. H., 283
There Will Be No Peace Dividend, 317
Transferring Income from the Rich to the Poor, 108

U.S. Civil Rights Commission, 207
U.S. Senate (See Clark Subcommittee; Special Committee on Aging; LaGuardia, Fiorello H.)

View of the Poverty Program, A, 167

Wages Should Be Left to the Fair and Free Competition of the Market, 38
Welfare System, The, 181
What Is Poverty?, 140
Why the Poor Remain Poor, 194
Why We Need Socialism in America, 319
Wilkerson, Doxey A., 264
William Committee (See Special Committee on Aging)
Working Girls of New York, The, 98

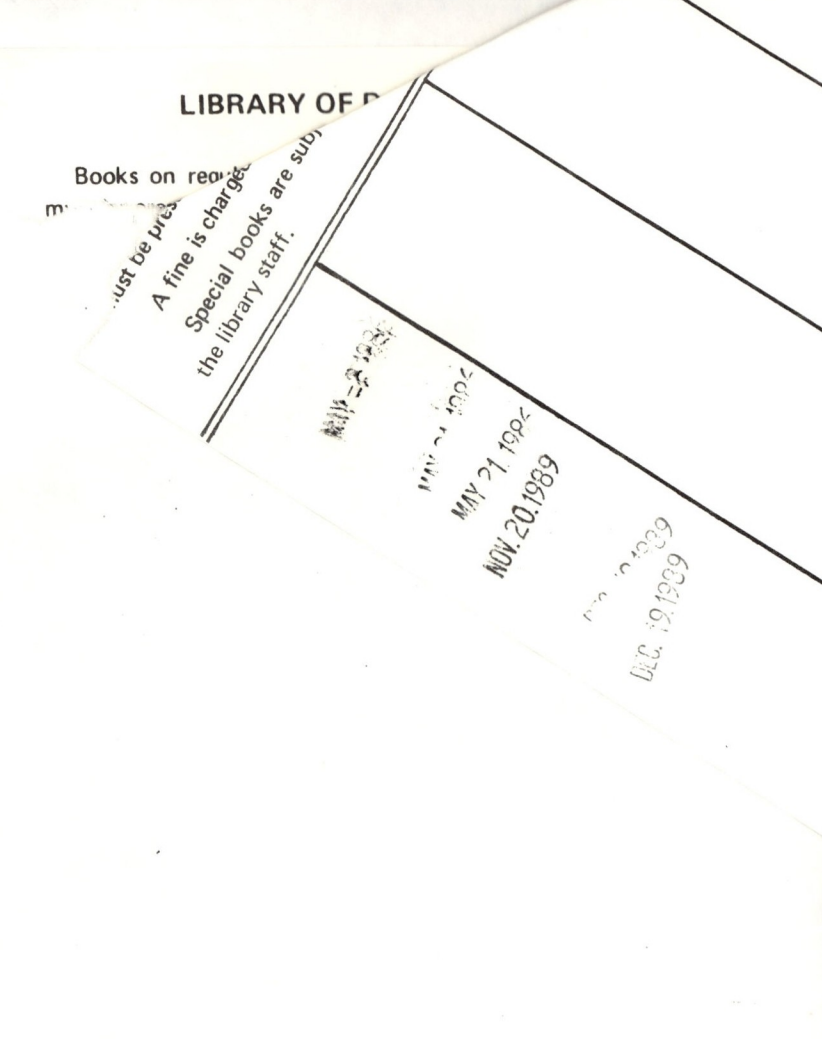